Global Research in Gender, Sexuality and Health

Series Editors

Ellen Annandale
Department of Sociology
University of York
York, UK

Xiaodong Lin
Department of Sociology
University of York
York, UK

Global Research in Gender, Sexuality and Health brings together original, forward-looking research on gender, sexuality and health at a time of far-reaching and complex global transformations in each of these areas. The associations between these realms are being reconfigured by global social change in different ways and with different consequences for the experience of illness and delivery of healthcare in local and national contexts. New experiences of health and illness are also being driven by the increased global mobility of bodies and illnesses and the growing securitization of illness. In turn, these are challenging conventional ways of thinking about gender, gender, sexualities and the body and call for novel conceptual approaches that are a better fit for an understanding of health in a 'global age'. This interdisciplinary series aims to showcase original research monographs and edited collections of interest to an international readership. Studies from the Global South are particularly encouraged, to help reflect on and revise knowledge of gender, sexuality and health beyond a Eurocentric perspective.

More information about this series at
http://www.palgrave.com/gp/series/15916

Courtenay Sprague

Gender and HIV in South Africa

Advancing Women's Health and Capabilities

palgrave
macmillan

Courtenay Sprague
University of Massachusetts
Boston, USA

University of the Witwatersrand
Johannesburg, South Africa

Global Research in Gender, Sexuality and Health
ISBN 978-1-137-55996-8 ISBN 978-1-137-55997-5 (eBook)
https://doi.org/10.1057/978-1-137-55997-5

Library of Congress Control Number: 2017964726

Printed on acid-free paper

This Palgrave Macmillan imprint is published by Springer Nature
The registered company is Macmillan Publishers Ltd.
The registered company address is: The Campus, 4 Crinan Street, London, N1 9XW, United Kingdom

Eyabo bonke abesifazane base Ningizimu Afrika abaphila noma abasengozini yesandulela-ngculazi.
(For all South African women living with or at risk of HIV)

Samkelisiwe Mquanaze, KwaZulu-Natal, September 1992

Samkelisiwe with her son at her mother's home in KwaZulu-Natal shortly before her death. Source: Mendel 2001, image 10/35. Reprinted with permission

Preface

The three photographs that appear in this work, including the arresting cover photo, are by the acclaimed South African-born photographer, Gideon Mendel. Gideon's photographs are distinctive, not only for their raw emotion and haunting beauty, but for their ability to portray the lived experience of families at key moments during the unfolding AIDS epidemic in sub-Saharan Africa. Gideon was one of the first photographers to cross the threshold into African homes and communities, and with their permission, to train his lens on individuals and families at the HIV epidemic's epicentre: calling attention to 'health as social justice' in the African Continent. In doing so, he was building on the practice of 'documentary genre' used by Peter Magubane and others (post-1976 Soweto uprising and earlier) to capture the bald brutality and cold-blooded injustice of the Nationalist government's apartheid regime (see Badsha, 1986).

Gideon's images powerfully render, not just the faces of people affected by HIV, but their stories. Each photograph has a caption that conveys what those individuals wanted to share at a time when the African AIDS (acquired immunodeficiency syndrome) epidemic was being ignored and the rising death toll uncounted. As Gideon writes in his work, *A Broken Landscape: HIV/AIDS in Africa*:

> I first began documenting HIV/AIDS in sub-Saharan Africa in the early 1990s. At the time, three-quarters of the world's 36 million people living with HIV/AIDS were in Africa. It was a slow burning tragedy on a monumental scale; one that was quietly decimating some of the poorest nations on Earth. (2001, p. 1)

I thank Gideon for his generous permission to reprint these moving photos. The full collection can be seen here: http://gideonmendel.com/a-broken-landscape/. As with Gideon's photo narratives—what people felt, the anxieties that gripped them—must continue to be located in the foreground as the HIV epidemic evolves.

Today 22.3% of all women in South Africa are living with HIV (Statistics South Africa [StatsSA], 2016a). Despite a massive HIV treatment programme in the public health system since 2004, South Africa leads the world in global HIV incidence in young women aged 15–24 years (UNAIDS, 2016a, 2016b). Moreover, HIV prevalence in South African pregnant women has stood at a constant 29–30% since 2004, while new HIV infections in women aged 50 and above are increasingly documented (see Fig. 1.1) (Government of South Africa, 2015a; Sprague & Brown, 2016; UNAIDS, 2013). These statistics are powered by quantitative techniques using large samples and they effectively tell a powerful story of the sustained high HIV prevalence and incidence in South African women and its pernicious effects on women's health as part of long-term trends. It is, however, the narratives and voices of women—the qualitative, lived experience—that is perhaps most important in informing how the research and policy community can gain greater purchase on HIV in women in particular social contexts.

The research presented in these pages adopts a joint public health and social justice lens to capture the complex dimensions of HIV in South African women. It investigates the opportunities to be healthy or 'capabilities' and agency of black South African women living with HIV. The central question asked by Amartya Sen's Capabilities Approach (CA) to human development (1999) is: what are people able to do and be? (1999). Martha Nussbaum rightly presses that question, asking, are women 'really able to do and to be these things, or are there impediments, evident or hidden, to their real and substantial freedom?' (2008, p. 1). In this work, the impediments to and enablers of women's health, agency and wellbeing are elicited through in-depth interviews (IDIs) conducted with 89 women living with HIV, and supplemented by interviews with 44 key informants. Spanning more than a decade, my research on black South African women living with the virus has primarily been qualitative in nature to elevate a needed focus on women's lived and social experiences of health and illness. It thus complements the large body of quantitative biomedical and epidemiological research on HIV in women—some of it analysed here—to inform social science understandings of the effects of HIV on women. Attention to some of the essential moral and social aspects of women's experiences of living with HIV are also captured but these continue to require further articulation by South African women and by women affected by HIV in other parts of the world.

Of note, the original findings, particularly when supplemented by the results from numerous other South African studies, underscore the principal role of structural constraints—especially intimate partner violence—to undermine black South African women's agency, and their process and opportunity freedoms. The manner by which these structural health determinants, notably adverse gender norms, interact with other influential factors to inhibit women's HIV care and adherence are documented here. These add to the growing body of evidence about social health inequalities, and how women experience systematic health differences in their daily world. The possibilities for promoting and protecting women's health while advancing their capabilities are also emphasised. The principal need for women to be able to exercise the rights they are afforded in South African law remains paramount, as do social policies and inter-sectoral action. Notably, two gender-transformative interventions (GTIs) undertaken in community-based settings illustrate that structural-level changes can be achieved (Chap. 7). Indeed, the core thesis of this work is that HIV in South African women constitutes a social justice problem, and one that is changeable.

Significantly, the women most at risk of acquiring HIV in South Africa, and most likely to die from HIV-related causes, are black women. Despite the process of social transformation that has been unfolding since the introduction of democracy in 1994, black women's health and prospects for human development have been—and continue to be—

poorer than for women of other race groups. The narrative of the South African woman on the cover, Samkelisiwe Mquanaze (from Kwazulu-Natal), is illustrative. In 2017, Samkelisiwe would have been 43 years of age. She was not able to live to the end of a normal lifespan. In the year of the photo (2000), treatment was unavailable in South Africa, and would remain out of reach for another four years. Today, HIV treatment has successfully extended the lives of many, both in Africa and globally. Yet, for black South African women, HIV remains a leading cause of premature deaths. As Samkelisiwe told Gideon: 'Normally I would be the one taking care of my mother, but now I am the baby again. She is looking after everyone in the family.' Samkelisiwe's words highlight the caregiving role borne by women, and their vulnerability to HIV, both characteristic features of many black South African women's lives. Despite women's rights in South African law, grave social and economic challenges bar many women from achieving good health and exercising their constitutional rights and freedoms to achieve their notions of the good life. While treatment remains imperative, it is only a partial answer, given the structural drivers that foster HIV acquisition among women.

Crossing the Threshold

Gideon notes that, as HIV treatment became available, instead of using harsh black and white images to depict people living with HIV, he turned to colour to reflect new life and hope. South Africa remains the global HIV epicentre, representing 18% of the global population living with HIV (UNAIDS, 2014b). While declines in HIV incidence and prevalence have been recorded for some, women continue to bear a disproportionate burden of HIV illness (SANAC, 2014). There are 3.9 million South African women living with HIV, one-fifth of total women of reproductive age (StatsSA, 2016a, p. 4). We are now at a different point in the HIV epidemic trajectory. Indeed, the HIV epidemic in women has reached a new threshold and marks a 'crucible' moment for South Africa. The current response, largely located in the public health system, has been insufficient to prevent new HIV infections in women. Consequently, I deliberately chose the stark black and white image of Samkelisiwe for the book's cover to reflect the ongoing, profound dimensions of the HIV epidemic for African and South African women. A fundamental paradigm shift and transformational change will be necessary to situate women and girls more securely on an optimal path of health and human development. This work suggests some possibilities for engaging with law, policy, the health system and community-based interventions to advance women's health and capabilities, while also attending to health inequities for black South African women. A changed HIV response that engages with structural factors facilitating HIV in women, including adverse gender norms, is possible but can only come from within South Africa, with the requisite political will and support.

In the last year of her life, Samkelisiwe told Gideon that she was very sad because she had wanted to participate in AIDS education events but was too weak to do so. It thus seems appropriate that Samkelisiwe should invite readers across the threshold and into this work on HIV, gender and health as social justice in South Africa.

Boston, MA, USA Courtenay Sprague

Permission from the following has generously been granted to reprint images, excerpts and illustrations.

Diderichsen, F., Evans, T., & Whitehead, M. (2001). Framework for elucidating pathways from social context to social and economic consequences. In the social disparities in health. In T. Evans et al. (Eds.), *Challenging Inequities to Health: From Ethics to Action*. Oxford: Oxford University Press.

Dunkle, K., & Decker, M. (2013). Gender-based violence and HIV: Reviewing the evidence for links and causal pathways in the general population and high risk groups. *American Journal of Reproductive Immunology, 69*(suppl. 1), 20–26.

Mendel, G. (2001). Photo images. In *A Broken Landscape: HIV/AIDS in Africa*. London: Blume.

Pilane, P. (2016, May 20). Sugar daddies, Shame the blessers, not the blessed. *Mail & Guardian* (South Africa).

WHO. (2013). Figure 2: Indirect and direct links between violence against women, HIV risk and uptake of services (Pathways 2 and 3), In *16 Ideas for Addressing Violence Against Women in the Context of the HIV Epidemic: A Programming Tool*. Geneva: WHO.

Acknowledgements

I am but one person among a global community of people deeply concerned about the problem of HIV in women, both in South Africa and elsewhere. It is necessary, then, to engrave into these pages the names of those involved in supporting this work. The University of the Witwatersrand (Wits) in Johannesburg has been my institutional home since 1999 and the University of Massachusetts Boston (UMB) since 2012. I remain grateful to my co-authors for allowing me to draw on our related published and unpublished research in South African clinical settings. I especially thank Vivian Black (Wits Medical School), Abigail Hatcher (Wits School of Public Health), Nataly Woollett (Wits Medical School), Stu Woolman (Wits Law School), Shelley Brown (Boston University, UMB), Jane Parpart (UMB) and Theresa Sommers (Tufts University, UMB).

The empirical research undertaken in this work relies on direct in-depth engagement with women living with HIV (Chap. 6). I offer a deep bow of gratitude to the 89 women living with HIV who are at the centre of this work. Their narratives of struggle, pain, suffering, joy and resilience have profoundly shaped my understanding of women's experiences of living with HIV, of gender, health, and *ubuntu: Ngiyabonga ngiyabonga.*

A profound thank you to the 44 key informants: South African health providers who are the backbone of health care delivery and undertake their work in the face of great obstacles; and to the key academic and policy experts who shepherd an exacting discourse on HIV, gender and justice in South Africa.

I remain indebted to the following colleagues and friends for their engaged involvement, strategic thinking, problem solving and key support during the conception, evolution and execution of this work: Caroline Wanjiku Kihato, Charisse Drobis, Melusi Mthembu, Nhlanhla N. Mathonsi, Laurie Zapalac, Louise Penner, Chris Bobel, Shelley Foster, Sara Divello, Laura Parrott, Brian Halley, Evelyn Schichner, Krish Sigamoney, Lisa Vetten, Leah Gilbert, Shireen Hassim, Anne Elton, Ines Ferreira, Sara Simon, Amy Heiden, Jonathan Klaaren, Kim Sacks, David Bilchitz and Shaun de Waal.

I thank Cathy Campbell (London School of Economics & Political Science), Jenevieve Mannell (University College London) and participants at a London workshop, as part of a special issue on women's agency in marginalised settings published in the journal, *Global Public Health*. My involvement deepened my thinking, both conceptually and practically, about South African women's agency and the institutional agency of the South African health system.

My thanks to the authors, publishers and editors who generously granted copyright permission to make use of their figures, models and diagrams.

Reviewers and editors make authors' work sharper. I am immensely grateful to the following colleagues who reviewed earlier sections and chapters, and whose deft intellectual contributions improved the work: Ellen Annandale, Vivian Black, Di Cooper, Andy Gibbs, Gillian MacNaughton, Jeff Pugh, Karen Ross, Nwabisa Shai, Stu Woolman and four anonymous reviewers commissioned by the Human Sciences Research Council of South Africa (HSRC) and Palgrave Macmillan. My heartfelt thanks to Ana Ferreira for both her skilful editing and expert comments.

Palgrave Macmillan colleagues in London and HSRC colleagues in Cape Town exhibited the utmost professionalism and good humour. I particularly thank Joshua Pitt, Joanna O'Neill, Holly Tyler, and Dominic Walker. Special thanks to the co-editors of the *Global Research in Gender, Sexuality and Health* series, Ellen Annandale and Xiaodong Lin, and the Advisory Board, and colleagues at the HSRC, especially Mthunzi Nxawe, for their commitment to this work, and the larger concern of HIV and health inequities for black South African women.

For their excellence in research support, I thank Bharathi Radhakrishnan, Kaitlyn Gorman, Micayla Freehan, Lyndsey MacMahon. I remain grateful to Michael Scanlon, who fastidiously prepared the index, edited the references, conducted research and reviewed chapters.

Rockefeller Foundation has long-supported the field of health equity. I was very fortunate to receive a scholarly residence to the Foundation's Bellagio Centre (a heavenly place of refuge), which created an invaluable space for thinking about capabilities for South African women living with HIV. *Grazie mille* to the Foundation's Claudia Juech, Pilar Palaciá and to fellow residents. For their keen insights, I especially thank Tsitsi Dangarembga, Suzanne Skevington, Andy Feldman and Anne Marie Kimball.

A hefty thank you to UMB colleagues, particularly Zong-Guo Xia and Laura Hayman, for awarding me a Healey Grant to fund some of the field research. For additional travel funding to South Africa and a semester release from full-time teaching, I warmly thank Darren Kew, Sammy Barkin, Eben Weitzman, David Matz, David Cash and Ira Jackson. For helpful comments on the Capabilities Approach at a brown bag conversation, I thank my colleagues in the Department of Conflict Resolution, Human Security & Global Governance. For their constant professionalism and care, I heartily thank Kelly Ward, Leigh Murphy and Roni Lipton. Warmest thanks to Cynthia Enloe, Winston Langley, David W. Pantalone and to my colleagues in the Nursing Department for their steadfast support of this work, especially Rosanna DeMarco, Jean Edward, Jacqui Fawcett, Emily Jones, Suzanne Leveille and Eileen Stuart-Shor.

My sincere thanks to my students in South Africa and the US who have shown great interest in my research over the years: It has been an honour to teach and to learn from them.

Owing to the difficult subject matter, this book was challenging to write. It has been suggested that the root word of 'friendship' in German means 'place of high safety'. For the shelter and joy of friendship, I thank Laura Bures, Karen Cha, Charisse Drobis, Mary Gardill, Caroline Wanjiku Kihato, Ambika Kapur, Jennifer Kirn, Heather McKay, Annalisa Lettinga, Helen Nicholson, Suzanne Sonneborn, James Tasker, Susana Tente and Laurie Zapalac.

Finally, I offer my gratitude to my parents—Deanna Rosser, and Dale and Mary Rosser—for their abiding love and support.

Contents

List of Abbreviations

AIDS	Acquired immune deficiency syndrome
ANC	Antenatal care
ARV	Antiretroviral
AZT	Zidovudine
BMJ	British Medical Journal
CA	Capabilities (or capability) approach
cART	Combination antiretroviral therapy
CDC	Centers for Disease Control and Prevention (US)
DALE	Disability-adjusted life expectancy
DALY	Disability-adjusted life years
DOH	South African Department of Health
DREAMS	Determined, resilient, empowered, AIDS-free, mentored, and safe women
GBD	Global burden of disease
GBV	Gender-based violence
GEF	Gender equality framework
GTI	Gender-transformative intervention
HiAP	Health in all policies
HICs	High-income countries
HIV	Human immunodeficiency virus
HPV	Human papilloma virus
HSRC	Human Sciences Research Council of South Africa

HSV-2	Herpes simplex virus type 2
IDIs	In-depth interviews
IMAGE	Intervention with Microfinance for AIDS and Gender Equity
iMMR	Institutional maternal mortality rate
IPV	Intimate partner violence
LMICs	Low- and middle-income countries
LTFU	Lost to follow up in HIV care
MDGs	Millennium Development Goals
MRC	South African Medical Research Council
MTCT	Mother-to-child HIV transmission
NHI	National Health Insurance South Africa
NSP	South African National Strategic Plan on HIV, STIs and TB
PLHIV	People living with HIV
PMTCT	Prevention of mother-to-child HIV transmission
PPP	Per person per day
QALY	Quality-adjusted life years
RADAR	Rural AIDS and development action research programme
RCT	Randomised controlled trial
ROI	Record of interviews
SANAC	South African National AIDS Council
SDGs	Sustainable Development Goals
SDH	Social determinants of health
SEF	Small Enterprise Foundation
SEM	Socio-ecological model
SES	Socioeconomic status
SRHR	Sexual and reproductive health and rights
SSA	Sub-Saharan Africa
StatsSA	Statistics South Africa
STIs	Sexually transmitted infections
STM	'Sexually transmitted marks'
TB	Tuberculosis
TRIPS	Trade-related aspects of intellectual property rights
UMB	University of Massachusetts Boston
UN	United Nations
UNAIDS	Joint United Nations programme on HIV/AIDS
UNDP	United Nations Development Programme
UNICEF	United Nations Children's Fund

US	United States of America
VAW	Violence against women
VAWG	Violence against women and girls
WHO	World Health Organisation
Wits	University of the Witwatersrand

List of Figures

List of Tables

1

Introduction

Securing health as a normative social goal and *addressing gender inequalities that undermine women's opportunities to be healthy*—these challenges, formidable on their own, comprise disparate yet interwoven threads that are inextricably bound together within the ongoing problem of human immunodeficiency virus (HIV) acquisition and the disproportionate burden of HIV illness among women.

Worldwide, 36.7 million people are living with HIV (UNAIDS, 2016a). Globally, HIV remains the leading cause of death in women of reproductive age (18–44 years) (World Health Organization [WHO], 2014a).[1] Ongoing HIV risk, prevalence and premature HIV-related deaths, particularly for key populations of women, continue to raise core questions for governments, societies and the international community, concerning not just 'health as social justice' but 'health and gender as social justice'. Justice is about fairness. Questions of justice in relation to HIV rush to the fore because HIV is fully preventable and treatable, and because HIV transmission is driven, in part, by social factors and processes (UNAIDS, 2014a, 2014b). These social factors are particularly salient for women in high HIV prevalence settings, such as South Africa, which represents over 18% of the global population living with HIV

C. Sprague, *Gender and HIV in South Africa*, Global Research in Gender, Sexuality and Health, https://doi.org/10.1057/978-1-137-55997-5_1

(UNAIDS, 2014b, see pp. 17–18). South Africa is one of 19 countries with the highest (and increasing) HIV incidence in young women (aged 15–24), globally. Seventeen others are also located in sub-Saharan Africa (SSA) (UNAIDS, 2016a, 2016b). The number of new HIV infections recorded in women (aged 15–24) in those countries totalled 450,000 in 2015: equivalent to 8600 new HIV infections in women per week (UNAIDS, 2016a, 2016b). Among these 19 countries, South Africa is the indisputable leader, owing, in part, to its large population size (e.g. relative to neighbouring Lesotho, Swaziland and Botswana). In this work, I use a health equity lens to investigate the opportunities to be healthy, or *capabilities* (Sen, 1999) of black South African women who are living with HIV. Based on the findings, I address a companion question: what more, if anything, does justice require of the South African government?

Today, HIV can be managed as a chronic condition, provided people have access to essential HIV medication or combination antiretroviral therapy (cART). Indeed, the survival and improvements in the quality of life of millions of people living with the virus can be attributed to cART (Marins et al., 2003; UNAIDS, 2014b, 2016c; Walensky, Paltiel, & Losina, 2006). In settings in the developing world, this very possibility exists as a result of a victorious global social justice campaign led primarily by civil society. Access to affordable HIV medicine has been the chief battleground for the global HIV community (comprising activists, researchers and other stakeholders), to press for health to be viewed as a public good and a social justice claim (Heywood, 2009). With pivotal leadership from the Global South, including from South Africa and Brazil, this global justice movement was also successful in garnering greater recognition of the right to health as a primary aspect of ensuring well-being in ways that reshaped the global health discourse (Galvão, 2005; Rosenberg, 2001). Global health can refer to the interacting, single system affecting health worldwide, and to the health of the world population. Indeed, there is no accepted definition of global health, but rather, a set of dominant features that characterise the evolving field, including the types of problems engaged, and levels and units of analysis. Nonetheless, there is agreement on several core principles, such as the need to value health as a public good and an appropriate social justice goal and to focus particularly on populations in the developing world, where 80% of the global population resides (see Frenk & Moon, 2013; Fried, Piot, Spencer, & Parker, 2012; Koplan et al., 2009; Merson, Black, & Mills, 2011). Health equity considerations associated with the HIV epidemic among women have increasing relevance for global and national health across the domains of research, policy and practice. They promise to refashion debates over global health justice, or greater equity in health, once again by bringing gender-based considerations, typically pushed to the sidelines, to the centre.

Health equity, the ability of diverse groups in society to achieve a certain standard of health, is a chief objective of social justice (Sen, 2002). While inequality and poverty are empirical notions that are measurable, judgements of equity require that normative social assessments be undertaken, largely within national, social contexts. Research and related work on equity in health thus take intuitive notions about fairness and then seek to make them explicit (Evans, Whitehead, Diderichsen, Bhuiya, & Wirth, 2001). By definition, health inequities have a social basis—or some degree of social causation (Braveman, 2006; Diderichsen, Evans, & Whitehead, 2001; Whitehead, 1990, 1992). Because health inequities are agreed to be socially produced to some extent, they are also viewed as modifiable, through particular social policies and interventions implemented over the long term, through approaches such as 'health in all policies' (HiAP) (Braveman & Gruskin, 2003; Koivusalo, 2010; Leppo, Ollla, Pena, Wismar, & Cook, 2013). Thus, and significantly, the use of the term health equity recognises the active role and the obligation of states to ameliorate inequities in groups and populations (Braveman & Gruskin, 2003).

Within the current HIV epidemic among women, research indicates, and this work affirms, that the battleground of justice in health has now shifted from 'just health care' (or justice in health care) to social or structural determinants of health (SDHs), including gender-related factors, as a key location on which greater equity in health for women depends. Significantly, for women (particularly, but not only) in high HIV prevalence locations, both improved HIV outcomes for those living with the virus and prevention of new HIV infections in women at risk of contracting HIV rest on moving the structural drivers that foster HIV risk and transmission from the periphery to the very core of the HIV response.

This is not to say that justice in health care, or ensuring HIV testing and treatment provision in health systems, should cease (UNAIDS, 2014a). Roughly 50% of Africans living with HIV still do not have access to cART, which underscores the continuing importance of health care and systems. On the contrary, it would be more accurate to envisage social structure and health systems as multiple, connected locations that affect people's opportunities to be healthy in ways that are relational, as this work demonstrates. These concentric spheres are perhaps most visible for women in the geographical location where the majority of people, 71%, are living with HIV and acquired immune deficiency syndrome (AIDS): SSA. When it comes to gender, HIV and advancing health equity, as ever, place matters, as does social context. In SSA, HIV transmission occurs primarily through heterosexual contact, and women comprise 58% of those living with HIV (UNAIDS, 2016a). That statistic not only reveals a feminised epidemic, but also points to the influential social health determinants, including the leading role of gender-related factors in continuing to foster HIV transmission, particularly for women in the high HIV prevalence setting of Southern Africa (Leclerc-Madlala, 2008a, 2008b; UNAIDS, 2016a, 2016b, 2016c).

Gender, a social concept, is influenced by sociocultural factors, rather than anatomical ones, and refers to characteristics, such as norms, behaviours and roles, that are not located in the person but are socially constructed (Butler, 2004; Moynihan, 1998). Gender norms refer to the beliefs and actions that define social relations and the expected roles and behaviours between individuals, according to their gender categories (see Connell, 1987, 1995). Adverse gender and sociocultural norms and practices play a crucial role in generating individual or group susceptibility to disease or health conditions, and in determining access to the enabling conditions and factors that protect and promote human health and development (Sen, Östlin, & George, 2007). Gender relations are ultimately about power and influence, and gender inequality undermines health and health-seeking opportunities, also influencing vulnerability and exposure to injury, abuse and disease, especially HIV (see Diderichsen et al., 2001) (Throughout this work, I use the term 'gender equality' instead of gender equity, in line with usage by the United Nations [UN] since the Beijing 1995 conference; see UN, 2001). Indeed, sexually transmitted infections (STIs) such as HIV offer a powerful telescope into gender, health and justice in relationship within larger social systems. As Correa, Parker, & Petchesky observe:

> As always, and everywhere, 'sex' is not only about bodies and desires but also the economies, systems of governance, cultural and religious norms, kinship structures, and power dynamics of all of these issues. (2008, p. 7)

Gender can be viewed as a social or structural determinant of health (SDH). Social determinants, broadly defined as the 'full set of social conditions in which people live and work', recognise that while the causal pathways are complex, social conditions, factors and processes do indeed produce ill health (Solar & Irwin, 2007, p. 4). In social context, the interface between structural processes (i.e., processes made possible by social actors, institutions and social relations) and the gender system comprise the gendered SDHs (Sen et al., 2007). The gender system, or gender order (Connell, 1995), can be seen as nested within (though fully integrated into) the larger social order. The gender order can be viewed as the manner by which a society attributes roles, expectations of behaviour, activities and responsibilities, including what is allowed and what is *verboden*. The extant literature, together with the original research findings presented in this work, will evince just how the social structure affects health and well-being for black South African women at risk or living with HIV.

Both sociology and political philosophy can inform social health science understandings of health equity and of HIV in women, as they do within these pages. Sociologists use the term 'structure' to refer to an array of social institutions, rules and norms that govern society and that constitute the social order, recognising, however, the evolving debates taking place over such constructs within disciplines (Giddens, 1984; Sewell, 1992). Political philosophers are concerned with how social justice—fairness and equality or the 'good life'—can be realised in society, through particular social and economic institutions and the legal system, with an emphasis on normative values and considerations that shape a given social order. The philosopher John Rawls called the social structure the basic structure, which he viewed as the location of justice (1971).

Within the capabilities approach (CA), Sen refers to structure as social arrangements, but also to social opportunities and economic facilities that influence what individuals are able to do and be (1999, see pp. 36–49; 2011).

In the social health sciences, structural factors or determinants are those that generate social stratification and divisions among social classes in society. Social stratification processes effectively locate individuals' or groups' social position within the social hierarchy and then determine the access of individuals or groups to the social and economic resources that are associated with power and status, education, and employment, which serve as influential determinants of health and well-being. Because structural factors associated with HIV transmission are rooted in society, they are viewed as 'socially governed' and capable of being changed (Sen et al., 2007, p. xii). Moreover, there is wide agreement, informed by a growing evidence base, that gender norms and factors affecting HIV transmission can be modified over the long term through targeted policies and selected interventions. Both HIV and intimate partner violence (IPV) risk can be reduced to some degree through prevention efforts, as will be illustrated through a review of the extant literature and a detailed focus on the IMAGE (Intervention with Microfinance for AIDS and Gender Equity) and Stepping Stones intervention (Chap. 7).

In terms of gender and HIV risk, South African men and women are not equal in their risk of contracting HIV or in their burden of HIV disease. Rather, gender plays an important role in shaping the HIV risk environment in South African social context, as does race (see Tables 2.1 and 2.2). Black South African women are more likely to acquire HIV, compared with men and with women of other race groups[2] (On these racial categories, which were socially constructed in South Africa, see footnote 2). Moreover, it is also black South African women who bear a disproportionate burden of HIV disease, compared with women of other race groups at all ages, and relative to men, from birth up to age 59 (Shisana et al., 2005, 2009, 2014; see Chap. 2, Tables 2.1 and 2.2). Alongside increasing HIV incidence in young women aged 15–24, HIV prevalence has remained elevated in black women aged 20–39 years, ranging from 17.4% to 31.6% (Shisana et al., 2014). At the same time, in black women aged 50 years and older, there has been an increase in new HIV infections that mirrors the increases in new HIV infections, coupled with the ageing of those already living with HIV in mature populations, both in SSA and in other global regions (Sprague & Brown, 2016; UNAIDS, 2013) (see Chap. 2, Tables 2.1 and 2.2). In comparison, HIV prevalence in South African women of other race groups reveals a striking contrast. For them, HIV prevalence is an estimated 0.8% or less (Shisana et al., 2014).

HIV has also been making a substantial contribution to premature mortality in black South African women, while reducing life expectancy and increasing maternal mortality as part of long-term trends for this population (Government of South Africa, 2015b; Msemburi et al., 2016; Stats SA, 2016). Recent improvements among these indicators are encouraging (Buchmann, Mnyani, Frank, Chersich, & McIntyre, 2015; Burton, 2013), but have so far failed to counteract the deleterious impact of HIV, which affects black South African women's prospects for human development and well-being, over the entire life course.

Black South African women constitute the largest proportion of women in the country, and those living with HIV currently comprise 3.9 million of the 7 million South Africans living with HIV (Stats SA, 2016). HIV thus represents one of the foremost health challenges for South Africa. Given South Africa's share of the global HIV epidemic (over 18%), what happens in South Africa has importance for the HIV problem and response at the global level, for countries in high HIV prevalence settings with similar HIV transmission dynamics, and with potential lessons for other settings as well. Indeed, high HIV risk and infection is also a lived reality for poorer women in other low- and middle-income countries (LMICs) and high-income country settings (HICs), including the US South, where women experience marked social disadvantage (Centers for Disease Control and Prevention [CDC], 2017a, b, 2018).

While economic factors play a significant role in HIV risk and can be seen as one among a set of structural drivers of HIV risk in women, it would be a mistake to think that HIV is about poverty alone.[3] If we look closely enough, and patiently work to untangle the tightly woven, disparate threads binding health and gender within the ongoing HIV epidemic among women, the social basis underlying HIV transmission in women will become more visible. Indeed, in the high HIV burden countries, a triumvirate of structural factors have been found to facilitate HIV transmission in women: poverty and economic inequality, gender inequality and social norms that condone violence, and social constructions of gender—femininities and masculinities (a focus of Chap. 2) (see Jewkes, Flood, & Lang, 2015; Jewkes, Levin, & Penn-Kekana, 2002; Jewkes, Martin, & Penn-Kekana, 2002; Jewkes, Penn-Kekana, & Rose-Junius, 2005). Additionally, HIV stigma, a social and an intersubjective process of discrediting or 'othering' individuals or groups, also plays an essential role in affecting women's agency once they acquire HIV, with consequences for their mental and physical health, and highly negative implications for women's HIV care linkage and adherence (these connections are discussed in Chaps. 3, 6 and 8; see Farmer, 1992; Goffman, 1963; Yang et al., 2007; HSRC, 2015; Link & Phelan, 2001).

Despite the large evidence that has accumulated on the role and influence of social or structural drivers in fostering HIV acquisition in women in South and Southern Africa (and elsewhere), most national strategic plans (NSPs) on HIV and AIDS—the steering policy documents governing epidemic responses in countries—continue to devote the largest share of their human and financial resources to HIV treatment for those individuals who have already contracted the virus. While these efforts are necessary and laudable, in South Africa, women's risk of acquiring HIV has not been offset by the massive effort to advance the rollout of HIV treatment begun in 2004 on the back of a reforming public health system: instead, it remains amplified (Coovadia, Jewkes, Barron, Sanders, & McIntyre, 2009; SANAC, 2014, see pp. 3, 8, 10; Sprague, 2009). Such systematic health differences related to HIV risk, burden of disease and premature mortality in black South African women, relative to other groups of South African women and men, can be located within global trends of increasing social health inequalities.

Global Health Improvements Alongside Increasing Social Health Inequalities

The 'big story' of global health has been unprecedented progress over the last 60 years (Bartley, 2017), akin to a health 'revolution'. Life expectancy for women, for example, has been rising across settings: exceeding 80 years of age in over 40 countries in 2014, with recent indications that it may cross the 90-year threshold by 2030 (Kontis et al., 2017). Even many LMICs have achieved improved life expectancy and reduced mortality for poorer populations (Hogan et al., 2010; WHO, 2014b). Notably, these advances in health have largely been attributed to SDHs, including improved socio-economic status (SES), living and working conditions, much of this driven by social policies. A more modest contribution has been generated by enhanced medical care (Marmot, 2015).

Nonetheless, these health gains have not been replicated across all world regions. Despite some reductions in mortality and gains in life expectancy attributed to cART in SSA as mentioned, HIV is persisting in undercutting the life chances of African women (UNAIDS, 2014b, 2016a). African women's poorer health outcomes are evident in their reduced life expectancy and elevated maternal mortality, relative to women in most other geographical settings (Bartley, 2017; Hogan et al., 2010; Marmot, 2015; Smith, Bambra, & Hill, 2015). A mounting evidence base has pointed to the increasing role of social factors in degrading health, particularly for groups who are already socially disadvantaged, such as for black women in South Africa. Differences in health outcomes between groups in society on the basis of race, class, income or geography—social health inequalities—are glaring. Systematic health differences raise fundamental questions about equity and fairness across and within many societies (Anand, Peter, & Sen, 2004; Evans et al., 2001). Indeed, health inequalities are a major theme of, and challenge for, global and national public health and governance (Frenk & Moon, 2013; Marmot, 2015).

The recognition of social determinants, and the social environment's role in disease risk and acquisition, must be rooted within an historical arc of health improvements. Health improvements among populations in the nineteenth century were associated with improvements in nutrition and in the environments in which people lived and worked; in the twentieth century, they were focused on individual behaviours to reduce smoking, as part of dominant epidemiological approaches (Marmot, 1998). The WHO's 1948 Constitution recognised the influence of social and political conditions on health. A nascent health equity agenda began to develop in earnest. The agenda built upon the scaffolding of WHO's Constitution, coupled with the 1978 Alma Ata Declaration, and the UK's Black Report (Black, Morris, Smith, & Townsend, 1980). The resulting agenda must be seen as a joint scientific-social justice venture involving very many actors, with advances made on the back of the groundwork laid, in part, with the very origins of the United Nations (UN) in the aftermath of the Second World War, including the establishment of the WHO as the UN's lead international health institution in 1946 (see WHO, 1988).

Revolutionary at the time, Alma-Ata and its 'Achieving Health for All by 2000' tag line had at least four salient features that were central in developing a global commitment to health equity. First, health was explicitly agreed to be a human right and an important social goal, with governments holding primary responsibility for the health of their citizens. Second, the importance of active participation of citizens in the planning and implementation of their health care was recognised. Third, primary health care was to be the unequivocal foundation of the health care systems of nations. Fourth, Alma-Ata identified gross inequalities in the health status of populations in the industrialised and developing countries, and intergroup inequalities within countries, and deemed them unacceptable (Alma Ata, 1978; Lawn et al., 2008). Such blatant social health inequalities became the catalyst for the emerging health equity research and policy agenda (Marmot, 2015; Marmot & Shipley, 2006; WHO, 2010). Further improvements in health, the evidence showed and many in the international health community agreed, required engaging with the social basis of ill health.[4]

Due to the high visibility and successful dissemination of the investigations cited, combined with successful social activism against the negative effects of globalisation, and dynamic political, social, health and demographic transitions underway in their countries, many policy stakeholders have become more aware of and willing to engage with persistent social health inequalities, including through the Sustainable Development Goals (SDGs). The SDGs aim to build on the MDGs (first established in 2000), while addressing critical gaps (*Lancet* Editorial, 2014; Stuart & Woodroffe, 2016). Since then, three noteworthy shifts can be identified that have relevance for health and gender as social justice and for gaining ground on the HIV epidemic in women. First is the expanding role of the social environment in influencing scientific thinking, not solely in the health sciences, but across a cluster of disciplines. Stern captures this development as 'social co-creation' (as co-authors and I have noted elsewhere, see Sprague, Scanlon, & Pantalone, 2017b):

> [T]he role of the social environment has become more emphasized in the emergence of language ... meaning ... morality ... identity ... and the self—all of which are now seen largely in the light of their social co-creation. (2013, p. 78)

Second is the potential for greater translation of research—particularly concerning the social basis undergirding ill health—into policy (Leppo et al., 2013). Third, and closely tied to the second, is a shift, captured in writings from political philosophy to sociology and public health, from a focus on *personal responsibility* for health and individual behaviour to a *social responsibility* for health that recognises the multiple social and biological determinants that influence health and social health inequalities within and across different countries (see Gupta, Parkhurst, Ogden, Aggleton, & Mahal, 2008; Marmot, 2015; Pogge, 2004; Wikler, 2004).

While social health inequalities and health inequities are terms used interchangeably, even within the public health community (see Dahlgren & Whitehead, 1992), the distinctions matter. Health inequities, the term used throughout this work, can be defined as a subset of health inequalities that are systematic, frequent, substantial, persistent (not random) and associated with social disadvantage (Braveman & Gruskin, 2003; Whitehead, 1990, 1992). Conceptions of equity in society are not acontextual or free-floating. Rather, they reflect deeply held social values tethered to a social, historical context that serve to anchor countries' notions of, what Aristotle called, 'the good' and, what other philosophers have called, the 'good life', including governance structures and institutions (1998, p. 207). Equity is a quintessentially ethical notion. While ethical discourse at the global level engages in debates about 'translocal' values, and seeks to shape global governance and goals, as Kleinman notes, ethical discourse is 'generated out of and applied in local worlds' (2004, p. 270). It is lived out at the local level in 'moral processes' that are tethered to local conditions and relations. This is why notions of health equity must be rooted within the ethics of the everyday, of the social experience of people, as Kleinman emphasises, and within social context (2004, p. 270).

Within political philosophy, ethics and the social health sciences, there has been attention to questions of what justice demands of states in relation to the health of citizens. Some theorists and public health scholars have made explicit reference to the problem of HIV and AIDS as a problem of justice. The theory-to-practice discourse has historically been dominated, however, by practical concerns over the lack of access to affordable essential medicines for poorer countries earlier in the epidemic (Heywood, 2009). There has been recognition by many scholars that HIV is particularly problematic because it is a preventable infection that results in high numbers of premature deaths, suggesting that a higher degree of avoidability is possible through government action (Ruger, 2006; Sen, 2002).

More generally, philosophers have been slow to give health (as opposed to health care) special moral significance because prominent philosophers, such as Rawls (1971, 1993), failed to engage with health (Ruger, 2006). Others, such as Daniels (1981, 2008), have asserted that health is not an appropriate focal point for evaluating social justice claims (Peter, 2004; Ruger, 2004a, 2004b). More recent and exciting scholarship on what health as social justice demands has resulted (Bartley, 2017; Marmot, 2015; Ruger, 2010; Venkatapuram, 2011). There has been some reference to but little substantive engagement of HIV acquisition in women as a social justice concern, however, that engages with the problem of gender inequality and gender-related norms from interdisciplinary perspectives and an eye toward states' obligations.

There has been concerted emphasis on addressing poor health outcomes and advancing health equity at global and national levels, though much of the dominant research and discourse fuelling policy on health equity has come out of the HICs, and maintains an emphasis on health care (Koivusalo, 2010), with a more recent push to advance universal health care (UHC), globally, as part of the SDGs. The US case is instructive for its focus on achieving access to health care as the frontline for health as social justice. This is particularly manifest in the Trump administration's commitment to roll back Obamacare as a way of releasing the government from commitments to expanding access to health care for the uninsured US population that were made under the Obama administration. Indeed, there is no system of UHC in the US. A right to health care is not recognised in US constitutional or statutory law, and the right to health enshrined in the International Covenant on Economic, Social and Cultural Rights has never been ratified by the US. Moreover, no US state has, to date, recognised health care as a human right in its constitution—although there are progressive states that have recognised health as a public good, such as Vermont. Hence, there is no path to demand UHC in the US via the courts: it must be done through legislation (see MacNaughton, Haigh, McGill, Koutsioumpas, & Sprague, 2015).

In contrast, upper middle-income countries such as South Africa and Brazil have a greater commitment to health as a human right than some HICs and LMICs. This includes the provision of essential medicines for the treatment of HIV, tuberculosis and other conditions (Bilchitz, 2006; Galvão, 2005; Government of South Africa, 1996; Lima, 2007; Teixeira, 2003). However, in these settings, resources are fewer, including for health infrastructure, care and staffing, and data on key indicators to monitor health and well-being are often incomplete or absent. This includes basic statistics, DHS data and civil registration systems (WHO, 2014b). Governance, civil society, legislation and social institutions to enact remedies in response to shortfalls in health achievements also vary to a large degree in the Global South. Moreover, these responses are not well documented in the international literature.

Alongside the global discourse, it is national authorities that formulate and deliver health policies in ways that create the conditions by which citizens and even non-citizens can be healthy (Vearey, 2010). In LMIC settings, the under-funded national public health systems typically provide the majority of health-promoting interventions and activities. Indeed, at the national and local levels in countries, structures of inequality can be reinforced or challenged by national authorities. This suggests that any hope of advancing health, and health as social justice, must fully engage with national health authorities, rooting responses in national, social context, governance and institutions. Yet, paradoxically, due to the influence of SDHs, research and action to address health inequities must engage with the structural-level domains, and factors that are connected to but exist outside of the reach of health system interventions: households, communities, schools, workplaces. This reinforces the need for greater intersectoral collaboration in country contexts, which has been emphasised by WHO (2010). Looking at a swath of countries across income settings, this reality suggests a very mixed picture in terms of strategies and points of intervention that would enable countries to address health inequities, including across the linked domains of accessing quality health care and SDHs, including gender. The policy discourse and the potential for addressing health inequity, through various mechanisms in law and policy, will differ among settings—and these are worth noting because health equity assessments will need to be diverse and varied, and paths to remedies will, similarly, vary.

As an upper middle-income country with decent health and physical infrastructure, South Africa possesses features of poorer-resource settings, as well as industrialised, resource-rich ones (with its early adoption of some technologies and significant contributions to medicine and public health research and practice. Recall that the first heart transplant was performed in Cape Town at Groote Schuur Hospital.) With its robust civil society, South Africa has been at the vanguard of the HIV epidemic response and its culture of activism against social injustice. The pursuit of greater gender equality can be situated within a larger struggle for social transformation that has been unfolding since independence in 1994. As a location of enquiry, the South African government's obligation to protect and advance women's health and their substantive equality in law and policy is substantial and highly progressive. Its health and HIV policies are noteworthy, making South Africa an important location for investigations that substantively link public health with law and human rights, like this one.

The 1996 Constitution established the primacy of fundamental values of equality and justice that would underpin a non-racial new democracy, giving shape to new institutions that were predicated on social equity, with laws and policies aimed at social transformation (Bilchitz, 2008; Woolman, 2008). The state's obligation towards citizens and even non-citizens is enshrined in the basic law (Government of South Africa, 1996). The 1996 Constitution sets forth a set of justiciable socio-economic rights, although it also establishes provisions for justifiable limitations on those rights (Woolman, 2008). Critics want a hard core of socio-economic rights or more, notes Woolman (2008; Bilchitz, 2006, 2008). Law academics and lawyers routinely grouse that socio-economic rights are weak in construction, as the focus is on 'progressive realisation' of those rights according to 'reasonable' plans and 'available resources' (Woolman, 2008).

There are 27 substantive provisions in the Bill of Rights that impose negative and positive duties on the South African state. South Africans possess the right of access to health care, food, water and social security in Section 27(1), the right to housing in Section 26(1), the right to bodily integrity within Section 12's right to freedom and security of the person, and within the Domestic Violence Act 116 of 1998, and in South Africa's commitment to the Convention on the Elimination of All Forms of Discrimination against Women (CEDAW) (Meyersfeld, 2003, 2008; Woolman & Sprague, 2015). Alongside the existence of these rights sit a range of governing policy frameworks and accompanying health policies to support women's health, which are located largely in the public health system (discussed in Chap. 3). Again, all of this makes South Africa relevant to many different social and economic contexts.

Thus far, there has been a vigorous engagement with HIV in South Africa as a public health concern, with some relevance for health as social justice in the published literature. The preponderance of scholarship on South Africa's HIV epidemic has emphasised distinct and significant lines of enquiry, from public health to sociology to political philosophy, law and policy. A prominent focus earlier in the HIV epidemic was on law and policy in the absence of HIV treatment, with a spate of studies emerging over the years to consider South Africa's obligations to treat its growing population living with HIV, using law, human rights and public health arguments (Heywood, 2003; Nattrass, 2004; Sprague & Woolman, 2006). There has been a great deal of research that investigates culture, health and sexuality and implications for women living with or at risk of HIV in South and Southern Africa (discussed in detail in Chap. 2). Gender, HIV and social justice have not been investigated sufficiently in the South African context. Indeed, there seems to be no enquiry to date that investigates the problem of high HIV prevalence, incidence and poor health outcomes in black South African women as a joint public health and social justice concern that engages with women's capabilities, while also considering the South African government's obligation in response to potential health inequities for women. This work is located in that lacuna. I engage with several dominant themes that link normative considerations to empirical research in public health, health sociology and law in ways that are relevant to other complex social problems with health dimensions. The analyses undertaken rely on interdisciplinary approaches to wrestle with these concerns.

Worth noting at this stage is the possibility for bringing various disciplines together, combining strengths and stretching their boundaries to address the distinctive aspects of HIV in women in ways that might have application for other social health problems. The opportunity to do so in relation to the HIV epidemic in women announces itself with renewed urgency. Indeed, HIV has contributed to reshaping conventional disciplinary lines of demarcation in fields, from medical or social anthropology to social epidemiology, health (or medical) sociology and others. The establishment of the subfield of health and human rights might perhaps be the most prominent example of a discipline that has arguably had the most positive impact on the community of people living with HIV, globally and nationally in South Africa (Gruskin, Mills, & Tarantola, 2007; Mann, 1997). Additionally, this is a key moment to maximise research methods in order to engage with multi-level determinants and factors, including social structure and processes of social stratification, that foster systematic health differences for socially disadvantaged groups and undermine their well-being. I discuss these possibilities in Chaps. 5 and 9 (see also Sprague, Scanlon, & Pantalone, 2017b).

Aims and Scope

To investigate the problem of HIV in black South African women and its influence on women's health, I adopt a dual public health and social justice lens and focus on two lines of enquiry: 1) What are HIV positive women's opportunities to be healthy—their capabilities—in this context? Based on the research findings, combined with results from other studies, 2) What more does justice demand of the state's HIV response, if anything? To engage these questions, I employ a range of bases of information and knowledge sources, from theories of health justice to empirical evidence, using interdisciplinary research methods. The assumption made is that doing so allows for profiting from the richness that multiple perspectives and methods offer. The inclusion of systematic reviews with larger datasets and statistical trend data offer the benefits of large samples and statistical power. The quantitative data are paired with original qualitative empirical research I conducted among 89 black South African women living with HIV in two provinces. A primary focus of that investigation is on gaining access to and elevating women's lived experience and their agency in social context. The work captured in these pages also draws from a well of related research I have undertaken, with my co-authors and individually, on black South African women living with HIV, as a principal concern, for over a decade. Taken together, I explore this problem and possible responses on four distinct levels, while drawing out lessons for other settings where possible:

1. At the theoretical level—primarily through the CA, which theorises 'health as social justice' as individuals' or groups' opportunities (capabilities) to be healthy. The use of this approach, I argue, has a number of distinct features and benefits (discussed further below, in Chaps. 4 and 9). Briefly, it makes a contribution to theorising health as social justice generally, and in ways that capture the complexities of women living with HIV particularly. The CA engages with social arrangements and structure, while going 'deep' into women's lived experiences of health and well-being. This is necessary because these dimensions are otherwise obscured. The CA generates an empirical quality-of-life assessment while also constituting a normative approach. Thus, it can move from theory to evidence in ways that serve to guide social evaluation and action—ultimately with a view to achieving greater equity in health (Chaps. 4, 6 and 8).
2. At the health system level, which comprises the point of health care and HIV services delivery for women. Equal opportunity or fair access to health care is usually the focal point of social justice claims. Given women's ongoing need for HIV services for their health, and even survival, it is fair to ask whether their access to and uptake of HIV care is assured and what impediments remain, if any, and the nature and extent of those impediments (Chap. 3).

3. At the social (community) level, where HIV risk is embedded and perpetuated, by engaging with social structure in communities, specifically gender and social norms that influence women's risk of HIV acquisition, and also, targeted interventions that seek to overturn these norms in the long term (Chap. 7).
4. At the law and policy level—through engagement with South Africa's constitutional obligation, health and HIV policy framework and the NSP. This recognises that analysing progress on health goals in policy and claims to justice for this population must be considered against the state's duty in policy and in the basic law (Chaps. 3 and 8).

Unravelling the distinct dimensions of this South African problem, the threats it poses to South African women's health and human development in this high HIV prevalence setting, requires a powerful conceptual framework—one that is able to offer a rich, deep, nuanced and complex understanding of women's well-being. Following extensive consideration of many frameworks—and their application in selected chapters of this work (see discussion of the socio-ecological model [SEM] in Chap. 3), the capability approach, also called the capabilities approach (CA), was elected.

The Capabilities Approach: A Conceptual Framework for Investigating Women's Opportunities to Be Healthy

The CA was first formulated by the social welfare economist and Nobel Laureate Amartya Sen (see 1992, 1999, 2011) and extended by his collaborator, the political philosopher Martha Nussbaum (2000, 2003, 2011). They have worked in concert and individually to develop the framework over the years and both pay special attention to women's well-being. I very briefly summarise elements of it here, while offering a more expansive treatment, with specific reference to the problem of HIV in black South African women, in Chap. 4.

The CA recognises human beings as having a set of 'capabilities' (short for capability set) that may expand or contract, depending on conditions, factors and institutions that are available to support these capabilities. The CA is a social justice approach to human development that is centrally concerned with considerations of quality of life. It is used in the social evaluation of well-being for individuals or groups, their social arrangements and assessments of policies aimed at social change (Robeyns, 2003). The CA is rich, both in its formulation of what capabilities constitute for individual human development (or that of groups) and in its attention to the process of social deliberation by which societies and governments would seek to address capability deprivations in key populations. Sen suggests that any social evaluation of capabilities must be done with reference to whether the real freedom of individuals has been expanded. He thus emphasises the centrality of freedom in the development process and the ability of individuals to have the substantive freedom to make choices that will expand their capabilities, or to make choices that allow them to construct a life of meaning, echoing the Aristotelian conceptions of the good life that underpin the CA (Sen, 1999).

The choice and relevance of the capabilities framework for this work are based on its incisive ability to probe and generate deeper insights into the fundamental capabilities question about what this particular group of South African women are able to do and be (Nussbaum, 2000; Sen, 1999). The CA thus serves as a complement to the focus on women's lived experiences of being HIV positive (Chap. 6). It assists in shedding light on women's agentic aspirations and constraints, their opportunity and process freedoms, within the South African context, which yields an analysis of greater depth and insight.

Additionally, the CA gives attention to women's particular health and development needs and constraints in society over the life course. It links health explicitly with human development processes. The approach allows for an empirical, comparative quality-of-life assessment along a range of indicators. The CA has been elected, too, for its consistency with South Africa's constitutional framework and entitlements in the basic law (Government of South Africa, 1996). Human rights in South African law parallel capabilities to an uncanny extent. Health equity is embedded within key policies of the South African health sector, where equity serves as a principle underlying the embrace of the National Health Insurance

(NHI) health sector reform. In sum, the CA offers a number of distinctive strengths in investigating the nature and magnitude of this problem. It is not without significant limitations, however (discussed in Chaps. 4 and 9).

Thus far, I have articulated the scope of this work, and the theoretical framework used to conceptualise and investigate this problem. I have set some of the issues of concern against the backdrop of global social health inequalities, drawing attention to changes in the research and policy discourse to embrace the social role and responsibility in health, and greater equity in health, while depicting the trends posed by HIV as an ongoing health threat for women in South and SSA. In the remainder of this introduction, I offer a thumbnail sketch of the chapters to come.

Road Map for the Journey: Preview of Chapters

Chapter 2 moves from empirical to normative considerations in three parts. In part one, I consider the magnitude of HIV in black South African women. Despite recent gains, the evidence base indicates that black South African women have high HIV-related premature mortality and lower life expectancy at birth, relative to South African women of other race groups. In part two, I engage with the complex set of factors that underpin high HIV risk and transmission among this population, spanning social and biological factors; discuss debates concerning women's constrained agency; and review the latest evidence. Taken together, health outcomes and social factors affecting this population paint a stark portrait of HIV's deleterious long-term effects on black South African women's health. In part three, I begin to apply normative considerations of health and social justice to the empirical evidence, concluding that reliance on a single information source in assessing justice in health (such as health outcomes) misleads, thus necessitating engagement with additional bases of information and evidence, starting with health care.

Chapter 3 shifts the site of investigation to black South African women's opportunities to access health and HIV care within the South African public health system as a minimum requirement of justice. It reviews

South Africa's national HIV policy framework, goals and progress in meeting them; and investigates access to and provision of health and HIV care in the public health system. Using the socio-ecological framework, primary barriers to HIV care and factors that influence HIV care linkage, dropout, adherence and retention are identified along four dimensions: intrapersonal, interpersonal, health systems and structural. A number of key gaps in both the policy and the health system response in relation to HIV among women are brought to light. The analysis reveals that health and HIV care, together with the policy framework, comprise layers within a multi-tiered, larger edifice of enabling or disabling conditions and locations that determine and support women's health. These, however, offer an inadequate base from which to gain an in-depth insight into HIV-positive women's prospects for health and well-being and greater equity in health for this population. I conclude that gaining such insight requires investigation into this population's opportunities to be healthy, or capabilities.

This chapter presents the conceptual framework used to shed light on the research problem: the CA. A set of guiding questions are taken up that radiate from HIV in women as a social justice and public health problem, and form part of ongoing South African national and global health debates. These encompass the special nature of health, viewing health as a normative social goal, debates associated with social valuations of health and the difficulties in locating health (as opposed to health care) within a moral social justice framework. Features of the CA, its relevance, strengths and limitations are communicated, as are the ways that the CA accommodates and answers these debates.

Chapter 5 locates the research methods applied in the empirical investigation within approaches that embrace a normative social justice commitment to undertaking research among vulnerable populations and to advancing equity in health. I highlight the South African context at the time of the study's inception, and the rationale for selecting qualitative methods against a background of quantitative HIV studies that had long dominated the published literature on cART and prevention of mother-to-child HIV transmission (PMTCT). I describe the strengths of qualitative research methods in health equity and social justice research, generally, and in investigating women's capabilities to be healthy particularly. I discuss methods debates in the social health sciences, and review some chief challenges introduced in studies such as this one. I highlight the potential for qualitative research methods to advance knowledge of health inequities, and suggest possibilities for such research methods to be beneficial for participants and researchers in ways that engage with social injustice.

Chapter 6 investigates women's opportunities to be healthy based on original empirical research conducted among a sample population of 89 South African women living with HIV and 44 key informants. I present women's lived experiences (offering an internal perspective) in accessing health and HIV services in four public health facilities in two provinces, distilling the dominant themes and influential factors that emerge from the narratives of women living with HIV across the sample. This is followed by health provider and key informant views (providing an external perspective). Following the presentation of the findings, I elaborate the themes in the discussion section, applying the CA to consider what the empirical results tell us about the health and well-being of these HIV positive women within this social context, and what the data suggest for women's capabilities along ten domains (Nussbaum, 2000). I ask this guiding question: do South African women living with HIV meet the threshold level of capabilities? This chapter reveals a set of capability deprivations for women, particularly in the domains of life, bodily health, bodily integrity and control over their material environment.

Chapter 7 explores the evidence on structural gender-transformative interventions (GTIs) undertaken in community settings. I present assumptions, evolution in concepts, criteria for and examples of, two GTIs which offer evidence about what is capable of being changed in relation to social factors and drivers that facilitate HIV risk and infection in social settings. I highlight the evidence of their effectiveness and limitations. Together, the findings from the two case studies—Stepping Stones and IMAGE—indicate that GTIs can protect against enhance women's capabilities by reducing HIV and IPV risk, reshaping gender norms and supporting gender equality. I also highlight distinct features that underpin the ability of these GTIs to be effective at creating structural-level change, closing with further debates and continuing challenges.

Chapter 8 conducts an assessment of whether the ongoing problem of HIV in black South African women constitutes a health inequity. Nested within the health equity analysis is a section that considers key capabilities in direct relation to human rights afforded to South African women in the basic law. The assessment concludes that (a) this problem does constitute a health inequity that is modifiable; (b) four central capabilities are undermined and these have direct counterparts in Sections 11, 12 and 27 of the South African Constitution; (c) the current government response to HIV in South African women is insufficient because it fails to attend to the social factors that foster HIV risk and transmission in women; (d) relational factors associated with the basic social structure are contributing to HIV in this population; and (e) this problem can be socially governed, which generates an obligation by agents of the State to take further action to ameliorate HIV in women and to facilitate the enjoyment of their rights. Moreover, the government and the South African National AIDS Council are aware of these structural drivers, but have failed thus far to address them fully in the NSP on HIV.

In the final section (i.e. Chap. 9), I reflect on the particular strengths of applying the CA to the problem, which may have relevance for other settings and other types of complex social problems. I highlight its distinguishing strengths and limitations, and close by offering a set of reflections, with selected areas for further research, policy and practice.

Notes

1. Health science publications typically seek the latest available data. Robust data from low- and middle-income countries (LMIC) settings are not always available, however. Publications cited in this work are those that specifically track, analyse and offer comparative data on key trends in particular population groups in these settings (such as women generally, African women, or young women aged 15–24). These publications may be several years old and still constitute the latest data. Additionally, the key (high-quality) reports cited and released in South Africa, such as the *South African National HIV Prevalence, Incidence and Behaviour and Survey* and the *National Burden of Disease Study for South Africa*, are released typically only every 3–5 years. With other works (e.g. on health equity or gender), I am highlighting significant foundational texts or reports, rather than the latest publication dealing with the subject matter.

The dearth of data in LMICs, a theme emerging from the Millennium Development Goals (MDGs) that is reaffirmed in this work, has important ethical and equity dimensions: the lack of and poor-quality data in LMICs raise questions concerning who is counted, and thus whose health and lives matter.

2. Race is a social construct. Today, prominent scientists agree that the biological basis of race is so weak as to require cessation in using racial categories in genetics research: 'Racial categories are weak proxies for genetic diversity and need to be phased out' (see Gannon, 2016, p. 1). I employ the racial categories here in the South African context, which were socially constructed, had a highly deleterious impact on people's life chances and experiences for decades (and which continues for many), and are still in use in data collection, in order for redress to occur (see Gutto, 2002; Habib & Bentley, 2008). These are African or black, coloured, white and Asian.
3. The award-winning author, film director and activist Tsitsi Dangarembga created a short film (17 minutes) that powerfully engages the struggles of a rural Zimbabwean woman seeking to care for a vulnerable AIDS (acquired immune deficiency syndrome) orphan, Tabitha, during the Zimbabwean economic crisis. The film underscores the essential role of family and community in sharing the burden of caring for their most vulnerable members, while highlighting the political determinants of health. *The Sharing Day* can be seen here: http://tve.org/film/the-sharing-day/.
4. Jong-wook (2003), former director general of the World Health Organization (WHO) (2003–2006), first sought to connect the global 'Health for All' campaign to the international HIV epidemic and to WHO's health equity agenda. Before his death, Jong-wook wrote that the most urgent objectives for WHO included the health-related MDGs and the '3 by 5' targets for HIV/AIDS treatment, which aimed to make essential HIV medication accessible to 3 million people, mainly in the poorest countries, by the end of 2005.

References

Alma-Ata Declaration. (1978). Retrieved October 19, 2017, from http://www.who.int/publications/almaata_declaration_en.pdf

Anand, S., Peter, F., & Sen, A. (Eds.). (2004). *Public Health, Ethics, and Equity*. Oxford: Oxford University Press.

Bartley, M. (2017). *Health Inequality: An Introduction to Concepts, Theories and Methods* (2nd ed.). Cambridge: Polity.

Bilchitz, D. (2006). The right to health. In S. Woolman & M. Bishop (Eds.), *Constitutional Law of South Africa* (2nd ed.). Cape Town: Juta Press, Chapter 56A.

Bilchitz, D. (2008). *Poverty and Fundamental Rights: The Justification and Enforcement of Socio-Economic Rights*. Oxford: Oxford University Press.

Black, D., Morris, J., Smith, C., & Townsend, P. (1980). *Inequalities in Health: Report of a Research Working Group*. London: Department of Health and Social Security.

Braveman, P. (2006). Health disparities and health equity: Concepts and measurement. *Annual Review of Public Health, 27*, 167–194.

Braveman, P., & Gruskin, S. (2003). Defining equity in health. *Journal of Epidemiology and Community Health, 57*(4), 254–258.

Buchmann, E., Mnyani, C., Frank, K., Chersich, M., & McIntyre, J. (2015). Declining maternal mortality in the face of persistently high HIV prevalence in a middle-income country. *BJOG, 122*(2), 220–227.

Burton, R. (2013). Maternal health: There is cause for optimism. *South African Medical Journal, 103*(8), 520–521.

Butler, J. (2004). *Undoing Gender*. New York: Routledge.

CDC. (2017a). *Selected National HIV Prevention and Care Outcomes in the United States*. [online]. Atlanta: CDC. Retrieved January 15, 2018 from https://www.cdc.gov/hiv/pdf/library/factsheets/cdc-hiv-national-hiv-care-outcomes.pdf

CDC. (2017b). *HIV Among Women*. [online]. Atlanta: CDC. Retrieved January 15, 2018, from http://www.cdc.gov/hiv/group/gender/women/

CDC. (2018). *HIV and AIDS in the United States by Geographic Distribution* [online]. Atlanta: CDC. Retrieved January 15, 2018, from https://www.cdc.gov/hiv/statistics/overview/geographicdistribution.html

Connell, R. (1987). *Gender and Power: Society, the Person and Sexual Politics*. Stanford: Stanford University Press.

Connell, R. (1995). *Masculinities*. Berkeley: University of California Press.

Coovadia, H., Jewkes, R., Barron, P., Sanders, D., & McIntyre, D. (2009). The health and health system of South Africa: Historical roots of current public health challenges. *Lancet, 374*(9692), 817–834.

Correa, S., Petchesky, R., & Parker, R. (2008). *Sexuality, Health and Human Rights*. New York: Routledge.

Dahlgren, G., & Whitehead, M. (1992). *Policies and Strategies to Promote Equity in Health*. Copenhagen: World Health Organization Regional Office for Europe.

Daniels, N. (1981). Health care needs and distributive justice. *Philosophy and Public Affairs, 10*(2), 146–179.
Daniels, N. (2008). *Just Health: Meeting Health Needs Fairly*. Cambridge: Cambridge University Press.
Diderichsen, F., Evans, T., & Whitehead, M. (2001). The social disparities in health. In T. Evans, M. Whitehead, F. Diderichsen, A. Bhuiya, & M. Wirth (Eds.), *Challenging Inequities to Health: From Ethics to Action* (pp. 12–23). Oxford: Oxford University Press.
Evans, T., Whitehead, M., Diderichsen, F., Bhuiya, A., & Wirth, M. (Eds.). (2001). *Challenging Inequities to Health: From Ethics to Action*. Oxford: Oxford University Press.
Farmer, P. (1992). *AIDS & Accusation, Haiti and the Geography of Blame*. Berkeley: University of California Press.
Frenk, J., & Moon, S. (2013). Governance challenges in global health. *New England Journal of Medicine, 368*, 936–942.
Fried, L., Piot, P., Spencer, H., & Parker, R. (2012). The changing landscape of global public health. *Global Public Health, 7*(Suppl. 1), S1–S4.
Galvão, J. (2005). Brazil and access to HIV/AIDS drugs: A question of human rights and public health. *American Journal of Public Health, 95*(7), 1110–1115.
Gannon, M. (2016, February 5). Race is a social construct scientists argue. *Scientific American*. Retrieved October 25, 2017, from https://www.scientificamerican.com/article/race-is-a-social-construct-scientists-argue/
Giddens, A. (1984). *The Constitution of Society*. Cambridge: Polity Press.
Goffman, E. (1963). *Stigma: Notes on the Management of Spoiled Identity*. Englewood Cliffs: Prentice-Hall.
Government of South Africa. (1996). The Constitution of the Republic of South Africa, Act No. 108 of 1996. Cape Town: South Africa.
Government of South Africa. (2015b). *Saving Mothers 2011–2013: Sixth Report on the Confidential Enquiries into Maternal Deaths in South Africa*. Pretoria: National Department of Health.
Gruskin, S., Mills, E., & Tarantola, D. (2007). History, principles, and practice of health and human rights. *Lancet, 370*(9585), 449–455.
Gupta, G., Parkhurst, J., Ogden, J., Aggleton, P., & Mahal, A. (2008). Structural approaches to HIV prevention. *Lancet, 372*, 764–775.
Gutto, S. (2002). *Equality and Non-discrimination in South Africa: The Political Economy of Law*. Wynberg: David Philip Publishers.
Habib, A., & Bentley, K. (2008). *Racial Redress and Citizenship in South Africa*. Cape Town: HSRC Press.

Heywood, M. (2003). Preventing mother-to-child HIV transmission in South Africa: Background, strategies and outcomes of the Treatment Action Campaign case against the Minister of Health. *South African Journal of Human Rights, 19*, 278–280.

Heywood, M. (2009). South Africa's Treatment Action Campaign: Combining law and social mobilization to realize the right to health. *Journal of Human Rights Practice, 1*(1), 14–36.

Hogan, M., Foreman, K., Naghavi, M., Ahn, S., Wang, M., Makela, S., et al. (2010). Maternal mortality for 181 countries, 1980–2008: A systematic analysis of progress towards Millennium Development Goal 5. *Lancet, 375*(9726), 1609–1623.

Human Sciences Research Council. (2015). *The People Living with HIV Stigma Index: South Africa 2014*. Pretoria: HSRC, South African National AIDS Council, and UNAIDS.

Jewkes, R., Flood, M., & Lang, J. (2015). From work with men and boys to changes of social norms and reduction of inequities in gender relations: A conceptual shift in prevention of violence against women and girls. *Lancet, 385*, 1580–1589.

Jewkes, R., Levin, J., & Penn-Kekana, L. (2002). Risk factors for domestic violence: Findings from a South African cross-sectional study. *Social Science & Medicine, 55*, 1603–1617.

Jewkes, R., Martin, L., & Penn-Kekana, L. (2002). Correspondence: The virgin cleansing myth: Cases of child rape are not exotic. *Lancet, 359*, 711.

Jewkes, R., Penn-Kekana, L., & Rose-Junius, H. (2005). "If they rape me, I can't blame them": Reflections on gender in the social context of rape in South Africa and Namibia. *Social Science & Medicine, 61*, 1809–1820.

Jong-wook, L. (2003). Global health improvement and WHO: Shaping the future. *Lancet, 362*, 2083–2088.

Kleinman, A. (2004). Ethics and experience: An anthropological approach to health equity. In P. Anand, F. Peter, & A. Sen (Eds.), *Public Health, Ethics, and Equity* (pp. 269–282). Oxford: Oxford University Press.

Koivusalo, M. (2010). The state of health in all policies (HiAP) in the European Union: Potential and pitfalls. *Journal of Epidemiology and Community Health, 64*(6), 500–503.

Kontis, V., Bennett, J., Mathers, C., Guangquan, L., Foreman, K., & Ezzati, M. (2017). Future life expectancy in 35 industrialised countries: Projections with a Bayesian model ensemble. *Lancet, 389*(10076), 1323–1335.

Koplan, J., Bond, T., Merson, M., Reddy, K., Henry, M., Sewankambo, N., et al. (2009). Towards a common definition of global health. *Lancet, 373*, 1993–1995.

Lancet Editorial. (2014). Women, children, and adolescents: The post-2015 agenda. *Lancet, 384*, 1159.

Lawn, J., Rohde, J., Rifkin, S., Were, M., Vinod, P., & Chopra, M. (2008). Alma-Ata: Rebirth and revision Alma-Ata 30 years on: Revolutionary, relevant, and time to revitalize. *Lancet, 372*, 917–927.

Leclerc-Madlala, S. (2008a). Age-disparate and intergenerational sex in Southern Africa: The dynamics of hypervulnerability. *AIDS, 22*(Suppl. 4), S17–S25.

Leclerc-Madlala, S. (2008b). Intergenerational/age-disparate sex and young women's vulnerability in Southern Africa. In *UNAIDS Technical Meeting on Young Women in HIV Hyper-Endemic Countries of Southern Africa*. Muldersdrift, South Africa: UNAIDS.

Leppo, K., Ollla, E., Pena, S., Wismar, M., & Cook, S. (2013). *Health in All Policies: Seizing Opportunities, Implementing Policies*. Helsinki: Finland Ministry of Social Affairs and Health.

Lima, N. (2007). Public health and social ideas in modern Brazil. *American Journal of Public Health, 97*, 1168–1177.

Link, B., & Phelan, J. (2001). Conceptualizing stigma. *Annual Review of Sociology, 27*, 363–385.

MacNaughton, G., Haigh, F., McGill, M., Koutsioumpas, K., & Sprague, C. (2015). The impact of human rights on universalizing health care in Vermont, USA. *Health & Human Rights Journal, 17*(2), 83–95.

Mann, J. (1997). Medicine and public health, ethics and human rights. *The Hastings Centre Report, 27*(3), 6–13.

Marins, J., Jamal, L., Chen, S., Marilisa, B., Hudes, E., Barbosa, A., et al. (2003). Dramatic improvement in survival among adult Brazilian AIDS patients. *AIDS, 17*, 1675–1682.

Marmot, M. (1998). Improvement of social environment to improve health. *Lancet, 351*, 57–60.

Marmot, M. (2015). *The Health Gap: The Challenge of an Unequal World*. London: Bloomsbury.

Marmot, M., & Shipley, M. (2006). Do socioeconomic differences in mortality persist after retirement? 25 year follow up of civil servants from the first Whitehall study. *British Medical Journal, 313*, 1177–1180.

Merson, M., Black, R., & Mills, A. (2011). *Global Health: Diseases, Programs, Systems and Policies* (3rd ed.). Burlington: Jones & Bartlett.

Meyersfeld, B. (2003). Reconceptualizing domestic violence in international law. *Albany Law Review, 67*, 371–426.
Meyersfeld, B. (2008). Domestic violence, health and international law. *Emory International Law Review, 22*, 61–112.
Moynihan, C. (1998). Theories in health care and research: Theories of masculinity. *BMJ, 317*, 1072–1075.
Msemburi, W., Pillay-van Wyk, V., Dorrington, R., Neethling, I., Nannan, N., Groenewald, P., et al. (2016). *Second National Burden of Disease Study for South Africa: Cause-of-Death Profile for South Africa, 1997–2012*. Cape Town: South African Medical Research Council.
Nattrass, N. (2004). *The Moral Economy of AIDS in South Africa*. Cambridge: Cambridge University Press.
Nussbaum, M. (2000). *Women and Human Development: The Capabilities Approach*. Cambridge: Cambridge University Press.
Nussbaum, M. (2003). Capabilities as fundamental entitlements: Sen and social justice. *Feminist Economics, 9*(2–3), 33–59.
Nussbaum, M. (2011). *Creating Capabilities*. Cambridge: Harvard University Press.
Peter, F. (2004). Health equity and social justice. In S. Anand, F. Peter, & A. Sen (Eds.), *Public Health, Ethics, and Equity* (pp. 93–106). Oxford: Oxford University Press.
Pogge, T. (2004). Relational conceptions of justice: Responsibilities for health outcomes. In S. Anand, F. Peter, & A. Sen (Eds.), *Public Health, Ethics, and Equity* (pp. 135–161). Oxford: Oxford University Press.
Rawls, J. (1971). *A Theory of Justice*. Cambridge, MA: Harvard University Press.
Rawls, J. (1993). *Political Liberalism*. New York: Columbia University Press.
Robeyns, I. (2003). Capability ethics. In H. LaFollette & I. Persson (Eds.), *The Blackwell Guide to Ethical Theory* (2nd ed.). New York: Blackwell.
Rosenberg, T. (2001). Drug companies are vincible. The AIDS crisis is solvable. *The New York Times Magazine*.
Ruger, J. (2004a). Health and social justice. *Lancet, 364*, 1075–1080.
Ruger, J. (2004b). Ethics of the social determinants of health. *Lancet, 364*, 1092–1097.
Ruger, J. (2006). Ethics and governance of global health inequalities. *Journal of Epidemiological and Community Health, 60*, 998–1003.
Ruger, J. (2010). *Health and Social Justice*. Oxford: Oxford University Press.
Sen, A. (1992). *Inequality Re-Examined*. Cambridge: Harvard University Press.
Sen, A. (1999). *Development as Freedom*. New York: Random House.

Sen, A. (2002). Why health equity? *Health Economics, 11*, 659–666.
Sen, A. (2011). *The Idea of Justice*. Cambridge: Harvard University Press.
Sen, G., Östlin, P., & George, A. (2007). Unequal, unfair, ineffective and inefficient gender inequity in health: Why it exists and how we can change it. In *Report of the Women and Gender Equity Knowledge Network of the Commission on Social Determinants of Health, Final Report to the Commission on Social Determinants of Health*. Geneva: WHO.
Sewell, W. (1992). A theory of structure: Duality, agency and transformation. *The American Journal of Sociology, 98*(1), 1–29.
Shisana, O., Rehle, T., Simbayi, L., Parker, W., Zuma, K., Bhana, A., et al. (2005). *South African National HIV Prevalence, Incidence and Communication Survey*. Cape Town: HSRC Press.
Shisana, O., Rehle, T., Simbayi, L., Zuma, K., Jooste, S., Pillay-van Wyk, V., et al. (2009). *South African National HIV Prevalence, Incidence and Communication Survey, 2008. A Turning Tide Among Teenagers?* Cape Town: HSRC Press.
Shisana, O., Rehle, T., Simbayi, L., Zuma, K., Jooste, S., Zungu, N., et al. (2014). *South African National HIV Prevalence, Incidence and Behaviour Survey, 2012*. Cape Town: HSRC Press.
Smith, K., Bambra, C., & Hill, S. (Eds.). (2015). *Health Inequalities: Critical Perspectives*. Oxford: Oxford University Press.
Solar, O., & Irwin, A. (2007). A conceptual framework for action on the social determinants of health. Discussion paper for the Commission on Social Determinants of Health (April). Geneva: WHO.
South African National AIDS Council (SANAC). (2014). *Progress Report on the National Strategic Plan for HIV, TB and STIs 2012–2016*. Pretoria: South African National AIDS Council.
Sprague, C. (2009). *Cui Bono: A Capabilities Approach to Understanding HIV 1192 Prevention and Treatment for Pregnant Women and Children in South Africa*. 1193 Doctoral thesis, University of the Witwatersrand.
Sprague, C., & Brown, S. (2016). Introduction: Local and global HIV aging demographics and research. In R. DeMarco & M. Brennan-Ing (Eds.), *HIV and Aging* (pp. 1–10). Basel: S. Karger.
Sprague, C., Scanlon, M., & Pantalone, D. W. (2017b). Qualitative methods to advance research on health inequities among previously incarcerated women living with HIV in Alabama. *Health Education & Behavior, 44*(5), 716–727.
Sprague, C., & Woolman, S. (2006). Moral luck: Exploiting South Africa's policy environment for an effective national antiretroviral treatment programme. *South African Journal on Human Rights, 22*(3), 337–379.

Stats SA. (2016). *Mid-Year Population Estimates 2016, Statistical Release P0302.* Pretoria: Statistics South Africa.
Stern, D. (2013). Intersubjectivity. In E. Person, A. Cooper, & G. Gabbard (Eds.), *The American Psychiatric Publishing Text—Book of Psychoanalysis* (pp. 77–92). Arlington, TX: American Psychiatric Publishing.
Stuart, E., & Woodroffe, J. (2016). Leaving no-one behind: Can the sustainable development goals succeed where the millennium development goals lacked? *Gender and Development, 24*(1), 69–81.
Teixeira, P. (2003). Universal access to AIDS medicines: The Brazilian experience. *Divulgaçao em Saúde para Debate, 27*, 184–191.
UNAIDS. (2013). *HIV and Aging: Special Supplement to the UNAIDS Report on the Global AIDS Epidemic 2013.* Geneva: UNAIDS.
UNAIDS. (2014a). *90-90-90: An Ambitious Treatment Target to Help End the AIDS Epidemic.* Geneva: UNAIDS.
UNAIDS. (2014b). *The Gap Report.* Geneva: UNAIDS.
UNAIDS. (2016a). *UNAIDS 2016 Estimates.* [online]. Geneva: UNAIDS. Retrieved February 8, 2017, from http://www.unaids.org/en/resources/documents/2016/HIV_estimates_with_uncertainty_bounds_1990-2015
UNAIDS. (2016b). *UNAIDS 2016 Guidance: HIV Prevention Among Adolescent Girls and Young Women. Putting HIV Prevention Among Adolescent Girls and Young Women on the Fast-Track and Engaging Men and Boys.* [online]. Geneva: UNAIDS. Retrieved February 8, 2017, from http://www.unaids.org/sites/default/files/media_asset/UNAIDS_HIV_prevention_among_adolescent_girls_and_young_women.pdf
UNAIDS. (2016c). *Global AIDS Update 2016.* Geneva: UNAIDS.
UN Office of the Special Adviser on Gender Issues and the Advancement of Women. (2001). Important concepts underlying gender mainstreaming: Concepts and definitions. Retrieved June 16, 2017, from http://www.un.org/womenwatch/osagi/conceptsandefinitions.htm
Vearey, J. (2010). *The persistent urban challenges of migration and informal settlements in the context of HIV.* Doctoral thesis, University of the Witwatersrand, Johannesburg, South Africa.
Venkatapuram, S. (2011). *Health Justice.* Cambridge: Polity Press.
Walensky, R., Paltiel, A., & Losina, E. (2006). The survival benefits of AIDS treatment in the United States. *Journal of Infectious Diseases, 194*(1), 11–19.
Whitehead, M. (1990). *The Concepts and Principles of Equity in Health.* Copenhagen: WHO Regional Office for Europe.

Whitehead, M. (1992). The concepts and principles of equity in health. *International Journal of Health Services, 22*(3), 429–435.
Wikler, D. (2004). Personal and social responsibility for health. In S. Anand, F. Peter, & A. Sen (Eds.), *Public Health, Ethics, and Equity* (pp. 109–134). Oxford: Oxford University Press.
Woolman, S. (2008). *Constitutional Law of South Africa* (2nd ed.). Cape Town: Juta Press.
Woolman, S., & Sprague, C. (2015). Nowhere to run, nowhere to hide: The absence of public policy as to how health care professionals should address intimate partner violence constitutes a breach of the rights to health and bodily integrity under the South African Constitution. *Cardozo Journal of Law & Gender, 22*(1), 29–74.
WHO. (1988). WHO: From Small Beginnings, Interview with Dr Szeming Sze. *World Health Forum, 9*, 29–34. Retrieved October 19, 2017, from http://apps.who.int/iris/bitstream/10665/46414/1/WHF_1988_9_1_p29-34.pdf
WHO. (2010). *A Conceptual Framework for Action on the Social Determinants of Health. Discussion Paper 2: Debates, Policy and Practice*. Geneva: WHO. Retrieved June 10, 2017, from http://www.who.int/sdhconference/resources/ConceptualframeworkforactiononSDH_eng.pdf
WHO (2014a). Women's health. Fact sheet number 334 (September). Retrieved May 30, 2017, from http://www.who.int/mediacentre/factsheets/fs334/en/
WHO. (2014b). *World Health Statistics, 2014*. Geneva: WHO.
Yang, L. H., Kleinman, A., Link, B. G., Phelan, J. C., Lee, S., & Good, B. (2007). Culture and stigma: Adding moral experience to stigma theory. *Social Science & Medicine, 64*(7), 1524–1535.

Part I

HIV, Gender and Health in Black South African Women

2

Health Outcomes and Social Factors Influencing Women's HIV Acquisition in Social Context

Part 1: HIV Trends in African Women Against Global Health Gains

Of an estimated 17.8 million women living with HIV, globally, the majority are located in sub-Saharan Africa (WHO, 2015). Of the global total, 3.9 million women are South Africans (Stats SA, 2015). Despite declines in HIV prevalence in some African countries, and UNAIDS' ambitious plan to end AIDS by 2030, new HIV infections in African women continue to increase, particularly in young women (15–24 years). It is not only young women who are at risk in sub-Saharan Africa and other settings, however. Mature women, aged 50 and older, are also becoming newly infected (UNAIDS, 2014b). UNAIDS and others have recently drawn attention to populations ageing with HIV globally (2013; Sprague & Brown, 2016). Significantly, UNAIDS and other health authorities had, historically, collected HIV prevalence data only up to age 49 in routine surveys, therefore HIV prevalence data for older populations has been neglected until more recently (Negin & Cumming, 2010).

C. Sprague, *Gender and HIV in South Africa*, Global Research in Gender, Sexuality and Health, https://doi.org/10.1057/978-1-137-55997-5_2

HIV Prevalence in South Africa: Unequal Distribution of HIV Infection

Prevalence—defined as the proportion of individuals in a selected population infected with the virus at a given point in time—offers a measure of cumulative risk of HIV infection (Gouws & Abdool Karim, 2005). Prevalence data have been routinely collected and reported in national South African surveys since 2002 (Shisana et al., 2005, 2009, 2014).[1] The data from these surveys illustrate that the burden of HIV disease is not distributed evenly among the South African population (see Tables 2.1 and 2.2). Among the total population, just over seven million are estimated to be living with HIV (Shisana et al., 2014; Stats SA, 2016). Breakdowns in HIV prevalence by gender and population grouping are shown in Table 2.1.

HIV prevalence data presented just above and below are based on the fourth population-based survey, conducted by the national Human Sciences Research Council (HSRC).

Burden of HIV by Age and Gender

Within the black South African population, nationally, men across all ages, have a lower HIV prevalence, 9.9%, compared to women, whose HIV prevalence is an estimated 14.4% (Shisana et al., 2014, p. xxv).

Table 2.1 HIV prevalence by race group and gender

Total population: 55,900,000	HIV prevalence overall: 12.7%	Ratio of population	%
Population aged 15–49 years living with HIV: 18.9%		Women Men	51 49

Source: Stats SA (2016) (for all data just above)

Population Group[a]	% of total	% HIV prevalence	HIV prevalence by Sex	%
Black	80.8	15	Women	14.4
Coloured	8.6	3.1	Men	9.9
White	8.0	0.6		
Indian/Asian	2.6	0.8		

Source: Shisana et al. (2014) (HSRC HIV prevalence data) for all data just above

[a]These are the original race groupings used to classify South Africans, which remain in use today (see Gannon, 2016)

Taking the analysis further yields an unequivocal result: black girls and women acquire HIV at higher levels than boys and men in every age bracket up to age 59 (Table 2.2).

Estimated HIV prevalence in pregnant women, reported in the latest (2013) annual antenatal care (ANC) survey, was 29.5% (Government of South Africa, 2015). Prevalence among pregnant women has persisted at this level—consistently high or moderately higher (just over 30%) since 2004 (Fig. 2.1).

With more recent reductions in AIDS mortality in South Africa and sub-Saharan Africa, people are living longer with HIV (Negin & Cumming, 2010; UNAIDS, 2013). Post-menopausal women are also at higher risk of acquiring HIV, owing to factors discussed later in the chapter (Blair, Paxton, & Kamb, 2012; Quinn & Overbaugh, 2005).

Commenting on the HIV burden in women versus men, Shisana et al. observe: 'This... difference between the sexes which highlights

Table 2.2 HIV prevalence by age and gender across the lifespan

HIV prevalence by age group	0–14 (%)	15–19 (%)	20–24 (%)	25–29 (%)	30–34 (%)	35–39 (%)	40–44 (%)	45–49 (%)	50–54 (%)	55–59 (%)	60+ (%)
Men	2.3	0.7	5.1	17.3	25.6	28.8	15.8	13.4	15.5	5.5	4.6
Women	2.4	5.6	17.4	28.4	36	31.6	28	19.7	14.8	9.7	2.4

Source: Shisana et al. (2014)

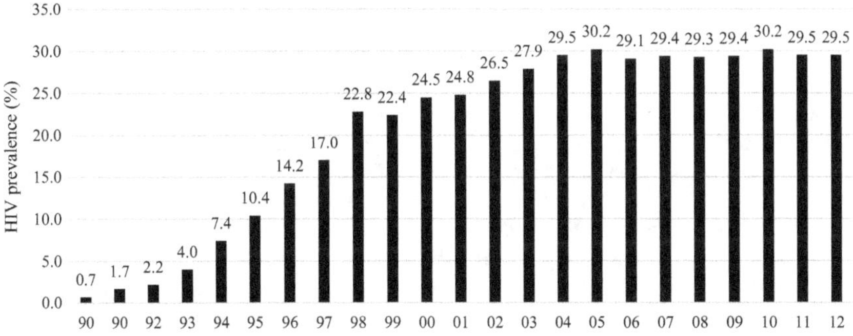

Fig. 2.1 Trends in HIV prevalence among pregnant women seeking antenatal care, South Africa, 1990–2012. Source: Government of South Africa, National Department of Health [DOH] (2013a)

that the brunt of the epidemic is still felt mainly among females' (quoted in van der Linde, 2013, p. 1). South Africa's *National Strategic Plan on HIV and AIDS, TB and STIs 2012—2016* (NSP) is the national policy steering document on HIV. The NSP recognises that girls will acquire HIV earlier than boys: 'On average, young females become HIV positive about five years earlier than males' (Government of South Africa, 2012, p. 25).

Unlike HIV prevalence, HIV incidence is not collected and reported annually using a uniform national data collection method (Gouws & Abdool Karim, 2005; SANAC, 2014). However, as noted in the South African National AIDS Council's (SANAC's) 2014 report on the HIV epidemic and response, HIV incidence for adults aged 15–49 years declined from 1.79% in 2008 to 1.47% in 2012 (based on the THEMBISA model). But not for all South Africans. HIV incidence among young women aged 15–24 increased and—at an estimated 2.83%—was the highest among all age groups. This compares with 0.82% in young men SANAC (2014, pp. 3, 8, 10). Subsequently, young women were designated a key affected population in the NSP. This demonstrates that the government and civil society are aware of the problem of rising HIV incidence in women.

Box 2.1 Study population: A subset of black South African women living with HIV

Throughout this work, I refer to the 'population'[2] as South African women living with HIV who are black. However, in the in-depth empirical research undertaken among the 89 women, the 'study population' are HIV positive women, pregnant or having given birth in the previous four months. Why focus on this population group of women when other groups of women, female sex workers for example, have higher HIV prevalence? There is a need, and an opportunity to do so, in ways that are unmatched in other groups of women. HIV prevalence in pregnant women has remained at about 30% (Government of South Africa, 2013a, 2015), and pregnant women living with HIV require timely access to and uptake of treatment and prevention to ensure optimal health outcomes for themselves and their infants.

These women are a population at risk of acquiring HIV, with a higher risk of illness and premature death: HIV infection increases the risk of maternal death (Pattinson, 2007). Women are also at high risk of violence during the perinatal period (Hatcher et al., 2014), defined by WHO (n.d.), as commencing from 22 completed weeks and ending seven completed days following birth. Because over 92% of South African women have at least one visit to a hospital for antenatal care during their pregnancy, it is possible to access them during routine visits, unlike more hidden or stigmatised populations, such as sex workers, who have higher HIV prevalence but are more difficult to reach, particularly in large numbers, in different provinces. Moreover, the public health system's infrastructure offers multiple points within the HIV care continuum to study women living with HIV as they flow through services during the perinatal period. Women have opportunities to receive HIV testing and counselling, to initiate cART, and other routine HIV services delivered in pregnancy and following postnatal care, when they transition to adult antiretroviral (ARV) clinics. Pregnancy is often the greatest opportunity for women to receive an HIV test, and it can be the first time women learn that they are HIV positive. From a research perspective, and one that is concerned with operational delivery of HIV services, this creates an opportunity to study a segment of the total HIV positive population of women in depth within the health system, and in relationship with their health providers, which is a crucial factor influencing women's health beliefs and behaviours. Lastly, following delivery, this population of women will transition to and become part of the larger pool of adult women living with HIV who will need lifelong and continuous HIV care.

Black South African Women: Life Expectancy Declines Against Global Gains

Life expectancy and maternal mortality in South Africa can be situated within global trends and the so-called 'global health revolution' (or significant advances in world health) referenced in the introduction. Life expectancy, notes WHO, is a summary measure of mortality rates at all ages. Measures for mortality are more accurate globally, in spite of large data gaps (WHO, 2014c, 2014d), than other measures of disability and disease (WHO, 2016a), hence its use as a standardised health indicator. For over five decades, life expectancy has been steadily rising (Kontis et al., 2017; WHO, 2014b). Since the early 1950s, life expectancy has increased by almost 30 years in some countries (WHO, 2014b). However, these survival gains have not been evenly distributed (Doyal, 2006). Many sub-Saharan African countries have experienced a resounding reversal (WHO, 2014b), largely due to AIDS-related mortality. (For reductions in particular African populations due to AIDS-associated mortality, see Jamison et al., 2006; Velkoff & Kowal, 2007.)

WHO 2014 data indicate that women's life expectancy at birth globally exceeded 80 years of age for women in 46 countries (2014b). This contrasts with a life expectancy of 58 years for women in the WHO African region, encompassing the range of low-, middle- and upper-middle income countries in sub-Saharan Africa. In South Africa, women's life expectancy has declined dramatically with recent improvements. From a high of 66 years in 1991, it declined sharply to reach a low of 52 years in 2005 (UN Statistical Division/UN Population Division, n.d.-a). During the period 2001–2006, South African women's life expectancy by province ranged from a low of 47 years in the poorer Free State province to a high of 62 years in the wealthier Western Cape (Stats SA, 2015, p. 12). By 2015, gains for women were achieved with life expectancy an estimated 64 years for women on average, ranging from 55 years in the Free State to 66 years in the Western Cape over the period 2011–2016 (Stats SA, 2015, p. 1). These gains were attributed to declines in child mortality, owing to prevention of mother-to-child transmission (PMTCT), and cART. The impact of HIV on South African women has thus been significant. In the absence of AIDS, women's life expectancy was projected to be 73 years. (For modelling assumptions, see Stats SA, 2015.)

Despite these notable improvements, life expectancy at birth for South African women in 2016, at 65 years, stands in marked contrast with women in Japan who can expect to live to age 87, and in Spain, Switzerland, Singapore and France who can expect to live to age 85. The difference in life expectancy reveals a gap of nearly roughly two decades (WHO, 2014b)—20 fewer years of life for African women. While population life expectancy is only broken down by gender in South African statistical trends, due to the absence of HIV in other race groups of South African women, disparities in life expectancy are also highly likely to be found between black South African women and women who have the highest attainable life expectancy: white South African women (Stats SA, 2016).

Going forward, life expectancy projections are worrying. Stats SA notes that the increases in life expectancy since 2005 have been attributed to cART. However, the national agency reports that by 2015, there was a 'stall in life expectancy' (Stats SA, 2015, p. 5). They observe, disturbingly, that it could also be 'in part due to the progression of the HIV/AIDS epidemic' (Stats SA, 2015, p. 5).

Mortality

The South African Medical Research Council (MRC) reported the leading causes of deaths in the population from 1997 to 2012, and found that for women and men HIV/AIDS and tuberculosis (TB) accounted for the highest proportion of deaths, an estimated 33.6% for adults and children (Msemburi et al., 2016, p. 5). They also estimated the leading causes of premature deaths over the same period, finding that HIV and AIDS occupies the top spot and contributes to 1851 years of life lost for the South African population of women in total (Msemburi et al., 2016, p. 13).

Shifting to maternal mortality, maternal health (and child health), is viewed by the international health community as a proxy for wider national health in many countries. Maternal health was also one of the eight MDGs, and the sole women's health development goal (WHO, 2014a). MDG 5 sought to reduce the maternal mortality rate by three-quarters and to achieve universal access to reproductive health by 2015. (See WHO, 2014d) Additionally, maternal mortality is preventable, with access to skilled birth attendants and emergency obstetric care (Hogan et al., 2010; Ronsmans & Graham, 2006; WHO, 2014b). A major focus of the SDGs moving forward is on targets that reduce preventable deaths, including maternal mortality, neonatal and child mortality. (see Islam, 2007; WHO, 2016a).

In the Southern African region, maternal mortality per 100,000 live births was 280 in 2013, compared to 209 globally and 12 in the high-income countries (Kassebaum et al., 2014). The published cause-of-death data from South Africa demonstrate that black South African women, particularly those of reproductive age, have been severely affected by HIV infection in terms of mortality (Bradshaw & Nannan, 2005; Pattinson, 2007; South Africa Every Death Counts Writing Group, 2008a, 2008b).

Since 1999, non-pregnancy-related infections have become the main cause of maternal mortality in South Africa, contributing to upwards of 40% of maternal deaths, with AIDS the single leading cause (Government of South Africa, 1999, 2012). By 2012, steady gains were made in reducing maternal mortality due to expanded cART coverage and improved maternal HIV testing (Government of South Africa, 2015). The sixth report on confidential enquiries into maternal deaths in South Africa found a 12.6% reduction in maternal deaths (2011–2013), against the previous period of reporting (2008–2010): this is evidence of notable progress (2015). The maternal mortality ratio, called the institutional maternal mortality ratio (iMMR) in South Africa (because most deaths take place in, and are reported by, health facilities or institutions) decreased from 176 per 100,000 live births in 2008–2010 to 154 per 100,000 live births in 2011–2013 (Government of South Africa, 2015). This source has non-pregnancy-related infections (primarily deaths in pregnant women with HIV) contributing to 34.7% of maternal deaths, a decline from 40.5% in the previous period (Government of South Africa, 2015). However, the MRC's national cause of death data estimate that indirect maternal factors (associated with TB and AIDS) were responsible for 39.9% of maternal deaths over a longer period: from 2008 to 2012 (they did not estimate the iMMR) (Msemburi et al., 2016).

Despite these marked improvements, the contribution of HIV to maternal deaths remains significant. The data reinforce the reality that South African women remain at risk of dying prematurely of HIV-related infections. In one Johannesburg audit of maternal deaths conducted from 2003 to 2012, for example, maternal mortality for women with HIV was still three times higher than for women who were HIV negative (Black, Morris, Smith, & Townsend, 2016). Glenda Gray, head of South Africa's MRC, has called maternal health, along with child health and infectious diseases, part of the 'unfinished agenda' of the international community (Msemburi et al., 2016, p. 1; Tinker, 2000).

In sum, over the last several years, there have been some gains in reducing maternal mortality against the long-term upward trend (Buchmann et al., 2015; Burton, 2013). However, in spite of the growing availability of HIV treatment since 2004, black women continue to acquire HIV at higher rates than women of other race groups. This is reflected in their poorer health outcomes, relative to other women. Life expectancy at birth is lower and maternal mortality is higher compared with women of other race groups who are HIV negative.

Part 2: Interrogating the Social Basis Underlying Differential HIV Risk in Black South African Women

Key Factors Facilitating HIV Transmission in Social Context

The indicators presented in the previous section underscore a core theme within South Africa that also reflects trends in social health inequalities at the global level, namely: opportunities to be healthy are highly unequal. HIV remains a persistent threat to women's health. Yet health and development indicators on their own may occlude complex aspects of health affecting particular populations—including this one—as much as they reveal principal trends. The web of factors that facilitate HIV risk in black South African women are not fully visible without some excavation to bring them into sharper view. What places these South African women at heightened risk of acquiring HIV from an early age? What are the factors facilitating new HIV infections, particularly in young black women?

Various disciplines have sought to investigate and describe the mechanisms by which social determinants produce physiological changes in the body—i.e., disease—in order to generate theories of how causal pathways link social conditions to differential health outcomes related to poor health. This work is being pursued in many fields. (For a helpful review, see Venkatapuram, 2011) Diderichsen stresses that many of these factors cluster among socially disadvantaged individuals 'living in underprivileged conditions' and these factors tend to 'interact with each other' (quoted in WHO, 2010, p. 3). He calls these 'long causal chains of mediating factors' (WHO, 2010, p. 3) (more on this below). The extant literature collected over more than a decade gives us a large base of evidence on social or structural factors that facilitate black women's risk of acquiring HIV in South Africa. In this section, I seek not to develop a theory about why social norms allow for risk of HIV and ill health. Rather, I offer an interpretive lens. I capture and report the available evidence on the complex phenomenon of HIV risk in social context. I map the set of variables that interact to generate risk for women. This includes the hypothesised pathway connecting gender inequality, violence against women (VAW), and masculinities to HIV risk (Dunkle & Decker, 2013; Heise & McGrory, 2016).

Understanding HIV Risk for Women in South and Southern Africa

The vast majority of HIV transmission cases among South African women occur during unsafe sex without a condom, through vaginal-penile or rectal-penile sex with an infected partner, which results in exposure of a woman's genital or anal mucosa to HIV in a man's seminal fluids (Blair et al., 2012). Avoiding new HIV infections in women and girls therefore necessitates an understanding the HIV 'risk environment' in which women are located and determinants that influence women's risk in social context, whether proximal or distal (Auerbach, Caceres, & Parkhurst, 2011; Parkhurst, 2014; Preston-Whyte, 2003).

Conceptualising Risk and Risk Factors

The concept of 'risk' in the health sciences refers to the risk of a negative health outcome (WHO, 2014e). Risk can be defined as 'probability of an adverse outcome, or a factor that raises this probability' (WHO, 2002, p. xiii). Risk factors are those influences that shape disease, illness or injury. HIV risk factors tend to vary by context, location and population (Rhodes, Singer, Bourgois, Friedman, & Strathdee, 2005). HIV risk is primarily associated with sexual risk behaviour and practices that increase exposure to and possibility of HIV infection, through oral, anal or vaginal sex without a latex or polyurethane condom. Additional HIV risk factors are associated with exposures of a person (the host) to the virus (the pathogen) in bodily fluids, including the exposure of a foetus or infant to HIV in utero, during labour, delivery and breastfeeding (UNAIDS, 1998). HIV can also be transmitted through blood or contaminated devices, such as needles (WHO, 2014e).

Risk does not connote blame, and the framing and communication of risk is important, particularly in differing cultural contexts. Social scientists have criticised the public health community for this language of 'risk' and the over-emphasis on regulating individual behaviours at the expense of structural ones. (See Gilbert, 1995; Gilbert & Selikow, 2011; Parkhurst, 2014).[3] The research shows that the way in which risk is framed to policymakers, scientists, the public and key affected groups can affect the outcome (WHO, 2002).

In Southern and South Africa, women's greater vulnerability to and risk of HIV acquisition is both social and biological, generating a thick literature by researchers who seek to understand how HIV prevention can be situated effectively within the larger risk environment (Cluver et al., 2013; Coates, Richter, & Caceres, 2008; Leclerc-Madlala, 2008a, 2008b; Pettifor, MacPhail, Anderson, & Maman, 2012; Selikow, Zulu, & Cedras, 2002). Gender inequalities are deeply embedded within the HIV risk environment at the structural level (discussed below).

The Structural Level: Gender, Sexuality and HIV Risk

Studies have demonstrated that social context, socioeconomic status and sociocultural gender norms and beliefs are significant factors in placing girls and women at risk of HIV in the Southern African region (Jewkes, Levin, & Penn-Kekana, 2002; Jewkes, Martin, & Penn-Kekana, 2002; Jewkes, Penn-Kekana, & Rose-Junius, 2005). The array of interacting factors is depicted in Fig. 2.3 At this juncture, it is helpful to engage with the slippery notion that is structure. Sewell writes that structure operates in social-scientific discourse 'as a powerful metonymic device…identifying some part of a complex social reality as explaining the whole,' (1992, p. 2). Here he urges that no definition can fully succeed in 'fixing the term's meaning' (1992, p. 2). It is like trying to grab the wind—it will evade your grasp. Rather, structure is represented in social patterns and rules. It is made manifest in social institutions: in the workplaces, schools and neighbourhoods we frequent and the social norms that govern expected and accepted behaviours, including patterns associated with sexuality and sexual desire (Correa, Petchesky, & Parker, 2008).

For the purposes of clarity, structure in this work refers to social, political or economic processes, as well as the social rules, norms and organisation that govern the dominant social order, which is a gendered order (Friedman & McKnight, 2003). Factors that underpin HIV risk are typically referred to as *social or structural drivers* (used interchangeably) by UNAIDS and others. (See Auerbach et al., 2011.) These drivers are associated with social determinants of health.

I discuss the shift to embrace the notion of structure within HIV prevention interventions in greater detail in Chap. 7. Here, I am unpeeling the layers to get at the core of social context and norms, including gendered expectations placed on women related to sex, social constructions of gender and women's behaviours in this social environment where gender, sexuality and ill health intersect with the political economy of the region. As Correa, Petchesky and Parker emphasise, 'Gender and sexuality are clearly located at the core of current 'real politics." They observe that

> [S]exuality research and thinking have barely started to explore ways of articulating the knowledge accumulated about the microphysics and the political economy of sex. (2008, p. 7)

They rightly remind us that sex is a representation of many interacting processes, contending that

> The vast diversity of how bodies and desires are located in space and time, and across the intersections of gender, race, class, age, and geography, makes us feel more like cartographers than bold theorists of sexual landscapes. (2008, p. 7)

In this social and economic context, the 'shaping' environment of HIV risk is one in which a small minority of black women are able to exercise full control and choice and to act on their desires—in other words, to demonstrate their agency due to a social context that determines black women's relative position in the social hierarchy. Colleagues such as Diderichsen, Evans, and Whitehead (2001) posit that pathways from social context to poor health outcomes functions via a set of four mechanisms: social stratification (I); differential exposure to disease or injury (II); differential vulnerability (III); and differential consequences (IV), leading to the social consequences of ill health—or health inequities. The causal social mechanisms are complex and interact. The following discussion indicates the way that social arrangements and social structure enable a cluster of HIV risk factors to operate in lockstep in ways that increase black South African women's risk of acquiring the virus (Fig. 2.2).

Social Position

Black South African women's social position in the social hierarchy tends to be lower relative to black men and to women of other race groups.

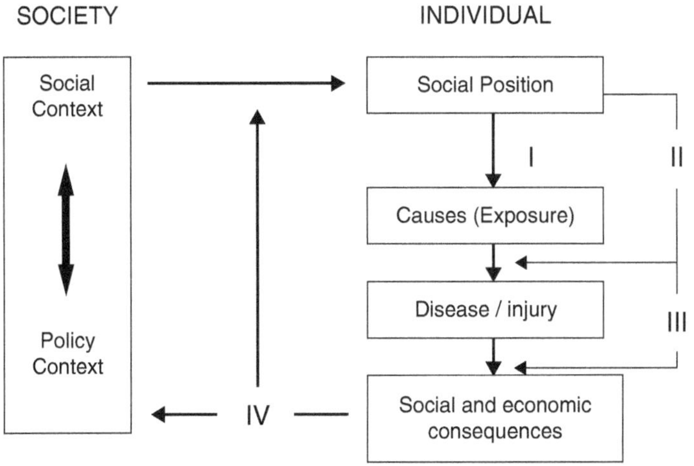

Fig. 2.2 Diderichsen et al. (2001) framework for elucidating pathways from social context to social and economic consequences

Social position here is distinct from socioeconomic status and can be seen as 'social standing'. While in some countries, like the US, social position is associated with SES (and composite measures that comprise it, like education and occupation), social position in South Africa is largely associated with race and with gender. Deliberate social stratification and development of a social hierarchy was effected systematically through apartheid policies. Social position comes with a set of social norms that determine accepted behaviours in the social hierarchy, with variation by social groups according to culture, ethnicity, gender, age and other identifiers (Diderichsen et al., 2001).

Socioeconomic Status

The lower social position of black women interacts with their SES, which also tends to be lower, relative to men and to women of other race groups. SES is a composite measure that generally includes three main factors: education, occupation and income. In South Africa, low SES largely correlates with low levels of educational attainment, which combine to create greater likelihood for girls and women to engage in unsafe sex (Ackermann & de Klerk, 2002; see Hargreaves & Glynn, 2002). Low SES also constrains women's agency by reducing the range of available protections women have to employ against HIV (e.g., contraception or condoms). If food is scarce, for example, women's perceptions of HIV risk and fears of HIV as a threat will be affected (i.e., avoiding HIV may not be the greatest priority).

Low SES comprises part of the risk environment and must be seen as one important factor among others. In South Africa, lower SES in women and girls has been associated with unsafe sexual behaviours, such as multiple, concurrent sexual partners and transactional sex (Hunter, 2002; Leclerc-Madlala, 2002). This creates exposure and vulnerability to HIV disease that is rooted in gender inequality, economic poverty and deprivation. Thus, black women are often born into unequal social and economic opportunities, including fewer opportunities for education and employment, along the life course. This, note Gilbert and Selikow (2011), predisposes women to poverty, malnutrition and lack of control over their own fertility (see also Ackermann & de Klerk, 2002; Gerntholtz, Gibbs, & Willan, 2011; Ramkissoon et al., 2006). Low SES also correlates with poor health and is a predictor of mental and physical health problems (Wilkinson & Marmot, 2003).

Low Economic Participation

South Africa has reported very low participation of women in formal employment, with an accompanying small percentage (less than 5%) of women making in excess of $1500 per year (Government of South Africa, 2013b). That is below the poverty line used by the government, the UN and OECD. The unemployment rate for South African women is high—an estimated 27% (Stats SA, 2016b). While poverty rates have decreased for some South Africans, the report notes that poverty is gendered, stating that

> Halving the share of the population earning less than $1.25 per person per day (PPP) is already achieved... Despite this progress, there are disturbing trends in terms of the differentiation of poverty outcomes according to generation and gender. (Government of South Africa, 2013b, p. 36)

The government maintains that '[i]n particular, youth and women remain disproportionately vulnerable to all forms of poverty defined under MDG 1' (Government of South Africa, 2013b, p. 36; see Bilchitz, 2008). In a setting with high HIV prevalence, like South Africa, economic vulnerability also introduces particular health vulnerabilities.

Childhood Sexual Abuse

Sexual abuse in childhood seems to facilitate an important risk pathway for girls that links different types of violence exposure to HIV risk, to increased HIV risk behaviours and eventual HIV transmission in particular social and familial contexts (see Table 2.3). Life course epidemiological models have made inroads in establishing how different socioeconomic

Table 2.3 South African studies investigating links between lifetime trauma and HIV, including abuse in childhood

- A cross-sectional survey of 298 pregnant women in Cape Town, South Africa examined the correlates of lifetime trauma exposure and found that 19.8% of women reported trauma exposure. *Trauma exposure* was *associated with prior termination of pregnancy, lifetime substance use, depression and history of STIs* (Myers et al., 2015).
- A comparative study examined childhood physical and sexual abuse and adult HIV risk behaviour in South Africa (two sites: Vulindlela and Soweto), Zimbabwe and Tanzania among 11,206 women and men aged 18–32 years. The study found a *strong correlation between childhood abuse and risk behaviours such as age at first sex, alcohol and drug use and various forms of IPV*. The prevalence of women who experience childhood sexual abuse was 2.4% in Vulindlela, 4.9% in Soweto, 2.1% in Tanzania and 4.4% in Zimbabwe, while the prevalence of reporting childhood sexual or physical abuse was 8% and 11.4% in the South African sites, 6.1% in Tanzania and 18.4%, in Zimbabwe, respectively (Richter et al., 2014).
- *A study* among 1415 women and 1367 men recruited *from 70 rural villages* in South Africa *explored the prevalence of childhood experiences of adversity and HIV infection*. Both women and men reported high rates of adversity, including physical punishment (89.3% and 94.4%), emotional abuse (54.7% and 56.4%), and sexual abuse (39.1% and 16.7%). *Among women, HIV infection was significantly associated with experiences of emotional abuse, sexual abuse and physical punishment*. The authors conclude their findings underscore *all forms of adversity (emotional, physical and sexual) increase risks for adverse health outcomes later in life for men and women*, and that *childhood exposure to adversity* in this setting *was very high* (Jewkes, Dunkle, Nduna, & Shai, 2010).

and psychosocial factors at various life stages function via 'social chains of risk' by influencing risk exposure to causal factors early in the lifespan, as part of a trajectory of psychological, social and biological risk chains (Kuh, Ben-Schlomo, Lynch, Hallqvist, & Power, 2003). Alcohol, substance use and untreated trauma also play a role for particular populations of women (see Heise & McGrory, 2016; Sprague, Scanlon, & Pantalone, 2017b). South African studies are highlighted below. Research connecting these factors is far from complete, however.

Early Sexual Debut

Sexual debut typically marks the onset of HIV risk. Early sexual debut, defined as sexual debut taking place at age 15 years or younger, contributes to HIV risk among adolescents and young women, due in part to the biological factors cited above (Harrison, O'Sullivan, Hoffman, Dolezal, & Morrell, 2006). Harrison et al. found in a cross-sectional household survey of South African men aged 15–24 years that 13.1% of men reported early sexual debut (range 9–14 years), forming what they term a 'distinct risk group' (2006, p. 259). However, such age ranges may shift over time, with changing HIV transmission dynamics. Stern and Cooper (2014) employed a narrative approach among a sample of 75 young South Africans, men and women, to elicit reflections on sexual debut. They found that young women cited pressure from male partners to debut, while young men reported that higher social status influenced the timing of first sex. Significantly, there was less attention to safe sex among young people in the sample overall (Stern & Cooper, 2014). Delayed onset of sex is therefore an important strategy to reduce HIV exposure and to protect adolescents from HIV (WHO, 2006b).

Age-Disparate Sexual Partnerships

Age-disparate sexual partnerships among older men and younger women are established in surveys and other South African studies (Shisana et al., 2009, 2014). In young South Africans, Harrison cites evidence pointing to associations between HIV infection and low school attendance or completion, together with parental absence, participation in sports or community organisations and the age of a partner (2008, p. 262; Pettifor et al., 2012). In routine surveys, Shisana et al. have documented this South African phenomenon, stating that 'These partnerships encompass intergenerational relationships, motivated by financial gain, normally between younger females and older males' (2009, p. 65). Research indicates that families may encourage women to partake in these partnerships:

> Such relationships are sometimes also condoned by families as a product of family members benefiting from the material proceeds of such relationships. (Shisana et al., 2009, p. 65)

HSRC researchers found that intergenerational sex increased significantly among women in the 15–19 age bracket during each of the three subsequent national HIV prevalence and behaviour surveys. Age of sexual partner presents a risk factor for HIV transmission because it allows youth exposure to older men who are in a higher HIV prevalence group (compared to men aged 15–19), thus increasing the probability that South African girls or women are exposed to HIV and may contract the virus (Shisana et al., 2009, p. 74). Recent research by Akullian et al. (2017) found that South African men in the age group 25–34 years posed a higher risk for transmitting HIV to women (compared to older men, 35 years and above) because men in that age cohort had recently acquired HIV, had particularly high viral loads, with low HIV testing and cART uptake. Such studies offer greater insight into the nature of HIV transmission and seroconversion dynamics. These studies, however, underscore that it is the structural factors that facilitate and encourage these age disparate partnerships that underpin HIV risk in women in South and Southern Africa.

Studies have found that men gain respect and esteem from having multiple sexual partners, including young women, and from being seen to exercise control over sexual relations, including decisions around condom use. There is significant research amassed that indicates South African men view young women as being less likely to be HIV positive: they see them as 'clean' and 'fresh' which makes them more desirable. The 'virgin cleansing' myth in which men thought that having sex with a virgin would cure of them of HIV and AIDS is still circulating (Jewkes et al., 2002; Ramjee & Daniels, 2013). Notably, President Jacob Zuma has shown off his penchant for acquiring new, young wives as part of polygamous practice as a cultural norm, to the intense dismay of feminists and the HIV research and activist community. Moreover, Zuma was acquitted in a legal case in which he was accused of raping a young family friend; he told the media he took a shower to reduce his risk of contracting HIV: thus confirming and communicating erroneous beliefs about HIV transmission to the South African public (*The Guardian*, 2006). The depiction of young women being sexually desirable and as playthings or objects over which men think they have ownership continues to be perpetuated by leaders in some of the highest echelons of the social order (Sen, Östlin, & George, 2007). Women in different quarters continue to contest men's perceptions and their dominance. Gasa's remarks are illustrative and her irritation evident:

> I find this insulting and affecting my dignity. I can speak whenever I want... I didn't come here as 'your woman'... We are not your women... We are equals. (Nomboniso Gasa, traditional leader, quoted in Albertyn, 2009, p. 165)

Social Constructions of Gender

Social constructions of gender in South Africa, as elsewhere, are fluid. The landscape of gender relations in South Africa since independence in 1994 is a changed terrain. The accent until recent years had been on women's rights and their empowerment. However, this is shifting to explore and to deepen studies of masculinities (Dworkin, Hatcher, Colvin, & Peacock, 2013; Dworkin, Treves-Kagan, & Lippman, 2013; Gennrich, 2013; Ouzgane & Morrell, 2005). Men's perceptions and attitudes towards women, the pressures men face within sociopolitical and economic arrangements, and in relation to women's aspirations must be located at the centre of these processes of social change.

For men, hegemonic masculinities emerge in a contested process among vying identities, as Connell and Messerschmidt (2005) explain. A dominant, accepted social construction of what it is to be a 'real man' at a particular point in time is given shape and reproduced in this manner. It is this notion of 'hegemonic masculinity' first coined by Connell (1987), that is associated with the subordination of females, and it is these notions of manhood that create the ideals by which men appear to judge their social success (Jewkes & Morrell, 2010, p. 3). There is wide agreement that there is more than one hegemonic masculinity in South Africa (thus it is more appropriate to refer to masculinities). It is these shifts that allow for greater traction in understanding ways that HIV risk in men and women can be mediated (See Gennrich, 2013; Jewkes & Morrell, 2012). (Discussed further in Chap. 7 and the Concluding Remarks)

Gender Socialisation

Sexual risk behaviour that renders South African women vulnerable to HIV is often associated with submissive and 'coercive' male-dominated relationships. A spate of studies in South and Southern Africa have illustrated that girls, adolescents and women, act on the basis of gender norms and expectations. This encompasses being submissive to male partners, being sexually available and affording men decision making power related to sex. (See Jewkes et al., 2002; Mathews, 2005; Stern, Buikema, & Cooper, 2016.) These sociocultural norms are established through gender socialisation practices. The establishment of such social practices are explained in the following comments made by health providers interviewed in five clinics or hospitals in Johannesburg and captured in a study my colleagues and I conducted to gauge South African health providers' perceptions of IPV in the women patients they see (Sprague, Hatcher, Woollett, & Black, 2015; Sprague, Hatcher, Woollett, Sommers, & Black, 2016a). All names are pseudonyms to protect health providers' identities.

Funi, a nurse, shares her perception of the gender hierarchy:

> They [men] are the controlling bodies in our society and in our homes. (Sprague et al., 2016a, p. 6)

Gugu, also a nurse, identifies the cultural practice of *lobola*, where a payment is offered to the bride's family during marriage, as one that is equivalent to ownership of the woman and enables the sanction of women through 'punishment':

> It is culture. The man is treated as superior …. Most power is given to the man. He is socialised he has a right to punish the woman. It is also because our parents have accepted *lobola* that leads to violence. The person feels he owns you. (Sprague et al., 2016a, p. 6)

HIV risk behaviour remains linked to sociocultural beliefs that encourage young women to allow male partners to have decision making authority, generally, and control related to sex, particularly, as part of accepted gender hierarchies and norms in this setting (Boonzaier, 2005; Connell, 1987, 1995; Harrison, 2008; Harrison et al., 2006). These are more evident in the excerpts below.

Lack of condom use, for example, is associated with some South African men's documented preference for dry sex—sex without lubrication or moisture—which increases HIV risk (Casale et al., 2011). As one participant, nurse Khosi states, women are expected to curb their natural sexual response to accommodate men's expectations:

> The partners will always say to them [women patients she sees], 'you are wet, you are cold' so the women will want anything they can put in the vagina to keep it dry .... [O]ne lady's ... partner said 'you are wet, go and wash'. If you think of [the] sexual act, when you get excited, what happens? (Sprague et al., 2016a, p. 7)

Similarly, a different participant communicates a common perception by men that if 'girls' do not comply with partners' demands for sex, they are not being monogamous:

> But these partners want sex because they believe if these girls don't give them sex, they are giving sex to other men. (unpublished from transcriptions, see Sprague et al., 2016a)

In an environment where women tend to lack economic means, 'holding onto their men'—pleasing or placating men through sexual behaviours—becomes normalised and is linked to women's economic security. These excerpts underscore the way that women's own sexual desires and preferences are effectively stifled in these instances—supplanted by fear and anxiety (Fig. 2.3).

One participant, sister Lebo, observes how men claim their authority and dominance in the gender hierarchy, even as she questions this norm, indicating her lack of agreement with it:

> South African men feel that they are entitled. You hear this from the taxi rank from the dress code—it makes them think that you want sex [based on what you are wearing] and because you are a woman you can't say no. But the dress code has nothing to do with it. If you go to the taxi rank you will hear all the comments. They think they are entitled to sex, there is something I don't understand from men thinking that the way that the woman dresses means they want sex. (unpublished from interview transcripts, see Sprague et al., 2016a)

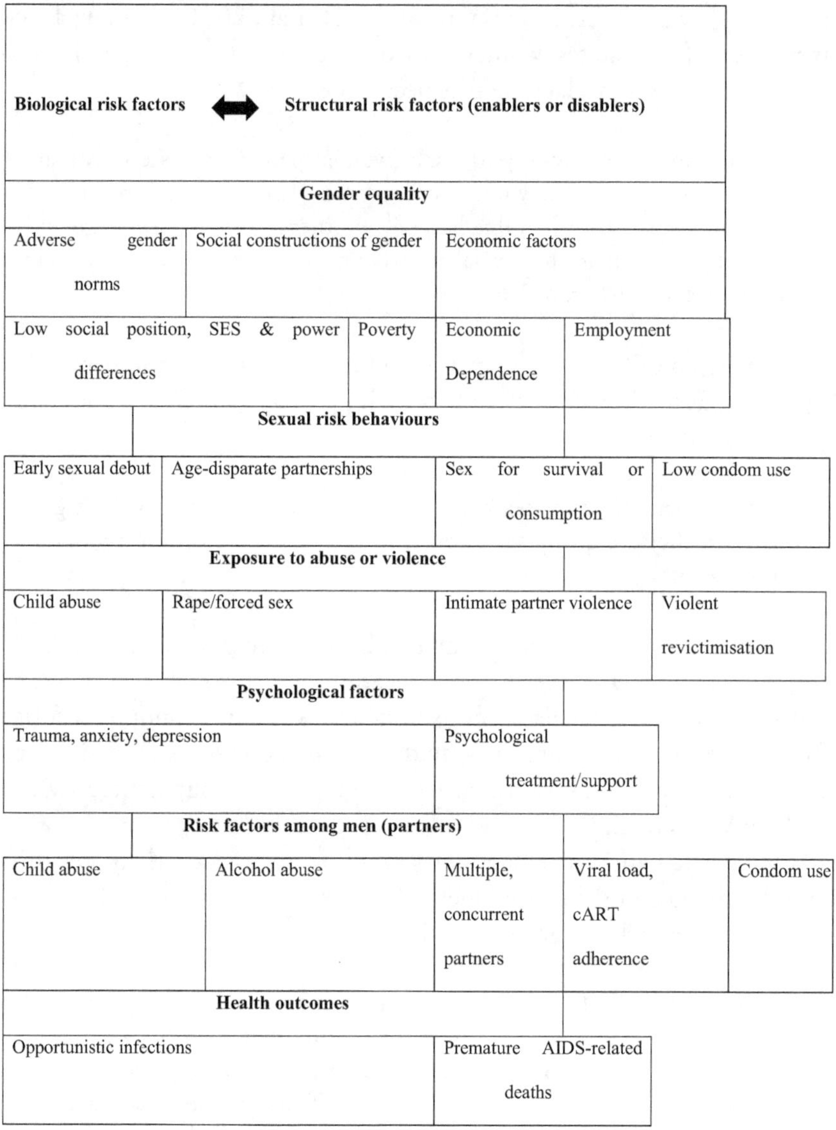

Fig. 2.3 HIV risk environment: Black South African women. Source: Sprague (2018). Constructed from the extant literature

Aspirations, Risk Practices and Women's Constrained Agency

Girls and women are seen to be motivated both by love and by material gain and the motivations prompting girls and women to have sex are evolving and complex (Selikow, Ahmed, Flisher, Mathews, & Mukoma, 2009), particularly with South Africa's greater integration into the global economy. Women still retain agency in this high HIV risk context but the potential negative effects on women's health are highly significant (Jewkes & Morrell, 2010). Scholars focused on the Southern Africa context acknowledge women's agency but differ on its role and intentions in sexual partnerships.

Sexual Agency

Sexual agency has been a focus of Jewkes and Morrell's (2010) research in South Africa. They observe that

> [g]ender inequalities give men considerable relational power over young women, particularly in circumstances of poverty and where sex is materially rewarded. Young women are often described as victims of men, but this inadequately explains women's observed sexual agency. (p. 1729)

Similarly, Casale et al. (2011) have pointed to studies that challenge conventional understandings of sexual behaviour among youth, both perceptions of young men and women. They highlight studies that emphasise the ways in which females are not wholly passive in unequal sexual partnerships with older men. They may choose to engage in such relationships for material gain and to increase their social status, gaining esteem both from expensive gifts but also by being seen with a 'powerful' man. In South Africa, there is a common term used by young women enrolled in our universities. They refer to their male partners as 'Ministers'—e.g., Minister of Education or Finance—high profile, wealthy men who meet their material and other needs (e.g., emotional needs and social status). Some ministers are more powerful and have more wealth, owing to their portfolio, and are deemed more attractive as a result. These university students are more educated than their counterparts in rural regions of the Eastern Cape and KwaZulu-Natal, yet they are also engaging in 'transactional' types of sexual behaviour to the detriment of their own health (Kaufman & Stavrou Stavros, 2004; Selikow et al., 2009). The newer social media 'Blessers' phenomenon among women of higher education and economic status is indicative of this exchange of sex for status among a higher socioeconomic group, also with higher educational attainment. Social media is used as a platform to link blessers (men) to blessees (women) that has a powerful reach. Journalist Pontsho Pilane captures this cultural phenomenon in her frank article, describing Rachel's situation (Box 2.2). This phenomenon is discussed further in Chap. 6.

Box 2.2 'Shame the blessers, not the blessed' (Pilane, 2016 excerpt)

I went to school with a girl I will call Rachel to protect her identity. She was four years older than me, and easily the most beautiful girl in our school. When she was in grade nine, she dated an older man from our neighbourhood. He would pick her up from school, give her money to do her hair and buy her clothes that ensured she was the best dressed on civvies day. Nobody ever told me that their relationship was wrong, but I remember everybody describing her as "fast" and "disrespectful". Some even called her a whore. Our mothers would warn us not to be like her—whatever it is they thought she was. Rachel was just 15 years old. This man was well into his 20s and had already fathered two children, but many boys envied him and other girls wanted him for themselves. By virtue of his manhood, he was immune from the animosity shown towards Rachel.

Last year I bumped into Rachel, and she was still as beautiful as I remembered. She was visiting her relatives back in our village—something she hadn't done in years. When I asked her why, she told me she doesn't come home because she is tired of being reminded of the mistakes she made as a teenager. She was tired of taking the blame for a relationship that, in effect, amounted to statutory rape.

What happened to the man? He is still happily married and lives comfortably in our neighbourhood. After impregnating Rachel when she was in grade 10, he went on to date even younger girls. He continued with his life, as unbothered and callous as ever.

Rachel—who was just a girl at the time of their affair—continues to be insulted and shamed, whereas he moved on swiftly and violated other girls. Rachel is one of the many girls who live with the trauma and backlash of statutory rape.

When I read about Health Minister Aaron Motsoaledi's three-year programme to "wean" schoolgirls off sugar daddies, aimed at reducing new HIV infections and teenage pregnancies, I remembered Rachel and how society failed to protect her.

His plan is good and noble, but the language used concerns me. Why do we think it is young women and girls who need the skills to avoid being exploited by sinister men? When will the focus be on these men, who prey on vulnerable young women? When will we stop letting them get away with it? When will these men be shamed for their actions?

Earlier this week, the hashtag #AntiBlessers was trending on Twitter. Unfortunately, it was not trending because people were calling out blessers (wealthy, probably married, men who date younger women), but because a woman who had just graduated tweeted: "#AntiBlessers. When young women are busy searching for blessers, we out here. Goal achieved!!!"

In less than 140 characters, this woman completely absolved the men in these "blesser" relationships of any responsibility—and slut-shamed the women.

Blessers and men like the one who pursued Rachel are never discussed. We do not chastise them or call them out; they are not shamed for using money to lure young women. In fact, in many cases, they are rewarded for their actions by gaining social capital. Men such as Kenny Kunene, who exploited young women and now slut-shames them, publicly weigh in on the issue of blessers.

I grew up with my mother warning me against taxi drivers. She would tell me how they would try to lure me in with their top-of-the-range sound systems. These drivers would constantly prey on schoolgirls, attempting to entice us with KFC or pocket money. To protect me from these taxi drivers, my mother made sure I used *skofo*—a privately hired taxi that collected us from school—until my matric year.

I grew up in an area where older men were always on the prowl for young girls. Schoolgirls would date men who worked in the mines and at the factories, because they would give them pocket money to buy "nice things"—in Rachel's case, and other instances, basic necessities such as toiletries and food for their families. We shake our heads at these girls but turn a blind eye to the deeds of the men, who are nothing more than sexual predators.

Source: Pilane (2016). Reprinted with permission.

Hunter (2002) considered sexual exchange practices through a study of two communities in northern KwaZulu-Natal (one of the provinces with the highest HIV prevalence for women of reproductive age): Matadeni and Isithebe. He drew sharp distinctions between sex for subsistence and sex for consumption (for material or economic reward or gains), interpreting this against the background of gendered material inequalities and lifestyles associated with a township and informal settlement. Hunter viewed the association between sex and gifts as a central factor driving multiple sex partnerships and reinforcing a construction of masculinity that he described as facilitating HIV transmission (2002). In 2003, Leclerc-Madlala built on Hunter's research, seeking to better understand women's agency by viewing their motivations and the subjective meanings they attached to their experiences of exchanging sex for material rewards. She writes of her findings:

> The language of 'survival sex' framed discussions about material expectations. Regardless of whether the women spoke about their 'need' for food or transportation, or their 'need' for fashionable items of clothing or outings to expensive hotel, all compensations by men were construed as helping to meet their 'needs'. (2003, p. 219)

Jewkes and Morrell (2012) highlight the changing social construction of gender and of masculinities and the different experiences of South African women in the peri-rural Eastern Cape. They report on women's experiences and their perceptions, commenting on how they make sense of their choices in a more rural context:

> Agency was most notable in particular stages of the dating 'game', especially relationship initiation. Constructions of desirable men differed but generally reflected a wish to avoid violence, and a search for mutual respect, sexual pleasure, romance, modernity, status and money. (2012, p. 1729)

Agency changed once girls or women entered into these relationships. They remark:

> Agency was constrained once relationships were consented to, as men expected to control their partners, using violent and non-violent methods.

> Women knew this and many accepted this treatment, although often expressing ambivalence. (2012, p. 1729)

They continue:

> A...third [agentic] position... rested not on a feminist challenge to patriarchy, but on an accommodation with men's power whilst seeking to negotiate greater respect and non-violence within relations with men. These multiple and dynamic femininities open up possibilities for change. They demonstrate the need to engage with women, both as victims of patriarchy and active supporters of the gender order... [to] validate women's agency, reduce violence and prevent HIV. (2012, p. 1729)

Notably, findings by Stern and Cooper (2014) indicate that South African women who are older may change their perceptions about their risk behaviours. These women reported looking back on the sexual risk behaviour undertaken by their younger selves, indicating that they did not understand the repercussions related to HIV risk. Some women reported that they would not opt to make the same choices. These women recognised they were influenced by factors that were temporal.

Connell, whose research on masculinities continues to shape the field, argues that in any society, there are many masculinities and not all are equally powerful as social forces (1995). The shaping and the reconstruction of gender through opportunities and interventions that allow for norms to shift are thus both important and complex. Jewkes and Morrell (2010) state that the men and women who adopt the resulting gender norms are following social convention, and may face difficulty if their behaviour contradicts what has been established as acceptable behaviour:

> [M]en and women who adopt these gender identities are following ideals with deep roots in social and cultural processes, and thus, they are models of behaviour that may be hard for individuals to critique and in which to exercise choice. Women who are materially and emotionally vulnerable are least able to risk experiencing sanctions or foregoing these rewards and thus are most vulnerable to their men folk. (p. 3)

Further research that engages masculinities, femininities and women's agency is essential in understanding potential points of HIV intervention, as well as suggesting possibilities for social change. I take this up in greater detail in Chap. 7.

Gender-Based Violence (GBV)

Across race groups, South African women face high levels of gender-based violence. I provide the UN definition, which I use throughout this work.

Rape and Forced Sex

Rape is a notifiable crime but one of the least notified crimes in South Africa; this includes child rape (Ackermann & de Klerk, 2002, p. 166). The difficulties in gathering accurate data also exist in the collection rape prevalence statistics. Mullick et al. state that 'studies point to gross underreporting of cases' (2010, p. 50). Data are problematic, fragmented and largely confined to cases reported to police or collected by researchers. Research by Jewkes, Vundule, Maforah, & Jordaan (2001, p. 737; Jewkes & Abrahams, 2002) highlights the frequency of rape in South Africa, stating that the 'majority of teens reported having had sex against their wishes and one in 10 had been raped'. They also found that two-thirds of participants had been beaten by a partner. A large survey conducted by Jewkes, Sikweyiya, Morrell, and Dunkle (2011) in the Eastern Cape and KwaZulu-Natal provinces in 2011 found that 27.6% of the 1738 men interviewed (aged 18–49) had raped a woman or girl, and 2.9% had raped a boy or man (Table 2.4).

Rape in South Africa is often termed 'forced sex'—to avoid the stigma associated with rape (Jewkes et al., 2006). A number of studies have documented that many women's first sexual experience in South Africa is forced (Jewkes et al., 2005). A study in Soweto conducted by researchers from the MRC found that 7% of participants' first sexual act was forced (Dunkle et al., 2004; see also Jewkes et al., 2006). In a study by Jewkes and colleagues, among a sample of respondents (both men who had perpetrated rape and those who had not), HIV prevalence was high: over 25% for those

Table 2.4 UN definitions for violence

The United Nations provides the following definitions of key terms: • *Violence against Women* is "any act of *gender-based violence* that results in, or is likely to result in, physical, sexual or mental harm or suffering to women, including threats of such acts, coercion or arbitrary deprivation of liberty, whether occurring in public or in private life." • *Sexual violence* is "any sexual act, attempt to obtain a sexual act, or other act directed against a person's sexuality using coercion, by any person regardless of their relationship to the victim, in any setting. It includes rape, defined as the physically forced or otherwise coerced penetration of the vulva or anus with a penis, other body part or object."

Source: WHO (2016b, p. 1)

in the 25–45 age bracket and over 40% for those 30–39 years of age. This study underscored that men who perpetrate rape may be at higher risk of having HIV, and that women who experience violence and forced sex are at increased risk of acquiring HIV (Jewkes et al., 2011). Forced sex can also be routinised within intimate partnerships.

Intimate Partner (Domestic) Violence

Globally, prevalence of IPV is estimated to range from 15% to 71% in women (WHO, 2013a). IPV is generally defined as behaviours by a present or past partner, whether attempted or completed, which cause psychological, physical or sexual harm (WHO, 2013a). IPV in South Africa is defined broadly as physical, sexual or psychological abuse and is a violation of South African law. (See Government of South Africa 1998; Woolman & Sprague, 2015.) High prevalence of IPV, across race groups of women, is well-documented in South Africa though estimates vary (Hoque, Hoque, & Kader, 2009; Human Rights Watch, 1995; Jewkes et al., 2009; Martin et al., 2006).

One study across three provinces in 1999 found lifetime prevalence of abuse by an intimate partner of 26.8% in the Eastern Cape, 28.4% in Mpumalanga, and 19.1% in the Northern Province (Jewkes et al., 2001). Research by Wits University researchers documented that more than 60% of women were regularly battered by partners or spouses and 50% to 60% of marriages were reported to involve physical and sexual violence (Wood, Maforah, & Jewkes, 1998). Yet IPV is routinely under-reported due to stigma and women's lack of confidence in the police services (Government of South Africa, 2009; Sprague et al., 2015, 2016a) (Table 2.5).

Table 2.5 IPV prevalence, femicide and links between gender-based violence, IPV and HIV

• Using data from the cross-sectional, nationally representative South African Stress and Health Study, *the prevalence of IPV among 1229 married and cohabitating women was 31%*. Women reporting IPV exposure were also more likely to practise HIV risk behaviours such as alcohol and drug use, and less likely to engage in health seeking behaviours (i.e., recent visit to a medical doctor) (Gass, Stein, Williams, & Seedat, 2010).
• The *link between gender-based violence, specifically IPV, and HIV risk* has been investigated in a small number of studies in South Africa. In one landmark study in the area of IPV and HIV, Dunkle and colleagues reported on a cross-sectional study of 1366 women presenting for ANC at four clinics in Soweto. They found that after adjusting for age, current relationship status and women's risk behaviours, *IPV was significantly associated with HIV positivity*, as were high levels of male control in a woman's current relationship (measured by the Sexual Relationship Power Scale) (Dunkle et al., 2004).
• A subsequent study followed a cohort of 1099 women aged 15–26 years in Eastern Cape Province for two years between 2002 and 2006 and found that 128 women seroconverted (HIV incident rate of 6.2 per 100 person-years). Importantly, in multivariable analyses *both low relationship power equity and more than one reported experience of IPV significantly increased the risk of incident HIV infection* (Jewkes et al., 2010), leading to several policy recommendations around reducing gender-based violence as a strategy to prevent HIV infection (Silverman, 2010). The study also raised some criticism for not including male partner characteristics (namely, multiple partnering by men) and issues in reverse causality (Castor, Cook, Leclerc-Madlala, & Shelton, 2010).
• A study led by the South African Medical Research Council investigated intimate femicide using a national mortuary based sample in 2009, following up on an earlier study using the same methods in 1999. The study found that while overall female homicides and intimate partner homicides had deceased, intimate homicides had decreased at a lower rate. *IPV was the leading cause of death of women homicide victims* (56%). The study found *no evidence that interventions to reduce IPV were working, and found no evidence that police investigations were improving* (i.e., no change in number of cases with no perpetrator data) (Abrahams, Mathews, Jewkes, Martin, & Lombard, 2012).

In 2013, the South African MRC, together with the WHO released a report entitled *Global and Regional Estimates of Violence Against Women: Prevalence and Health Effects of Intimate Partner Violence and Non-Partner Sexual Violence* (WHO, 2013b). The report cites growing evidence of the link between IPV and increased vulnerability to HIV and other STIs. Various mechanisms are highlighted, including direct infection from forced sexual encounters with partners, general effects from prolonged exposure to violence and stress and limited control over timing and circumstances of sexual intercourse (e.g., negotiation of safe sex through condom use). Work on the causal pathways between IPV and HIV risk has been undertaken by Dunkle and Decker (2013) who propose two primary pathways: (1) direct transmission from an infected perpetrator; and (2) increased vulnerability due to experiences of violence. They stress, however, that the causal pathways are likely complex, multifaceted and linked to individual factors and social gender norms that may differ across settings (Dunkle & Decker, 2013; see Fig. 2.4). One systematic review investigating these links is highlighted below (Table 2.6).

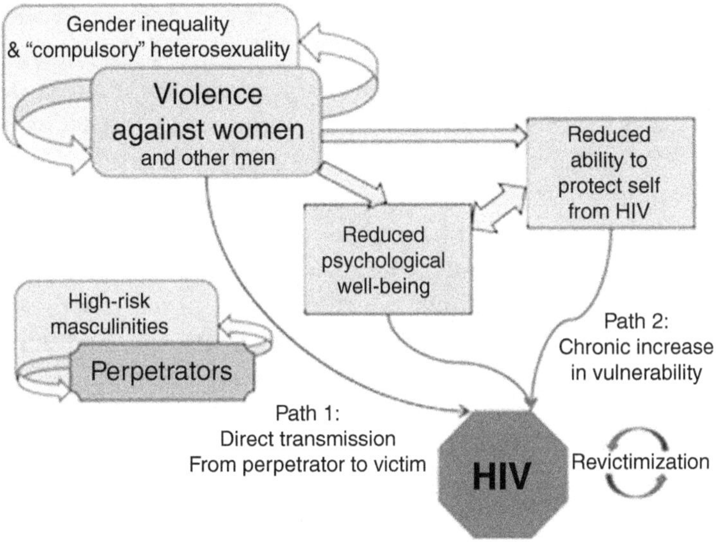

Fig. 2.4 Pathways linking gender inequality, VAW, masculinities to HIV risk. Source: Dunkle & Decker (2013)

Table 2.6 Reviewing the evidence: HIV and IPV (Focus on African women)

• A recent study used updated Demographic and Health Surveys from 2004 to 2012 conducted in 10 sub-Saharan African countries (not including South Africa) as well as additional exposure-level variables to define IPV. While the previous study used only physical and/or sexual violence, the authors in this study also calculated emotional violence, controlling behaviour by a partner and any combination of these. The study found that *almost 40% of all women in the sample reported experiencing some form of IPV, with physical violence (29%) being the most common*. The prevalence of HIV was 14–16% among women who reported any IPV and 10% among those who reported experiencing no IPV. In pooled regressions across all sites, *experiencing physical violence, emotional violence and controlling partner behaviour were significantly associated with higher odds of HIV infection*, while experiencing sexual violence was not significantly associated with HIV. The authors argued that their study likely found positive associations between IPV and HIV where the previous study had not due in part to their inclusion of indicators of violence combined with male controlling behaviour, *suggesting that a more nuanced definition of IPV and controlling behaviour is important* (Durevall & Lindskog, 2015).

Biological Factors

Biological and physiological factors also play a significant role in women's vulnerability to HIV through heterosexual contact (Quinn & Overbaugh, 2005). However, a clear grasp of the biology that is associated with HIV sexual transmission is not fully established (Klot, Auerbach, & Berry, 2013). Estimates of sexual transmission are conducted in two ways: the probability (1) per sexual act, which gauges the risk of infection per sexual contact; or (2) per partner, which measures cumulative risk of HIV infection over the course of numerous sexual contacts in a given partnership (Boily et al., 2009; Garnett & Røttingen, 2001). The probability of HIV transmission (estimated per sex act or per partner) depends on both the infectiousness of the HIV positive partner and the susceptibility of the uninfected woman. Her susceptibility overall depends on factors that include her biologic, genetic, immunological, behavioural and other factors, as well as those of the partner. (see Boily et al., 2009; Quinn & Overbaugh, 2005.)

Biologically, women are more susceptible to HIV than men due to the greater surface area of mucous membranes in the vagina and cervix that are exposed during sex (and potentially the uterus). Immaturity of the vaginal tract; inflammation and ulcerations caused by pre-existing STIs; vaginal and cervical lesions; microabrasions; hormonal factors; and hormonal contraception use all play a role in women's susceptibility (Klot et al., 2013). Microtears occur in women's vaginal tissue as a result of sex, and bleeding and abrasions create opportunities for HIV infection. Young women (especially below age 18) are at increased risk due to an immature cervix. In young women, thinner cells line the cervix all the way down to the vagina and HIV can penetrate the vaginal wall more easily; younger women are also at increased risk of HIV because their genital tracts are under-developed, which means that tearing and infection of the genital tract occurs more easily during sex (Blair et al., 2012). Older women who have gone through menopause are also at increased risk because the lining of the uterus has become thinner and the vagina drier; lack of lubrication during sex facilitates tearing and bleeding. This has relevance for South African men's sexual preference for dry sex, a practice that increases women's risk of HIV acquisition (Blair et al., 2012).

Regarding other biological factors creating susceptibility to HIV in women, some studies have indicated elevated risk of HIV acquisition during pregnancy, which could be attributed to immune responses or to hormonal changes (e.g., high levels of oestrogen and progesterone are produced in pregnancy), possibly affecting mucosa in the genital tract or creating other immunological effects (WHO, 2006a, 2006b). STIs are viewed as co-factors that may render women more susceptible to HIV (Quinn & Overbaugh, 2005). There is now substantial evidence that the presence of specific STIs, including herpes simplex type 2 (HSV-2), are linked to increased risk of HIV transmission (CDC, 1998; Ramjee, Kamali, & McCormack, 2010; Wasserheit, 1992). A recent systematic review found evidence from 57 longitudinal studies that HSV-2 increases the risk of HIV acquisition (Looker et al., 2017). This is highly significant because sub-Saharan Africa has the highest prevalence of HSV-2: 417 million people aged 15–49 years were estimated to have herpes simplex virus type 2 in 2012 (Looker et al., 2017). Additionally, bacterial vaginosis and syphilis are common infections for Southern African women. Individuals with STIs are often asymptomatic, which makes treatment difficult and creates delays (Connolly, Ramjee, Sturm, & Abdool Karim, 2002). A lack of awareness about STI symptoms, low levels of STI knowledge and low access to primary health care and reproductive health services hinder STI management and control (Chersich & Rees, 2008). In one randomised controlled trial (RCT), Ramjee et al. (2008) found that women in three South African sites were three times more likely to acquire an STI than participants in the Tanzanian and Zambian sites. STI treatment interventions in RCTs have demonstrated limited success, however (Padian et al., 2010). Pre-exposure prophylaxis is more promising and has shown to be effective for some women (Cohen et al., 2011).

In response to the evidence, experts have called for improved interventions against STIs, particularly those generating increased risk for HIV in women (e.g., HSV-2 and human papillomavirus). Vaccines and additional methods for STI diagnosis and treatment are needed (Fast & Kaleebu, 2010; Hayes et al., 2010). Microbicide interventions have been conducted in South Africa over a number of years. The CAPRISA 004 study conducted in the global HIV epicentre of KwaZulu-Natal—an area situated along the southeast coast of South Africa—demonstrated proof that a topical microbicide gel could substantially reduce HIV infections and reduce genital herpes infections (Abdool Karim & Baxter, 2010). Nevertheless, subsequent trials (VOICE and FACTS 001) were unable to confirm this effectiveness, primarily due to poor adherence among young women, which was attributed to gender-related factors (Doggett et al., 2015. For a review, see Ramjee et al., 2010). These interventions also underscored the role of gender hierarchies and adverse gender norms in the development of technologies and mechanisms to protect and promote women's health, particularly in the high HIV prevalence countries (Abdool Karim & Baxter, 2010).

In summing up section two, social and structural factors are playing a highly significant role, in shaping this high HIV risk environment for women. Unlike biological factors, social and structural factors are changeable. These factors encompass a complex array of social constructions of gender, masculinities and femininities, gender hierarchies and norms surrounding men's sexual preferences, as well as intimate partner violence, with new hypotheses that connect gender inequality and high-risk masculinities to increased HIV risk (Dunkle & Decker, 2013).

Part 3: Moving from Empirical Evidence to Normative Considerations

Taking stock momentarily, a range of indicators and evidence has been reviewed in this chapter. Health measures (indicators) reviewed in part one are important in establishing differences in health status, and in the distribution of health determinants, between groups (groups of South African women in this case) in a given population. On their own they do not, however, offer sufficient insight into normative considerations associated with health as social justice in this population, or how things ought to be for this population to attain a higher standard of health. Deeming systematic differences in health as *health inequities* must be based on a process of *social evaluation* that is linked to *social valuations of health* in a given society. *Social valuations* of health are grounded in normative considerations and social values about what is unacceptable and unfair, in this case in relation to the persistent problem of HIV in South African women.

To move forward, we need the empirical evidence and the hard data generated by health and development statistics (i.e., health indicators), to track, monitor and improve health and to address health inequities. The evidence is a starting point. In LMICs, generating data is a major challenge. But it is not the only one. At a general level, Sen notes that explicit valuation is needed to assess individual advantage or disadvantage in relation to social progress (1999, see pp. 30–34). This, he argues, must be thrown open to public scrutiny and debate. At issue here is the moral nature and basis for addressing health disparities in vulnerable or marginalised groups who experience systematically poor health outcomes, relative to other groups.

Producing more equitable health outcomes also requires locating health policies within broader social welfare policies and commitments on governments that have competing demands on their economic resources. Actions taken to ameliorate poor health outcomes may need to be grounded in a strong rationale that governments should do more to address health inequities than they are already doing.

To date, despite early work in health promotion in Latin America, much of the work to move from the empirical evidence to normative assessments and action, the writing and the doing, has taken place predominately in continental Europe and the UK (Koivusalo, 2010; Leppo, Ollla, Pena, Wismar, & Cook, 2013). In other geographic locations, the discourse is nascent (such as in some LMICs), fraught (e.g., in the US), and in other regions, gains might not advance rapidly in geographic locations that have embraced new forms of nationalism. Documented cases of HiAP have tended to be pursued in societies with an already strong health sector, note Leppo et al. (2013), which also have capacity for coordination across multiple sectors; demonstrate societal commitment to social goals that advance health and wellbeing; and have financial, human and technical resources (2013). These authors state that 'such conditions are often weak or absent in low-income settings' (2013, p. 44). In identifying and addressing important health inequities in a society, there is some complexity in moving from evidence to normative judgments to action to address them: given different resource levels, data availability and governance systems across countries. Government interventions to improve health sometimes need 'to be fought for' and 'civil society [has] played a vital role' in advocating for health improvements (Leppo et al., 2013, p. 28). This has certainly occurred in South Africa, with the social mobilisation for essential HIV medicines. The distribution of HIV infection in women and their poor health outcomes throw into sharper focus the need for normative social justice approaches to engage with potential health inequities in South Africa. What is required is some forging of explicit connections that allow for movement from the empirical evidence to normative justice arguments that can gain purchase in practical policy implementation. This requires reviewing the empirical evidence and linking the health data to normative considerations of justice.

The empirical data seem to point to an initial reading of unfairness and injustice, because, as indicated, women are at higher risk of acquiring HIV over the lifespan; they carry a disproportionate burden of HIV; their life expectancy is roughly 20 years less than that for South African women of other race groups; and their HIV-related mortality is higher. These differences in health outcomes for black South African women throw harsh light on the very different health profiles for this population, relative to other groups in society. They raise fundamental questions about equity and fairness in South Africa, questions that may have relevance for other settings (Anand, Peter, & Sen, 2004; Evans, Whitehead, Diderichsen, Bhuiya, & Wirth, 2001). But these outcomes still require further investigation. Some caution must be noted. As Sen emphasises, approaches to health justice that take a single-dimensional view, e.g., on health outcomes only, may lead theorists and decision makers astray.

Take, for example, the 'fair innings' distributional argument by Williams (1998). Fair innings implies that equity in health care should encompass 'distributing [health] care in such a way as to get as close as is feasible to an equal distribution of health' (Culyer & Wagstaff, 1993, quoted in Sen, 2004b, p. 30). Williams, in his fair innings analysis, finds that the difference between life expectancy for males and females is even greater than that between social classes in the UK (1998). The data show that women tend to live longer than men due to a natural survival advantage for women at every stage in the life course. This is typically true except in societies with female excess mortality, like China and India, where deliberate social interventions take place that forcibly limit women's natural advantage. (See Sen, 1990) Such interventions include sex-selective abortions of female foetuses or infants and restrictions on food access or intake, due to preferences for boys (Sen, 1990). The inter-group differences in the UK between men and women in terms of life expectancy might signal inequities that need to be addressed. However, additional information is needed to assess whether this is a health equity: is this phenomenon truly unfair and unjust?

Williams, in his 'aha moment' claims that on the basis of male to female differences in life expectancy, 'We males are not getting fair innings' (1998, p. 327, quoted in Sen, 2004b, p. 30). Sen swoops in to offer a reality check, akin to 'not so fast!' He stresses that if equalising male and female survival to flatten women's advantage to overcome a 'natural inequality' were the goal, this could be achieved by using allocations in health care to guide health policy. In this scenario, men would be offered more and better care, and women would be denied it, offered less, or health care of poor quality. This would generate a deliberate social intervention, part-Kafkaesque and part-Orwellian, by controlling health care access to seek to produce an outcome where men and women are more equal. Would this intervention produce a fair and just result?

This example reveals that the type of information used in the assessment of fairness and equity in health is crucial because there is nothing unjust about this phenomenon of life expectancy differences between men and women in the UK. While there could potentially be interventions that would improve men's health, this is a natural difference and inequality between men and women, as opposed to an unnatural one that constitutes an inequity. Proposing to deny or limit women's health care would be questionable in terms of ethics and justice. Thus, from a distributional justice perspective focused on health outcomes, what sounds fair and reasonable, may actually produce greater injustice, while generating a dystopian reality. This is why, Sen (1990) and Pogge (2004) stress, that in any assessment of health equity, when looking at health achievements—life expectancy, in this example—the *process* by which outcomes were achieved must be given consideration. Additional evidence would be needed to support a finding and make a claim that the Government or state agents must do more than they are doing at present because there are competing resources and obligations on (limited) state coffers. As Wikler notes, 'We also need a moral account, a compelling argument that health inequalities represent or constitute an injustice that places a claim on society's resources' (2004, p. 114).

A major argument that could be—and typically is—raised at this stage, has to do with this population of South African women's access to health care. The point could be made that perhaps insufficient access to HIV care is the most obvious intervention to address poor health outcomes for black South African women; and that the demands of justice really only require health and HIV care. A bastion of arguments can be drawn from communitarian, libertarian, procedural democracy and welfare economics to support fair opportunity to access health care. What is this population's access to health and HIV care? In response, the next chapter investigates access to HIV programmes in the South African public health system as a pre-requisite to improve their health and HIV outcomes, which could be viewed as a minimum requirement of justice in the South African context, in keeping with the basic law.

Notes

1. Led each time by Dr Olive Shisana of the HSRC. For the methodology and other details of the survey, see Shisana et al. (2014).
2. When I refer to the 'population' or 'group' (a public health convention), I am referring to black or African South African women. When I refer to the 'study population' I am referring to the group of women studied in the empirical investigation (design and methods described in Chap. 5, and findings presented in Chap. 6), and described in detail in Box 2.1.

3. The emphasis on the individual in public health control efforts has been criticised by anthropologists and sociologists because it assumes that individuals have full and free agency, and it considers individual behaviour outside of the full composition of social, economic, political and cultural forces that shape behaviour (Gupta et al., 2008; Parkhurst, 2014). All people engage in sexual practices and relationships rooted within social contexts and gender norms situated within larger social systems and institutions that comprise the gendered social order.

References

Abdool Karim, S., & Baxter, C. (2010). Microbicides and their implications in HIV prevention. *Indian Journal of Medical Research, 132*(6), 656–659.

Abrahams, N., Mathews, S., Jewkes, R., Martin, L., & Lombard, C. (2012). *Every Eight Hours: Intimate Femicide in South Africa 10 Years Later!* [online]. Tygerberg: South African Medical Research Council. Retrieved November 1, 2016, from http://www.mrc.ac.za/policybriefs/everyeighthours.pdf

Ackermann, L., & de Klerk, G. (2002). Social factors that make South African women vulnerable to HIV infection. *Health Care for Women International, 23*(2), 163–172.

Akullian, A., Bershteyn, A., Klein, D., Vandormael, A., Bärnighausen, T., & Tanser, F. (2017). Sexual partnership age pairings and risk of HIV acquisition in rural South Africa. *AIDS, 31*(12), 1755–1764.

Albertyn, C. (2009). 'The stubborn persistence of patriarchy'? Gender equality and diversity in South Africa. *Constitutional Court Review, 2*(1), 165–208.

Anand, S., Peter, F., & Sen, A. (Eds.). (2004). *Public Health, Ethics, and Equity.* Oxford: Oxford University Press.

Auerbach, J., Caceres, C., & Parkhurst, J. (2011). Addressing social drivers of HIV/AIDS for the long-term response: Conceptual and methodological considerations. *Global Public Health, 6*(Suppl 3), S293–309.

Bilchitz, D. (2008). *Poverty and Fundamental Rights: The Justification and Enforcement of Socio-Economic Rights.* Oxford: Oxford University Press.

Black, V., Black, A., Rees, H., Guidozzi, F., Scorgie, F., & Chersich, M. (2016). Increased access to antiretroviral therapy is associated with reduced maternal mortality in Johannesburg, South Africa: An audit from 2003–2012. *PLoS ONE, 11*(12), e0168199.

Blair, J., Paxton, L., & Kamb, M. (2012). HIV and AIDS in women. In M. Goldman, R. Troisi, & K. Rexrode (Eds.), *Women and Health* (2nd ed., pp. 505–522). Boston: Academic Press.

Boily, M., Baggaley, R., Wang, L., Masse, B., White, R., Hayes, R., et al. (2009). Heterosexual risk of HIV-1 infection per sexual act: A systematic review and meta-analysis of observational studies. *Lancet Infectious Diseases, 9*(2), 118–129.

Boonzaier, F. (2005). Woman abuse in South Africa: A brief contextual analysis. *Feminism & Psychology, 15*(1), 99–103.

Bradshaw, D., & Nannan, N. (2005). Mortality and morbidity among women and children. In *South African Health Review 2006* (pp. 127–150). Health Systems Trust: Durban.

Buchmann, E., Mnyani, C., Frank, K., Chersich, M., & McIntyre, J. (2015). Declining maternal mortality in the face of persistently high HIV prevalence in a middle-income country. *BJOG, 122*(2), 220–227.

Burton, R. (2013). Maternal health: There is cause for optimism. *South African Medical Journal, 103*(8), 520–521.

Casale, M., Rogan, M., Hynie, M., Flicker, S., Nixon, S., & Rubincam, C. (2011). Gendered perceptions of HIV risk among young women and men in a high-HIV-prevalence setting. *African Journal of AIDS Research, 10*(1), 301–310.

Castor, D., Cook, S., Leclerc-Madlala, S., & Shelton, J. (2010). Intimate partner violence and HIV in South African women. *Lancet, 376*(9748), 1219–1220.

Centers for Disease Control and Prevention (CDC). (1998). HIV prevention through early detection and treatment of other sexually transmitted diseases—United States. *Morbidity and Mortality Weekly Report, 47*(12), 1–24.

Chersich, M., & Rees, H. (2008). Vulnerability of women in Southern Africa to infection with HIV: Biologic determinants and priority health sector interventions. *AIDS, 22*(Suppl. 4), S27–S40.

Cluver, L., Boyes, M., Orkin, M., Pantelic, M., Molwena, T., & Sherr, L. (2013). Child-focused state cash transfers and adolescent risk of HIV infection in South Africa: A propensity-score-matched case-control study. *Lancet Global Health, 1*(6), e362–e370.

Coates, T., Richter, L., & Caceres, C. (2008). Behavioural strategies to reduce HIV transmission: How to make them work better. *Lancet, 372*(9639), 669–684.

Cohen, M., Chen, Y., McCauley, M., Gamble, T., Hosseinipour, M., Kumarasamy, N., et al. (2011). Prevention of HIV-1 infection with early antiretroviral therapy. *New England Journal of Medicine, 365*, 493–505.

Connell, R. (1987). *Gender and Power: Society, the Person and Sexual Politics*. Stanford: Stanford University Press.

Connell, R. (1995). *Masculinities*. Berkeley: University of California Press.

Connell, R., & Messerschmidt, J. (2005). Hegemonic masculinity: Rethinking the concept. *Gender Society, 19*(6), 829–859.

Connolly, C., Ramjee, G., Sturm, A., & Abdool Karim, S. (2002). Incidence of sexually transmitted infections among HIV positive sex workers in KwaZulu-Natal, South Africa. *Sexually Transmitted Diseases, 29*(11), 721–724.

Correa, S., Petchesky, R., & Parker, R. (2008). *Sexuality, Health and Human Rights*. New York: Routledge.

Diderichsen, F., Evans, T., & Whitehead, M. (2001). The social disparities in health. In T. Evans, M. Whitehead, F. Diderichsen, A. Bhuiya, & M. Wirth (Eds.), *Challenging Inequities to Health: From Ethics to Action* (pp. 12–23). Oxford: Oxford University Press.

Doggett, E., Lanham, M., Wilcher, R., Gafos, M., Karim, Q., & Heise, L. (2015). Optimizing HIV prevention for women: A review of evidence from microbicide studies and considerations for gender-sensitive microbicide introduction. *Journal of the International AIDS Society, 18*(1), 20536.

Doyal, L. (2006). How well are women worldwide? *Lancet, 367*(9526), 1893–1894.

Dunkle, K., & Decker, M. (2013). Gender-based violence and HIV: Reviewing the evidence for links and causal pathways in the general population and high risk groups. *American Journal of Reproductive Immunology, 69*(Suppl. 1), 20–26.

Dunkle, K., Jewkes, R., Brown, H., Gray, G., McIntyre, J., & Harlow, S. (2004). Transactional sex among women in Soweto, South Africa: Prevalence, risk factors and associations with HIV infection. *Social Science & Medicine, 59*(8), 1581–1592.

Durevall, D., & Lindskog, A. (2015). Intimate partner violence and HIV in ten sub-Saharan African countries: What do the Demographic and Health Surveys tell us? *Lancet Global Health, 3*(1), e34–e43.

Dworkin, S., Hatcher, A., Colvin, C., & Peacock, D. (2013). Impact of a gender-transformative HIV and antiviolence program on gender ideologies and masculinities in two rural, South African communities. *Men and Masculinities, 16*(2), 181–202.

Dworkin, S., Treves-Kagan, S., & Lippman, S. (2013). Gender-transformative interventions to reduce HIV risks and violence with heterosexually-active men: A review of the global evidence. *AIDS and Behavior, 17*(9), 2845–2863.

Evans, T., Whitehead, M., Diderichsen, F., Bhuiya, A., & Wirth, M. (Eds.). (2001). *Challenging Inequities to Health: From Ethics to Action*. Oxford: Oxford University Press.

Fast, P., & Kaleebu, P. (2010). HIV vaccines: Current status worldwide and in Africa. *AIDS, 24*(Suppl. 4), S50–S60.

Friedman, S., & McKnight, K. (2003). What is the role of structural interventions in HIV prevention? [online]. San Francisco: University of San Francisco. Retrieved June 20, 2017, from https://caps.ucsf.edu/uploads/pubs/FS/structural.php

Gannon, M. (2016, February 5). Race is a social construct scientists argue. *Scientific American*. Retrieved October 25, 2017, from https://www.scientificamerican.com/article/race-is-a-social-construct-scientists-argue/

Garnett, G., & Røttingen, J. A. (2001). Measuring the risk of HIV transmission. *AIDS, 15*(5), 641–643.

Gass, J., Stein, D., Williams, D., & Seedat, S. (2010). Intimate partner violence, health behaviours, and chronic physical illness among South African women. *South African Medical Journal, 100*(9), 582–585.

Gennrich, D. (2013). *Men and Masculinities in South Africa: Men Making a Difference*. Pietermaritzburg: ACSA/Sonke Gender Justice.

Gerntholtz, L., Gibbs, A., & Willan, S. (2011). The African women's protocol: Bringing attention to reproductive rights and the MDGs. *PLoS Medicine, 8*(4), 1–4.

Gilbert, L. (1995). Sociology and the "New Public Health" in South Africa. *South African Journal of Sociology, 26*, 115–124.

Gilbert, L., & Selikow, T. (2011). "The epidemic in this country has the face of a woman": Gender and HIV/AIDS in South Africa. *African Journal of AIDS Research, 10*(Suppl. 1), 325–334.

Gouws, E., & Abdool Karim, Q. (2005). HIV infection in South Africa: The evolving epidemic. In S. Abdool Karim & Q. Abdool Karim (Eds.), *HIV/AIDS in South Africa* (pp. 48–66). Cambridge: Cambridge University Press.

Government of South Africa. (1998). Domestic Violence Act 116 of 1998. Cape Town: South Africa.

Government of South Africa. (1999). *Saving Mothers Report on Confidential Enquiries into Maternal Deaths in South Africa*. Pretoria: National Department of Health.

Government of South Africa. (2009). *A Study of the Factors Contributing to SAPS Non-Compliance with the Domestic Violence Act*. [online]. Pretoria: National Department of Health. Retrieved January 1, 2016, from http://govza.gcis.gov.za/tn/node/521070

Government of South Africa. (2012). *National Strategic Plan on HIV, STIs and TB 2012–2016*. Pretoria: National Department of Health.

Government of South Africa. (2013a). *The 2012 National Antenatal Sentinel HIV and Herpes Simplex Type-2 Prevalence Survey, South Africa*. Pretoria: National Department of Health.

Government of South Africa. (2013b). *MDG Country Report: The South Africa I Know The Home I Understand*. Pretoria: Government of South Africa.

Government of South Africa. (2015). *Saving Mothers 2011–2013: Sixth Report on the Confidential Enquiries into Maternal Deaths in South Africa*. Pretoria: National Department of Health.

Gupta, G., Parkhurst, J., Ogden, J., Aggleton, P., & Mahal, A. (2008). Structural approaches to HIV prevention. *Lancet, 372*, 764–775.

Hargreaves, J., & Glynn, J. (2002). Educational attainment and HIV-1 infection in developing countries: A systematic review. *Tropical Medicine & International Health, 7*(6), 489–498.

Harrison, A. (2008). Hidden love: Sexual ideologies and relationship ideals among rural South African adolescents in the context of HIV/AIDS. *Culture, Health and Sexuality, 10*, 175–189.

Harrison, A., O'Sullivan, L., Hoffman, S., Dolezal, C., & Morrell, R. (2006). Gender role and relationship norms among young adults in South Africa: Measuring the context of masculinity and HIV risk. *Journal of Urban Health: Bulletin of the New York Academy of Medicine, 83*(4), 709–722.

Hatcher, A., Woollett, N., Pallitto, C., Mokoatle, K., Stockl, H., MacPhail, C., et al. (2014). Bidirectional links between HIV and intimate partner violence in pregnancy: Implications for prevention of mother-to-child transmission. *Journal of the International AIDS Society, 17*, 19233.

Hayes, R., Watson-Jones, D., Celum, C., van de Wijgert, J., & Wasserheit, J. (2010). Treatment of sexually transmitted infections for HIV prevention: End of the road or new beginning? *AIDS, 24*(Suppl. 4), S15–S26.

Heise, L., & McGrory, E. (2016). *Greentree II: Violence Against Women and Girls, and HIV—Report on a High-Level Consultation on the Evidence and Implications*. Greentree Estate, NY: STRIVE.

Hogan, M., Foreman, K., Naghavi, M., Ahn, S., Wang, M., Makela, S., et al. (2010). Maternal mortality for 181 countries, 1980–2008: A systematic analysis of progress towards Millennium Development Goal 5. *Lancet, 375*(9726), 1609–1623.

Hoque, M., & Kader, S. (2009). Prevalence and experience of domestic violence among rural pregnant women in KwaZulu-Natal, South Africa. *South African Journal of Epidemiology and Infection, 24*(4), 34–37.

Human Rights Watch. (1995). *Violence Against Women in South Africa: The State Response to Domestic Violence and Rape*. New York: Human Rights Watch.

Hunter, M. (2002). The materiality of everyday sex: Thinking beyond prostitution. *African Studies, 61*(1), 99–120.

Islam, M. (2007). The safe motherhood initiative and beyond. *Bulletin of the World Health Organization, 85*(10), 735.

Jamison, D., Feachem, R., Makgoba, M., Bos, E., Baingana, F., Hofman, K., et al. (Eds.). (2006). *Disease and Mortality in Sub-Saharan Africa* (2nd ed.). Washington, DC: World Bank.

Jewkes, R., & Abrahams, N. (2002). The epidemiology of rape and sexual coercion in South Africa: An overview. *Social Science & Medicine, 55*(7), 1231–1244.

Jewkes, R., Abrahams, N., Mathews, S., Seedat, M., Van Niekerk, A., Suffla, S., et al. (2009). Preventing rape and violence in South Africa: Call for leadership in a new agenda for action. In *MRC Policy Brief.* Pretoria: Medical Research Council.

Jewkes, R., Dunkle, K., Koss, M., Levin, J., Nduna, M., Jama, N., et al. (2006). Rape perpetration by young, rural South African men: Prevalence, patterns and risk factors. *Social Science & Medicine, 63*(11), 2949–2961.

Jewkes, R., Dunkle, K., Nduna, M., & Shai, N. (2010). Intimate partner violence, relationship power inequity, and incidence of HIV infection in young women in South Africa: A cohort study. *Lancet, 376*(9734), 41–48.

Jewkes, R., Levin, J., & Penn-Kekana, L. (2002). Risk factors for domestic violence: Findings from a South African cross-sectional study. *Social Science & Medicine, 55*, 1603–1617.

Jewkes, R., Martin, L., & Penn-Kekana, L. (2002). Correspondence: The virgin cleansing myth: Cases of child rape are not exotic. *Lancet, 359*, 711.

Jewkes, R., & Morrell, R. (2010). Gender and sexuality: Emerging perspectives from the heterosexual epidemic in South Africa and implications for HIV risk and prevention. *Journal of the International AIDS Society, 13*(1), 6.

Jewkes, R., & Morrell, R. (2012). Sexuality and the limits of agency among South African teenage women: Theorising femininities and their connections to HIV risk practices. *Social Science & Medicine, 74*, 1729–1737.

Jewkes, R., Penn-Kekana, L., & Rose-Junius, H. (2005). "If they rape me, I can't blame them": Reflections on gender in the social context of rape in South Africa and Namibia. *Social Science & Medicine, 61*, 1809–1820.

Jewkes, R., Sikweyiya, Y., Morrell, R., & Dunkle, K. (2011). Gender inequitable masculinity and sexual entitlement in rape perpetration in South Africa: Findings of a cross-sectional study. *PLoS ONE, 6*(12), e29590.

Jewkes, R., Vundule, C., Maforah, F., & Jordaan, E. (2001). Relationship dynamics and teenage pregnancy in South Africa. *Social Science & Medicine, 52*(5), 733–744.

Kassebaum, N., Bertozzi-Villa, A., Coggeshall, M., Shackelford, K., Steiner, C., Heuton, K., et al. (2014). Global, regional, and national levels and causes of maternal mortality during 1990–2013: A systematic analysis for the Global Burden of Disease Study 2013. *Lancet, 384*(9947), 980–1004.

Kaufman, C., & Stavrou Stavros, E. (2004). Bus fare please: The economics of sex and gifts among young people in urban South Africa. *Culture, Health and Sexuality, 6*(5), 377–391.

Klot, J., Auerbach, J., & Berry, M. (2013). Sexual violence and HIV risk. *American Journal of Reproductive Immunology, 69*(1), 5–19.

Koivusalo, M. (2010). The state of health in all policies (HiAP) in the European Union: Potential and pitfalls. *Journal of Epidemiology and Community Health, 64*(6), 500–503.

Kontis, V., Bennett, J., Mathers, C., Guangquan, L., Foreman, K., & Ezzati, M. (2017). Future life expectancy in 35 industrialised countries: Projections with a Bayesian model ensemble. *Lancet, 389*(10076), 1323–1335.

Leclerc-Madlala, S. (2002). Youth HIV/AIDS and the importance of sexual culture and context. *Social Dynamics, 28*, 20–41.

Leclerc-Madlala, S. (2008a). Age-disparate and intergenerational sex in Southern Africa: The dynamics of hypervulnerability. *AIDS, 22*(Suppl. 4), S17–S25.

Leclerc-Madlala, S. (2008b). Intergenerational/age-disparate sex and young women's vulnerability in Southern Africa. In *UNAIDS Technical Meeting on Young Women in HIV Hyper-Endemic Countries of Southern Africa*. Muldersdrift, South Africa: UNAIDS.

Leppo, K., Ollla, E., Pena, S., Wismar, M., & Cook, S. (2013). *Health in All Policies: Seizing Opportunities, Implementing Policies*. Helsinki: Finland Ministry of Social Affairs and Health.

Looker, K. J., Elmes, J. A. R., Gottlieb, S. L., Schiffer, J. T., Vicker, P., Turner, K. M. E., et al. (2017, August 23). Effect of HSV-2 infection on subsequent HIV acquisition: An updated systematic review and meta-analysis. *Lancet Infectious Diseases* (online). https://doi.org/10.1016/S1473-3099(17)30405-X

Martin, S., Li, Y., Casanuevam, C., Harris-Britt, A., Kupper, L., & Cloutier, S. (2006). Intimate partner violence and women's depression before and during pregnancy. *Violence Against Women, 12*(3), 221–239.

Mathews, C. (2005). Reducing sexual risk behaviours: Theory and research, successes and challenges. In S. Abdool Karim & Q. Abdool Karim (Eds.), *HIV/AIDS in South Africa*. Cambridge: Cambridge University Press.

Msemburi, W., Pillay-van Wyk, V., Dorrington, R., Neethling, I., Nannan, N., Groenewald, P., et al. (2016). *Second National Burden of Disease Study for South Africa: Cause-of-Death Profile for South Africa, 1997–2012*. Cape Town: South African Medical Research Council.

Mullick, S., Teffo-Menziwa, M., Williams, E., & Jina, R. (2010). Women and sexual violence. In F. Padarath (Ed.), *South African Health Review 2010*. Durban: Health Systems Trust.

Myers, B., Jones, H., Doherty, I., Kline, T., Key, M., Johnson, K., et al. (2015). Correlates of lifetime trauma exposure among pregnant women from Cape Town, South Africa. *International Journal of Mental Health and Addiction, 13*(3), 307–321.

Negin, J., & Cumming, R. (2010). HIV infection in older adults in sub-Saharan Africa: Extrapolating prevalence from existing data. *Bulletin of the World Health Organization, 88*, 847–853.

Ouzgane, L., & Morrell, R. (Eds.). (2005). *African Masculinities: Men in Africa from the Late Nineteenth Century to the Present*. New York: Palgrave.

Padian, N., McCoy, S., Balkus, J., & Wasserheit, J. (2010). Weighing the gold in the gold standard: Challenges in HIV prevention research. *AIDS, 24*, 621–635.

Parkhurst, J. (2014). Structural approaches for prevention of sexually transmitted HIV in general populations: Definitions and an operational approach. *Journal of the International AIDS Society, 17*(1), 19052.

Pattinson, R. (2007). Maternal health. In *South African Health Review 2006* (pp. 89–99). Durban: Health Systems Trust.

Pettifor, A., MacPhail, C., Anderson, A., & Maman, S. (2012). "If I buy the Kellogg's then he should [buy] the milk": Young women's perspectives on relationship dynamics, gender power and HIV risk in Johannesburg, South Africa. *Culture, Health & Sexuality, 14*(5), 477–490.

Pilane, P. (2016). Sugar daddies: Shame the blessers, not the blessed. [online]. *Mail & Guardian* (South Africa). Retrieved May 5, 2017, from http://mg.co.za/article/2016-05-19-shame-the-blessers-not-the-blessed

Pogge, T. (2004). Relational conceptions of justice: Responsibilities for health outcomes. In S. Anand, F. Peter, & A. Sen (Eds.), *Public Health, Ethics, and Equity* (pp. 135–161). Oxford: Oxford University Press.

Power, S. (2003). The AIDS Rebel. [online]. *The New Yorker*. Retrieved February 2, 2017, from http://www.newyorker.com/magazine/2003/05/19/the-aids-rebel

Preston-Whyte, E. (2003). Contexts of vulnerability: Sex, secrecy and HIV/AIDS. *African Journal of AIDS Research, 2*(2), 89–94.

Quinn, T., & Overbaugh, J. (2005). HIV/AIDS in women: An expanding epidemic. *Science, 308*(5728), 1582–1583.

Ramjee, G., & Daniels, B. (2013). Women and HIV in sub-Saharan Africa. *AIDS Research and Therapy, 10*(1), 30.

Ramjee, G., Kamali, A., & McCormack, S. (2010). The last decade of microbicide clinical trials in Africa: From hypothesis to facts. *AIDS, 24*(Suppl. 4), S40–S49.

Ramjee, G., Kapiga, S., Weiss, S., Peterson, L., Leburg, C., Kelly, C., et al. (2008). The value of site preparedness studies for future implementation of phase 2/IIb/III HIV prevention trials: Experience from the HPTN 055 study. *Journal of the Acquired Immune Deficiency Syndromes, 47*(1), 93–100.

Ramkissoon, A., Coutsoudis, A., Coovadia, H., Mthembu, P., Hlazo, J., & Smit, J. (2006). Options for HIV positive women. In *South African Health Review 2006* (pp. 315–332). Durban: Health Systems Trust.

Rhodes, T., Singer, M., Bourgois, P., Friedman, S., & Strathdee, S. (2005). The social structural production of HIV risk among drug users. *Social Science & Medicine, 61*(5), 1026–1044.

Richter, L., Komarek, A., Desmond, C., Celentano, D., Morin, S., Sweat, M., et al. (2014). Reported physical and sexual abuse in childhood and adult HIV risk behaviour in three African countries: Findings from Project Accept (HPTN-043). *AIDS and Behavior, 18*(2), 381–389.

Ronsmans, C., & Graham, W. (2006). Maternal mortality: Who, when, where, and why. *Lancet, 368*, 1189–2000.

Selikow, T., Ahmed, N., Flisher, A., Mathews, C., & Mukoma, W. (2009). I am not "Umqwayito:" A qualitative study of peer pressure and sexual risk behaviour among young adolescents in Cape Town, South Africa. *Scandinavian Journal of Public Health, 37*, 107–112.

Selikow, T., Zulu, B., & Cedras, E. (2002). The Ingagara, the Regte and the Cherry: HIV/AIDS and youth culture in contemporary urban townships. *Agenda, 53*, 22–32.

Sen, A. (1990). More than 100 million women are missing. *New York Review of Books, 37*(20), 20 December 1990 [online]. Retrieved January 11, 2018, from http://ucatlas.ucsc.edu/gender/sen100m.html

Sen, A. (1999). *Development as Freedom*. New York: Random House.

Sen, A. (2004b). Health achievement and equity: External and internal perspectives. In S. Anand, F. Peter, & A. Sen (Eds.), *Public Health, Ethics, and Equity* (pp. 263–268). Oxford: Oxford University Press.

Sen, G., Östlin, P., & George, A. (2007). Unequal, unfair, ineffective and inefficient gender inequity in health: Why it exists and how we can change it. In *Report of the Women and Gender Equity Knowledge Network of the Commission on Social Determinants of Health, Final Report to the Commission on Social Determinants of Health*. Geneva: WHO.

Sewell, W. (1992). A theory of structure: Duality, agency and transformation. *The American Journal of Sociology, 98*(1), 1–29.

Shisana, O., Rehle, T., Simbayi, L., Parker, W., Zuma, K., Bhana, A., et al. (2005). *South African National HIV Prevalence, Incidence and Communication Survey*. Cape Town: HSRC Press.

Shisana, O., Rehle, T., Simbayi, L., Zuma, K., Jooste, S., Pillay-van Wyk, V., et al. (2009). *South African National HIV Prevalence, Incidence and Communication Survey, 2008. A Turning Tide Among Teenagers?* Cape Town: HSRC Press.

Shisana, O., Rehle, T., Simbayi, L., Zuma, K., Jooste, S., Zungu, N., et al. (2014). *South African National HIV Prevalence, Incidence and Behaviour Survey, 2012.* Cape Town: HSRC Press.

Silverman, J. (2010). Key to prevent HIV in women: Reduce gender-based violence. *Lancet, 376*(9734), 6–7.

South Africa Every Death Counts Writing Group. (2008a). Every death counts: Use of mortality audit data for decision making to save the lives of mothers, babies, and children in South Africa. *Lancet, 371*, 1294–1304.

South Africa Every Death Counts Writing Group. (2008b). *Every Death Counts: Saving the Lives of Mothers, Babies, and Children in South Africa.* Cape Town: National Department of Health, Medical Research Council, University of Pretoria, Save the Children and UNICEF.

South African National AIDS Council (SANAC). (2014). *Progress Report on the National Strategic Plan for HIV, TB and STIs 2012–2016.* Pretoria: South African National AIDS Council.

Sprague, C., & Brown, S. (2016). Introduction: Local and global HIV aging demographics and research. In R. DeMarco & M. Brennan-Ing (Eds.), *HIV and Aging* (pp. 1–10). Basel: S. Karger.

Sprague, C., Hatcher, A., Woollett, N., & Black, V. (2015). How nurses in Johannesburg address intimate partner violence in female patients: Understanding IPV responses in low and middle-income country health systems. *Journal of Interpersonal Violence, 32*(11), 1591–1619.

Sprague, C., Hatcher, A., Woollett, N., Sommers, T., & Black, V. (2016a). "They can't report abuse; they can't move out. They are at the mercy of these men." Exploring connections between intimate partner violence, gender and HIV in South African clinical settings. *Culture, Health & Sexuality, 27*, 1–15, Epub 2015.

Sprague, C., Scanlon, M., & Pantalone, D. W. (2017b). Qualitative methods to advance research on health inequities among previously incarcerated women living with HIV in Alabama. *Health Education & Behavior, 44*(5), 716–727.

Statistics South Africa (Stats SA). (2015). *Mid-Year Population Estimates 2015, Statistical Release P0302.* Pretoria: South Africa.

Stats SA. (2016). *Mid-Year Population Estimates 2016, Statistical Release P0302.* Pretoria: Statistics South Africa.

Stats SA. (2016b). *Labour-Force Survey, Quarter 2.* Pretoria: Statistics South Africa.

Stern, E., Buikema, R., & Cooper, D. (2016). South African women's agency in relation to hegemonic masculinity in the context of intimate partner violence. *Global Public Health, 11*(1–2), 135–152.

Stern, E., & Cooper, D. (2014). Experiences and conceptualizations of sexual debut from the narratives of South African men and women in the context of HIV/AIDS. *African Journal of AIDS Research, 13*(2), 121–131.

The Guardian. (2006, May 8). Jacob Zuma cleared of rape. Retrieved July 1, 2017, from https://www.theguardian.com/world/2006/may/08/aids.southafrica

Tinker, A. (2000). Women's health: The unfinished agenda. *International Journal of Gynecology and Obstetrics, 70*, 149–158.

UN Statistical Division/UN Population Division. (n.d.-a). *South Africa, Life Expectancy at Birth (Female), 1960–2014*. [online]. New York: United Nations. Retrieved January 15, 2018, from http://data.worldbank.org/indicator/SP.DYN.LE00.FE.IN?locations=ZA

UNAIDS. (1998). *Mother to Child Transmission of HIV: UNAIDS Technical Update*. Geneva: UNAIDS.

UNAIDS. (2013). *HIV and Aging: Special Supplement to the UNAIDS Report on the Global AIDS Epidemic 2013*. Geneva: UNAIDS.

UNAIDS. (2014b). *The Gap Report*. Geneva: UNAIDS.

van der Linde, I. (2013). *HIV/AIDS in South Africa: At Last the Glass is Half Full*. [online]. Pretoria: HSRC. Retrieved January 15, 2018, from http://www.hsrc.ac.za/en/media-briefs/hiv-aids-stis-and-tb/plenary-session-3-20-june-2013-hiv-aids-in-south-africa-at-last-the-glass-is-half-full

Velkoff, V., & Kowal, P. (2007). *Population Aging in Sub-Saharan Africa: Demographic Dimensions 2006*. Washington, DC: US Census Bureau.

Venkatapuram, S. (2011). *Health Justice*. Cambridge: Polity Press.

Wasserheit, J. (1992). Epidemiologic synergy: Interrelationships between human immunodeficiency virus infection and other sexually transmitted diseases. *Sexually Transmitted Diseases, 9*, 61–77.

Wikler, D. (2004). Personal and social responsibility for health. In S. Anand, F. Peter, & A. Sen (Eds.), *Public Health, Ethics, and Equity* (pp. 109–134). Oxford: Oxford University Press.

Wilkinson, R., & Marmot, M. (Eds.). (2003). *Social Determinants of Health: The Solid Facts*. Copenhagen: WHO Regional Office for Europe.

Williams, A. (1998). If we are going to get a fair innings, someone will need to keep the score. In M. L. Barer, T. E. Getzen, & G. L. Stoddart (Eds.), *Health, Health Care and Economics* (pp. 319–330). New York: Wiley.

Wood, K., Maforah, F., & Jewkes, R. (1998). 'He forced me to love him': Putting violence on the adolescent sexual health agenda. *Social Science & Medicine, 47*, 233–242.

Woolman, S., & Sprague, C. (2015). Nowhere to run, nowhere to hide: The absence of public policy as to how health care professionals should address intimate partner violence constitutes a breach of the rights to health and bodily integrity under the South African Constitution. *Cardozo Journal of Law & Gender, 22*(1), 29–74.

WHO. (2002). *The World Health Report, 2002: Reducing Risks, Promoting Healthy Life*. Geneva: WHO.

WHO. (2006a). *Sexual and Reproductive Health for Women Living with HIV/AIDS: Guidelines on Care, Treatment and Support for Women Living with HIV/AIDS and Their Children in Resource-Constrained Settings*. Geneva: WHO.

WHO. (2006b). *Defining Sexual Health: Report of a Technical Consultation on Sexual Health*. Geneva: WHO.

WHO. (2010). *A Conceptual Framework for Action on the Social Determinants of Health. Discussion Paper 2: Debates, Policy and Practice*. Geneva: WHO. Retrieved June 10, 2017, from http://www.who.int/sdhconference/resources/ConceptualframeworkforactiononSDH_eng.pdf

WHO. (2013a). *Responding to Intimate Partner Violence and Sexual Violence Against Women, WHO Clinical and Policy Guidelines*. Geneva: WHO.

WHO. (2013b). *Global and Regional Estimates of Violence Against Women: Prevalence and Health Effects of Intimate Partner Violence and Non-Partner Sexual Violence*. Geneva: WHO.

WHO (2014a). Women's health. Fact sheet number 334 (September). Retrieved May 30, 2017, from http://www.who.int/mediacentre/factsheets/fs334/en/

WHO. (2014b). *World Health Statistics, 2014*. Geneva: WHO.

WHO. (2014c). *Civil Registration: Why Counting Births and Deaths Is Important. Fact Sheet No. 324*. Geneva: WHO.

WHO. (2014d). *MDG 5: Improve Maternal Health*. [online]. Geneva: WHO. Retrieved November 6, 2014, from http://www.who.int/topics/millennium_development_goals/maternal_health/en/

WHO. (2014e). *Risk Factors*. [online]. Geneva: WHO. Retrieved November 6, 2014, from http://www.who.int/topics/risk_factors/en/

WHO. (2015). *Global Health Observatory Data*. [online]. Geneva: WHO. Retrieved January 14, 2017, from http://www.who.int/gho/database/en/

WHO. (2016a). *World Health Statistics 2016: Monitoring Health for the SDGs*. Geneva: WHO.

WHO. (2016b). Violence against women, intimate partner and sexual violence against women fact sheet, updated November 2016. [online]. Geneva: WHO. Retrieved January 22, 2017, from http://www.who.int/mediacentre/factsheets/fs239/en/

WHO. (n.d.). Maternal and perinatal health. Retrieved June 30, 2017, from http://www.who.int/maternal_child_adolescent/topics/maternal/maternal_perinatal/en/

3

HIV Care: Prevailing Trends, Barriers and Paradoxes

From the trends and data analysed in Chap. 2, it is clear that black South African women are bearing a disproportionate burden of HIV disease, relative to South African men and to women of other race groups (Shisana et al., 2014). Moreover, HIV is shaping women's health outcomes in ways that are antithetical to healthy human development. By implication, black women will continue to require an enabling HIV policy framework, and access to and provision of HIV prevention, treatment and support to mitigate and manage HIV over the life course. From the perspective of health and social justice, a range of theories and frameworks can be used to argue that 'health as social justice' should support the introduction of health policies and some level of access to health care for citizens by their governments, typically with some attention to vulnerable populations. Broadly, these theories include utilitarian, egalitarian, communitarian, and libertarian theories, as well as welfare economics, and procedural democracy. (For a review and summary, see Ruger, 2010.) In South Africa, Section 27 of the Bill of Rights in the 1996 Constitution spells out the progressive health care provisions afforded South Africans in the basic law:

> *Health care, food, water and social security* 27. (1) Everyone has the right to have access to—(a) health care services, including reproductive health care;

C. Sprague, *Gender and HIV in South Africa*, Global Research in Gender, Sexuality and Health, https://doi.org/10.1057/978-1-137-55997-5_3

> (b) sufficient food and water; and (c) social security, including, if they are unable to support themselves and their dependants, appropriate social assistance. (2) The state must take reasonable legislative and other measures, within its available resources, to achieve the progressive realisation of each of these rights. (3) No one may be refused emergency medical treatment. (Government of South Africa, 1996, p. 10)

Access to some level of health and HIV care can thus be seen as a minimum requirement of justice by the State to address the ongoing problem of HIV. This chapter investigates whether women are able to access timely, quality HIV programmes from the public health system, where combination antiretroviral therapy and prevention of mother-to-child HIV programmes have been freely available since 2004. I use the following questions as a guide: What is the existing HIV policy framework, and what is the picture of HIV care and service provision for women who seek care in the public health system, including cART and PMTCT programmes? What are the main barriers facing women and what additional insights can be gleaned when viewing access to health care as a principal domain for securing wellbeing, i.e., what is neglected or absent? I focus primarily on pregnant and postpartum HIV positive black South African women requiring cART and PMTCT as the study population. This does not reflect all South African women but captures a significant percentage of women of reproductive age, with high HIV prevalence—29 to 30%—since 2004 (Government of South Africa, 2015a)—as well as key aspects and challenges vis-à-vis HIV care among this group of women that may be relevant to other women. (The main rationale for a focus on this study population has been provided in Chap. 2).

To answer the above questions, I integrate results from South African studies, and from sub-Saharan Africa more broadly, as part of recent systematic reviews. I synthesise a large set of recent data, teasing out the dominant trends to gain a more comprehensive analytical picture of cART/PMTCT access and uptake, nationally. These systematic reviews offer the best available data on South African women's access to HIV care, while complementing the results of the original in-depth qualitative research (presented in Chap. 6). The advantage of harnessing the statistical power of large samples is to overcome the limitations of qualitative research conducted with a smaller sample of the study population. I rely on the socio-ecological framework to present the results from the data synthesis along four dimensions: intrapersonal; interpersonal; health systems; and structural. This allows for viewing the health system in relation to other important dimensions that influence women living with HIV in need of HIV care (Kaufman & Stavrou Stavros, 2014). Based on the gaps emerging from the analytical review undertaken here, I highlight where additional research is needed in Chap. 9.[1]

The HIV Policy Framework

From an HIV care perspective, fostering timely cART initiation for women who are newly diagnosed is critical, both nationally and globally (WHO, 2010). At the same time, continuous HIV care (retention in care and management of HIV) must be achieved, with strong adherence and viral suppression to ensure optimal HIV outcomes for women (WHO, 2016). Yet these cannot be assumed simply because a treatment programme exists in public health systems or because a woman starts on cART. Fortunately, HIV policy frameworks in South Africa and elsewhere, particularly in high HIV prevalence settings, have recognised the crucial assumption that access to HIV care does not equate to optimal HIV outcomes. Indeed, global and national policymakers have set goals, targets and objectives in recognition of this. This includes policy objectives specifically focused on women, to improve—not only their access to treatment—but uptake of cART, retention in HIV care, adherence and viral suppression.

In beginning to answer the guiding questions, it is useful to view South Africa's progress against established HIV targets. The UNAIDS 90/90/90 global goals for 2020 are outlined below (UNAIDS, 2014a). Then the South African NSP goals for all adults are presented (Tables 3.1–3.3), followed by those explicitly for women (Tables 3.4 and 3.5).

Table 3.1 National Strategic Plan (NSP) on HIV, STIs and TB, 2012–2016: five main goals

The NSP outlines a set of goals for zero new HIV infections, zero new infections due to mother-to-child HIV transmission, zero preventable deaths due to HIV and zero discrimination associated with HIV. In line with these goals, the report set five goals to be achieved by end-2016:

1. Reduce new HIV infections by at least 50%, using combination prevention approaches;
2. Initiate at least 80% of eligible patients on cART, with 70% alive and on treatment 5 years after initiation;
3. Reduce new TB infections and TB-related deaths by 50%;
4. Ensure an enabling, accessible legal framework that protects and promotes human rights to support NSP implementation;
5. Reduce self-reported HIV and TB-related stigma by at least 50%.

Sources: Government of South Africa (2012); SANAC (2014)

Table 3.2 Progress on NSP Goal 1: reduce new HIV infections (all adults) by at least 50%

- SANAC's latest progress report found national HIV prevalence increased since the 2008 survey, from 10.6% to 12.2%.
  - Among adults aged 25 and older, HIV prevalence increased from 15.5% in 2002 to 19.9% in 2012.
  - Among adults aged 15–49, HIV prevalence increased from 15.6% in 2002 to 18.8% in 2012.
- HIV incidence for adults aged 15–49 years of age declined from 1.79% in 2008 to 1.47% in 2012 (THEMBISA model).
- However, *among young women* (aged 15–24), *HIV incidence at 2.83%, was the highest among all age groups*, and compares with 0.82% in young men.

  Conclusion: *Adult HIV incidence declining but the 50% reduction was not met by end-2016*—with young women continuing to drive up HIV incidence rates.

Source: SANAC (2014, pp. 3, 8, 10)

Recall that the NSP (2012–2016) is the steering document and framework guiding South Africa's national HIV response and represents the fifth such plan, and the third country-wide consultation (SANAC, 2014). Note that gender-disaggregated data are not readily available for all targets.

Table 3.3 Progress on NSP Goal 2: initiate at least 80% of eligible patients on cART, with 70% alive and on treatment 5 years after initiation

By end-March 2013, *2.3 million people* were on cART in the South African public sector.

- Two estimates of cART coverage using the THEMBISA model are shown:
  - Using South African criteria for adult cART initiation of CD4 < 350, cART coverage = *57%*
  - Using new UNAIDS definition of 'treat all' regardless of CD4 cell count (of total population living with HIV), *cART coverage = 36%* (global coverage of cART = 46%)

  Conclusion: *NSP goal 2 was not met.*

Note: no gender-disaggregated results available in SA.

Retention in HIV Care and Viral Suppression (South Africa)

- New data set from national cohort outcome database; covers 791,430 treatment-naïve adults and children who started cART between 2004 and March 2013:
  - Of patients who initiated cART, *65% were women*
  - For 522,636 adults starting cART by end-FY 2011/2012, *59.0% were retained in care* at end-FY 2012/2013
  - *Less than half of patients remaining in care* above (FY 2012/2013) *had a viral load available in the database. Among those who did, 76.6% of adults were virally suppressed* (defined as <400 copies/mL).

No results disaggregated by gender.

Comparative Stats: Sub-Saharan Africa and US

- In 2013, UNAIDS estimated that in SSA, *39%* of adults living with HIV were receiving cART, with *29%* of the overall population living with HIV *virally suppressed*. In contrast, in the US, *74.5%* were linked to HIV care (74.1% for men, 76.2% for women), *56.5%* were retained in care (56.3% for men, 57.1% for women), and viral suppression was an estimated *54.7%* (55.5% for men and 52.3% for women) (CDC, 2017a).

  Conclusion: Significant improvement in expanding enrolment in South African cART programmes was needed to meet the target of 80%. The target was not met. However, retention and viral suppression were relatively high, and higher than other settings, including the US (SANAC, 2014).

Note: NSP Goal 3: reduce TB infections and deaths was not reviewed

Global UNAIDS 90/90/90 Targets (by 2020)

In 2014, UNAIDS released a report outlining ambitious targets to end the HIV/AIDS epidemic called the 90–90–90 Treatment Target (2014a), setting treatment targets beyond the 2015 treatment target deadlines

Table 3.4 NSP Strategic Objectives 1, 2 and 4 specific to women

- Strategic Objective 1 *to Address the Social and Structural Drivers of HIV*:
  - Sub-Objective 1.1: to "*Mainstream HIV and TB and its gender and rights-based dimensions into the core mandates of all government departments and all SANAC sectors.*" (p. 32)
  - Sub-Objective 1.3: "*Implement interventions to address gender inequities and gender-based violence as drivers of HIV and STIs.*" (p. 35)
- Strategic Objective 2 *to Prevent New HIV Infections*
  - Sub-Objective 2.2 to "*Make accessible a package of sexual and reproductive health services*" (p. 41)
  - Sub-Objective 2.3 to "*Prevent transmission of HIV by reducing mother-to-child transmission (MTCT) to at least 2% at 6 weeks and to less than 5% at 18 months by 2016.*" (p. 42)
  - Sub-Objective 2.7 to "*Address sexual abuse and improve services for survivors of sexual assault.*" (p. 45)
- Strategic Objective 4: *to Ensure Protection of Human Rights and Increased Access to Justice*
  - This section of the NSP specifically notes the human right of women living with HIV to access sexual and reproductive health services, adding that "Women living with HIV in particular have fertility desires which must be protected, respected and addressed. Curricula for training health care providers in these areas must be prioritized; such curricula should include a module on human rights." (p. 53)

Source: Government of South Africa (2012)

called for in the 2011 Political Declaration on HIV and AIDS. The *90–90* target advocates rapid scale-up of HIV testing and treatment (including moving towards a test-and-treat approach) with these aims:

- By 2020, 90% of all people living with HIV will know their HIV status.
- By 2020, 90% of all people with diagnosed HIV infection will receive sustained antiretroviral therapy.
- By 2020, 90% of all people receiving antiretroviral therapy will have viral suppression.

Table 3.2 gives an indication of HIV incidence in South Africa. SANAC's latest progress report devotes a page to the types of incidence studies conducted in South Africa from 2008 to 2012, and also explains how the calculations are estimated using various models as well as the respective strengths and limitations of each (SANAC, 2014, p. 8).[2]

To summarise, the NSP policy framework is strong in formulation, with clear targets and objectives. However, it is weak in setting indicators and creating accountability mechanisms. A review of the NSP reveals that government officials are aware of the evidence, the key trends and the factors influencing HIV risk and transmission for women and girls. The 2012–2016 NSP has been criticised by TAC and SECTION 27 colleagues, however, for being overly technical; lacking accountability and implementation plans; being difficult to translate into implementation on the ground; and lacking even rough budget estimates associated with key activities (Davis, 2017). In the latest NSP progress report (2016), which is largely uncritical of government's response, SANAC does note that while 'strong emphasis is placed on structural drivers…social drivers…are not included as clearly articulated goals or indicators' (2016, p. 36). It is, SANAC notes, 'necessary to understand the relation between social and structural drivers and gender vulnerabilities of HIV-vulnerable sub-populations' (2016, p. 36), such that analysis can inform the identification of key indicators. SANAC recommends a consensus workshop to identify lead entities to do so. In short, this indicates clear awareness by government of social factors that foster HIV acquisition in women. However, it also evinces a continuing emphasis on keeping what is at the centre of new HIV infections—structural factors associated with gender—at the outskirts of the response. Moreover, the report notes that the NSP fails to include core programmes and indicators, 'making it difficult to measure the response' (2016, p. 89).

The HIV Care Continuum

I now shift into an analysis of HIV care in the public health system, which comprises the centrepiece of the HIV response in South Africa and where the vast majority of state and external funds are directed (Government of South Africa, 2012). The HIV care continuum was developed as a conceptual tool to capture different 'phases' of care (see Gardner, McLees, Steiner, Del Rio, & Burman, 2011; Horstmann et al., 2010; McNairy & El-Sadr, 2012). The continuum model is a useful visual to map what continuous HIV care entails and where drop-

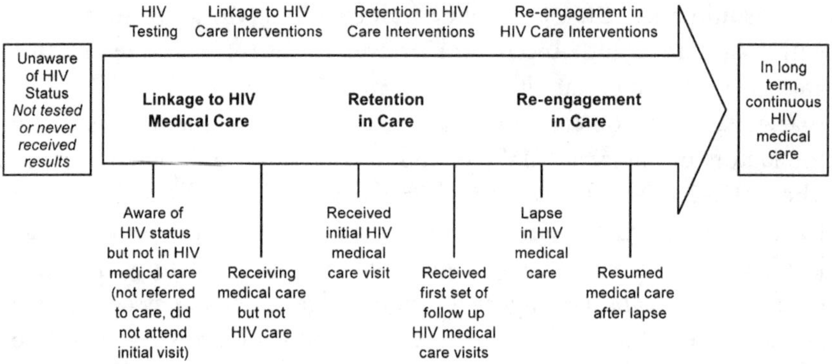

Fig. 3.1 Typical HIV care continuum for adults. Sources: Adapted from Health Resources and Services Administration, HIV/AIDS Bureau (2006, p. 4)

out and lapses occur. Figure 3.1 depicts five main stages and points along the care trajectory. These encompass: (1) HIV diagnosis, (2) linkage to HIV care, (3) initiation of cART, (4) retention in HIV care, and (5) viral suppression (Gardner et al., 2011). Achieving optimal HIV outcomes, including reduced HIV-related morbidity and mortality as well as prevention through decreased risk of transmission, depend on continuous engagement in HIV care throughout the life course. It requires re-engagement when lapses in treatment and drop out of care occur. This can take place at any stage, as shown below (Gardner et al., 2011). This diagram is somewhat misleading because it looks like a linear path for a person living with HIV to achieve continuous (lifelong) HIV care, and it looks simple—but it is not. In reality, for many people living with HIV, care is characterised more accurately as an elliptical process. Their perceptions of HIV care and their linkage patterns can change over time. This is true particularly for those living with the virus for many years, and not just for black South African women (see Sprague & Simon, 2014; Sprague, Radhakrishnan, Brown, Sommers, & Pantalone, 2017a). While Fig. 3.1 looks static, it represents a particularly dynamic interplay between the system of care, the patient and health providers, over the longer-term. For people living with HIV seeking treatment, perceptions of HIV care are influenced by household-level and community-level factors, e.g., HIV stigma, expectations of accepted social norms, including gender norms. Furthermore, encounters with health providers are influential in the type and quality of care individuals receive—particularly women in the perinatal period—as well as influencing individuals' perceptions, attitudes and experiences of care, all of which affect their subsequent health behaviours. Psychological aspects, including anxiety, stress and/or depression, influence cART adherence and retention in care, to be discussed shortly.

A typical care continuum for pregnant women in the South African health system is more complex with additional points of care needing to be traversed—often between wards as well as between facilities—which other population groups would not have to navigate.

South African Women Living with HIV: More Likely to Access HIV Care but Disproportionate Care Needed

Black South African women living with HIV are somewhat paradoxical as a population. The research literature to date indicates that this population, particularly pregnant women, are more likely to know their HIV status, to access HIV treatment and experience health benefits associated with cART, including reduced morbidity, mortality and improved life expectancy, compared to South African men (Huerga et al., 2016; Lippman et al., 2016). However, these outcomes need further critical assessment. South African women are also at disproportionately higher risk of acquiring HIV, compared to men, particularly young women (aged 15–24 years) whose HIV incidence rates are two to three times higher than young men's (as indicated in Table 3.3 above) (Shisana et al., 2014). Women's burden of disease and HIV care needs are greater as a result. The research also indicates that pregnancy is significantly associated with being lost to follow up (LTFU) and more women are likely to be lost, compared with men (Wang et al., 2011).

Additionally, access to HIV care does not equate to quality of life, wellbeing or optimal HIV outcomes (e.g., viral suppression). Note that data are lacking for marginalised groups of women—including female sex workers and women who have been detained or incarcerated (UNAIDS, 2014b). Sexual minority women (lesbian, bi-sexual, transgender, intersex and other socially excluded groups), the disabled, as well as women over age 50, are not well represented in the current published literature (Baral et al., 2013; Negin & Cumming, 2010; Sprague & Brown, 2016). These groups tend not to seek health or HIV care and remain less visible to authorities due to intersecting stigma, judgement and fears of criminalization and ageism, among other factors (UNAIDS, 2014b). This suggests a far more complex picture for key populations than is presented in the extant evidence on cART and PMTCT in African and South African women.

Key Trends from Sub-Saharan and South Africa

Here I draw on the extant literature to identify and populate factors into these categories to map the levels of influence on women patients. These primary barriers are categorised and summarised in Table 3.5. In the next section, barriers are characterised at different 'levels of action' in the socio-ecological model, namely, intrapersonal, interpersonal, health care system and structural. The socio-ecological model or framework is a theory of change, and an intervention approach, that locates individuals (and their human development) within layers that comprise a larger ecological system of change. It has its origins in Bronfenbenner's early work to develop an ecological framework for human development that also captures biological processes (1979). It has been developed in different fields, and has also been used to investigate the aetiology of abuse and neglect in children and in women (Heise, 1998). It has since been widely adapted, particularly in research on violence prevention and action by WHO and the US Centers for Disease Control and Prevention (Krug et al., 2002). The framework depicts differing, though interacting, levels of analysis and influence; it both explains their interaction and the resulting effect; offers a theory of change; and directs action in accordance with the levels of influence. As WHO notes, this approach is

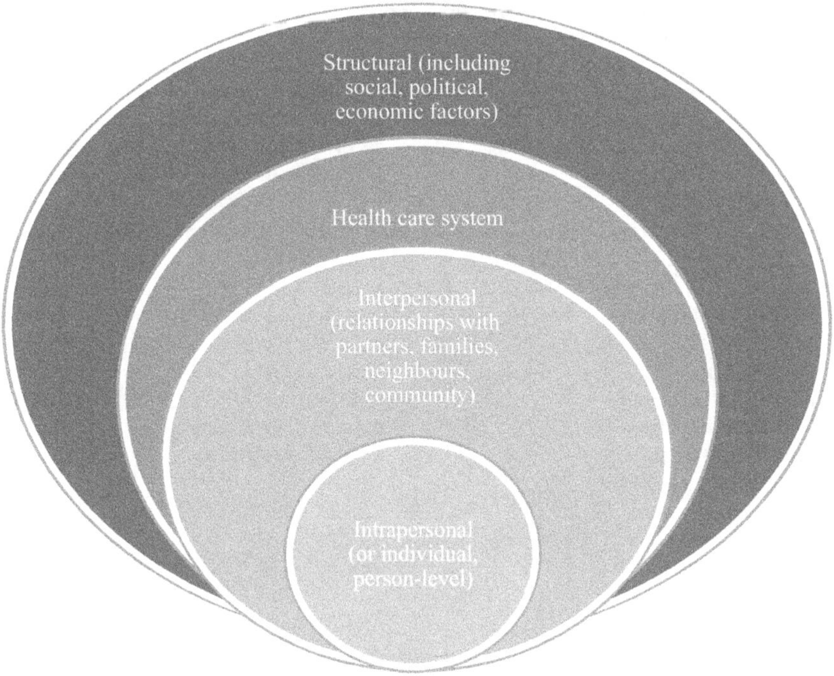

Fig. 3.2 Factors affecting HIV care for South African women: adapted from the *Socio-ecological framework*. Source: Adapted from Bronfenbrenner (1979)

'useful to identify and cluster intervention strategies based on the ecological level in which they act' (2017, p. 1). Note that these levels are fluid and overlapping as barriers can operate on multiple levels simultaneously or at different times, such as intimate partner violence and gender-based violence (Kaufman, Cornish, Zimmerman, & Johnson, 2014). I discuss limitations of the framework at the end of the chapter.

Health Systems' Factors

The health system mirrors social norms, and offers glimpses into women's structural environments and constraints, while revealing access to health care as an important health determinant. It can thus be viewed as both a

Table 3.5 Primary barriers to HIV treatment for South African women

Intrapersonal	Interpersonal	Health System	Structural
Women's lack of knowledge of cART or PMTCT or treatment guidelines	Non-disclosure of status to partner, families, community	Fragmented care systems, complicated referrals between wards/facilities	Economic (cost of services, transport)
Practical demands of managing cART treatment	Intimate partner violence	Poor quality of care, low provider knowledge	Rural residence
Poor mental health (emotional distress, depression)		Shortage of staff, long queues, drug stockouts	Gender inequality
Women of younger age and first time mothers associated with poorer PMTCT outcomes		Confidentiality concerns: HIV testing and care resulting in stigma	Human rights violations (SRHR)
		Poor treatment of women by providers	Gender-based violence and Intimate partner violence[b]
		Poor patient-provider relationships or interactions[a]	
Stigma as multi-level cross-cutting barrier (across all levels)			
→	→	→	→ →

[a]Note that relationships between patients and providers could be characterised as interpersonal to some extent. However, I am deliberately locating this within the level of the health system, as it is taking place in, and amenable to, intervention at that level

[b]I locate IPV both as interpersonal and as structural to reflect that dual reality

primary and a social health determinant. In reviewing the trends over time, overall there has been an astonishing increase in cART for South African pregnant women over the past decade, with the WHO estimating that 95% of pregnant women living with HIV accessed cART for PMTCT in 2015, a steep increase from less than 15% in 2005 (WHO Global Health Observatory Data, 2015; UNAIDS, 2005; Sprague, 2009). The following barriers, cited in the literature, are associated with the health system itself. These are elements that women must navigate and negotiate as they proceed through care.

Fragmentation of HIV Care, Lack of Linkage Between Facilities (or Wards) That Serve Women and Poor Referral Networks Characterise Care Continuum

Systematic reviews from sub-Saharan Africa as well as studies from South Africa find fragmented care between different HIV services (e.g., PMTCT and adult HIV care); lack of integration of HIV and reproductive health services, with gaps in referrals systems; and weak linkages between services, including these shown below.

Themes on Barriers to cART in LMICs and South Africa

Primary themes that emerge from the literature are as follows. A systematic review by Ferguson et al. (2012) to investigate linkage from HIV testing to HIV care among women testing HIV positive through pregnancy-related services in LMIC identified various barriers at the health systems level. In terms of health systems, *lack of continuity in care, gaps in referral processes and weak linkages between PMTCT and general HIV treatment services*, as indicated above, were highlighted in studies from Malawi and Kenya (Levy, 2009; Otieno et al., 2010). Additionally, a study in 2011 reviewed 39 published articles and policy papers on challenges in cART scale up in South Africa, and identified *four major themes on barriers to scale up*: (1) *lack of integration of ART services in general care; (2) greater need for comprehensive HIV services* (related to psycho-social and economic dynamics of HIV); (3) *rising costs of expanded treatment for public health system; and, (4) provider and human resource shortages*. Unfortunately, no mention of gender was made in the review (Wouters, Heunis, Michielsen, Van Loon, & Meulemans, 2011) (Fig. 3.2).

Overall, a principal finding captured in the extant literature is that poor quality of care remains a steadfast concern for women patients in the South African public health system, shown below. This can be attributed to operational delivery at clinic level, to health providers and to governance of the system.

Quality of Care, Low Provider Knowledge and Lack of Training

- A review of 42 studies on barriers to cART among pregnant and postpartum women globally found key health systems barriers were: *poor communication and coordination among and across health system actors; poor clinical practices (i.e., not following guidelines); and gaps in provider training*. The review identified few interventions to improve the maternal HIV care cascade. Those that did demonstrated the importance of multi-level and multi-pronged interventions (Colvin et al., 2014).
- A study using questionnaires and focus group discussions among 45 women who gave birth to children living with HIV after 2008 in Soweto, South Africa, explored women's perceptions of PMTCT (and why it failed to prevent infection in their cases). *Women raised a number of problems at various levels, including failure of providers to follow infant or maternal ARV guidelines* (Laher et al., 2012).
- A qualitative study among public providers at HIV clinics in Cape Town, South Africa found *low knowledge among providers about safer conception methods, which limited provider abilities to counsel and support patients in achieving their fertility desires*. The authors argued that further training and support is essential to provide comprehensive sexual and reproductive health care and to protect the human rights of women living with HIV (Moodley, Cooper, Mantell, & Stern, 2014).

Shortages of Staff and Supplies (Including Stockouts of Antiretrovirals)

Since the beginning of the 2004 ARV rollout, stockouts have been consistent in some locations. Long wait times for clinic services are a persistent feature documented in studies, and the cost of services (e.g., for transport) have all been identified as barriers to effective cART and PMTCT for women. These are detailed below.

Drug Stockouts in South Africa

In June 2016, the Stop Stock outs Project—a coalition of NGO and civil society groups in South Africa—released its 3rd annual report on drug stock outs, including ARVs (Stop Stockouts Project, 2016).

The annual survey attempts to reach all public health facilities in the country, reaching 2804 facilities in 2015. The survey found that *one in four facilities had experienced at least one stockout of ARVs or TB medicines in the past three months*, with little change from the results of the previous survey. Significantly, *one in five stockouts of ARVs or TB medicines in the past 3 months resulted in patients leaving the facility with no medication.* Among facilities experiencing stockouts in the past three months, *70% lasted longer than one month.* The report concludes that while it anticipates South Africa to move to the 'test-and-treat' (UNAIDS, 2014a) approach advocated by the WHO/UNAIDS, significant improvements in supply chain management, monitoring and emergency response mechanisms will need to be achieved (Stop Stockouts Project, 2016).

Poor Treatment of Women by Providers and Relational Factors

Poor care experiences have been documented as contributing to poorer engagement in HIV services among women living with HIV in a number of studies in South Africa and other African countries, with some of these highlighted below.

Confidentiality Concerns Cited by Women

Lack of confidentiality has been cited as a consistent barrier to HIV treatment and uptake in services for some women. A recent qualitative study in the North West Province of South Africa found that men and women reported delaying or avoiding attending health services due to concerns about confidentiality, including that there were separate services for HIV at the clinic (e.g., waiting rooms for patients) and providers sometimes revealed HIV status to others in the community, particularly in rural areas. The same study surveyed 26 health facilities in low resource sub-districts of the province and found that 54% reported not having a confidentiality policy in place related to HIV care (Treves-Kagan et al., 2016).

Poor Patient-Provider Relationships

Studies are summarised as follows.

- A qualitative study used semi-structured interviews (n = 50) and a focus group discussion (n = 8) with women initiating cART during pregnancy at the Witkoppen Health and Welfare Centre—a primary care clinic in Fourways (Johannesburg), and one of the few at the time to offer *Option B+ HIV treatment.* The study sought to investigate barriers to retention in cART care among postpartum women. Women participants in the study identified several perceived barriers to HIV care after delivery. These were related to provider views and included the belief among providers that mothers care more about their child's health than their own (29.2%); being treated as 'ignorant' or 'irresponsible' by providers (16.7%); or simply treated poorly overall (12.5%) (Clouse et al., 2014).
- A systematic review on barriers to the uptake of cART for PMTCT in sub-Saharan Africa, including South Africa, found that women reported poor staff-client interactions in health settings as a major health system barrier to PMTCT (Duff, Kipp, Wild, Rubaale, & Okech-Ojony, 2010; Gourlay, Birdthistle, Mburu, Iorpenda, & Wringe, 2013; Levy, 2009).

Intrapersonal Barriers

Women's Lack of Knowledge of cART, PMTCT and Treatment Guidelines

Women's knowledge of PMTCT and cART for HIV treatment has been identified as a barrier to accessing treatment and adhering to treatment guidelines in several studies. Qualitative inquiry among pregnant and postpartum women has revealed low knowledge of HIV treatment as a barrier to care (Ferguson et al., 2012; Gourlay et al., 2013; Hodgson et al., 2014; Laher et al., 2012; Nachega et al., 2012).

Practical Demands of Time and Travel in cART Management Affects Adherence

In addition to knowledge of HIV treatment, the practical demands of adhering to cART treatment—including time to collect medication from the pharmacy and understanding how to manage treatment guidelines and balance employment commitments—have been identified as challenges for pregnant and postpartum South African women (Clouse et al., 2014). This has been highlighted in systematic reviews of studies across sub-Saharan Africa as well (Hodgson et al., 2014).

Younger Age and Being First Time Mother Associated with Poorer Outcomes

For pregnant women in South Africa, younger age and being a first-time mother are associated with poorer health outcomes, such as later presentation for ANC, greater LTFU and greater risk for maternal HIV transmission to the infant (Technau et al., 2014; Woldesenbet et al., 2015). Horwood, Butler, Haskins, Phakathi, and Rollins (2013) conducted interviews with 19,093 mothers with infants <16 weeks attending immunisation clinics at six sites in KwaZulu-Natal between 2008 and 2009. Among mothers living with HIV, adult mothers were significantly more likely to have a CD4 cell test prior to pregnancy, to have received a CD4 cell test result (84.4% vs. 75.7%) and to have received the recommended PMTCT regimen (81.2% vs. 76.7%). Among women living with HIV, the overall MTCT rate was 7.0%, and the likelihood of MTCT was significantly higher among adolescent mothers (10.8% of infants infected) compared to adult mothers (6.6%) (Horwood et al., 2013).

Poor Mental Health Affects Adherence and Retention

Depression, a significant health concern for women living with HIV, is associated with poorer adherence and retention in HIV treatment, both nationally and globally. The studies below highlight research based in South Africa and in other LMICs.

Studies Documenting Poor Mental Health Among HIV Positive Women

- Barriers to adherence among pregnant women, globally, were identified in a systematic review of 51 studies on cART adherence during and after pregnancy, including *emotional distress, depression (particularly in the postpartum period) and substance use* (Nachega et al., 2012). *Postpartum depression was found to be a major barrier to adherence*, particularly *for women in low-income countries where mental health services are more limited.* Moreover, a recent systematic review found *rates of postpartum depression among women in low-income countries to be 31.3%*, and suggested that *postpartum depression may be higher among women in developing countries*, compared to developed countries (Villegas, McKay, Dennis, & Ross, 2011).
- A global survey among 480 *women living with HIV across 94 countries found 82%* of respondents *reported depression symptoms*. There was *a 3.5-fold increase in mental distress after HIV diagnosis*. Women identified *links between poor mental health and increased barriers to sexual and reproductive health, including rejection and social exclusion, problems sleeping, challenges engaging in sexual and intimate relationships, increased substance use and sexual risk, and human rights violations* (Orza et al., 2015).

Interpersonal Barriers

HIV Non-disclosure to Partners and Other Family Members

At the interpersonal level, several studies have investigated the role of HIV disclosure—i.e., whether women feel able to share their HIV positive status with partners, family members, friends or others, including peers. Data from South Africa illustrate a link between disclosure of status, partner violence and access and adherence to HIV treatment (Hatcher et al., 2014). These studies have found that a lack of partner involvement and fear of disclosure to families/partner/friends are major barriers to care. Abigail Hatcher, Nataly Woollett and other colleagues at the University of the Witwatersrand and WHO have undertaken valuable research that illuminates these direct and indirect links more readily, including the role of partner violence (Hatcher et al., 2014), discussed below under structural barriers.

Structural Barriers

For women living with HIV, the larger context of their social, political and economic environment has received little attention in published research. Historically, this dearth of literature reflects the more dominant biomedical, epidemiology-based focus on individual behaviours and on quantitative studies in HIV research. Recent research, however, is emerging that engages these factors (Kaufman et al., 2014). Characterising how women access care within this broader environment is critical to achieving a more holistic understanding of the larger HIV epidemic and how it disproportionately affects women in South and sub-Saharan Africa.

Economic Factors and Low Socioeconomic Status (SES) Associated with Poorer Access to HIV Care, Increased Dropout and Higher AIDS-Related Mortality

Economic barriers encompass a spectrum, from lower income overall to lack of funds for specific health-related needs, such as transport to clinics and household needs, such as food. Reviewing studies from sub-Saharan and South Africa (identified below) (note that some of these studies did not have analyses by gender) found the following highlighted below.

Economic Factors Affecting HIV Care Access and Outcomes

Studies among women have documented the interaction between transport, drop out of care, SES and low educational attainment.

- *Transport*: Several *studies of women in poorer-resourced, low-income settings* within South Africa and in other sub-Saharan African countries *found difficulty with transportation (including both cost and availability) to attend clinic services as a significant barrier to care* (Ferguson et al., 2012; Hodgson et al., 2014; Laher et al., 2012).
- *Dropout*: A study using a cross-sectional survey sampled 9803 mothers across South Africa who had brought their infants in for immunisations at one of 580 nationally representative public health facilities in 2010. Overall, *31.7% of mothers were HIV positive and more than a third (34.9%) had dropped out of PMTCT care at one or more stages, with increased dropout being associated with low SES and low educational attainment* (Woldesenbet et al., 2015).

The SANAC report on NSP Strategic Objective 1 notes little progress in reducing poverty, citing the global economic recession as a contributing factor. Additionally, the report states that *young women are disproportionately unemployed*. Using 2012 data, *54% of men were unemployed compared to 71% of women* (SANAC, 2014).

Some studies documenting economic barriers to HIV care among women and men also found higher risk of mortality associated with low SES, compared to those with higher SES.

- *Risk of mortality*. A meta-analysis of 10 studies conducted in South Africa, including over 175,000 patients, found *individuals of low SES* (based on income, assets or employment) *had at least a 50% higher risk of dying from HIV, compared to individuals of high SES*, while level of education was not a significant predictor or mortality. The analysis did not explore mortality and SES by gender (Probst, Parry, & Rehm, 2016).
- An additional study explored the economic consequences of AIDS mortality on South African households using a large, longitudinal

dataset and *found evidence that poorer households are at higher risk for AIDS, rather than AIDS leading to impoverishment at the household level*, and households losing a family to AIDS experience further impoverishment, but are less explained by losing an employed member of household. Finally, these colleagues argue that the *data demonstrate that expanded access to cART has "not changed the socioeconomic gradient observed in AIDS deaths"* (Ardington, Barnighausen, Case, & Menendez, 2014, p. 48).

Rural Residence

Factors associated with HIV treatment outcomes in rural versus urban areas need greater attention in South Africa. Some studies suggest that rural South African women are likely to face higher barriers in accessing and adhering to treatment compared to urban women (Sprague, 2009). Additional results are highlighted below.

Data on Rural Populations

- In one prospective cohort study of 6690 adults (75% female) from Soweto (urban) and Mpumalanga (rural) enrolled from 2003 to 2010, Otwombe, Petzold, Modisenyane, Martinson, and Chirwa (2014) found a *higher mortality rate* per 100 person-years *in rural participants versus urban* participants. Overall, *11% died in the rural cohort compared to 7% in the urban cohort.* Rural participants were more likely to enrol in HIV care at an older age (36.4 vs. 32.7 years); report a household income <R1000; be unemployed (86.7% vs. 70.7%); have a lower median BMI (24.9 vs. 21.0); and have lower median CD4 at treatment initiation (178 cells/mm^3 vs. 303 cells/mm^3). But they were more likely to be on cART at the end of the study (70.0% vs. 36.8%). Overall, *rural participants were more likely to die shortly after treatment initiation* (likely due to later treatment initiation) *compared to urban participants* who were more likely to die >12 months after treatment initiation (Otwombe et al., 2014).

- A different study calculated uptake of cART in six primary care clinics in the subdistrict of Hlabisa in KwaZulu-Natal to investigate factors associated with treatment access and initiation (Cooke, Tanser, Barnighausen, & Newell, 2010). Using demographic, HIV surveillance and GIS data, the authors estimated that the mean uptake of cART in the catchment areas of the six clinics was 21%, with uptake among women slightly higher (21.8%) compared to men (19.2%). The authors found that cART uptake was not associated with education level, household assets or urban versus rural locale; however, uptake was strongly associated with distance to the nearest primacy health care facility. *They found a negative association between cART uptake and distance to facility* (see also Peltzer et al., 2010).

IPV, Gender-Based Violence and HIV

A 2013 WHO report entitled *Global and Regional Estimates of Violence Against Women: Prevalence and Health Effects of Intimate Partner Violence and Non-Partner Sexual Violence* (WHO, 2013a) estimates that 35% of women worldwide have experienced physical and/or sexual IPV or non-partner sexual violence. The report commissioned a systematic review that identified three large (over 1000 participants) prospective cohort studies from India, South Africa and Uganda exploring the link between IPV and HIV and other sexually transmitted infections. They found an increased risk of HIV and other STIs among women who reported IPV, with the study from South Africa showing the clearest association between IPV and HIV with an odds ratio of 1.52 (Jewkes, Dunkle, Nduna, & Shai, 2010).

The WHO report concludes that further research is needed to understand the link between IPV and HIV, and between IPV, HIV and other health outcomes, including reproductive and child health, mental health (particularly depression and anxiety) and injuries (WHO, 2013a). Figure 3.3 specifies the likely effect on services uptake.

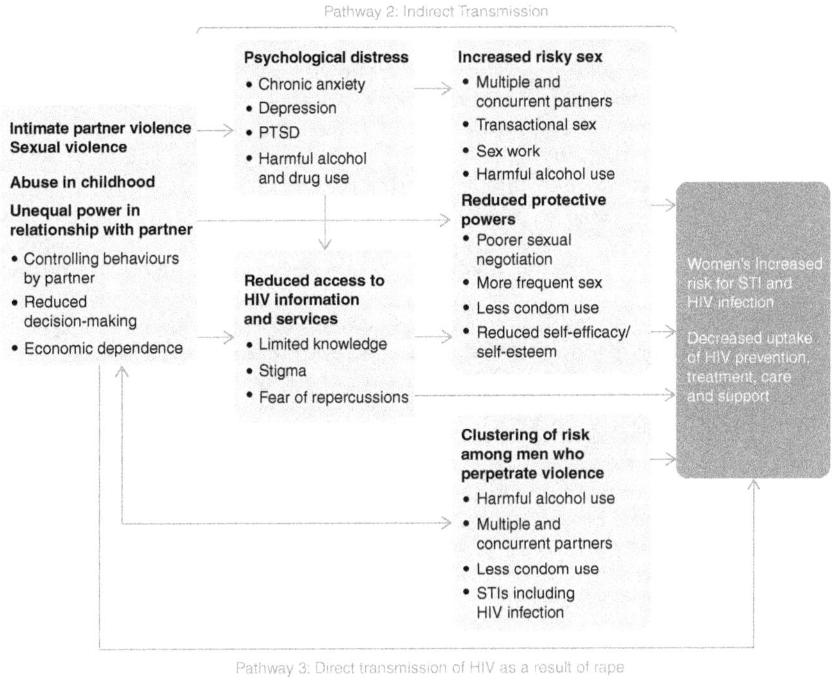

Fig. 3.3 Indirect and direct links between violence against women, HIV risk and uptake of services (Pathways 2 and 3). Source: WHO (2013c)

Box 2.1 IPV and HIV links

- A study using nationally representative Demographic and Health Surveys conducted in 10 countries (7 in sub-Saharan Africa, and the Dominican Republic, Haiti and India) between 2003 and 2007 investigated the association between reported physical and/or sexual violence by a women's most recent partner and HIV status. The study was conducted among women aged 15–49 years of age and controlled for demographic and socioeconomic variables. It found no country-specific nor pooled association between physical and/or sexual IPV with HIV (Harling, Msisha, & Subramanian, 2010). *South Africa was not included in the study as South Africa does not have Demographic and Health Surveys data on IPV and other forms of gender-based violence*, and the authors note this as a potential weakness since the evidence of a link between IPV and HIV has been strongest in South Africa (Harling et al., 2010).

- A more recent study used updated Demographic and Health Surveys from 2004 to 2012 conducted in 10 countries (all in sub-Saharan Africa *but, again, not including South Africa, per above*) as well as additional exposure-level variables to define IPV (Durevall & Lindskog, 2015). While the previous Harling et al. (2010) study used only physical and/or sexual violence, Durevall and Lindskog also calculated emotional violence, controlling behaviour by a partner and any combination of these. The study found that almost 40% of all women in the sample reported experiencing some form of IPV, with physical violence (29%) being the most common (2015).
  In this same study, HIV prevalence was 14–16% among women who reported any IPV and 10% among those who reported experiencing no IPV. In pooled regressions across all sites, the experience of physical violence, emotional violence and controlling partner behaviour was significantly associated with higher odds of HIV infection; while experiencing sexual violence was not significantly associated with HIV. The authors argued that their study likely found positive associations between IPV and HIV where the previous study had not, due in part to their inclusion of indicators of violence, combined with male controlling behaviour. This suggests that a more nuanced definition of IPV and controlling behaviour is important (Durevall & Lindskog, 2015).

Pregnant women living with HIV may be especially at risk of IPV:

- A systematic review of IPV among pregnant women in sub-Saharan Africa found a reported IPV prevalence among 13 studies between 2 and 57% with a meta-analysis showing an estimated prevalence of 15.23%. Adjusting for confounding, five studies also showed a significant association between HIV infection and IPV during pregnancy (odds ratio 1.48–3.10), suggesting that HIV is a significant risk factor for IPV during pregnancy (Shamu, Abrahams, Temmerman, Musekiwa, & Zarowsky, 2011). Three of the studies were from South Africa and showed higher rates of IPV overall (past 12 months before pregnancy) with IPV during pregnancy between 30% and 35% (Dunkle et al., 2004; Hoque & Kader, 2009; Mbokota & Moodley, 2003).

The 2014 UNAIDS *Gap Report* highlights gender-based violence as a significant factor that increases the risk for HIV acquisition and also decreases women's ability to effectively engage in HIV testing and treatment (2014b, p. 31). The report notes the complex issues that contribute to inaccessible health services for both adolescent girls and young women, including: their autonomy in decision making about their own health and health care; laws surrounding age of consent for HIV testing and access to sexual and reproductive health care; lack of access to quality comprehensive sexual education information; and adverse gender norms that limit access to contraception and family planning and enable condom use to be negotiated. Less access to primary and secondary education also significantly impacts adolescent girls' health outcomes, including having less knowledge about sexual and reproductive health, including protecting against HIV.

The 2015 People living with HIV (PLHIV) Stigma Index report notes that 'social factors that drive the epidemic, such as sexual assault, gender inequality, gender-based violence, and alcohol and substance use, have not been adequately addressed' (HSRC, 2015, p. xviii). They highlighted that *indicators mentioned in the* **NSP 2012–2016** *on the number of women reporting incidents of GBV to the South African police services* (see Sprague, Hatcher, Woollett, & Black, 2015; Woolman & Sprague, 2015), *and the percentage of women who have experienced physical or sexual violence within the last year, were not reported*; and *data were unavailable, suggesting that GBV continues to be neglected within the inter-sectoral HIV response*.

HIV Stigma: Multi-level, Cross-cutting Barrier to HIV Care

Multiple studies have cited HIV stigma as a cross-cutting barrier to HIV care for women and men (Gourlay et al., 2013; Greeff et al., 2010; Hodgson et al., 2014; Treves-Kagan et al., 2016). The evidence suggests that HIV stigma, whether anticipated, experienced or self-stigma, continues to be an impediment to women needing to access and be retained in care (Laher et al., 2012). In 2015, the HSRC in collaboration with the SANAC Human Rights Technical Task Team released the results from the *People Living with HIV Stigma Index* that surveyed people living with HIV across 18 districts of South Africa in 2014 (HSRC, 2015). In total, 10,473 people living with HIV took part in the survey (65% female), with 36% of respondents reporting they experienced some form of stigma and discrimination.

Human Rights Violations

Human rights concerns and violations against women living with HIV are well-documented. Women are more likely to experience human rights violations, gender-based violence, harmful gender norms and poorer mental health, particularly depression, as noted. This means that black South African women's challenges to health and wellbeing are considerable. Table 3.6 provides an excerpt on key concerns from the PLHIV Stigma Index Report (HSRC, 2015; see also Narasimhan et al., 2016).

NSP strategic objective 4 clearly situates the government's HIV response within a human rights framework. It specifically notes the human right of women living with HIV to access sexual and reproductive health services, adding that 'Women living with HIV in particular have fertility desires which must be protected, respected and addressed. Curricula for training health care providers in these areas must be prioritised; such curricula should include a module on human rights' (Government of South Africa, 2012, p. 53). Many women have reported coercive treatment, including 7% of women who reported forced sterilisation due to their HIV status (HSRC, 2015). Additionally, HSRC notes continuing high dropout rates from school, especially for young girls. They contend that additional social grants need to be strengthened as data show that these grants help girls stay in school longer and are protective against HIV. Additional results are summarised below.

Results of Human Rights Studies and Surveys

- A study by MacCarthy and colleagues examined the literature published between 2009 and 2011 on pregnancy-related decisions and needs as well as the rights of women living with HIV, and included 214 published articles (125 peer-reviewed, 40 conference abstracts, 49 grey literature). The authors of the study highlighted several key issues raised in the literature:
  - In many settings *contraceptive options for women living with HIV are limited*, e.g., condoms are unavailable or women do not have the autonomy to negotiate their use, and other contraceptive

options are limited by issues of availability, affordability and quality. The study also found *widespread reports of forced and coerced sterilisations among women living with HIV, while access to safe abortions is often limited.* Among pregnant women, the study found that the *health needs of the foetus and infant are often prioritised over that of the mother.* The authors recommended that more importance be placed on human rights-based approaches to addressing pregnancy-related needs of women living with HIV. This could include involving women living with HIV in the design and implementation of research studies, interventions and policies (MacCarthy, Rasanathan, Ferguson, & Gruskin, 2012).

- A literature review by Kumar and colleagues explored the current state of knowledge on human rights and the sexual and reproductive health of women living with HIV (Kumar, Gruskin, Khosla, & Narasimhan, 2015). The review included 40 peer-reviewed articles and seven from grey literature published between 2011 and 2014 and found that *while human rights language has been incorporated* in the study of sexual and reproductive health of women living with HIV, *there are few data on how to implement and monitor those rights programmatically.* In addition, the authors found that *the published literature selectively addresses specific rights rather than addressing human rights comprehensively in sexual and reproductive health.* The authors conclude that *the review indicates a need for more research into interventions to improve the security of human rights related to the sexual and reproductive health of women living with HIV* and to inform programme design and policy making more broadly.
- Significantly, *gender inequality was cited as a key barrier to all aspects of protecting women's rights in sexual and reproductive health care for women living with HIV.*

In concluding this chapter, several analytical insights can be drawn. First, while the NSP reflects important target areas for policy, the indicators, frameworks and implementation to take these forward are, crucially, absent. This is particularly so with regard to human rights and structural factors that enable HIV acquisition in women, as well as for engaging with GBV and IPV (SANAC, 2016).

Second, it is clear that a number of gaps still need to be addressed in the operational delivery of HIV services in the South African public health system. However, and significantly, impressive strides have been made in introducing cART and PMTCT, since the initiation of the ARV rollout in 2004 (Sprague, Chersich, & Black, 2011; Woolman, Sprague, & Black, 2009). This can be attributed to dedicated health providers offering care in South African clinical settings and to an enabling government policy on HIV care and services.

Third, a strength of the socio-ecological model is its ability to illuminate the ways in which the health system must be seen as just one in a number of intersecting levels that influence women's health. The visual depiction of the model reveals the health system as one layer in a larger 'sandwich' of layers (Fig. 3.2) each of which could be viewed as an enabler or disabler for women, particularly in relation to health and HIV care. A key point that emerges is this, which presents another paradox: while intrapersonal concerns can be dealt with to some degree by the health system, interpersonal and structural levels also fundamentally affect women's access to HIV care and services in the health system. Although the health system does not formally recognise these factors, the interpersonal and structural-level determinants are likely to continue to negatively shape the health behaviours and outcomes of women, while serving to undermine the existing HIV policy and services that are available. Improved health for women will depend on recognition of these multiple sites of engagement for health protection and promotion. I probe and discuss this in more detail in the empirical research findings, Chaps. 6 and 8.

Fourth, the socio-ecological framework has important strengths but offers an inadequate lens to ensure a robust understanding of health and wellbeing for women living with HIV—their opportunities to be healthy—in the South African context. The limitations of this model, as applied to this population, are several. The framework does not engage with or offer insight into this population's fears, anxieties, health beliefs and experience, and their agency (both aspirational and constrained). Such factors not only shape women's health and health behaviours, but also their daily struggles and social experience of being HIV positive, particularly as socially disadvantaged black women. Nor does the framework offer a normative view of health and human development—an evaluative standard or judgement by which to assess whether the population's health reaches an acceptable level. Nor does it attach a moral basis to the protection of women's health and their human rights.

The existing literature reviewed in this chapter indicates that while health and HIV care are essential, achieving greater understanding of women's health and equity in health—what justice in health demands for this population—requires looking beyond health and HIV care to those other levels and layers, using appropriate frameworks to do so. It is important to consider what women living with HIV are able to do and be: *their opportunities to be healthy or capabilities*. This enlarges the base of information about health and health equity considerably, as will be seen. To engage with these considerations, an even more powerful analytical framework that can generate insight into multiple factors and processes and consider how they interact within and across some of these levels is required. In the next chapter, I introduce the capabilities framework, explaining how, despite shortcomings, its design and strengths should allow for overcoming the limitations outlined.

Table 3.6 Reproductive health and human rights concerns

Reproductive health concern	%
Coerced by health care professional on choice of infant feeding practice due to HIV status	23
Coerced by health care professional about method of giving birth due to HIV status	14
Coerced by health care professional to terminate the pregnancy due to HIV status	5
Not provided with information about healthy pregnancy and motherhood, as part of PMTCT programme	5
Lack of access to HIV treatment for PMTCT during pregnancy	3
Were refused cART for PMTCT during pregnancy	1

Source: HSRC (2015)

Notes

1. This chapter does not provide a substantive overview of health systems' level changes and health reforms over the past decade, which, has been described elsewhere. See Cooper et al. (2016, 2004); Coovadia, Jewkes, Barron, Sanders, and McIntyre (2009); Ramkissoon et al. (2006); Schneider, Barron, and Fonn (2006); for changes in health systems' delivery of HIV services for pregnant and postpartum women, see Sprague (2009); Sprague, Chersich, and Black (2011).
2. These incidence studies encompass longitudinal studies (following HIV negative individuals over time who seroconvert to become HIV positive) or use data from cross-sectional surveys among the same population conducted at different time points (synthetic cohort approach). Assays have been used to detect recent HIV infections, as have mathematical models using HIV prevalence data (SANAC, 2014, p. 8). SANAC's report devotes a table to three main sources of these estimates: the HSRC household surveys, which used an assay approach and a synthetic cohort approach, and the THEMBISA and Spectrum mathematical models. All sources, with the exception of the HSRC assay, present comparative results at different time intervals, with differing results.

References

Ardington, C., Barnighausen, T., Case, A., & Menendez, A. (2014). The economic consequences of AIDS mortality in South Africa. *Journal of Development Economics, 111*, 48–60.

Baral, S., Poteat, T., Stromdahl, S., Wirtz, A., Guadamuz, T., & Beyrer, C. (2013). Worldwide burden of HIV in transgender women: A systematic review and meta-analysis. *Lancet Infectious Diseases, 13*(3), 214–222.

Bronfenbrenner, U. (1979). *The Ecology of Human Development: Experiments by Nature and Design*. Cambridge: Harvard University Press.

CDC. (2017a). Selected national HIV prevention and care outcomes in the United States. [online]. Atlanta: CDC. Retrieved January 5, 2018, from https://www.cdc.gov/hiv/pdf/library/factsheets/cdc-hiv-national-hiv-care-outcomes.pdf

Clouse, K., Schwartz, S., Van Rie, A., Bassett, J., Yende, N., & Pettifor, A. (2014). 'What they wanted was to give birth; nothing else': Barriers to retention in option B+ HIV care among postpartum women in South Africa. *Journal of Acquired Immune Deficiency Syndromes, 67*(1), e12–e18.

Colvin, C., Konopka, S., Chalker, J., Jonas, E., Albertini, J., Amzel, A., et al. (2014). A systematic review of health system barriers and enablers for antiretroviral therapy for HIV-infected pregnant and postpartum women. *PLoS ONE, 9*(10), e108150.

Cooke, G., Tanser, F., Barnighausen, T., & Newell, M. (2010). Population uptake of antiretroviral treatment through primary care in rural South Africa. *BMC Public Health, 10*, 585.

Cooper, D., Harries, J., Moodley, J., Constant, D., Hodes, R., Mathews, C., et al. (2016). Coming of age? Women's sexual and reproductive health after twenty-one years of democracy in South Africa. *Reproductive Health Matters, 24*(48), 79–89.

Cooper, D., Morroni, C., Orner, P., Moodley, J., Harries, J., Cullingworth, L., et al. (2004). Ten years of democracy in South Africa: Documenting transformation in reproductive health policy and status. *Reproductive Health Matters, 12*(24), 70–85.

Coovadia, H., Jewkes, R., Barron, P., Sanders, D., & McIntyre, D. (2009). The health and health system of South Africa: Historical roots of current public health challenges. *Lancet, 374*(9692), 817–834.

Davis, R. (2017). HIV and TB: New government plan raises concerns over practicalities and politics. [online]. *Daily Maverick*. Retrieved January 15, 2017, from https://www.dailymaverick.co.za/article/2017-04-11-hiv-tb-new-government-plan-raises-concerns-over-practicalities-and-politics/#.WUKvwhPysYE

Duff, P., Kipp, W., Wild, T., Rubaale, T., & Okech-Ojony, J. (2010). Barriers to accessing highly active antiretroviral therapy by HIV positive women attending an antenatal clinic in a regional hospital in western Uganda. *Journal of the International AIDS Society, 13*, 37.

Dunkle, K., Jewkes, R., Brown, H., Gray, G., McIntyre, J., & Harlow, S. (2004). Transactional sex among women in Soweto, South Africa: Prevalence, risk factors and associations with HIV infection. *Social Science & Medicine, 59*(8), 1581–1592.

Durevall, D., & Lindskog, A. (2015). Intimate partner violence and HIV in ten sub-Saharan African countries: What do the Demographic and Health Surveys tell us? *Lancet Global Health, 3*(1), e34–e43.

Ferguson, L., Grant, A., Watson-Jones, D., Kahawita, T., Ong'ech, J., & Ross, D. (2012). Linking women who test HIV positive in pregnancy-related services to long-term HIV care and treatment services: A systematic review. *Tropical Medicine and International Health, 17*(5), 564–580.

Gardner, E., McLees, M., Steiner, J., Del Rio, C., & Burman, W. (2011). The spectrum of engagement in HIV care and its relevance to test-and-treat strategies for prevention of HIV infection. *Clinical Infectious Diseases, 52*(6), 793–800.

Gourlay, A., Birdthistle, I., Mburu, G., Iorpenda, K., & Wringe, A. (2013). Barriers and facilitating factors to the uptake of antiretroviral drugs for prevention of mother-to-child transmission of HIV in sub-Saharan Africa: A systematic review. *Journal of the International AIDS Society, 16*, 18588.

Government of South Africa. (1996). The Constitution of the Republic of South Africa, Act No. 108 of 1996. Cape Town: South Africa.

Government of South Africa. (2012). *National Strategic Plan on HIV, STIs and TB 2012–2016*. Pretoria: National Department of Health.

Government of South Africa. (2015a). *2013 National Antenatal HIV Prevalence Survey*. Pretoria: National Department of Health.

Greeff, M., Uys, L., Wantland, D., Makoae, L., Chirwa, M., Dlamini, P., et al. (2010). Perceived HIV stigma and life satisfaction among persons living with HIV infection in five African countries: A longitudinal study. *International Journal Nursing Studies, 47*(4), 475–486.

Harling, G., Msisha, W., & Subramanian, S. (2010). No association between HIV and intimate partner violence among women in 10 developing countries. *PLoS ONE, 5*(12), e14257.

Hatcher, A., Woollett, N., Pallitto, C., Mokoatle, K., Stockl, H., MacPhail, C., et al. (2014). Bidirectional links between HIV and intimate partner violence in pregnancy: Implications for prevention of mother-to-child transmission. *Journal of the International AIDS Society, 17*, 19233.

Health Resources and Services Administration, HIV/AIDS Bureau (HRSA) (US). (2006). *Linkage to HIV Care*. Rockville, MD: Health Resources and Services Administration.

Heise, L. (1998). Violence against women: An integrated, ecological framework. *Violence against Women, 4*(3), 262–290.

Hodgson, I., Plummer, M., Konopka, S., Colvin, C., Jonas, E., Albertini, J., et al. (2014). A systematic review of individual and contextual factors affecting ART initiation, adherence, and retention for HIV-infected pregnant and postpartum women. *PLoS ONE, 9*(11), e111421.

Hoque, M., & Kader, S. (2009). Prevalence and experience of domestic violence among rural pregnant women in KwaZulu-Natal, South Africa. *South African Journal of Epidemiology and Infection, 24*(4), 34–37.

Horstmann, E., Brown, J., Islam, F., Buck, J., & Agins, B. D. (2010). Retaining HIV-infected patients in care: Where are we? Where do we go from here? *Clinical Infectious Diseases, 50*(5), 752–761.

Horwood, C., Butler, L., Haskins, L., Phakathi, S., & Rollins, N. (2013). HIV-infected adolescent mothers and their infants: Low coverage of HIV services and high risk of HIV transmission in KwaZulu-Natal, South Africa. *PLoS ONE, 8*(9), e74568.

Huerga, H., Van Cutsem, G., Ben Farhat, J., Reid, M., Bouhenia, M., Maman, D., et al. (2016). Who needs to be targeted for HIV testing and treatment in KwaZulu-Natal? Results from a population-based survey. *Journal of Acquired Immune Deficiency Syndromes, 73*(4), 411–418. https://doi.org/10.1097/QAI.0000000000001081.

Human Sciences Research Council. (2015). *The People Living with HIV Stigma Index: South Africa 2014*. Pretoria: HSRC, South African National AIDS Council, and UNAIDS.

Jewkes, R., Dunkle, K., Nduna, M., & Shai, N. (2010). Intimate partner violence, relationship power inequity, and incidence of HIV infection in young women in South Africa: A cohort study. *Lancet, 376*(9734), 41–48.

Kaufman, M., Cornish, F., Zimmerman, R., & Johnson, B. (2014). Health behavior change models for HIV prevention and AIDS care: Practical recommendations for a multi-level approach. *Journal of Acquired Immune Deficiency Syndromes, 66*(Suppl. 3), S250–S258.

Krug, E. G., et al. (Eds.). (2002). *World Report on Violence and Health*. Geneva: World Health Organisation.

Kumar, S., Gruskin, S., Khosla, R., & Narasimhan, M. (2015). Human rights and the sexual and reproductive health of women living with HIV—A literature review. *Journal of the International AIDS Society, 18*(Suppl. 5), 20290.

Laher, F., Cescon, A., Lazarus, E., Kaida, A., Makongoza, M., Hogg, R., et al. (2012). Conversations with mothers: Exploring reasons for prevention of mother-to-child transmission (PMTCT) failures in the era of programmatic scale-up in Soweto, South Africa. *AIDS and Behavior, 16*(1), 91–98.

Levy, J. (2009). Women's expectations of treatment and care after an antenatal HIV diagnosis in Lilongwe, Malawi. *Reproductive Health Matters, 17*(33), 152–161.

Lippman, S. A., Shade, S. B., El Ayadi, A. M., Gilvydis, J. M., Grignon, J. S., Liegler, T., et al. (2016). Attrition and opportunities along the HIV care continuum: Findings from a population-based sample, North West Province, South Africa. *Journal of Acquired Immune Deficiency Syndromes, 73*(1), 91–99. https://doi.org/10.1097/QAI.0000000000001026.

MacCarthy, S., Rasanathan, J., Ferguson, L., & Gruskin, S. (2012). The pregnancy decisions of HIV positive women: The state of knowledge and way forward. *Reproductive Health Matters, 20*(Suppl. 39), 119–140.

Mbokota, M., & Moodley, J. (2003). Domestic abuse—An antenatal survey at King Edward VIII Hospital, Durban. *South African Medical Journal, 93*(6), 455–457.

McNairy, M., & El-Sadr, W. (2012). The HIV care continuum: No partial credit given. *AIDS, 26*(14), 1735–1738.

Moodley, J., Cooper, D., Mantell, J., & Stern, E. (2014). Health care provider perspectives on pregnancy and parenting in HIV positive individuals in South Africa. *BMC Health Services Research, 14*, 384.

Nachega, J., Uthman, O., Anderson, J., Peltzer, K., Wampold, S., Cotton, M., et al. (2012). Adherence to antiretroviral therapy during and after pregnancy in low-income, middle-income, and high-income countries: A systematic review and meta analysis. *AIDS, 26*(16), 2039–2052.

Narasimhan, M., Orza, L., Welbourn, A., Bewley, S., Crone, T., & Vazquez, M. (2016). Sexual and reproductive health and human rights of women living with HIV: A global community survey. *Bulletin of the World Health Organization, 94*(4), 243–249.

Negin, J., & Cumming, R. (2010). HIV infection in older adults in sub-Saharan Africa: Extrapolating prevalence from existing data. *Bulletin of the World Health Organization, 88*, 847–853.

Orza, L., Bewley, S., Logie, C. H., Crone, E. T., Moroz, S., Strachan, S., et al. (2015). How does living with HIV impact on women's mental health? Voices from a global survey. *Journal of the International AIDS Society, 18*(Suppl. 5), 20289.

Otieno, P., Kohler, P., Bosire, R., Brown, E., Macharia, S., & John-Stewart, G. (2010). Determinants of failure to access care in mothers referred to HIV treatment programs in Nairobi, Kenya. *AIDS Care, 22*(6), 729–736.

Otwombe, K., Petzold, M., Modisenyane, T., Martinson, N., & Chirwa, T. (2014). Factors associated with mortality in HIV-infected people in rural and urban South Africa. *Global Health Action, 7*, 25488.

Peltzer, K., Friend-du Preez, N., Ramlagan, S., & Anderson, J. (2010). Antiretroviral treatment adherence among HIV patients in KwaZulu-Natal, South Africa. *BMC Public Health, 10*, 111. https://doi.org/10.1186/1471-2458-10-111.

Probst, C., Parry, C., & Rehm, J. (2016). Socioeconomic differences in HIV/AIDS mortality in South Africa. *Tropical Medicine and International Health, 21*(7), 846–855.

Ramkissoon, A., Coutsoudis, A., Coovadia, H., Mthembu, P., Hlazo, J., & Smit, J. (2006). Options for HIV positive women. In *South African Health Review 2006* (pp. 315–332). Durban: Health Systems Trust.

Ruger, J. (2010). *Health and Social Justice*. Oxford: Oxford University Press.

Shamu, S., Abrahams, N., Temmerman, M., Musekiwa, A., & Zarowsky, C. (2011). A systematic review of African studies on intimate partner violence against pregnant women: Prevalence and risk factors. *PLoS ONE, 6*(3), e17591.

Shisana, O., Rehle, T., Simbayi, L., Zuma, K., Jooste, S., Zungu, N., et al. (2014). *South African National HIV Prevalence, Incidence and Behaviour Survey, 2012*. Cape Town: HSRC Press.

South African National AIDS Council (SANAC). (2014). *Progress Report on the National Strategic Plan for HIV, TB and STIs 2012–2016*. Pretoria: South African National AIDS Council.

South African National AIDS Council (SANAC). (2016). *Enhanced Progress Report, National Strategic Plan for HIV, TB and STIs 2012–2016*. Pretoria: SANAC.

Sprague, C. (2009). *Cui Bono: A Capabilities Approach to Understanding HIV Prevention and Treatment for Pregnant Women and Children in South Africa*. Doctoral thesis, University of the Witwatersrand.

Sprague, C., & Brown, S. (2016). Introduction: Local and global HIV aging demographics and research. In R. DeMarco & M. Brennan-Ing (Eds.), *HIV and Aging* (pp. 1–10). Basel: S. Karger.

Sprague, C., Chersich, M., & Black, V. (2011). Health systems weaknesses constrain access to PMTCT and maternal HIV services in South Africa: A qualitative enquiry. *AIDS Research and Therapy, 8*, 10.

Sprague, C., Hatcher, A., Woollett, N., & Black, V. (2015). How nurses in Johannesburg address intimate partner violence in female patients: Understanding IPV responses in low and middle-income country health systems. *Journal of Interpersonal Violence, 32*(11), 1591–1619.

Sprague, C., Radhakrishnan, B., Brown, S., Sommers, T. E., & Pantalone, D. (2017a). Southern women at risk: Narratives of familial and social HIV risk in justice-involved US women in Alabama. *Violence & Victims, 32*(4), 728–753. Epub 2016.

Sprague, C., & Simon, S. (2014). Understanding HIV care delays in the US South and the role of the social-level in HIV care engagement/retention: A qualitative study. *International Journal for Equity in Health, 13*(28), 1–14.

Stop Stockouts Project. (2016). *2015 Stock Outs National Survey, 3rd Annual Report—South Africa*. Johannesburg: Medecins Sans Frontieres, Southern African HIV Clinicians Society, Section 27, Rudasa, Treatment Action Campaign, Rural Health Advocacy Project.

Technau, K., Kalk, E., Coovadia, A., Black, V., Pickerill, S., Mellins, C., et al. (2014). Timing of maternal HIV testing and uptake of prevention of mother-to-child transmission interventions among women and their infected infants in Johannesburg, South Africa. *Journal of Acquired Immune Deficiency Syndromes, 65*(5), e170–e178.

Treves-Kagan, S., Steward, W., Ntswane, L., Haller, R., Gilvydis, J. M., Gulati, H., et al. (2016). Why increasing availability of ART is not enough: A rapid, community-based study on how HIV-related stigma impacts engagement to care in rural South Africa. *BMC Public Health, 16*, 87.

UNAIDS. (2014a). *90-90-90: An Ambitious Treatment Target to Help End the AIDS Epidemic*. Geneva: UNAIDS.

UNAIDS. (2014b). *The Gap Report*. Geneva: UNAIDS.
UNAIDS. (2005). *Epidemiological Fact Sheets on HIV/AIDS and Sexually Transmitted Infections, 2005 Update (South Africa)*. Geneva: UNAIDS.
Villegas, L., McKay, K., Dennis, C., & Ross, L. (2011). Postpartum depression among rural women from developed and developing countries: A systematic review. *Journal of Rural Health, 27*(3), 278–288.
Wang, B., Losina, E., Stark, R., Munro, A., Walensky, R. P., Wilke, M., et al. (2011). Loss to follow-up in a community clinic in South Africa—Roles of gender, pregnancy and CD4 count. *South African Medical Journal, 101*(4), 253–257.
Woldesenbet, S., Jackson, D., Lombard, C., Dinh, T. H., Puren, A., Sherman, G., et al. (2015). Missed opportunities along the prevention of mother-to-child transmission services cascade in South Africa: Uptake, determinants, and attributable risk (the SAPMTCTE). *PLoS ONE, 10*(7), e0132425.
Woolman, S., & Sprague, C. (2015). Nowhere to run, nowhere to hide: The absence of public policy as to how health care professionals should address intimate partner violence constitutes a breach of the rights to health and bodily integrity under the South African Constitution. *Cardozo Journal of Law & Gender, 22*(1), 29–74.
Woolman, S., Sprague, C., & Black, V. (2009). Why state policies that undermine HIV lay counsellors constitute retrogressive measures that violate the right of access to health care for pregnant women and infants. *South African Journal on Human Rights, 24*, 102–123.
WHO. (2010). *A Conceptual Framework for Action on the Social Determinants of Health. Discussion Paper 2: Debates, Policy and Practice*. Geneva: WHO. Retrieved June 10, 2017, from http://www.who.int/sdhconference/resources/ConceptualframeworkforactiononSDH_eng.pdf
WHO. (2013a). *Global and Regional Estimates of Violence Against Women: Prevalence and Health Effects of Intimate Partner Violence and Non-Partner Sexual Violence*. Geneva: WHO.
WHO. (2013b). *16 Ideas for Addressing Violence Against Women in the Context of the HIV Epidemic a Programming Tool*. Geneva: WHO.
WHO. (2015). *Global Health Observatory Data*. [online]. Geneva: WHO. Retrieved January 14, 2017, from http://www.who.int/gho/database/en/
WHO. (2016). *Consolidated Guidelines on the Use of Antiretroviral Drugs for Treating and Preventing HIV Infection: Recommendations for a Public Health Approach—Second Edition*. Geneva: WHO.
WHO. (2017). *The Ecological Framework*. [online]. Geneva: WHO. Retrieved June 15, 2017, from http://www.who.int/violenceprevention/approach/ecology/en/
Wouters, E., Heunis, C., Michielsen, J., Van Loon, F., & Meulemans, H. (2011). The long road to universal antiretroviral treatment coverage in South Africa. *Future Virology, 6*(7), 801–812.

4

Conceptualising Justice in Health as Opportunities to Be Healthy (Capabilities)

This chapter serves to lay the groundwork for and establishes the rudiments of the Capabilities Approach. Initial presentation and discussion of the CA here is meant to allow for a fuller analysis about what black South African women are able to 'do and be' in South African society in the presentation and interpretation of the findings in Chaps. 6 and 8. I engage a set of guiding questions that radiate from the research problem and are part of national and global health debates: What is the special nature of health? What is the proper object of a social justice claim: health or health care? And what is the state's role and responsibility in addressing widening health inequities? Within this terrain, I explore themes that encompass health protection and promotion as a normative social goal; debates associated with social valuations of health; the lack of attention to and difficulties in locating health (as opposed to health care) within a moral social justice framework; and the ways in which the CA addresses some of these difficulties (Nussbaum, 2000; Sen, 1999).[1] I then highlight additional features of the approach, its relevance for the research problem, strengths and limitations.

C. Sprague, *Gender and HIV in South Africa*, Global Research in Gender, Sexuality and Health, https://doi.org/10.1057/978-1-137-55997-5_4

Aristotelian Foundations: Justice as Equality in Some Sense

The pursuit of a just, fair society, and how that society should be optimally arranged and governed for the benefit of its citizens has been a focal point of debate since ancient times. (See Cicero, 2013.) It has also characterised more recent political and social deliberations among newer democracies, such as South Africa (Woolman, 2008). Over the centuries, political philosophers have given expansive consideration to the normative relationship between state and society, and the necessary prerequisites for citizens to shape a life of meaning, also called the 'good life' (Rawls, 1971). Western political philosophy's ideas of justice, and the core ideas of the social welfare economist, Amartya Sen and the political philosopher, Martha Nussbaum, have been shaped by those of Aristotle. Sen explains that the notion of *functionings* within the CA 'has distinctly Aristotelian roots' (1999, p. 75). Functionings, for Sen, 'reflect the various things a person may value doing or being' (Sen, 1999, p. 75). Sen is invoking Aristotle's notion of *ergon*, referring to 'the function or task of something', but specifically in relation to the human being (Crespo, 2012, p. 58; Sen, 1992). 'Aristotle, while looking for the content of happiness, states that this is the chief good of the human being and that it consists in his function,' writes Crespo (2012, p. 58). For Nussbaum, Aristotle is paramount. She fully grounds her conception of capabilities within an Aristotelian account of 'the good' (Nussbaum, 1988a, 1988b, 1992). In reference to this notion, Aristotle wrote:

> In the state, the good aimed at is justice; and that means what is for the benefit of the whole community. Now all men believe that justice means equality in some sense… [but] they are in limited agreement [as to equality of what]. (1998, p. 207)

In the Aristotelian view, the good or goal we seek within the state is justice, or what benefits the whole community. Sen has noted, this means equality—but equality of what? Aristotle indicates that we have limited agreement on justice as 'equality in some sense'. South Africa, as well as other countries, gives content to such considerations of justice or some form of equality in the health space through their national constitutions and in the basic law.

South Africa's historic democratic process of extended public consultation and engagement preceding the adoption of the Constitution of South Africa, 1996, engaged questions about how justice could be actualised, particularly for the majority of South Africans who had been disenfranchised—i.e., black South Africans. These questions were not esoteric then, nor are they today. The Bill of Rights and Constitution established the primacy of fundamental values of equality and justice that would underpin a nonracial new democracy, giving shape to social institutions, arrangements, and the very content of laws and policies, with the aim of social transformation. The Constitution's founding provisions embrace: (a) human dignity, including the 'achievement of equality and the advancement of human rights and freedoms'; (b) non-racialism and non-sexism; (c) the supremacy of the Constitution and the rule of law; and (d) universal adult suffrage (a national voter's roll, routine elections and a multi-party system of democracy) (Government of South Africa, 1996, 'Founding Provisions', p. 3). When it comes to health and health care in South Africa and elsewhere, questions concerning 'equality of what' have been answered to some degree through social reasoning and evaluation. They have been given content, not only in provisions within the Constitution and Bill of Rights, but also in the way these health care provisions, policies and reforms have been enacted in social policies that promote health and social welfare (Dubihlela & Dubihlela, 2014; United Nations Children's Fund [UNICEF] South Africa, 2012).

Current health policies in the public health system enacted in the post-apartheid era embrace equity in health and health care (Government of South Africa, 1996). These are visible most recently in the proposed National Health Insurance (NHI) scheme (Government of South Africa, 2015). Health financing, budgetary processes and appropriations governed by public officials, the elected representatives of the people, indicate the level of government and public support for health. Societal values are captured in key principles that underpin the delivery of health and social services, including the *Batho Pele* principles (meaning 'people first' in Sesotho) (Department of Public Service and Administration, 1997).

These principles and other rights can be found in laminated plastic posters affixed to the once white walls—now an ashen grey—in the public health system. The posters proudly proclaim patients' rights, even as patients limp by them to seek their place in the queue, and doctors dash past. And nurses, social workers, lay counsellors—stationed in the wards at the coalface of public health care with the most direct and most frequent contact with patients—steadfastly seek to live out those demands (see Marks, 1994). The posters proclaim a right to health care that exists in South Africa. For the observer, they also serve as a reminder that having a right to health care is not equivalent to having good health or even quality health care, and that securing health is far more complex.

The Special Nature of Health

To comprehend the importance attached to health as a social justice concern, excerpts from philosophers, ancient and contemporary, are illustrative. The descriptions here are thin, rather than thick, but they allow for a glimpse into understanding the rationale for attaching a normative, moral basis to health—one that is necessary to promote the health of groups and populations, nationally and globally.

Health has been recognised as a special good, and the foundation of other goods, throughout the ages. In highlighting the writings of a series of philosophers who spoke of the special nature of health, Anand observes that Democritus, the ancient Greek philosopher, wrote in the fifth century BCE: 'without health nothing is of any use, not money nor anything else' (Anand, 2004, pp. 16–17). Descartes, regarded as the father of modern Western philosophy (Russell, 2004), declared in 1637 in *Discours de la Methode* that health is the highest good: 'the preservation of health is… without doubt the first good and the foundation of all other goods of this life' (quoted in Anand, 2004, p. 17). The recognition that health is necessary for other things is also articulated by the father of modern economics, Adam Smith, who opines that 'the person who has lost his whole fortune, if he is in good health, feels nothing in his body'. Connecting health with happiness in his remark, Smith observes that 'if a man has good health, is out of debt, and has a clear conscience, what can be added to his happiness?' (2010, p. 15). Similarly, the philosopher-transcendentalist, Ralph Waldo Emerson, wrote that 'the first wealth is health' (2017, p. 21). More recently, the French philosopher-physician, Georges Canguilhem, commented on the way health makes all things appear possible, stating that 'health is a feeling of assurance in life to which no limit is fixed' (1991, p. 201). Thus, from these diverse and influential thinkers, health is characterised as having essential qualities. The key message here is that health is regarded as critical for its own sake, i.e., it has *intrinsic value*, and—because it allows for other things—its value is also *instrumental* (Anand, 2004; Ruger, 2006, p. 999; Sen, 1999, pp. 13–15). It is considerations of this kind that have shaped normative notions of health and social justice, introducing questions about how we define and advance health and how quality of life can be protected—as well as how health can be assessed or measured.

A working definition of health thus becomes essential for scholars and practitioners, policy makers and even for the public. To provide a uniform conception that will ground considerations in this work, I rely on a definition of health formulated over 70 years ago. Ever-debated and imprecise, this definition is located within the Preamble of the WHO's founding constitution and has been used as a touchstone globally (the definition was developed by Dr Brock Chisholm of Canada, Dr Gregorio Bermann of Argentina, Dr Szeming Sze of China, and improved upon by Dr HS Gear of South Africa, see WHO, 1988).

Box 4.1 WHO definition of health

Health is a state of complete physical, mental and social wellbeing and not merely the absence of disease or infirmity (WHO, 1946, entered into force, 1948).

The strength of the WHO (1946) definition is its embrace of a notion of wellbeing that goes beyond ill health and that includes mental health. This must be seen as an enlightened inclusion in the 1940s, given that mental health has been and remains neglected around the world. By 2001, for example, WHO had noted that one in four families globally 'has at least one member currently suffering from a mental or behavioural disorder' (2002, p. 21). But WHO's conceptualisation of health has limitations which have been identified and even lamented (Saracci, 1997). Doll, for instance, decries that it is 'a fine and inspiring concept and its pursuit guarantees health professionals unlimited opportunities for work in the future… But it is not of much practical use for specialists in public health medicine who need to compare the states of health in different communities and at different times' (1992, p. 933). The broad WHO definition offers a 'basement level' entry point into health as a multi-layered concern. To climb from the ground level upwards requires further work, or even a ladder to move us further along this conceptualisation of what health and wellbeing comprise. Fortunately, the rich writings of Amartya Sen and other thinkers can assist us in this regard (see Anand, Peter, & Sen, 2004).

Quality of Life and Premature Death

Philosophers have raised a set of concerns about health in relation to ill health, to quality of life and to premature death. Nagel emphasises that securing health is necessary to enable what Aristotle termed the good, and other philosophers have termed the good life, and to which Sen refers to as a 'life we have reason to value' (1999, p. 14). Nagel writes:

> What we find desirable in life are certain states, conditions, or types of activity. It is *being* alive, *doing* certain things, having certain experiences that we consider good. (1979, p. 13)

On this basis, Nagel stresses the moral dimensions associated with premature death, stating that 'it is the loss of life, rather than the state of being dead…that is objectionable' (1979, p. 3). Sen characterises these losses due to disability, morbidity and mortality in his typically-understated yet pointed way, observing that 'we are not able to do much if we are disabled or ceaselessly bothered by illness, and we can do very little indeed if we are not alive' (Sen, 2004b, p. 28). By implication, if we are constantly plagued by ill health, then our desires, actions and intentions are sharply curtailed. If we are dead, we are clearly not able to do much at all. Nagel extends this realisation to draw out the implication, stating that 'death, no matter how inevitable, is an abrupt cancellation of indefinitely extensive possible goods' (1979, p. 10).

It is this notion of indefinitely extensive possible goods that begins to hint at the rather nebulous view of what good health comprises—going beyond our WHO stock definition—and the ramifications for one's ability to function and, indeed to flourish, in its absence. With good health, anything is possible. With ill health, the range of indefinite possibilities becomes narrowly circumscribed. Nagel then pinpoints a core concern—not solely being robbed of life, but the loss of opportunity to live a long life. Nagel is moving the ethical dimension of ill health into the foreground. He draws a comparison using the example of Keats and Tolstoy: 'The death of Keats at 24 is generally regarded as tragic; that of Tolstoy at 82 is not,' he writes (1979, p. 9). To sharpen the point, Nagel highlights the different valuation of a lost life for a young man, compared to one who has lived a full life, stating that 'Keats' death deprived him of many years of life which were allowed to Tolstoy; so in a clear sense Keats' loss was greater' (1979, p. 9). There is a gain to society when a life is lived according to an average lifespan. Tolstoy's voluminous, brilliant works have been a precious contribution to humankind. The genius of Keats was lost. Here a key message can be gleaned from Nagel's astute philosophical reflections. They foster an understanding of the 'social valuation of health'. This includes the importance of quantitative indicators and qualitative understandings that allow us to value health as a social good, and to determine when health and life is compromised, whether through disability or preventable deaths that rob us of beloved members of our communities. Nagel's insights point to the need to quantify health and quality of life measures with a view to establishing comparative indicators among and between populations.

Within the health sciences, this quantification has been captured through a range of measures. The GBD (developed by Murray & Lopez, 1996) has been adopted by the WHO to generate standard measures that account for disability and premature mortality due to disease, injuries, accidents, illnesses and other health conditions in populations, as part of their DALY calculations across world regions (for an explanation, see WHO, 2016d). The GBD thus captures the gap between the ideal and the actual. Other measures include quality-adjusted life years (QALY) and disability-adjusted life expectancy (DALE) (Murray & Lopez, 1996). In different societies, the ability to live a long and healthy life varies; it is the result of many determinants that influence health over the life course. There is a large evidence base indicating that particular health needs must be met for other developmental capabilities to follow. Children's optimal development and growth depends upon promoting key aspects that shape their health and brain function, including adequate nutrition alongside many other factors within their external environment and social health determinants: human development and life course theories have advanced the evidence base in this regard (Bronfenbrenner, 1979; Elder, 1998; Hertzman, 2010). The converse is true, i.e., that adverse experiences, such as exposure to violence and abuse in childhood, have been shown to affect the developmental pathway, with intertwined psychological and physiological effects, documented in research on biological embedding, foetal origins research and violence against women (Barker, 1992; Heise & McGrory, 2016; Hertzman, 1999, 2010; Osmani & Sen, 2003). In this manner, health in early life can be viewed as foundational for human development processes, with biological, environment, familial and social factors playing a role.

In addition to those health determinants, what it means to be healthy is socially constructed, both in how society and individuals within communities, view illness and health (the social meaning ascribed to good or ill health) and the social effects for those who experience ill health. Social conceptions of health and valuations of health in society also determine the ways in which health funding for medical and social science and innovation is prioritised and thus what type of health knowledge is utilised and valued in society (Greenhalgh et al., 2016). The social construction of illness and the cultural meanings ascribed to ill health have a long history in sociology (Charmaz, 1991; Foucault, 1977; Freidson, 1970; Glaser & Strauss, 1965; Goffman, 1963) and is distinct from biomedicine. Nonetheless, research on stigma, for example, increasingly highlights the manner by which stigma as a social process has moral-somatic consequences (affecting physical health states) and moral-emotional consequences (affecting emotional health) (Yang et al., 2007), which reinforce the social-medical aspects of social processes, such as stigma and discrimination against those who are excluded or pushed to the margins of society.

In the case of both endemic factors that threaten health (such as violence, poverty and substance abuse), and epidemics (such as influenza, Ebola or HIV), society determines what health threats are acceptable and what actions must be taken to protect health. This is a recognition of social values and tolerance of factors and social conditions that shape health negatively, whether it is child marriage, domestic violence, hazing rituals of young people, or female genital mutilation. Such practices can be sanctioned or challenged by public policy and norm setting.

Social Values and Social Policy

In certain contexts, the state's role in addressing the needs of the community through specific health or education policy and service provision is commonplace, but the role and extent of state intervention in enhancing social welfare varies by country, and the respective social values. The extensive literature on social policy addresses the way states envisage their responsibility for social security, improved welfare and protection, as well as policies that foster health (Mkandawire, 2001; Titmuss, 1974). Social policy adherents recognise that promoting and protecting social welfare might not result from *laissez-faire* market economics, thus requiring particular interventions on the part of the state (Leppo, Ollla, Pena, Wismar, & Cook, 2013). The South African government's responsibility in this sphere is vast. As Hassim has written, 'South Africa is regularly described as the developing world's largest and most generous welfare state' (2007, p. 1). This is manifest in grants to support female-headed households and for child support (Dubihlela & Dubihlela, 2014; UNICEF South Africa, 2012). The Ministry of Health highlights how the NHI has been envisaged as a health financing system designed to pool funds to ensure access to 'quality, affordable personal health services for all South Africans based on their health needs, irrespective of their socioeconomic status'

(Government of South Africa, 2015, p. 1). This presents a key problem and source of debate for many countries that rely on market-based economic systems to drive the organisation and delivery of services, including health care and social services, as is the case in the United States. The risk is that health becomes a private good, and that good health is only available for purchase. This can create a conflict between values located within constitutional frameworks that articulate many countries' historical notions of justice, fairness and equality, how market-based systems function, and the degree of state intervention. As Dahl writes, 'without government intervention and regulation a market economy inevitably inflicts serious harm on some persons; and those who are harmed or expect to be harmed will demand government intervention' (1998, p. 174; Karger, Midgely, & Brown, 2003, pp. 3–18). South Africa has retained a highly progressive commitment to equity and justice in social services provision generally, and in health and health care specifically. The South African government outlines its view of the state's constitutional commitment towards health in its discussion of the proposed NHI, also highlighting the kind of South Africa that the state is committed to shaping, stating the following:

> NHI implementation is consistent with the constitutional commitment for the state to take reasonable legislative and other measures, within its available resources, to achieve the progressive realisation of the right to have access to health care services including reproductive health care. Implementation of NHI is a reflection of the kind of society we wish to live in: one based on the values of justice, fairness and social solidarity. (Government of South Africa, 2015, p. 12)

In addition, the document reinforces the NHI vision that health care in South Africa should not be determined by market mechanisms, stating that:

> [i]mplementation of NHI is consistent with the global vision that health care should be seen as a social investment and therefore should not be subjected to market forces where it is treated as a normal commodity of trade. (Government of South Africa, 2015, p. 12)

How this vision translates into health for all, and particularly for historically and socially disadvantaged groups in South Africa such as black women, is a continuing concern.

Just Health or Just Health Care?

It is because health is intrinsic, instrumental, a product of social and biological factors, is socially constructed, that it requires social protection. Social evaluation of justice as 'equality' in the health sphere has launched fiery debates over affordable health care in some HICs, as well as over access to affordable essential medicines for preventable and treatable diseases that continue to plague populations in the LMICs, in the form of avoidable deaths. Many scholars and practitioners, together with citizens, agree that the state's role is to create optimal arrangements for advancing health through laws and codes that routinely regulate the health and safety of populations and public institutions that promote and advance health (Krieger & Birn, 1998). To grasp the conditions by which health is secured, including enabling policies, much of the literature has been dominated by *equality of opportunity to be healthy*, which has historically centred on access to health care. On this basis, some nations make health care available to citizens and residents because they regard the health of their citizens as too important to be left entirely to chance or to market mechanisms. Some nations, including South Africa, go further to protect and promote the health of non-citizens, including migrant populations (see Vearey, 2010). Marmot, Friel, Bell, Houweling, and Taylor (2008) observe that almost all high-income countries (with exceptions, such as the US) organise their health care systems around the principle of universal coverage[2]—an approach requiring that everyone has access to the same range of services, according to preferences and needs, regardless of social status, income or other criteria.

In terms of how societies locate health and address social health inequities, health as a social goal—and greater equity in health among a population—would seem obvious, note Peter and Evans (2001). Yet underlying this seemingly simple proposition is a labyrinth of intricate issues related to the meaning of health and how it is assessed, what good health encompasses, and factors that affect the distribution of health status across and within populations (Evans, Whitehead, Diderichsen, Bhuiya, & Wirth, 2001, p. 25). As Peter and Evans point out, in the philosophical literature, theories of social justice are quiet on health broadly and health inequalities specifically: 'Turning to the literature on moral and political philosophy, one finds few direct efforts to deal with health equity. Theories of social justice are generally silent on the topic of health' (2001, p. 3). Ruger argues that philosophers have been slow to give health (as opposed to health care) any special moral significance because philosophers, such as Rawls and Daniels, make the assumption that health is not an appropriate focal point for evaluating social justice claims (2004a, 2004b). Egalitarian theories typically focus on the distribution of certain goods such as health care, whereas utilitarian theories stress the utilities of satisfaction, desire and preference. Liberal theories of justice, notably that of Rawls, have viewed health as a natural good. Rawls did not give an account of health care in his theory of social justice (1971). Ruger reflects on Rawls' assertion that health and vigour are 'natural goods'; she notes that Rawls seems to see these natural goods as being influenced by the basic structure but indirectly (Ruger, 2004a, p. 1075). In contrast to these natural goods, Rawls developed a list of primary goods society is meant to safeguard to some extent. Nussbaum writes that 'Rawls' evident concern is that no society can guarantee health to its individuals' (2000, p. 88). Rawls is viewed as the dominant voice on social justice theory for more than a generation and his views have had great influence. On this point, Sen emphasises that we should attend not only to the distribution of primary goods, but also to how effectively people are able to *use* those goods to pursue their ends. Sen has stated that the primary goods focus is insufficient, as it does not take into account individual health (and functioning) and environmental health, among other issues (see Sen, 1992, pp. 26–28; see also Robeyns, 2003, pp. 9–10). Sen points out that looking at available goods or resources is not the same as looking at the choices one has to pursue those goods (1992, p. 38). This is a particularly salient point for many groups that lack power in society to act on their aspirations, particularly women; and it underscores the importance of choice as a strength of the CA (Nussbaum, 2000).

On this point, Nussbaum has highlighted Rawls's inattention to classes of individuals in his theory of justice, who might not be 'competent contracting adults'. She writes that 'Rawls explicitly omits...the more extreme forms of need and dependency' (2008, p. 27). Women—as well as children and the disabled—in many settings are characterised by dependency, as part of their social roles, gender hierarchies and economic arrangements that may not foster women's inclusion. All of these are determinants that shape women's health (Annandale & Hunt, 2000; Östlin, George, & Sen, 2001).

Regarding 'just health' vs. 'just health care' Daniels and others suggest that the demand for equality of access or entitlement to health services—rather than good health—is the proper claim that should be lodged. Daniels has viewed health as an inappropriate object, emphasising that action which promotes health, such as a demand for entitlement to health services, is the appropriate focus (1981, 2008). Ruger, a major proponent of the CA, disagrees with Daniels. She stresses that one must not assume that more and better health care is all that is needed to improve health. The main effect of health care may depend on the type of care and often on other factors (2004a, p. 1076, 2010). Sen concurs, stating that '[w]e must go beyond the distribution of health care to get to an adequate understanding of health achievement and capability' (2004b, pp. 23–24).

Peter and Evans stress that even turning to bioethics and medical ethics, a major focus of debate has been on the rationalisation of greater equality in health care and the rights of individual patients (2001), although this is changing. Indeed, combing the public health literature churns up more in the way of moral ethics over the last few years to get to grips with these concerns (Arras, Fenton, & Kukla, 2015; Gostin, 2010; Ruger, 2010). The human rights field has been forging ahead in this lacuna. Before his death, the physician, Jonathan Mann (who headed WHO's global AIDS programme), a pioneer in building the health and human rights field, lamented that although public health began as a social movement, 'at least in its contemporary form, [it] is struggling to define and articulate its core values' (1997, p. 8). Others disagree with this assessment (Krieger & Birn, 1998).[3] In a theory-building article seeking to overcome divisions between medicine and ethics on the one hand, and public health and human rights[4] on the other, Mann remarked on a long-standing 'absence of an ethics of public health' (1997, p. 8). He stressed that public health identifies societal-level factors that determine health status, but that public health does not engage those factors directly. To address this gap, he called for a greater ethics of public health through the building of bridges to connect those disciplines, with a view to strengthening coherence and identity, and through the selection of professional roles and responsibilities to take this forward by marshalling the strengths of each (1997; see also Gruskin, Mills, & Tarantola, 2007).

Over time, the developing evidence base has revealed that health care is insufficient to secure health and wellbeing (Marmot, 2015; Marmot et al., 2008). Social health inequalities are well-documented and stark (Evans et al., 2001). Debates have emerged in recent years that have recognised not just the importance of social determinants but political determinants that typically lie beyond the reach of health care and that fundamentally shape health. This was elevated onto the global agenda by the Lancet/University of Oslo Commission on Global Governance of Health (Ottersen et al., 2014). Over time, many states have come to embrace this evidence more readily. There are diverse considerations in relation to health, Sen emphasises. He urges health decision makers, in considering health inequities, to return to the Aristotelian question, 'equality of what?' or 'equity in what form?' (2002, p. 660). He pushes us to consider health—but never in isolation. In the CA, health is holistic and considerations of health should, similarly, reflect this. Sen notes that 'health equity is most certainly not just about the distribution of health, not to mention the even narrower focus on the distribution of health care' (2002, p. 659). I will return to this shortly.

In recent times, in the transnational space of global health, the stark inequalities in people's ability to be healthy have reached new heights. Global stakeholders who play a role in health governance and those who work in the health space—health officials, researchers, NGO health programmers, civil society—have increasingly agreed that health should be viewed as a public good, not a commodity to be bought or traded (Koplan et al., 2009; Merson, Black, & Mills, 2011). This new terrain of global health with an emphasis on equity and justice is not a natural outgrowth of the global order. It is, I would argue, the result of a scorched earth making way for a new and fertile ground. Health as social justice lay in the hands of actors working persistently at multiple levels to change the landscape of health, nationally and globally. When it comes to the global HIV epidemic, a primary handmaiden has been civil society, and some enlightened governments, such as Brazil, and other international actors, including UN agencies (see Parker, 2003). In South Africa, social mobilisation at the grassroots level, led by the Treatment Action Campaign, together with the power of litigation, led by the AIDS Law Project (renamed SECTION 27) have been crucial in establishing the HIV response (Heywood, 2009; Power, 2003). At the same time, the justice agenda that embraced equity in health and health care was part of the vision of South Africa's new democracy enshrined within the Bill of Rights and South Africa's constitutional commitments (Bilchitz, 2006).

In spite of gains, greater clarity is needed over equity in relation to the health of those governed—or to how health equity is conceived of or assured within a just society. The debate turns on the nature and reach of such a social justice claim. There has been comparatively little scholarship, both to conceptualise *good* health, and to locate health more firmly within an accepted, moral social justice framework with some teeth. Against this background, Sen's CA provides an approach that conceptualises health holistically and robustly. The CA offers, not a full-fledged theory of justice, but a normative framework for social evaluation of health inequities and deprivations in capabilities for groups in society.

The Capabilities Approach

As a normative framework, the CA is both broad and flexible (Alkire, 2005). Capability is chiefly concerned with considerations of quality of life and used in the evaluation of wellbeing for individuals or groups, their social arrangements, as well as assessments of policies aimed at social change (Robeyns, 2003). It has a primary focus on the *ends* of wellbeing; and development within the CA assumes those ends should be discussed in relation to people's ability to be and do what they themselves value (Robeyns, 2003, p. 6). The CA embraces two principal ideas: (1) valuable beings and doings, called functionings; and (2) freedom (opportunity freedom and process freedom) (Alkire, 2005). Capability, Sen writes, 'represents the various combinations of functionings (beings and doings) that the person can achieve' (1992, p. 40). If capability risks sounding like a pipe dream, it is not. It is envisaged by Sen and others as being concrete and achievable. What are examples of capabilities? The United Nations Development Programme (UNDP) highlights some of the essential ones:

> The most basic capabilities for human development are to lead long and healthy lives, to be knowledgeable, to have access to the resources needed for a decent standard of living and to be able to participate in the life of the community. (2011, p. 1)

Moreover, UNDP has stressed that when choices are not available, many life opportunities remain out of reach.

In the CA, health is viewed as a form of freedom, while ill health is seen as its opposite (Peter, 2000). Health is regarded as a central capability. Health capability is defined as 'an individual's ability to achieve good health' and it includes an individual's ability to 'be free of preventable morbidity and mortality' (Ruger, 2006, p. 999). Sen notes that 'health is among the most important conditions of human life and a critically significant constituent of human capabilities which we have reason to value' (2002, p. 660). Sen maintains '[t]he fact that health is central to our wellbeing needs emphasis, as does the equally basic recognition that the freedoms and capabilities that we are able to exercise are dependent on our health achievements' (2004a, p. 28). Gasper observes that the very core of the CA is 'an insistence on referring to a wide range of types of information, notably about how people actually live—what they do and are—and their freedom—what they are able to do and be' (2002, p. 340). The key assumption made by the CA is that any evaluation of 'the good life' can and must be determined through a social process. The strength of the approach is its ability to ask particular questions of relevance to health and health equity, especially for women (Alkire, 2005, p. 124; Nussbaum, 2000). This is discussed in more detail below.

One's capability can be viewed as a set of vectors of functionings. Functionings are a core aspect of the CA. They demonstrate 'the person's freedom to lead one type of life or another...to choose from possible livings' (Sen, 1992, p. 40). Sen indicates functionings have roots in Aristotelian ideas (1999, p. 75). Aristotle suggested we must 'first ascertain the function of man' and explore life 'in the sense of activity' as the 'basic block of normative analysis' (Sen, 1999, p. 73). Functionings can be seen as actual achievements—they are a composite of what people *are* in their lives. Functionings are both the ends and means of human life, like development itself (Alkire, 2004, p. 5). Achieved functionings are measurable and comparable across individuals, groups or populations. Examples of achieved functionings are health and development indicators referenced previously, including life expectancy or literacy. Viewed in total, an individual's actual achievements can be referred to as a *functioning vector*. Use of a vector allows for viewing change and movement over time, in keeping with approaches to health and human development such as the life course approach. A life course approach recognises that needs shift along with different life stages during childhood, adolescence and reproductive years, for example (Elder, 1998; Kuh, Ben-Schlomo, Lynch, Hallqvist, & Power, 2003). Significantly, capabilities can expand as we go through life, or they can contract. Alkire has depicted capability expansion as a parachute inflating, and capability deprivation as the parachute contracting. One can visualise the parachute: losing its air, shrinking in size and becoming lifeless (2004, p. 15).

Sen communicates that the crystalline focus of the CA is a layered, rich, complex conception—not one that is only centred on outcome. It has a focus 'not just on what a person actually ends up doing, but also on what she is in fact able to do, whether or not she makes use of that opportunity' (Sen, 2009, p. 235). In other words, it is the capability *to choose* between possible achievements or livings. One example is choosing one's political or religious affiliation (Sen, 2009, pp. 235–238). Alkire provides examples to shine a light on functionings, which can be general (the capability to be nourished), complex (participation in community life, self-respect); they can be primary or elemental, including 'escaping morbidity and mortality' (2004, p. 5). Gasper adds that functioning is nearly always an operational proxy for capability (2007, p. 347). An additional principal idea within the CA is freedom.

Process and Opportunity Freedoms

Freedom occupies a central place in the CA. Sen's notion of freedom is never static; it is rich and expansive. While freedom may seem opaque, as Alkire eloquently notes, we all have an intuitive sense of what freedom is, namely:

> [t]he 'good life' is partly a life of genuine choice, and not one in which the person is forced into a particular life—however rich it might be in other respects. (2003, p. 5)

(Note that the Aristotelian aspects of the CA are evident here.) Capability expansion is seen to occur in alignment with the notion of 'development as freedom' the title of Sen's 1999 work, for which he won that not insignificant award, the Nobel Prize in Economics (Sen, 1999). The idea is to expand a person's capability set and thus her ability to create a life she has reason to value (Alkire, 2003, 2005). Sen emphasises that freedom has both process and opportunity aspects. This includes processes that enable freedom of decision and of action, and the actual opportunities people enjoy, given their material, social and personal circumstances (1999, p. 17; see also Sen, 2009, pp. 18–19). *Process* suggests people's real opportunities to be 'agents'—to affect processes within their own lives and in their communities and societies (Alkire, 2004, p. 7). *Opportunity* refers to individuals' ability to achieve functionings they deem of value, or valuable outcomes (Sen, 1999, p. 291). In this way, 'process' in social and political decisions is not only a means but constitutive of the ends of development (Sen, 1999). The process and opportunity aspects of freedom need to both be assessed. Sen uses the example of choosing fasting as a political act, as Gandhi did, to consider freedom in relation to choices and preferences. Fasting was a deliberate choice to starve. To be afforded that choice, Gandhi needed the option to eat, if he had so chosen. This is a form of freedom. Someone who is starving is not choosing to fast; they are not free to eat (Sen, 1999, p. 292). This is the very opposite of freedom and illustrates the fine distinctions between process and opportunity in freedom that comprise a significant dimension of the CA.

Agency

Within the CA, the notion of participation in human development is central. That individuals, particularly women, are active agents in their own development has been at the core of Sen and Nussbaum's conceptions of the CA. Agency must be determined and defined within social context and social norms, and it should not be oversimplified. In the CA, agency 'recognises that individuals often have values and goals (such as preserving the environment, purchasing free trade products or opposing injustice, tyranny and oppression) that transcend and sometimes even conflict with personal well-being' (Clark, 2005, p. 5; see Sen, 1985, 1992). The importance here is viewing individuals as members of society who have an agentic role in economic, social and political life. As Sen notes, this view has a bearing on numerous public policy issues, including in health.

Thus far I have discussed central aspects of the CA but not all. Sen hastens to stress that it is necessary to ask, in any assessment exercise, how the valuation is to be selected, stating that

> in arriving at an agreed range for social evaluation (for example, in social studies of poverty), there has to be some kind of 'reasoned consensus' on weights, or at least on a range of weights. (1999, pp. 78–79)

He emphasises further that '[t]his is a 'social choice' exercise, and it requires public discussion and a democratic understanding and acceptance' (1999, pp. 78–79). The CA has six dominant features, identified by Gasper (2002), which are helpful in grasping Sen's multifaceted, thick ideas. These have evolved over time and have been advanced in various ways by different scholars, while being adapted to many different fields. They are: (1) an orientation to use a variety of sources of information for understanding and determining wellbeing; (2) a language to describe the variety; (3) the categories of basic capabilities and threshold levels; (4) a prioritisation among categories, the 'prioritisation of capability' (as opposed to other measures); (5) a principle of prioritisation for groups—to be done through democratic deliberation and through public debate; and (6) a principle of prioritisation of capabilities for individuals is to be reasoned (Gasper, 2002).

The Moral Importance of Health and Implications

Adherents of the CA, such as Ruger, respond to the bias in ethical theory against health (as opposed to health care) as the focal variable of social justice, by suggesting that 'we lack a moral framework' for viewing health, and that a particular strength of the capability view of health is that it provides us with just such a moral underpinning (2006, p. 1002; see also Ruger, 2010). If the social covenant in South Africa and other nations is truly to be characterised by justice and equality for all, we need a theory of social justice that includes a sufficient conception of health: one that is inclusive of all people, those who are dependent and disabled, especially those who are ill, and those who care for them, women and children, as well as other groups; one that looks at the health and development prospects of and quality of life for all people within our particular social context and their entitlements. Sen emphasises that

> [we] cannot ignore the role of health in human life and the opportunities that persons, respectively, have to achieve good health—free from escapable illness, avoidable afflictions and premature mortality. (2002, p. 660)

Equity in Health Sen pays particular attention to equity in health. Sen's concern in the CA, echoing Aristotle, is the space in which equality is evaluated. Sen observes that equality is not reducible to 'one space only' (whether resources, utilities, achieved quality of life or capabilities) (2009, p. 297). He states that '[e]quity in the achievement and distribution of health gets thus incorporated and embedded in a larger understanding of justice' (2002, p. 660). The CA thus takes up central questions of relevance in this work, generally, that of how health and equality figure in a just society, specifically HIV as a continuing problem affecting black South African women. Part of the rationale for choosing the CA to understand HIV and its implications for women is indeed the ways in which freedom from escapable illness and premature death are explicitly identified and addressed within the CA. According to the Approach, if we regard human health as central to human development, then losses in health functioning can be seen as unjust because they reduce the capacity for individuals to develop and to flourish (Ruger, 2006). Ruger further notes that 'we value human life equally and deprivations in health capability constitute threats to human flourishing' (2006, p. 999). Ruger draws out the moral implications associated with deprivations in health capability due to HIV and AIDS, maintaining that

> policies that deny antiretroviral drugs to patients with HIV/AIDS, as happens in sub-Saharan Africa and other parts of the world, are morally troubling. (2006, p. 999)

This is so, she continues, 'not only because they constitute subminimal healthcare [and] reduce individuals' opportunity for employment' the 'moral concern is the reduced capability for physical and mental functioning, or even for being alive' (2006, p. 999). Ruger stresses that if health is diminished, very many other capabilities and freedoms remain out of reach; thus health is required to achieve other capabilities.

Women in the Capabilities Approach

Why we would want a social justice framework that engages women's health and human development as key concerns might be obvious for some. When looking at the relevance of this approach for women, we see that human development, health and wellbeing have been undermined for many women in particular settings around the world. As we saw in the previous chapter, poor health achievements along indicators of life expectancy and maternal mortality, as well as premature mortality, are visible for black women of low social position and low SES. Nussbaum describes women's development needs in this way:

> Women in much of the world lack support for fundamental functions of a human life. They are less well nourished than men, less healthy, more vulnerable to physical violence and sexual abuse. (2002, p. 124)

She continues: 'They are much less likely than men to be literate, and still less likely to have preprofessional or technical education'

(2002, p. 124). Education can be a route to economic independence, to job security and other types of wellbeing. Not only are many women unable to access this pathway, they, Nussbaum highlights, bear the burden of care for the family, assuming the 'double day' of work—i.e., they may conduct domestic or other work by day, and then fulfil the obligations of child care and housekeeping as a 'second shift'. Nussbaum concludes that in all these ways, women's social and political circumstances are distinctive and have direct importance for women's capabilities (2002, p. 124). Langer and co-authors, in a recent *Lancet Commission on Women and Health* (2015), concur that women are typically the caregivers, catering to the needs of others, even as their own health needs are often neglected. Moreover, women's work is underpaid and undervalued in society, professionally: women comprise the majority of community health care workers, globally, and they are famously underpaid, lack job security and the formal benefits that typically accompany salaried occupations.

In acknowledging the ways that the CA responds to women's special development needs, Nussbaum stresses that Sen's cognisance of gender justice issues has shaped his formulation of the Approach. She highlights, throughout Sen's career, including his work on the CA, 'Inequalities between women and men have been especially important in Sen's thinking.' She continues: 'achievement of gender justice in society has been one of the most central goals of his theoretical enterprise' (2003, p. 33).

Nussbaum makes her own singular and highly significant contribution to conceptualising the CA in relation to women's particular health and development needs. She has developed a list of ten central capabilities that serve as essential preconditions for a just society. The first three on Nussbaum's list most directly pertain to health but they all have some bearing on wellbeing. They recognise reproductive health and freedom from violent assault. There is explicit mention of 'being able to have good health, including reproductive health' and 'not dying prematurely' as well as choice in matters of reproduction and sexual satisfaction (Nussbaum, 2000, pp. 78–80). Thus, her central capabilities articulate and address important considerations that flow from the research problem, which is not just a theoretical problem but a major health and development challenge for women in South and Southern Africa, and elsewhere. In Nussbaum's interpretation of the CA, we can only have an adequate theory of social justice 'if we are willing to make claims about fundamental entitlements' and capabilities offers us a valuable approach to address this question (2003, pp. 1–2). Nussbaum's list of capabilities creates an account of those required entitlements. She emphasises: 'All are of central importance and all are distinct in quality' (2002, p. 131). Hence, in the Nussbaum view, the CA comprises an indivisible set of combined capabilities, and the goal is to pursue each capability for each person, treating each person as an end. With these (enumerated) as threshold levels of capability, the social goal is getting every person above the threshold to satisfy the requirement of equality (Peter & Evans, 2001, p. 28). I provide the full list of Nussbaum's central capabilities in the analysis in Chap. 6.

Strengths and Limitations of Capabilities as a Conceptual Framework

What happens when a society does not offer a threshold level of capabilities to its members? We already know that many women with HIV are not 'able to live to the end of a human life of normal length' (Nussbaum, 2000, p. 78). What can be done? The CA specifically discusses the particular problem at hand—premature death. There are some differences between Sen and Nussbaum in how to address shortfalls in capabilities, however. Chiefly, in contrast to Nussbaum, Sen does not endorse a list of capabilities. Instead, he throws it back to social evaluation and the process of democratic deliberation, and believes that societies must decide how to take a social evaluation forward. Ruger takes a stronger stance on states' obligations, and potentially that of non-state actors. She argues that global health inequities pose ethical challenges for the global health community that must be addressed (2006). Anand, too, stresses that 'ill-health reduces the full scope of human agency. If we see health in this way, then inequalities in health constitute inequalities in capability to function' (2004, pp. 17–18). But they pose even more pressing questions for our national and local communities who have to live with the consequences. In post-apartheid South Africa, how can questions of the good life for all citizens be taken up—one that includes freedom from premature illness and death for women? I discuss this in more detail in Chaps. 6, 8, and 9.

With regard to strengths, any conceptual framework is an organising device; a way of seeing. It allows us to map and understand phenomena and, if appropriate, it may direct action. Given that our research problem centres on premature illness and death for women living with HIV, the first major advantage of the CA—unlike social contract theory, or utilitarian, income or poverty-based development frameworks—is that it pays due attention to illness and premature death for women. It connects health to social considerations of fairness, justice and equity. It also recognises that health and human development are relational and that women have been overlooked in theories of justice. (It offers much more, and these distinct features are drawn out in Chap. 9).

Second, if we turn to the basic problem of women's exclusion from theories of social justice, the CA gives us proper traction in moving towards a fuller, enhanced notion of health and human development for women specifically, as well as for other marginalised or neglected populations, including children born to women with HIV. Women are not viewed as an appendage of men, but as their own agents. As Nussbaum notes, too often women are not treated as ends in themselves, as 'persons with a dignity that deserves respect from laws and institutions. Instead, they are treated as mere instruments of the ends of others—reproducers, caregivers, sexual outlets, agents of a family's general prosperity' (2000, p. 2).

Third, an important asset of the CA is clarity about the objective, as Alkire (2005) notes. She contends that '[a]ccording to the capability approach, the objective of both justice and poverty should be to expand the freedom that deprived people have to enjoy valuable beings and doings' (2005, p. 117). This generates a person-centred approach to health and human development. Fourth, the CA is both a human rights and human development approach where rights can be understood as social and material preconditions for development, and as constitutional guarantees that require government action, legal protection and enforcement. This approach fits with the rights entitlements afforded women in South African law. Fifthly, as mentioned, this normative approach assists in clearly articulating, at a minimum, what basic justice does require vis-à-vis development and flourishing for women; it allows for an empirical quality of life assessment to be undertaken within the study population.

There are several limitations, however. In Nussbaum's approach, a concrete list of essential preconditions also leaves itself open to criticism and multiple interpretations. Not everyone will agree on what is 'essential' and whether the current list fits the bill. There are concerns about pluralism and diversity lodged by feminists. As Quillen notes, 'feminist scholars want first to acknowledge the complexities of a female subjectivity constituted amid shifting and irreconcilable discourses, without as a result denying female agency' (2001, p. 87; see also Charlesworth, 2000).

Other critics contend that Nussbaum's conception of social justice 'relies upon an untheorised and an ahistorical liberal state' (Feldman & Gellert, 2003). These same critics assert that Nussbaum ignores the specific historical place of states within a changing global political economy; and 'accounting for the positioning of states within such a global context reveals the importance of states' differing relations to other states, transnational institutions, and their citizenry' (Feldman & Gellert, 2003). Equally, as noted, the CA is a paradigm, not a fully formed theory of justice. In Sen's own words:

> [c]apability is, in fact, no more than a perspective in terms of which advantages and disadvantages of a person can be reasonably assessed. That perspective is significant on its own, and it is also critically important for theories of justice and of moral and political evaluation.

He proceeds to explain that

> [a] theory of justice has to be alive to both the fairness of the processes involved and to the equity and efficiency of the substantive opportunities that people can enjoy. (2009, pp. 296–297)

Sen's concern, again, is the space in which equality is evaluated; the multiple dimensions in which equality matters are not 'reducible to equality in one space only' (2009, p. 297). Thus, though his sense of a social evaluation process can begin to point the way, the demands of procedural fairness are beyond what capabilities can address (Sen, 2005, pp. 155–156; Sen, 2009).

A further limitation can be put forward. As Clark notes, 'Public action also plays an important role in supporting capabilities directly and providing political pressure for state intervention in times of crisis and hardship', however, additional work is needed to 'bring out the policy implications' of the CA (2005, p. 11). Here Clark is pointing to one of the gaps in the CA: that it is under-formulated. Gasper offers a counter-argument, suggesting that such under-formulation may have advantages. He puts this is the following way:

> Does vagueness about the content of the capability approach and about how it relates to other bodies of work—human development, human security, 'development as freedom', Sen's work as a whole—really matter? Underdefinition allows everyone to perceive space for themselves in a project. It gives, fittingly, a lot of freedom for people of varied backgrounds to grow out from a small kernel in diverse ways. (2002, p. 336)

But herein lies the difficulty. As Gasper himself points out, underdefinition can often lead, temptingly, to throwing up one's hands and walking away: '[i]It remains unpersuasive to those who look for clarity, let alone precision. The risk increases that 'anything goes' during the inevitable simplifications in operationalization' (2002, p. 337). Lastly, any framework inevitably leaves things out that may be as important as what remains. The CA makes certain claims about what individuals require. However, the structures and systems that underpin those conditions are not easily taken into account (Quillen, 2001). Whether capabilities can be realised or not may depend in whole or in part on these structures. How these structures perpetuate entrenched social norms, and how norms and social arrangements might be changed, including gender norms, are critical to the exercise of women's capabilities. This is particularly important, given the structural factors that underpin HIV risk in South African women, as seen in Chap. 2. Whether the CA can sufficiently engage with these remains to be seen. I discuss this in further detail in Chap. 6.

How the Capabilities Approach Is Used in This Project

My goal in using the Capabilities Approach in this work is to achieve greater understanding of the capabilities and potential capability deprivations among a sample of 89 black South African women who are living with HIV. I do this by: (1) applying the theory of capabilities (and the specific capability dimensions identified by Sen and Nussbaum) to the findings of the empirical research on HIV positive women (presented and discussed in Chap. 6); (2) connecting the results of the CA analysis to other indicators, as part of the health equity assessment undertaken in Chap. 8, and to the normative moral framework that the CA offers, thus enabling the consideration of the implications for women's rights (in Chap. 7 and the Conclusion) that are afforded women in South Africa's basic law (e.g., the Constitution); (3) reflecting on how the theory illuminates the problem in ways that are often obscured, while analying the strengths and limitations of applying the CA to this research concern.

Effective conceptual frameworks allow us to generate deeper insight into research phenomena and to understand research concerns in new and powerful ways, which may inform theory and practice. When it comes to complex health concerns like HIV, the alignment between the framework, the concern and the social context is critical. To that end, the CA offers an important framework for viewing good health as an appropriate social justice goal in South Africa, despite a number of limitations. The CA analysis has the potential to yield insights for women living with HIV who face significant constraints to their agency. I argue that the value of the CA centres on its attention to developing a more comprehensive account of what good health entails, while addressing the specific needs of women—in sharp contrast with other approaches that fail to do so (Nussbaum, 2008). The CA's focus on process and opportunity freedoms also aligns with South Africa's commitment to establishing a new social order premised on 'the democratic values of human dignity, equality and freedom' (Government of South Africa, 1996, p. 5). Such an approach may also be relevant to a range of other countries and settings since health policies and goals are embedded in the constitutions and policies of countries, yet the reality of good health for citizens remains elusive in many nations. While there is no easy solution to the complex problem of HIV in black South African women, the CA offers a normative framework to guide this inquiry, and potentially, to advance knowledge in ways that will inform social evaluation in response.

Notes

1. Also called the Capabilities Approach, I use both terms.
2. The health system is not unique in its embrace of principles of equity, however. The transformation of all other sectors is underpinned by principles of equity in keeping with the transition to democracy and the development of a new post-apartheid social order.
3. For a series of country case studies and analyses of 'the evidence of impact' of applying human-rights based approaches to health, see the special issue of *Health & Human Rights Journal* (2015). 'Evidence of the Impact of Human Rights-Based Approaches to Health', *17*(2). Countries or settings analysed include India, Mexico, Kenya, Peru, Germany, England, Wales, the US and Ukraine. Issues covered also include women's health, and child and adolescent health; as well as maternal and sexual reproductive health: http://www.hhrjournal.org/. For a U.S. case study of these issues in the state of Vermont, see MacNaughton, Haigh, McGill, Koutsioumpas, and Sprague (2015).
4. This view is not held by Krieger and Birn (1998) and others who emphasise that health and social justice have always been tied in a common pursuit and that major advances in health have also contributed to building a just society (see, for example, Starfield, 2006). Nonetheless, the global HIV epidemic has drawn attention to the manner by which public health control efforts and criminalisation policies targeted at those living with HIV conflict with the advancement and protection of human rights and human dignity.

References

Alkire, S. (2003). *The Capability Approach as a Development Paradigm?* Document part of training course preceding the 3rd International Conference on the Capability Approach, Pavia, Italy, 7 September.

Alkire, S. (2004, September). *The Capability Approach and Human Development Presentation*. Oxford University, 1–15.

Alkire, S. (2005). Why the capability approach? *Journal of Human Development, 6*(1), 115–135.

Anand, S. (2004). The concern for equity in health. In S. Anand, F. Peter, & A. Sen (Eds.), *Public Health, Ethics, and Equity* (pp. 15–20). Oxford: Oxford University Press.

Anand, S., Peter, F., & Sen, A. (Eds.). (2004). *Public Health, Ethics, and Equity*. Oxford: Oxford University Press.

Annandale, E., & Hunt, K. (2000). Gender inequalities in health: Research at the crossroads. In E. Annandale & K. Hunt (Eds.), *Gender Inequalities in Health* (pp. 1–35). Philadelphia: Open University Press.

Aristotle. (1998). *The Nicomachean Ethics* (C. Taylor, Trans.). Oxford: Oxford University Press.

Arras, J., Fenton, E., & Kukla, R. (2015). *The Routledge Companion to Bioethics*. New York: Routledge.

Barker, D. (Ed.). (1992). *Fetal and Infant Origins of Adult Disease*. London: BMJ Books.

Bilchitz, D. (2006). The right to health. In S. Woolman & M. Bishop (Eds.), *Constitutional Law of South Africa* (2nd ed.). Cape Town: Juta Press, Chapter 56A.

Bronfenbrenner, U. (1979). *The Ecology of Human Development: Experiments by Nature and Design*. Cambridge: Harvard University Press.

Canguilhem, G. (1991). *On the Normal and the Pathological*. New York: Zone Books.

Charlesworth, H. (2000). Martha Nussbaum's feminist internationalism. *Ethics, 111*(1), 64–78.

Charmaz, K. (1991). *Good Days, Bad Days: The Self in Chronic Illness and Time*. New Brunswick: Rutgers University Press.

Cicero, M. (2013). *On the Republic and On the Laws* (D. Fott, Trans.). Ithaca, NY: Cornell University Press.

Clark, D. (2005). *The Capability Approach: Its Development, Critiques and Recent Advances*. [online]. Manchester: University of Manchester. Retrieved January 17, 2017, from http://www.gprg.org/pubs/workingpapers/pdfs/gprg-wps-032.pdf

Crespo, R. F. (2012). The capabilities approaches and Aristotelian practical reason. *Revista de Instituciones, Ideas y Mercados, 57*, 57–86.

Dahl, R. (1998). *On Democracy*. New Haven: Yale University Press.

Daniels, N. (1981). Health care needs and distributive justice. *Philosophy and Public Affairs, 10*(2), 146–179.

Daniels, N. (2008). *Just Health: Meeting Health Needs Fairly*. Cambridge: Cambridge University Press.

Department of Public Service and Administration, Government of South Africa. (1997). *Batho Pele—"People First." White Paper on Transforming Public Service Delivery*. [online]. Pretoria: Department of Public Service and Administration. Retrieved January 16, 2017, from http://www.dpsa.gov.za/dpsa2g/documents/acts&regulations/frameworks/white-papers/transform.pdf

Doll, R. (1992). Health and the environment in the 1990s. *America Journal of Public Health, 82*(7), 933–941.

Dubihlela, J., & Dubihlela, D. (2014). Social grants impact on poverty among the female-headed households in South Africa. *Mediterranean Journal of Social Sciences, 5*(8), 160–167.

Elder, G. (1998). The life course as developmental theory. *Child Development, 69*(1), 1–12.

Emerson, R. (2017). *The Conduct of Life*. North Charleston: CreateSpace Independent Publishing.

Evans, T., Whitehead, M., Diderichsen, F., Bhuiya, A., & Wirth, M. (Eds.). (2001). *Challenging Inequities to Health: From Ethics to Action*. Oxford: Oxford University Press.

Feldman, S., & Gellert, P. (2003). Central capabilities and entitlements: A critique of Nussbaum's Ahistorical and Universalist Western Liberal Claims. In *Annual Meeting of the American Sociological Association*. Atlanta: American Sociological Association.

Foucault, M. (1977). *Discipline and Punish: The Birth of the Prison*. New York: Vintage.

Freidson, E. (1970). *Profession of Medicine: A Study of the Sociology of Applied Knowledge*. New York: Harper & Row.

Gasper, D. (2002). Is Sen's capability approach an adequate basis for considering human development? *Review of Political Economy, 14*(4), 435–446.

Gasper, D. (2007). What is the capability approach? Its core, rationale, partners and dangers. *Journal of Socio-Economics, 36*(3), 335–359.

Glaser, B., & Strauss, A. (1965). *Awareness of Dying*. Chicago: Aldine Transaction.

Goffman, E. (1963). *Stigma: Notes on the Management of Spoiled Identity*. Englewood Cliffs: Prentice-Hall.

Gostin, L. (2010). *Public Health Law and Ethics: A Reader*. Berkeley: University of California Press.

Government of South Africa. (1996). The Constitution of the Republic of South Africa, Act No. 108 of 1996. Cape Town: South Africa.

Government of South Africa. (2015). White paper on national health insurance (11 December). National health insurance for South Africa: Towards universal health coverage. Version 40. Government Gazette No. 39506. Pretoria: National Department of Health.

Greenhalgh, T., Annandale, E., Ashcroft, R., et al. (2016). An open letter to The BMJ editors on qualitative research. *BMJ, 352*, i563.

Gruskin, S., Mills, E., & Tarantola, D. (2007). History, principles, and practice of health and human rights. *Lancet, 370*(9585), 449–455.

Hassim, S. (2007). Social justice, gender and developmental social welfare in South Africa. In *Conference on Social Justice*. Johannesburg: University of the Witwatersrand.

Health & Human Rights Journal. (2015). Special Issue 'Evidence of the impact of human rights-based approaches to health'. *17*(2). Retrieved June 1, 2017, from http://www.hhrjournal.org/

Heise, L., & McGrory, E. (2016). *Greentree II: Violence Against Women and Girls, and HIV—Report on a High-Level Consultation on the Evidence and Implications*. Greentree Estate, NY: STRIVE.

Hertzman, C. (1999). The biological embedding of early experience and its effects on health in adulthood. *Annals of the New York Academy of Sciences, 896*, 85–95.

Hertzman, C. (2010). Framework for the social determinants of early child development. In *Encyclopedia on Early Childhood Development*. Montreal: Université de Montréal.

Heywood, M. (2009). South Africa's Treatment Action Campaign: Combining law and social mobilization to realize the right to health. *Journal of Human Rights Practice, 1*(1), 14–36.

Karger, H., Midgely, J., & Brown, C. (2003). *Controversial Issues in Social Policy*. Boston: Allyn and Bacon.

Koplan, J., Bond, T., Merson, M., Reddy, K., Henry, M., Sewankambo, N., et al. (2009). Towards a common definition of global health. *Lancet, 373*, 1993–1995.

Krieger, N., & Birn, A. (1998). A vision of social justice as the foundation of public health. *American Journal of Public Health, 88*(11), 1603–1606.

Langer, A., Meleis, A., Knaul, F., Atun, R., Aran, M., Arreola-Ornelas, H., et al. (2015). Women and health: The key for sustainable development. *Lancet, 386*(9999), 1165–1210.

Leppo, K., Ollla, E., Pena, S., Wismar, M., & Cook, S. (2013). *Health in All Policies: Seizing Opportunities, Implementing Policies*. Helsinki: Finland Ministry of Social Affairs and Health.

MacNaughton, G., Haigh, F., McGill, M., Koutsioumpas, K., & Sprague, C. (2015). The impact of human rights on universalizing health care in Vermont, USA. *Health & Human Rights Journal, 17*(2), 83–95.

Mann, J. (1997). Medicine and public health, ethics and human rights. *The Hastings Centre Report, 27*(3), 6–13.

Marks, S. (1994). *Divided Sisterhood: Race, Class and Gender in the South African Nursing Profession*. New York: St. Martin's Press.

Marmot, M. (2015). *The Health Gap: The Challenge of an Unequal World*. London: Bloomsbury.

Marmot, M., Friel, S., Bell, R., Houweling, T., & Taylor, S. (2008). Closing the gap in a generation: Health equity through action on the social determinants of health. *Lancet, 372*(9659), 1661–1669.

Merson, M., Black, R., & Mills, A. (2011). *Global Health: Diseases, Programs, Systems and Policies* (3rd ed.). Burlington: Jones & Bartlett.

Mkandawire, T. (2001). *Social Policy in a Development Context*. Geneva: United Nations Research Institute for Social Development.

Murray, C., & Lopez, A. (Eds.). (1996). *The Global Burden of Disease: A Comprehensive Assessment of Mortality and Disability from Diseases, Injuries, and Risk Factors in 1990 and Projected to 2020*. Cambridge: Harvard University Press.

Nagel, T. (1979). *Mortal Questions*. Cambridge: Cambridge University Press.

Nussbaum, M. (1988a). Nature, function and capability: Aristotle on political distribution. *Oxford Studies in Ancient Philosophy, 1*(1), S145–S184.

Nussbaum, M. (1988b). Non-relative virtues: An Aristotelian approach. *Midwest Studies in Philosophy, 13*, 32–53.

Nussbaum, M. (1992). Human functioning and social justice: In defense of Aristotelian essentialism. *Political Theory, 20*, 202–246.

Nussbaum, M. (2000). *Women and Human Development: The Capabilities Approach*. Cambridge: Cambridge University Press.

Nussbaum, M. (2002). Capabilities and social justice. *International Studies Review, 4*(2), 123–135.

Nussbaum, M. (2003). Capabilities as fundamental entitlements: Sen and social justice. *Feminist Economics, 9*(2–3), 33–59.

Nussbaum, M. (2008). Foreword: Constitutions and capabilities: Perception against Lofty Formalism, The Supreme Court 2006 Term. *Harvard Law Review, 121*(4), 1–79.

Osmani, S., & Sen, A. (2003). The hidden penalties of gender inequality: Fetal origins of ill-health. *Economics and Human Biology, 1*, 105–121.
Ottersen, O., Dasgupta, J., Blouin, C., Buss, P., Chongsuvivatwong, V., Frenk, J., et al. (2014). The political origins of health inequity: Prospects for change. *Lancet, 383*(9917), 630–667.
Parker, R. (2003). Building the foundations for the response for HIV/AIDS in Brazil: The development of HIV/AIDS policy, 1992–1996. *Divulgaçao em Saúde para Debate, 27*, 143–183.
Peter, F. (2000). *Health Equity and Social Justice*. Cambridge: Harvard Center for Population and Development Studies.
Peter, F., & Evans, T. (2001). Ethical dimensions of health equity. In T. Evans, M. Whitehead, F. Diderichsen, A. Bhuiya, & M. Wirth (Eds.), *Challenging Inequities to Health: From Ethics to Action* (pp. 25–33). Oxford: Oxford University Press.
Power, S. (2003). The AIDS Rebel. [online]. *The New Yorker*. Retrieved February 2, 2017, from http://www.newyorker.com/magazine/2003/05/19/the-aids-rebel
Quillen, C. (2001). Feminist theory, justice and the lure of the human. *Signs, 27*(1), 87–122.
Rawls, J. (1971). *A Theory of Justice*. Cambridge, MA: Harvard University Press.
Robeyns, I. (2003). Capability ethics. In H. LaFollette & I. Persson (Eds.), *The Blackwell Guide to Ethical Theory* (2nd ed.). New York: Blackwell.
Ruger, J. (2004a). Health and social justice. *Lancet, 364*, 1075–1080.
Ruger, J. (2004b). Ethics of the social determinants of health. *Lancet, 364*, 1092–1097.
Ruger, J. (2006). Ethics and governance of global health inequalities. *Journal of Epidemiological and Community Health, 60*, 998–1003.
Ruger, J. (2010). *Health and Social Justice*. Oxford: Oxford University Press.
Russell, B. (2004). *History of Western Philosophy*. New York: Simon & Schuster.
Saracci, R. (1997). The World Health Organisation needs to reconsider its definition of health. *BMJ, 314*(7091), 1409–1410.
Sen, A. (1985). *Commodities and Capabilities*. Amsterdam: North Holland.
Sen, A. (1992). *Inequality Re-Examined*. Cambridge: Harvard University Press.
Sen, A. (1999). *Development as Freedom*. New York: Random House.
Sen, A. (2001). Health equity, perspectives, measurability and criteria. In T. Evans, M. Whitehead, F. Diderichsen, A. Bhuiya, & M. Wirth (Eds.), *Challenging Inequities to Health: From Ethics to Action* (pp. 69–75). Oxford: Oxford University Press.
Sen, A. (2002). Why health equity? *Health Economics, 11*, 659–666.

Sen, A. (2004a). Why health equity? In S. Anand, F. Peter, & A. Sen (Eds.), *Public Health, Ethics, and Equity* (pp. 21–34). Oxford: Oxford University Press.

Sen, A. (2004b). Health achievement and equity: External and internal perspectives. In S. Anand, F. Peter, & A. Sen (Eds.), *Public Health, Ethics, and Equity* (pp. 263–268). Oxford: Oxford University Press.

Sen, A. (2005). Human rights and capabilities. *Journal of Human Development, 6*(2), 151–166.

Sen, A. (2009). *The Idea of Justice*. Cambridge: Harvard University Press.

Smith, A. (2010). *The Theory of Moral Sentiments*. London: Penguin.

Starfield, B. (2006). State of the art in research on equity in health. *Journal of Health Politics, Policy and Law, 31*(1), 11–32.

Titmuss, R. (1974). *Social Policy*. London: Allen and Unwin.

UNDP. (2011). "Basic capabilities". From UNDP website [no longer accessible]. Retrieved February 2, 2017, from http://hdr.undp.org/en/humandev

UNICEF South Africa/Department of Social Development. (2012). *The South African Child Support Grant Impact Assessment: Evidence from a Survey of Children, Adolescents, and Their Households*. Pretoria: UNICEF South Africa.

Vearey, J. (2010). *The persistent urban challenges of migration and informal settlements in the context of HIV*. Doctoral thesis, University of the Witwatersrand, Johannesburg, South Africa.

Woolman, S. (2008). *Constitutional Law of South Africa* (2nd ed.). Cape Town: Juta Press.

World Health Organisation [WHO]. (1946). *Preamble to the Constitution of the World Health Organization*. [online]. Geneva: WHO. Retrieved June 2, 2017, from http://www.who.int/suggestions/faq/en/print.html

WHO. (1988). WHO: From Small Beginnings, Interview with Dr Szeming Sze. *World Health Forum, 9*, 29–34. Retrieved October 19, 2017, from http://apps.who.int/iris/bitstream/10665/46414/1/WHF_1988_9_1_p29-34.pdf

WHO. (2002). *The World Health Report, 2002: Reducing Risks, Promoting Healthy Life*. Geneva: WHO.

WHO. (2016d). *About the Global Burden of Disease (GBD) Project*. [online]. Geneva: WHO. Retrieved January 15, 2018, from http://www.who.int/healthinfo/global_burden_disease/about/en/

Yang, L. H., Kleinman, A., Link, B. G., Phelan, J. C., Lee, S., & Good, B. (2007). Culture and stigma: Adding moral experience to stigma theory. *Social Science & Medicine, 64*(7), 1524–1535.

Part II

Capabilities for Black South African Women: Gender as a Structural Health Determinant

5

Methodological Considerations and Research Methods to Advance Social Justice

In this chapter, I locate the work within a set of methodological considerations that directly inform social science understandings of the problem of HIV in black South African women. Such concerns also shape the HIV response, i.e., the ability of researchers and practitioners to use appropriate research methods to gain greater purchase on the high HIV incidence and HIV prevalence that have persisted in women despite the national response. I highlight the South African context at the time of the study's inception, and the rationale for selecting qualitative methods against a background of quantitative HIV studies that had long-dominated the published literature on cART and PMTCT in African women until fairly recently. I describe the strengths of qualitative research methods in health equity and social justice research generally, and in investigating women's capabilities to be healthy particularly. I discuss methods debates in the social health sciences; and review some of the ethical challenges introduced in studies such as this one. I also highlight the potential contribution of qualitative research methods to improving knowledge of health inequities in marginalised groups in ways that can be beneficial, both for researchers and participants.

C. Sprague, *Gender and HIV in South Africa*, Global Research in Gender, Sexuality and Health, https://doi.org/10.1057/978-1-137-55997-5_5

Context Setting

The research methods used in this work developed, evolved and are rooted within a specific time and geographical place, i.e., the high HIV prevalence setting of South Africa. The empirical research was designed in 2007 when HIV prevalence was an estimated 18% in the general South African population, and an estimated 30% in pregnant women, where it has remained (Government of South Africa, 2012; Shisana et al.; 2014; UNAIDS/WHO, 2008). At that time, fewer than 15% of HIV positive pregnant women were going forward for cART, as the single most important lifesaving intervention to arrest and manage HIV.

South Africa introduced a large-scale public sector HIV treatment programme, which was freely available in the public health system starting in mid-2004. This was earlier than most other African countries (with the exception of Botswana). Thus, at the time, little was known about individual, systems, structural and other barriers to HIV care confronting women (Sprague, 2009; Sprague, Chersich, & Black, 2011). Indeed, by 2007 I could find no published report or study with qualitative evidence that documented or engaged with HIV positive women's experiences, barriers, fears and anxieties in relation to taking HIV medication. This justified the selection of qualitative research methods applied here, with a focus on women's lived experiences in accessing HIV services within their social context and circumstances.

The period immediately following 2004 was a time of great urgency for HIV medication to be made available to South Africans living with HIV—then an estimated 5.7 million—who had been denied lifesaving drugs under the Mbeki administration (UNAIDS, 2005). In one study, Chigwedere, Seage, Gruskin, Lee, and Essex estimated that during the period that HIV medicines were deemed 'too expensive' by the government, over 330,000 South Africans died (2008). The devastating consequences for those individuals unable to benefit from treatment, and their families, are, however, incalculable.

In contrast with the LMICs, by the late 1990s, treatment had already become accessible for people living with HIV in the high-income countries. Survival rates and quality of life were improving markedly, made possible by the shift from a single drug, e.g., zidovudine (AZT), to highly active antiretroviral therapy (Walensky, Paltiel, & Losina, 2006). The medical advances associated with combination antiretroviral therapy heralded a radical shift. By enabling viral suppression in people living with the virus, HIV could be managed as a chronic condition (Broder, 2010). Wolffers highlights the dramatic results reported by a EuroSida study in 1998, where death rates in Europe due to HIV were less than one-fifth of those in 1995, stating '[m]uch of this improvement could be explained by the introduction of...combination therapy' (2000, p. 268). A resulting wave of optimism engulfed North America, Europe and Australia. However, in the developing countries, the situation differed markedly. Around the same time, UNAIDS issued a press release on World AIDS Day (1 December), reporting that 2.5 million people had died of AIDS-related causes in that year: 10% more HIV infections than the previous year, with 95% of those deaths occurring in LMICs. Wolffers observes that

> [t]he gap is seen by many as due largely to variations in the availability of medication. Though lack of access to medical treatment is one aspect of this gap, the main issue may be differences in the context of the epidemic and the most effective ways of dealing with it that follow from the context. (2000, p. 268)

Wolffers presciently identifies two simultaneous aspects that would come to define the global HIV epidemic and the accompanying response. First, the gap in treatment access between high-income and low- and middle-income settings turned on questions of equity. The ability of countries in the developing world to pay for expensive medications moved into sharp focus. Lifesaving medication for a deadly illness had become available, but *cui bono?*: who benefits from scientific progress? (Sprague, 2009; see Scanlon et al., 2017). Access to essential HIV medicines thus became the focal point of social justice campaigns waged in different locations around the world, but increasingly, as part of a larger global social justice movement. South African civil society, together with Brazil, Thailand, UN agencies and other actors, led the charge for treatment in the developing world (Heywood, 2009; Parker, 2003; Punpanich, Ungchusak, & Detels, 2004; Sprague & Woolman, 2006; Teixeira, 2003).

When Brazil ignored TRIPS (trade-related aspects of intellectual property rights) stipulations under the World Trade Organisation, announcing a universal HIV treatment programme for all those living with HIV, the HIV research and activist community were astounded (Rosenberg, 2001). In 1996, Brazil became the first developing country to treat people living with HIV through a publicly-funded programme (Teixeira, 2003). Moreover, the country defied objections, notably lodged by the World Bank, that HIV medications were too expensive and that adherence could not be achieved in a developing country (Parker, 2003). In a path-breaking move, Brazil introduced local manufacture of generic drugs to ensure a sustainable supply of ARVs. By moving so early in containing its burgeoning HIV epidemic, the country achieved astonishingly positive results in cutting hospital admissions, reducing AIDS deaths, preventing new HIV infections, all while maintaining good adherence (Marins et al., 2003; Sprague & Woolman, 2006). None of this was lost on the South Africans.

Second, Wolffers hints at the broader social context in countries, suggesting that perhaps treatment was only one piece—albeit a large one—in a much bigger puzzle. Nevertheless, a social justice response to HIV predicated on medical treatment would become a *leitmotif* of the global and the South African story. Following an extended social mobilisation campaign, combined with a series of successful court cases led by the Treatment Action Campaign, the AIDS Law Project and others, the country's social mobilisation for affordable treatment in the public health system met with a triumphant end. The South African Cabinet approved a national, state-funded HIV treatment programme to be established in the public health system in 2004 (Heywood, 2009). It was a moral victory, capping immensely difficult years, particularly as South African AIDS activists fought against the same individuals, now in positions in the new government, who had previously been their comrades during the struggle against apartheid (Power, 2003).

Treatment Action Campaign, Durban, July 2000

A protest march through the streets of Durban organised by the Treatment Action Campaign (TAC) during the 'Breaking the Silence' International AIDS Conference. The protesters were demanding free access to proper antiretroviral drug therapy for people with HIV or AIDS in South Africa and all other African countries. Source: Mendel (2001), image 34/35. Reprinted with permission

The end of the civil society campaign was just the beginning of the long years of implementation in an under-resourced public health system, however. With over five and a half million South Africans living with HIV then, most of whom required HIV medication, it was unclear how willing people would be to take ARVs, with their reported toxic side effects. Myths had circulated about the drugs being a plot of Western governments to kill Africans and the Government had strenuously denied a link between HIV and AIDS during the Mbeki administration, sowing some confusion among people (Power, 2003; Steinberg, 2008). During the period 2004–2009, comprising the first five years of the public sector treatment programme, researchers committed to removing barriers to lifesaving medication began to try to understand the impediments to accessing HIV treatment. While the urgency of the growing generalised HIV epidemic and lack of treatment galvanised the national research community, it also shaped the choice of our research designs and methods. Many senior scientists would make important contributions, nationally and internationally, to advancing understanding of varied dimensions of HIV that would inform the field (see Abdool Karim & Abdool Karim, 2005; Black et al., 2008; Campbell, 2003; Dickinson, 2009; Gilbert, 2012; on Gray and McIntyre, see Cohen, 2000; Preston-Whyte, 2003; and Jewkes, see bibliography).

Meanwhile, some of the junior HIV researchers were moving into the coalface to launch some of the first highly interdisciplinary applied social science HIV studies. Populations elected for research investigation, often as part of doctoral research, were marginalised and vulnerable, whether sex workers (Richter, 2013), migrants (Vearey, 2010), children (Chersich, 2007) or pregnant women (Sprague, 2009). The resulting studies focused on multi-level barriers to treatment, prevention, perceptions around and use of condoms, health behaviours and attitudes about taking treatment, sex preferences, gender, and health systems' barriers. Against this background, interdisciplinary approaches that could bridge the medical and social divides, and engage with multiple layers and levels of analysis, in social context, were essential.

Making Normative Social Justice Commitments in Research Designs and Methods

Given the imperatives of social transformation that were core to South Africa's new democracy, the long denial of medication for South Africans living with HIV, and the country's history of social mobilisation against oppression, HIV researchers in South Africa had been acculturated to concerns of equity and justice. Indeed, the social justice kernel likely attracted HIV researchers to the fold. While health became the new site of struggle in which to grapple with social injustice, the historical context fostered an HIV response in South Africa with treatment as a medical response to a problem of justice (Gilbert, 1995, 2012; Gilbert & Gilbert, 2004). Given the earliest cases of deep discrimination and social stigma attached to HIV across LMIC and HIC settings, it seems the disease was always located in the crosshairs of medicine and social justice. (For discussion of the US setting, see Bayer & Oppenheimer, 2000; Fauci, 2008; Shilts, 1988).

Against this backdrop, the interdisciplinary methods I employed to investigate the research problem have been situated similarly in these crosshairs. They can thus be located within applied social science research methods, used within South Africa, that are fully interdisciplinary and seek to engage with multi-centric concerns that radiate from HIV as a public health and social problem for socially disadvantaged, black women. In the South African context, researchers located their studies within a longer arc of social equity concerns that pre-existed, but were exacerbated by, HIV. Given the context, the research methods that were developed to investigate the virus might be different from other settings. Due to South Africa's history of injustice and the long march to democracy, there may also be greater confidence by researchers in South Africa [compared to some other settings) in the value of deploying normative social justice research methods to engage with inequities. The changes in the national South African discourse and understanding about HIV as a fully 'social epidemic' that is evident—not hidden—emerged over a number of years, with researchers continuing to adapt their research design and methods to better grasp how structural and social factors intersected with biomedical ones. Such interdisciplinary approaches are increasingly called for and used in different settings within the emerging field of global health, however, and they reflect an increasing socialisation within the health sciences (Frenk, Goméz-Dantas, & Chacón, 2011; Godoy-Ruiz, Cole, Lenters, & McKenzie, 2016).

Box 5.1 Socialising the health sciences

While research is generally defined as a systematic investigation of a well-defined concern that aims to contribute to knowledge (Frankfort-Nacmias, Nacmias, & DeWaard, 2014), research in the social health sciences is regarded as both a 'scientific and a social process' (Jacobsen, 2012, p. 5). That statement captures a principal strength of the social-scientific partnership that is implicit in the social health science paradigm, while hinting at their underlying tensions. The social health science marriage has been gaining ground. It is one fusing the health sciences' historical grounding—with one foot in the natural sciences and study of natural phenomena as they relate to health and disease (e.g., bodily systems, processes and cellular or immunological responses)—and the other planted in the social science investigation of the social world. This encompasses social factors, institutions and forces that shape the health of individuals and groups within society. Historically, the natural sciences and social sciences were largely bifurcated along two tracks. Today, though, the clear boundary that once separated them has been muddied, and some of the partitions dividing them have collapsed. The result is that today's health sciences have become increasingly 'social' even while they often retain a historical grounding in biomedicine, which introduces advantages and limitations in equal measure (Nass, Levit, & Gostin, 2009). This has of course happened along different trajectories and to varying degrees in diverse contexts.

The purpose of briefly highlighting this ground here is this: it is the possibilities these paradigms introduce for addressing complex health problems that, I argue, will either thwart or will transfigure the HIV research community's efforts to get to grips with the structural factors that foster black South African women's risk of acquiring HIV (Gupta, Parkhurst, Ogden, Aggleton, & Mahal, 2008; Parkhurst, 2014). As a research community, our ability to utilise possibilities for engaging with structural health determinants, like gender, depends, in part, on moving away from individualised HIV prevention efforts and the dominant biomedical paradigm long associated with HIV research (see Parkhurst, 2014; Piot, 2006).

Social Justice Research Methods for Social Transformation: The 'Hidden Power of Method'

Proponents of social justice research methods claim that it is through the *method* of engaging marginalised groups and communities—the interactive process of data collection—that change, and ultimately transformation, occurs. It is method that not only trains its lens to critically question *what is*, but it is through methods applied in the research investigation, the *how*, that the process of change can be enacted, not just by researchers, but by participants engaged in the research process. Just as the post-colonial and feminist epistemologies (i.e., the study of knowledge, including the nature, extent and sources of knowledge) recognise the 'knowing' authority of those in the margins to speak of marginalisation, as Tazreiter, Weber, Pickering, Segrave, and McKernan note, qualitative and mixed methodological approaches to social change recognise the 'hidden power of method' in this regard (2016, p. 20).

The transformative or emancipatory paradigm perspective contends that the advancement of social good occurs through the direct engagement of those who are marginalised in the research process (Marti & Mertens, 2014; Mertens, 2007, 2011; Tazreiter et al., 2016). Using method in this way means eliciting the view of the social world from those marginalised. Concentrating on capturing the voices of socially excluded individuals or groups during the research encounter may create opportunities for change on multiple levels, including for interviewer and interviewee (Tuhiwai Smith, 1999). I will take up these considerations over the course of the chapter.

This work utilises primarily qualitative methods to investigate the research problem as part of the empirical research study. Some of the merits and demerits of qualitative methods thus warrant brief discussion.

Qualitative Methods in HIV and Equity Research

Within South Africa and many other settings, there has been an historic, dominant influence of quantitative approaches to problems associated with public health and disease. These have had primacy in the published research literature as a longstanding trend. Indeed, the *British Medical Journal* (*The BMJ*) was recently taken to task for eschewing publication of qualitative research. The following rejection letter *The BMJ* editors sent to researchers from McGill was first tweeted and later published:

> Thank you for sending us your paper. We read it with interest but I am sorry to say that qualitative studies are an extremely low priority for *The BMJ*. Our research shows that they are not as widely accessed, downloaded or cited as other research. We receive over 8000 submissions a year and accept less than 4%. We do therefore have to make hard decisions on just how interesting an article will be to our general clinical readers, how much it adds, and how much practical value it will be. (quoted in Greenhalgh et al., 2016)

As a rejoinder, 76 senior academics, led by Greenhalgh et al. (2016) at Oxford University, collaborated on an open letter to the journal. They challenged *The BMJ* to develop a 'proactive, scholarly, and pluralist approach to research that aligns with its stated mission', with a formal policy on mixed methodology and qualitative research to become part of the explicit criteria for judging the merits of submissions (Greenhalgh et al., 2016, p. 3). At first the journal editors declined the invitation. This unleashed a storm of debate among researchers concerning the strengths and limits of quantitative, qualitative and mixed methods knowledge paradigms, and the perception of their value by journal editors and reviewers (Loder, 2016). To their credit, *The BMJ* editors published the letters, allowing the debate to unfold within the pages of the journal. Greenhalgh and colleagues' open letter was viewed over 32,000 times by January 2016, prompting the editors to reverse course. *The BMJ* subsequently announced they would be calling for qualitative expertise and review. (See Daniels et al.'s, 2016 call for fair publication of qualitative research in health systems.)

The BMJ example underscores the heated debates over epistemic difference concerning what types of research knowledge are given priority and are valued in the sciences and in societies. The debates raised by *The BMJ* debate ultimately led to researchers not only pointing to the critiques of qualitative research, of which there are many valid ones, but also illuminating its signature strengths.

Qualitative research methods are agreed to be suitable for research investigations into a web of complex relational individual, social and contextual factors that affect marginalised populations, particularly (Charmaz, 1999; Daniels et al., 2016; Popay & Graves, 2000; Sprague, Scanlon, & Pantalone, 2017b). Such methods are predicated on an inductive approach that allows the data to emerge without forcing participant responses into narrow tick box approaches (Ritchie & Lewis, 2012). Enquiries of a qualitative nature are often rooted within naturally-occurring settings (e.g., a local clinic) in order to position the investigation within locations where health or illness is experienced and also socially constructed. Context, timing and place become part of the setting as a direct source and key aspect of the study, like a character in a play or television show, similar to the way in which New York City was a character in television shows like *Seinfeld* and *Sex and the City*, and Johannesburg was the backdrop for *Egoli* ('City of Gold', laden with symbolic meaning). It is worth highlighting here, too, that a rural versus an urban setting can determine the opportunities, available choices and threats that shape daily interactions and experience, including opportunities to be healthy.

Qualitative approaches are also noteworthy for their use of a 'wide angle' or 'long lens' to gain in-depth perspective (Bogdan & Biklen, 2006). They often rely on interpretive description to explore and analyse underlying meanings and patterns of social behaviour (Neuman, 2007). As such, qualitative research is typically regarded as engaging with research phenomena through direct experience. The focus is on the meaning and beliefs attached by participants to illness, instead of the positivist concern with measurement ascribed to quantitative studies (Charmaz, 1999; Le Compte & Schenoul, 1999; Moustakas, 1994). From the research process, rather than testing a hypothesis, a picture 'emerges' of how participants describe their social world. The nature of the research process is thus flexible, adaptive and generative (Neuman, 2007; Robson, 1993).

The Internal

It must be recognised that health—or rather, illness—is an intimate concern, particularly for, in this research, black South African women affected by HIV. The threat of ill health has a kind of raw power for most people. A diagnosis of cancer, HIV or other illness reorders one's priorities fairly quickly, and can itself be life changing by introducing the spectre of death (Kalanithi, 2016). Pregnant or postpartum women are primed to pay attention to health concerns that affect them and their infants. A positive

HIV test result thus sparks high emotion in this population, bringing with it the anxiety of uncertainty, confusion, fear of being robbed of good health and the effects of this on their children. Qualitative health research allows for a curtain to be drawn back, and a view of the very interior of people's lives, or what is referred to as the 'internal', to be seen by the researcher. Kleinman suggests that it is such intimate experience that represents the flow of 'everyday actions in a local world' where participants are absorbed in certain things 'that…matter greatly' (2004, pp. 269–270). Local worlds, he emphasises, are 'the grounds of human lives'. In highlighting the moral dimension of this social experience, daily life is rendered onto a larger canvas of concerns where local concerns intersect with universal ones—sickness, struggle and mortality—and with resilience and strength too. Kleinman writes:

> The moral is defined by local processes concerning lived values that are at stake… Among the things that matter are…threats to local practices and values. (2004, p. 270)

The special contribution of qualitative research lies in its ability to 'go deep' to access this interior world and to connect the local lived or *emic* (in contrast to *etic*) experiences to sociocultural processes and practices, rooted in societies—some of which may foster ill health in women: IPV for instance (Farmer, 1992). To collect data that will engage and uncover the internal requires deliberate design and methods choices. Sen writes about the selection of data collection techniques in this way:

> in getting a grip on what counts as illness, how it arises and how healing can be done, any kind of exclusive reliance on externally observed clinical symptoms and remedial connections cannot but be at least partly deceptive. (2004, p. 265)

He characterises the complexity underlying the choice of data collection technique in this manner:

> If 'illness and pain are rooted in the person' then the kind of detached statistic on which economists and medical statisticians frequently rely may have to be very seriously supplemented by more involved scrutiny of how people comprehend [illness]. (2004, pp. 263–264)

Sen points to the limitations of methods that fail to engage study participants and fail to tap their interior worlds. He reminds us that when researchers are seeking to investigate health inequities, the 'relative simplicity of easily measurable statistics, the form of data emerging from external observations...is not a good enough reason to opt in that direction' (2004b, p. 264). Here Sen is referring to surveys and their limitations in capturing the internal perspective. To wit, Carrotte et al. (2016) published an article, rather cheekily titled, '*I am yet to encounter any survey that actually reflects my life*'.

Researchers can employ qualitative in-depth interviews (IDIs) as a vehicle by which to gain access to thick and rich descriptions that depict lived experience. Here I would emphasise the importance of interviews as a specific qualitative research technique for doing so, particularly the collection of narratives from research participants (Narratives are long associated with social science research methods across different fields, see Bertaux, 1981.)

In health equity research, narratives can be a crucial part of untangling the web of processes that result in systematic health differences between groups, and poor health among marginalised groups (Popay & Graves, 2000). The storytelling aspect within narrative approaches can serve as a tool that amplifies the voice of participants, while extending them agency that is often less accessible to them, particularly when the illness or health experience of participants is stigmatised and concealed from others, as is typical with HIV and IPV. The storytelling aspect can assist researchers in uncovering nuance by creating the opportunity to probe the interactive dimensions that affect women's agency in familial and social context (Wang & Geale, 2015). In this manner, through qualitative in-depth interviews, researchers explore and interpret the meaning participants ascribe to events, as well as temporal, contextual, familial and situational factors (Denzin & Lincoln, 2011) that influence the content and consequences of those events in the participants' lives.[1]

The External

Nevertheless, even as researchers elect qualitative methods for its advantages in capturing the internal view, they recognise it has limitations. The internal is, by definition, subjective. It has a necessary counterpoint, however: the external. This implies 'external' to the study participant. In health equity studies like this one, dangers lurk in emphasising one approach to the exclusion of others, and researchers must be cognisant of these traps. Sen observes:

> Judgments of health equity as well as aggregate achievements in health care are inescapably dependent on the *assessment* of individual states of health… there is a conceptual contrast between the 'internal' view of health, as seen by the person in question, and the 'external' views that others may take of the person's state of health. (2004b, p. 263)

In health equity research, if researchers want to enact changes that improve health, the internal and the external are both important to capture. Sen reminds us that each serves a purpose. What is to be avoided, he emphasises, is 'the narrowness and limitation of choosing either the internal *or* the external' (p. 268). In determining an optimal approach, the answer we come to is not one or the other but both (2004b, p. 264)[2]

To supplement the internal in this study, it was necessary to gain insight into external perspectives. The participants, women living with HIV, were enmeshed in a set of social-structural processes that needed further excavation to become more visible, particularly in relation to gender. Gaining this view meant investigating relational aspects and institutions, encompassing the health system and health providers, social structures (including the household), and social norms and processes. To do so, I drew on multiple, independent data sources, highlighted in Tables 5.1 and 5.2, presented and discussed in the next section.

Electing Qualitative Design and Methods in cART Research on South African Women Living with HIV

cART/PMTCT research on pregnant women was, at the time of the field research, wholly characterised by a quantitative approach and focus, primarily on the PMTCT 'cascade'. The cascade refers to the risk of HIV transmission to the child as the mother proceeds through each stage in

Table 5.1 Data collection techniques and sites

Techniques	Sites	Number
In-Depth Interviews		
Participants: HIV positive women (pregnant or postpartum)	1. Eastern Cape: Peri-urban 2. Johannesburg: Urban Facilities (4): Public clinic (1), Public hospitals (3); Ward types (4): antenatal care, maternity, postnatal, and paediatric	**89**
	Type and location	**Number**
Key informants of two types: (a) Health providers within health facilities	Physicians, nurses, health professionals: interviewed in same sites and facilities as above	**20**
(b) Key experts, e.g., in gender, health, human rights, maternal health, HIV	Academics in health, gender and social policy, research agencies (MRC, HSRC) Interviewed in office locations, cafes with one by skype	**24**
Total		**133**
Supplementary Data Collection		
Medical file of each patient	Viewed on-site in clinics and hospitals	
Digital recordings	All interviews were recorded except for 41 participants who declined	
Record of interviews (ROIs)	ROIs were distinctive points that emerged about participant or key informant stories related to capabilities	
Field notes	Theorising about ideas and relationships across interviews and data	
Participant observation	Observations in health facilities, procedures, the flow of patients through queues, services and patterns in the facilities, patient-health provider encounters and about reflexivity	

the continuum of HIV services. Typically, the cascade serves to map variable risk as HIV services drop off and the risk of maternal HIV transmission to the child increases. (For more on the cascade, see Gimbel et al., 2016; Rawizza et al., 2015.) This approach has placed the focus on child health and preventing paediatric HIV. While child health is undoubtedly

Table 5.2 Data sources for analyses

Research articles and related literature:	Refereed journal articles, including systematic reviews, conference abstracts, research presentations
Policy documents and reports:	Grey literature, Dept of Health documents, posters, guidelines (press releases, NSP, SANAC and NGO reports)
National health data sources:	DHIS, ANC prevalence surveys; HSRC HIV surveys; HIV household surveys; STATS SA; Saving Mothers reports; SANAC reports; NSP reports; DoH reports, including MCH and PMTCT strategies; Dept of Social Development, StatsSA, South Africa Every Death Counts, MRC Burden of Disease Research Unit
International health and HIV data, including those referencing South Africa	UNAIDS, WHO, UNICEF reports, statistics, trends, and guidelines
Law, legal sources, legal analyses and social policies	Bill of Rights, 1996 Constitution, Constitutional Court judgments, Wits Centre for Applied Legal Studies
	Books, journal articles, systematic reviews, narrative or thematic reviews; STRIVE data and reports (LSTHM), MRC 'What Works' to Prevent Violence (funded by DFID/UKAID), Data and reports from the MRC Gender and Health Unit, brochures, pamphlets

important, women's health is equally so. The fact that women should be viewed as agents, apart from their role as child bearers, should be stating the obvious. However, this is not the lived reality for the many women, worldwide, whose health is neglected (Kabira et al., 1997; Langer et al., 2015). This is particularly so for women in sub-Saharan Africa who have some of the worst health outcomes globally (Hogan et al., 2010; Tinker, 2000; WHO, 2014b). In the absence of qualitative research, I thus elected qualitative design and methods to shed light on this research concern.

Although studies and published literature link cART for pregnant and postpartum women closely with PMTCT, the distinct focus of this investigation was on women's health, in contrast with maternal or child health. It also encompassed women's capabilities. That included probing HIV positive black South African women's process and opportunity freedoms within the context of their 'social world'; their agency (the range of agentic desires to actions); their lived experiences of being HIV positive and of seeking care; and their reported experiences in relation to Nussbaum's central capabilities.

The ethical protocol for the study was constructed over a nine-month period. I navigated questions about access to clinics and the population, appropriate sites and locations, ethical responsibilities and protection for a vulnerable population of HIV positive women, participant recruitment and related, and sought multiple permissions. Ethics approval for the study was received from the University of the Witwatersrand (M080119), the University of Massachusetts Boston (2013133), Walter Sisulu University, and the provincial departments of health in Gauteng and the Eastern Cape.

Study Setting and Methods

Data collection and analyses were undertaken over two time periods. In-depth interviews with 89 study participants (women living with HIV) and 20 health providers (encompassing nurses, doctors, HIV counsellors and social workers) were conducted in two geographic locations and four public health facilities, and were supplemented with 24 key informant interviews, over the periods 2008–2009 and 2014–2016 (Table 5.1). The rationale for the second time period was to collect another round of data in order to consider women's capabilities in light of the array of economic, social and political changes in society and in health systems' operational delivery of cART and PMTCT. In other words, to update and capture more recent data and analyses from women living with HIV and from key informants.

The research took place in the largest city in Gauteng province, and one of the largest cities in the Eastern Cape. Johannesburg, which occupies the northern part of South Africa quite close to Botswana to the west and Swaziland to the east, was chosen for its urban location. The Eastern Cape location, situated 400km from Durban on the southeast coast and approximately 230 km from East London, was elected for its less-resourced environment. The goal in the Eastern Cape was to recruit and engage women in interviews who were from predominantly rural or peri-urban areas, where women had to travel longer distances to seek HIV services. Additional socio-demographic information by province is provided in Chap. 6.

Sites and Sampling Procedures

One public hospital in central Johannesburg served as the key research site. As a tertiary hospital, it provided the array of HIV services at a single site: antenatal care including HIV testing, cART initiation, maternal delivery, postnatal (or postpartum) care, and paediatric care (including infant HIV testing). However, points in the HIV care continuum were located in different wards (antenatal, postnatal, maternity, labour and paediatric wards).

In contrast, in the Eastern Cape, interviews were conducted in three public health facilities: two main public hospitals and one clinic. The two hospitals were linked, were on the same grounds adjacent to one another, shared resources (such as a photocopier), and were managed by one CEO. Only one of the two hospitals offered the full range of care: ANC, cART initiation, maternal delivery, postnatal care, and paediatric HIV treatment and care. The health clinic provided antenatal care, postnatal care, and HIV testing, counselling, treatment and provision of ARV prophylaxis to the child, as part of antenatal HIV care, but did not perform maternal deliveries (women delivered in the nearby hospitals). The clinic was located roughly four kilometres from the two public hospitals.

To gain differing external perspectives on HIV care provision, barriers and enablers for pregnant and postpartum women, as well as the policy and structural environment, I conducted in-depth interviews with three types of interviewees, collecting and using multiple data sources, to allow for triangulation. Triangulation is defined as mixing two or more types of data in order to obtain distinct, independent views on the concern being studied. It is viewed as a form of data validation that introduces greater rigour into qualitative studies (Olsen, Holborn, & Haralambos, 2004). Engaging with different stakeholders and relying on a range of sources enabled me to verify emerging patterns from the findings, thus overcoming potential bias or misinterpretation; it also generated in-depth understanding of this complex social phenomenon (Denzin & Lincoln, 2011).

All participants and key informants were identified using purposive sampling (Ritchie & Lewis, 2012); other sampling methods employed are noted below. Initial access to clinics occurred through the intervention of colleagues who were medical doctors working in local research entities that were affiliated with the sites.

Study Population—Black Women Participants Living with HIV

Recruitment of participants occurred with the assistance of nurses, lay counsellors and doctors, i.e., health providers. Women who met the eligibility criteria were recruited, e.g., women who: (1) had verbally agreed to be interviewed; (2) were aged 20 and older; (3) were pregnant or had given birth within the previous four months; and (4) had cART and PMTCT indicated in their patient file. (This meant that health providers had confirmed participants' HIV status and treatment had been recommended though perhaps not initiated).

Women's experiences of care were set against a backdrop of a changing health system. Women had to navigate points of care across different wards and sometimes different physical locations as part of the HIV care continuum for pregnant and postpartum women (discussed in Chap. 3). To do so, they had to engage with health providers. Providers would guide them operationally through the continuum of HIV prevention and care, and emotionally, through provision of psychological support (Sprague, 2009). Key to the study, then, was depicting what took place in those 'health encounters' with providers, which influenced women's care, health behaviours and their attitudes to HIV.

Key Informants (a): Health Providers with Knowledge of the Study Population

In-depth interviews, using semi-structured question guides, were conducted over the same time periods with 20 health providers, who were selected due to their work with women patients as part of antenatal care/

labour/delivery/maternity care/PMTCT programmes. Providers were located in the same facilities as the women participants seeking HIV services and were interviewed in the health system. Additional health providers were recruited on-site with the assistance of head nurses in the wards, as part of snowball sampling. These key informants had a view of women's health needs, their behaviours, and insights into the service delivery taking place in their facility, as well as having a perspective on the role and effectiveness of other health providers in providing HIV services, and operational health systems' constraints to HIV care.

Significantly, nurses, lay counsellors and social workers typically came from the same communities as women patients (although nurses would have secure employment and higher social status compared to their patients). This group of health providers thus had quite intimate knowledge of the challenges women faced; and of accepted sociocultural norms in families and communities, and gendered expectations of women. Interviews were based on a semi-structured guide tailored to the knowledge of this group, and focused on teasing out their insights along key capability domains (described in Chap. 6).

Key Informants (b): Subject Experts in Relevant Research and Policy Domains

Using purposive sampling, I interviewed 24 high level key informants who were experts in HIV, gender, women's health, sexual and reproductive health and rights, maternal health, maternal HIV, health services and systems, health policy, HIV interventions, social policy, constitutional law, human rights (right to health, substantive equality, protection from domestic or intimate partner violence), feminism, and violence against women. These interviews focused on the policy framework and policy response, as well as the translation of research into practice to support women's health and their capabilities. Interviews were based on a semi-structured guide customised to this group. Interviews with expert key informants took place in various office locations, with one interview taking place by phone and another on Skype.

I supplemented the primary interview data for each group with a typed record of each interview that had women's answers on specific capabilities questions; field observations for all respondents; and digital recordings for all but 41 respondents who declined consent for recording across all categories of IDIs (Denzin & Lincoln, 2011; Robson, 1993). In total, 133 in-depth interviews were conducted. Table 5.1 shows the distribution.

The majority of participant interviews took place in English and lasted 45 minutes on average. The question guide allowed for probing the following areas: women's socio-demographic and economic characteristics; perceptions of health and perceptions of support (including with HIV disclosure/adherence) from family/partners/friends; experience with the health system: HIV testing, counselling and follow up; experience discussing health with health providers; knowledge and beliefs about cART and PMTCT; availability, access to and uptake of cART and PMTCT, (including barriers and enablers); other aspects of living with HIV, including psycho-social aspects: stress, fear, anxiety, factors influencing mental health and coping.

Note that these semi-structured questions were an initial point of entry to probe much more deeply into the spectrum of women's experiences and their capabilities. Each participant was given a sandwich or muffin and cold drink. Sometimes the interview would begin in English and the participant and I would quickly ascertain that our communication was not optimal. In those cases, I called in a colleague to assist with the translation. The translators, two women and one man, were post-graduate students or researchers with great interest in HIV in women. All were black South Africans: two were from the Eastern Cape and one was from Gauteng. These colleagues were highly attuned to local sociocultural dynamics and processes, including gender norms and constructions, as well as HIV myths and stigma. I trained each person in qualitative methods and in the interview and ethics protocol we used. Working together, the translators and I would revert to isiXhosa in the Eastern Cape or isiZulu in Gauteng (the dominant language in each location), in accordance with the preference of the interviewee. I made use of simultaneous translation in the interviews (e.g., the translator asked the women questions and then back translated them into English immediately, so that I could ask for probes and prompts). We did this in a supportive way so that participants knew we cared about their health and their experiences, and were taking the time to capture important details.

As part of ensuring the quality and the reliability of the qualitative data, I was concerned about perceptions of participants and concerns about their trust in me as a foreigner (i.e., to disclose intimate details about their health and lives). Due to the back translation in interviews, I was present during almost all interviews and was able to directly observe potential threats to the credibility of the data, such as social desirability (Ritchie & Lewis, 2012). I debriefed with colleagues to inquire about this, and discarded six interviews where I knew that women were not being open. I also kept a Likert scale in the record of interview, indicating my perception of the level of trustworthiness associated with each participant interview (the level of trustworthiness is based on the degree to which thick and rich narrative accounts were forthcoming; see Anfara, Brown, & Mangione, 2002; Denzin & Lincoln, 2011). I repeated this practice with the key informants.

Because I participated in almost all of the interviews, I could navigate ethical dilemmas that arose, such as linking women manifesting signs of distress to HIV counsellors on-site, and not proceeding with interviews when women appeared fearful or doubtful. (Ethical concerns are discussed in greater detail shortly.). I worked with the translators to discuss patterns in the health system and among patients. As we sought to ascertain events and experiences—typically because of the chaotic nature of the health system—these could be somewhat puzzling (discussed further below and in Chap. 6). In the debriefings with the colleagues translating, we agreed that the women seemed to like, and even relish, the rare opportunity to share their stories and to engage with us about their health (Dickson-Swift, James, Kippen, & Liamputtong, 2007). Working with translators also served as a form of peer evaluation later (Denzin & Lincoln, 2011). There was thus a strong two-way learning process taking place between the translators and me: we learnt from one another. They were building research capacity and I was developing cultural acumen. This underscores the importance and value of working in research teams, which is typically the case in many health science research studies, and in culturally appropriate ways.

Data Management and Analysis

Data, both transcriptions and coding, were managed using Microsoft Excel and Microsoft Word, within an encrypted password protected computer. Code numbers were assigned to participants and key informants. Open coding and then narrative analysis was used to identify the dominant themes. Initial dominant themes were based on a coding structure that emerged from the interviews. Primary themes were constructed from the accounts across the interviews. Attention was paid to relative importance, frequency and consistency across the narratives. I refined the emerging themes in an iterative fashion over many months, constantly returning to the transcripts and to my participant observation and field notes to compare and contrast the coding framework with these other documents (called constant comparative analysis) (Anfara et al., 2002). As part of a long, laborious process of working through the data collected, I revised and refined, revised and refined, working out the analysis, iteratively, over many months as the themes began to take shape and were verified by continual return to the transcriptions. Over time, the analysis yielded a set of patterns and narrative quotations that supported the analytical themes (presented in Chap. 6) (Charmaz, 1999; Ritchie & Lewis, 2012).

Challenges and Responsibilities in the Research Process

Kleinman suggests that 'the relationship between the moral and the ethical should be at the heart of efforts on behalf of health equity' (2004, p. 271). If working with vulnerable populations to gain access to their interior worlds has value in bringing those voices into the knowledge domain in health equity research, it also introduces a set of challenges, risks and responsibilities for the researcher. This includes managing the quality of the research process, potential bias, acknowledging the researcher's positionality, practising reflexivity, establishing quality control checks and means of verification, while managing ethical dilemmas. Essential to ensuring the quality of qualitative research is recognising and taking steps to minimise bias. Bias can be avoided at the design stage by ensuring that there is no pre-determined outcome or agenda to the study, including conflicts of interest. Ensuring that high quality qualitative data are collected is also made possible by the construction of question guides that do not lead participants towards specific answers, but allow them the space to reflect and respond naturally. Another crucial aspect in addressing the reliability of qualitative data is continuous engagement in self-reflexivity, including recognising one's positionality and how it might affect the data being collected.

In terms of my positionality, I was not an indigenous person speaking on behalf of my community (an insider) (Alcoff, 1994). I was an outsider-insider, which afforded me certain advantages in winning trust, but also created challenges. As a white woman but not a white South African, I had some distance from any negative associations or stereotypes attributed by black South Africans to their white counterparts (Bozzoli & Nkotsoe, 1991; Rabe, 2003). My accent was strange to people, though my university, Wits University, was local and identifiable, which likely gave people comfort in the familiar. I had been working either on or in South Africa since 1999, which constituted a formative period of building knowledge of sociocultural dynamics, prior to the first set of interviews in clinical settings, which I then built on in the succeeding years. As a university-based academic, deeply entrenched in various teaching and research roles, I was part of a growing HIV community of researcher-academic-professional-activists. I worked with, and under the guidance of, South Africans. I was able to access patients by relying on partnerships with colleagues who were medical doctors or researchers working in the public health system, deeply engaged in the rollout of ARVs and in treating patients with HIV, particularly my long-time colleague, Vivian Black, a maternal HIV doctor who established the first maternal HIV clinic in Johannesburg.

To sharpen my skills and abilities in order to establish trust, I took other steps along the way: I used my body language, my words, tone of voice, my listening skills, conversational isiZulu, isiXhosa (read: very rudimentary), and drew on a reservoir of empathy to bridge the perceived divides of race, class and education, and to enter the local world of participants. It is worth noting, too, that I did not see HIV as something *out there*. HIV was part of my own local world: I have had a family member living with HIV since the early 1990s. My experience may have been different to participants but in this way the epidemic connected, rather than divided; it allowed for a bridge.

Quality control checks can be introduced in the data collection stage by engaging regularly in self-reflexivity, i.e., routinely reflecting on whether trustworthiness is being achieved in the conduct of interviews, recognising the signs of social desirability (also called reactivity), where participants may tell you what they think you want to hear. In this way, researchers have to be willing to look for those signs, and to make changes in questions and dynamics that might negatively influence the quality of the data being gathered (Kuehner, Ploder, & Langer, 2016). During the interviews, I had to be willing to step aside if I felt I was not getting thick and rich high quality data, e.g., if my personal characteristics were not instilling trust in participants and I was willing to do so, though this was not necessary.[3] I employed controls for credibility (reliability, in quantitative language), such as cross-verification of member accounts with other researchers in the field and validation with key informants and researchers with knowledge of participants' characteristics and behaviours as a proxy form of member checking (Denzin & Lincoln, 2011; Ritchie & Lewis, 2012).

Navigating Ethical Dimensions

Across study types, ethical considerations typically encompass: respect for (the dignity of) each person; beneficence (do no harm); and justice (who benefits from the research and who bears its burdens?) (Cox & McDonald, 2013; Kingori, 2013). Those are merely the entry point, however. In the field, the actual ethics that emerge 'on the ground' are diverse and have different layers and dimensions. Indeed, Heimer fittingly calls these 'wicked ethics' (2013).

For researchers in the social health sciences who investigate justice and equity concerns for individuals or groups pushed to the margins of society, ethical issues are rooted in the study's conception. These span questions about whom we choose to study and how we choose to do so; to issues of dissemination and beyond, e.g., what happens to the data; and who benefits from the research undertaken? This is the ethical 'accountability' implication of social science research, i.e., that public research funds should be used in ways that tackle the most pressing social problems. As Marti and Mertens observe, '[i]n a context of scarcity of resources… [c]itizens and societies need to see in which ways social science research is contributing to improve their lives and communities' (2014, p. 207).

An added challenge requiring active, careful management was the potential coercion of participants during the empirical research. This is the case particularly in IDIs, when conversations engage study participants selected to participate because they are marginalised or vulnerable (Liamputtong, 2006). The underlying power dynamics between researchers and the researched and other differences in gender, race, class and language need to be recognised and managed appropriately. Researchers under tight timelines to collect data in the field should not be pushing for more participant interviews, responses or disclosures. At times this threat comes not from the researcher, but from those involved in participant recruitment (i.e., health providers often do a first check that the participant meets eligibility criteria and the researcher verifies prior to seeking informed consent). For example, in this study, a number of times the nurses instructed me and the translators to interview women who had given birth several hours before, and to do so at their bedsides. In several cases, we quickly ascertained that those women, eyes filled with exhaustion and sheets stained with blood, were in no position to freely consent to be interviewed. We scurried away to leave the women in peace, whispering apologies over our shoulders as we hastily retreated from the hospital room. This example underscores that the ethical researcher has to find her own ethical footing amid a landscape strewn with potential traps and even landmines.

In addition, attention needs to be paid to the careful management of participants' disclosures and potential distress and how they would be managed during the research process. In studies of a sensitive nature, including HIV and violence studies, participants may recall stressful and even traumatic situations. Indeed, many women described learning they had received a positive HIV test result as a shocking, life-altering event, and I had to manage women's fresh responses (e.g., a woman could have learnt she was HIV positive for the first time the same morning I interviewed her), while determining whether any next steps for additional psychosocial support were needed (women were meant to receive routine post-test HIV counselling in the health system).

These realities require that any researcher entering into an in-depth 'engagement' with participants must have adequate preparation to manage these disclosures, and it may also require possession of a set of characteristics, and possibly even a disposition, which may be different than for other types of research (Liamputtong, 2006). Knowing how to deal with distress, when and how to link study participants to psychosocial support and when referral for clinical treatment is required. Understanding our obligations therein is *de rigueur*. However, managing the unique ethical aspects that emerge on the spot, and they always do, is a constant task, and there is no textbook for the ethical conundrums that emerge. Training, supervision, mentorship and guidance of researchers is all essential. Ultimately, one learns and is schooled in the field through repeated experience and management of these ethical concerns, and efforts to understand and to meet the ethics of obligation that go beyond published guidelines (Dickson-Swift et al., 2007). Researchers must be aware of and recognise that 'ethical discourse' is generated 'out of and applied in local worlds' that are part of local conditions and 'taken up on moral processes'; these are aspects of what is most 'at stake' for individuals (Kleinman, 2004, p. 270).

While the 'do no harm' principle remains for the researcher to uphold, it is merely a departure point—a sign posted at the edge of the shore before diving into the participant interview. It is in the interview that the participant, through an act of blind faith, chooses to entrust her story to the researcher. This becomes an invitation, a dance, and one executed by the researcher with care, with deft skill. The researcher must practise empathic listening, probing, clarifying, speaking when necessary, even while 'holding' the person's story and journey with attention, gingerly, with dignity and respect: perhaps with the same care with which you would hold a butterfly that has alighted onto your palm.

While HIV is becoming a chronic condition today, for many it remains a stigmatised way of life. Thus, sharing one's health status and personal experiences with strangers seated on the other side of a table in a hospital or clinic remains an act of untold trust. This compact creates an awesome responsibility on the part of the research community, as we are forced to make sense of seemingly incomprehensible realities. Interviewing became a way of witnessing suffering: an act of documentation; of holding the woman's truth; of recognising and acknowledging suffering and sorrow; while lending the woman dignity by containing and acknowledging her experience. At times, the moral, ethical world would require us to bear witness to the indescribable.

For example, during the research interviews, women were often most distressed about their infants' health. We observed the indomitable strength of the woman who held up her tiny infant who had contracted HIV. Lavishing affection on him, she told us that he survived four hospital admissions for TB, pneumonia and three blood transfusions—all before he was nine months of age. One young woman had three children who died (stillbirths and a drowning). She said she was hoping, as she patted her pregnant tummy, that this one would be healthy. She relayed all this with calm courage. When one participant's baby was given the paediatric test for HIV, and determined to be HIV negative, the mother beamed with joy. In that instant, we researchers could see the depth of her emotion. The anxiety, converted into obvious relief, was written on the face of that earnest woman who was unspooling her story to two strangers. As we gently tried to hold the threads of her narrative together, we researchers were not inert objects sitting on our chairs like slabs of stone. 'One eye sees, the other feels' as Klee once wrote (1968). In those moments, we cast off our cloaks of professional distance, adding our exuberant exclamations of 'congratulations!'. After the interview, my colleague translating turned to me, wanting I think, to continue to hold onto that golden moment of sheer possibility, exclaiming: 'One new HIV infection averted today!' Extending my hand upwards to him for a high-five, a wide grin taking over my face, I replied with an equally jubilant, 'Yes!'.

In this way, qualitative research allows for entering into the participants' journey, to accompany them where they have been, and to listen to what they have felt and experienced. In an interview setting, this dialogue means that the interview itself is a dynamic process of engagement, of interaction. It means that the participant, through an unfolding of their narrative, will take the interviewer through a passage that gives entry into her interior world. Here, equity and ethics converge in powerful ways and both the interviewer and interviewee may be altered. The process of taking part in such research can be an act of change, for the participant and for the interviewers (Lincoln & Guba, 1985; Mertens, 2007, 2011). Through the interview process, the participant and the researcher have crossed a threshold, arriving at a new destination together. There is even the possibility, a glimpse of, new hope and even a new world.

In these situations, where we researchers may be perceived as the 'other', we draw on our common humanity to construct a bridge that will transport us past differences in language, culture and experience to a safe place—where time, place, urgency, the hurly burly of life are paused. My colleagues who translated and I worked to create this place for the women we interviewed to speak freely. The safe landing we erected was firmly rooted in the South African concept of *ubuntu*, which translates roughly as 'I am because you are'. It is at once an expression of our universal profound shared humanity and a representation of communal values in South Africa. It was rare for women to be engaged in this way, and while they spoke, we wanted them to feel that time was suspended and that nothing was more important than them and their story in that moment. This had the quality of what T.S. Eliot describes as 'the still point of the turning world' (1971).

In terms of benefits and risks, findings from a range of research studies on the effects of research participation, regardless of gender, also reveal that the majority of participants report important benefits when they take part, with no greater risk of re-traumatisation or re-victimisation. Nonetheless, participation in sensitive research, where participants discuss aspects of violence or abuse, can never take the place of clinical treatment, whether for trauma, depression or HIV (Decker, Naugle, Carter-Visscher, Bell, & Seifert, 2011; Disch, 2001). For researchers, there are also risks of secondary or vicarious trauma as stories of abuse, neglect, and violence emerge (McCann & Pearlman, 1989). The research community has noted the need for training, breaks and support to mitigate the effects of vicarious trauma (Sexual Violence Research Initiative, 2015).

In concluding this chapter, this work exemplifies how social health science research methods have shifted to take on health and social justice concerns that are complex, interdisciplinary and global in magnitude (Crenshaw, 1989). It is in the teeth of transnational health threats like HIV that the nature of scientific inquiry, the questions we ask, and the research methods we use to answer them, have been refashioned. In South Africa, these have been rooted in the recognition that human dignity and equality needed to be reclaimed against a background of government policies that undermined hard-won constitutional principles of the new democracy (Heywood, 2003, 2009; Woolman, 2008). HIV was only the newest chapter in a long history of social inequities experienced by black South Africans. The South African methodological story is thus one about a national HIV research community that developed a responsive research agenda to engage and take on HIV as a pressing justice concern in fresh and innovative ways and in a manner compatible with agreed understandings that forms of social oppression would be contested in the new South Africa. The process of social transformation thus extends to the research domain as a site in which to engage with problems of equity. Social transformation is catalysed, not only in what we choose to study, i.e., HIV as a problem of social justice, but in the methods by which we investigate inequities, using normative approaches to equity, such as through the Capabilities Approach. Social transformation can be further embedded in research designs and methods that explicitly embrace normative social justice commitments, and that allow for dynamics of change to co-occur within the research encounter (Tazreiter et al., 2016). Qualitative research methods are recognised as particularly skilful in engaging within and across multiple levels and inter-linked factors in ways that assist in illuminating social processes and structures that shape health inequities for specific populations (Campbell & Mannell, 2016; Popay & Graves, 2000). Qualitative research methods, particularly through narrative accounts, also afford participants' greater agency in sharing their experiences, and making sense of life events, during the research process (Wang & Geale, 2015). The benefits of using such methods can be bidirectional for researchers and participants (Tazreiter et al., 2016).

Finally, research enquiries like this one, and others that use qualitative or mixed methods approaches that embed a normative commitment to equity, recognise that entering into the lived experience of socially marginalised individuals does not weaken the research lens and analysis of researchers. On the contrary, it strengthens it. As positioned subjects within the research process, researchers are able to document deprivations and rights violations, while witnessing the rich dimensions of social experience. Through this engagement, researchers can better investigate the complex processes underlying health inequities, while recognising that pain and suffering are universal threads that connect individuals to one another, as understood by the South African notion of *ubuntu*. Researchers are stakeholders enmeshed in the social hierarchy who play a role in reconstructing dominant social and gender norms. Researchers are in a position to advance social change on multiple levels: by shaping the research agenda, influencing what knowledge is valued in societies, and taking agentic action to advance health equity and social change within the social and institutional structures they occupy.

Notes

1. Research methods that engage marginalised groups of women are increasingly encouraged to be gender-responsive. For instance, research undertaken in the US on gender-responsive data collection involving previously incarcerated women found that women place a high value on relationships, and that data collection involving women should employ relational approaches where researchers can engage with participants face to face, through in-depth interviews (Staton-Tindall, n.d.).
2. One brief example may be illustrative of the value of collecting independent sources to unravel the complexity of the patient experience of seeking care in the labyrinthine public health system. When I interviewed one participant, she told me that she was turned away at one clinic, and she thought it might be because she was HIV positive, i.e., she thought she was being stigmatised. However, when I interviewed the health providers, they described strategies they used to manage the high patient load (evident in the long queues and innumerable patients to attend to). In providers' descriptions, they explained that turning patients away and telling them to go to a different, neighbouring clinic was one strategy they employed to manage the patient demand. These strategies emerged in

more than one health provider interview. In this case the patient attributes the health provider's actions to HIV stigma when, in fact, they seemed to be attributed to health providers' coping strategies.

3. This became a source of worry in the field research. When I first arrived in the Eastern Cape, one researcher (a nurse) shared a disturbing anecdote with me. She explained that she had provided translation for an American researcher. When the Eastern Cape colleague interviewed the participants in Xhosa, the American researcher was present in the interviews. The participants would explain their experience with the health system and they would insist: 'But don't tell the white woman that!' After hearing this, I became worried that I might face the same difficulty. I told the translators to watch for this, and if it occurred, to let me know immediately after the interview. Thankfully, it never occurred.

References

Abdool Karim, S., & Abdool Karim, Q. (Eds.). (2005). *HIV/AIDS in South Africa*. Cambridge: Cambridge University Press.

Alcoff, L. (1994). The problem of speaking for others. In S. Weisser & J. Fleischner (Eds.), *Feminist Nightmares: Women at Odds: Feminism and the Problem of Sisterhood* (pp. 285–309). New York: New York University Press.

Anfara, V., Brown, K., & Mangione, T. (2002). Qualitative analysis on stage: Making the research process more public. *Educational Researcher, 31*(7), 28–38.

Bayer, R., & Oppenheimer, G. (2000). *AIDS Doctors. Voices from the Epidemic: An Oral History*. New York: Oxford University Press.

Bertaux, D. (Ed.). (1981). *Biography and Society: The Life History Approach in the Social Sciences*. Beverly Hills, CA: Sage.

Black, V., Hoffman, R., Sugar, C., Menon, P., Venter, F., Currier, J., et al. (2008). Safety and efficacy of initiating highly active antiretroviral therapy in an integrated antenatal and HIV clinic in Johannesburg, South Africa. *Journal of Acquired Immune Deficiency Syndrome, 49*(3), 276–281.

Bogdan, R., & Biklen, S. (2006). *Qualitative Research in Education: An Introduction to Theory and Methods*. New York: Allyn & Bacon.

Bozzoli, B., & Nkotsoe, M. (1991). *Women of Phokeng: Consciousness, Life Strategy, and Migrancy in South Africa, 1900–1983: Social History of Africa*. London: Heinemann.

Broder, S. (2010). The development of antiretroviral therapy and its impact on HIV-1/AIDS pandemic. *Antiviral Research, 85*(1), 1–38.

Campbell, C. (2003). *Letting Them Die: Why HIV/AIDS Prevention Programmes Fail.* Bloomington: Indiana University Press.

Campbell, C., & Mannell, J. (2016). Conceptualising the agency of highly marginalized women: Intimate partner violence in extreme settings. *Global Public Health, 11*(1–2), 1–16.

Carrotte, E., Vella, A., Bowring, A., Douglass, C., Hellard, M., & Lim, M. (2016). 'I am yet to encounter any survey that actually reflects my life': A qualitative study of inclusivity in sexual health research. *BMC Medical Research Methodology, 16*(1), 86.

Charmaz, K. (1999). Stories of suffering: Subjective tales and research narratives. *Qualitative Health Research, 9*(3), 362–382.

Chersich, M. (2007). *Preventing HIV in Infants in Eastern and Southern Africa by Improving Access to HIV Testing, Maternal Health and Quality Services.* Doctoral thesis, Ghent University.

Chigwedere, P., Seage, G., Gruskin, S., Lee, T., & Essex, M. (2008). Estimating the lost benefits of antiretroviral drug use in South Africa. *Journal of Acquired Immune Deficiency Syndrome, 49*(4), 410–415.

Cohen, J. (2000). McIntyre and Gray have a will and a way. *Science, 288*(5474), 2163.

Cox, S., & McDonald, M. (2013). Ethics is for human subjects too: Participant perspectives on responsibility in health research. *Social Science & Medicine, 98*(C), 224–231.

Crenshaw, K. (1989). Demarginalizing the intersection of race and sex: A black feminist critique of antidiscrimination doctrine, feminist theory and antiracist politics. *The University of Chicago Legal Forum, 140*, 139–167.

Daniels, K., George, A., Howard, N., Koleva, G., et al. (2016). Fair publication of qualitative research in health systems: A call by health policy and systems researchers. *International Journal for Equity in Health, 15*(1), 98.

Decker, S., Naugle, A., Carter-Visscher, R., Bell, K., & Seifert, A. (2011). Ethical issues in research on sensitive topics: Participants' experiences of distress and benefit. *Journal of Empirical Research on Human Research Ethics, 6*(3), 55–64.

Denzin, N., & Lincoln, Y. (2011). *Handbook of Qualitative Research.* Thousand Oaks: Sage.

Dickinson, D. (2009). *Changing the Course of AIDS: Peer Education in South Africa and Its Lessons for the Global Crisis.* Ithaca, NY: Cornell University Press.

Dickson-Swift, V., James, E., Kippen, S., & Liamputtong, P. (2007). Doing sensitive research: What challenges do qualitative researchers face? *Qualitative Research, 7*(3), 327–353.

Disch, E. (2001). Research as clinical practice: Creating a positive research experience for survivors of sexual abuse by professionals. *Sociological Practice: A Journal of Clinical and Applied Sociology, 3*(3), 221–239.

Eliot, T. (1971). *Four Quartets*. New York: Houghton Mifflin Harcourt.

Farmer, P. (1992). *AIDS & Accusation, Haiti and the Geography of Blame*. Berkeley: University of California Press.

Fauci, A. (2008). Twenty-five years of HIV. *Nature, 453*, 289–290.

Frankfort-Nacmias, C., Nacmias, D., & DeWaard, J. (2014). *Research Methods for the Social Sciences*. New York: Worth Publishers.

Frenk, J., Gomez-Dantas, O., & Chacon, F. (2011). Global health in transition. In R. Parker & M. Sommer (Eds.), *Handbook of Global Public Health* (pp. 11–17). London: Routledge.

Gilbert, L. (1995). Sociology and the "New Public Health" in South Africa. *South African Journal of Sociology, 26*, 115–124.

Gilbert, L. (2012). 'Upstream/downstream'—Locating the 'social' in health promotion and HIV/AIDS in South Africa? *South African Review of Sociology, 43*(1), 62–77.

Gilbert, T., & Gilbert, L. (2004). Globalisation and local power: Influences on health matters in South Africa. *Health Policy, 67*(3), 245–255.

Gimbel, S., Rustagi, A., Robinson, J., Kouyate, S., Coutinho, J., Nduati, R., et al. (2016). Evaluation of a systems analysis and improvement approach to optimize prevention of mother-to-child transmission of HIV using the Consolidated Framework for Implementation Research. *Journal of Acquired Immune Deficiency Syndrome, 72*(Suppl. 2), S108–S116.

Godoy-Ruiz, P., Cole, D., Lenters, L., & McKenzie, K. (2016). Developing collaborative approaches to international research: Perspectives of new global health researchers. *Global Public Health, 11*(3), 253–275.

Government of South Africa. (2012). *National Strategic Plan on HIV, STIs and TB 2012–2016*. Pretoria: National Department of Health.

Greenhalgh, T., Annandale, E., Ashcroft, R., et al. (2016). An open letter to The BMJ editors on qualitative research. *BMJ, 352*, i563.

Gupta, G., Parkhurst, J., Ogden, J., Aggleton, P., & Mahal, A. (2008). Structural approaches to HIV prevention. *Lancet, 372*, 764–775.

Heimer, C. (2013). 'Wicked' ethics: Compliance work and the practice of ethics in HIV research. *Social Science & Medicine, 98*, 371–378.

Heywood, M. (2003). Preventing mother-to-child HIV transmission in South Africa: Treatment Action Campaign case against the Minister of Health. *South African Journal of Human Rights, 19*, 278–280.

Heywood, M. (2009). South Africa's Treatment Action Campaign: Combining law and social mobilization to realize the right to health. *Journal of Human Rights Practice, 1*(1), 14–36.

Hogan, M., Foreman, K., Naghavi, M., Ahn, S., Wang, M., Makela, S., et al. (2010). Maternal mortality for 181 countries, 1980–2008: A systematic analysis of progress towards Millennium Development Goal 5. *Lancet, 375*(9726), 1609–1623.

Jacobsen, K. (2012). *Introduction to Health Research Methods: A Practical Guide*. Sudbury: Jones & Bartlett.

Kabira, W. M., Gachukia, E. W., & Matiangi, F. O. (1997). The effect of women's role on health: The paradox. *International Journal of Gynecology & Obstetrics, 58*, 23–34.

Kalanithi, P. (2016). *When Breath Becomes Air*. New York: Random House.

Kingori, P. (2013). Experiencing everyday ethics in context: Frontline data collectors perspectives and practices of bioethics. *Social Science & Medicine, 98*, 361–370.

Klee, P. (1968). *The Diaries of Paul Klee 1898–1918*. Berkeley: University of California Press.

Kleinman, A. (2004). Ethics and experience: An anthropological approach to health equity. In P. Anand, F. Peter, & A. Sen (Eds.), *Public Health, Ethics, and Equity* (pp. 269–282). Oxford: Oxford University Press.

Kuehner, A., Ploder, A., & Langer, P. (2016). Introduction to the special issue: European contributions to reflexivity. *Qualitative Inquiry, 22*(9), 699–704.

Langer, A., Meleis, A., Knaul, F., Atun, R., Aran, M., Arreola-Ornelas, H., et al. (2015). Women and health: The key for sustainable development. *Lancet, 386*(9999), 1165–1210.

Le Compte, M., & Schenoul, J. (1999). *Designing and Conducting Ethnographic Research*. Sausalito: AltaMira Press/Sage.

Liamputtong, P. (2006). *Researching the Vulnerable: A Guide to Sensitive Research Methods*. Thousand Oaks: Sage.

Lincoln, Y., & Guba, E. (1985). *Naturalistic Inquiry*. Thousand Oaks: Sage.

Loder, E. (2016). Qualitative research and *The BMJ*: A response to Greenhalgh and colleagues' appeal for more. *BMJ, 352*, i641.

Marins, J., Jamal, L., Chen, S., Marilisa, B., Hudes, E., Barbosa, A., et al. (2003). Dramatic improvement in survival among adult Brazilian AIDS patients. *AIDS, 17*, 1675–1682.

Marti, T., & Mertens, D. (2014). Mixed methods research with groups at risk: New developments and key ideas. *Journal of Mixed Methods Research, 8*(3), 207–211.

McCann, L., & Pearlman, L. (1989). Vicarious traumatization: A framework for understanding the psychological effects of working with victims. *Journal of Traumatic Stress, 3*, 131–149.

Mendel, G. (2001). *A Broken Landscape: HIV/AIDS in Africa*. London: Blume.

Mertens, D. (2007). Transformative paradigm: Mixed methods and social justice. *Journal of Mixed Methods Research, 1*(3), 215–225.

Mertens, D. (2011). Mixed methods as tools for social change. *Journal of Mixed Methods Research, 5*(3), 195–197.

Moustakas, C. (1994). *Phenomenological Research Methods*. London or Thousand Oaks, CA: Sage.

Nass, S., Levit, L., & Gostin, L. (Eds.). (2009). *Beyond the HIPAA Privacy Rule: Enhancing Privacy, Improving Health Through Research*. Washington, DC: National Academies Press, Institute of Medicine Committee on Health Research and the Privacy of Health Information.

Neuman, L. (2007). *Social Research Methods: Qualitative and Quantitative Approaches* (5th ed.). Boston, MA: Allyn and Bacon.

Olsen, W., Holborn, M., & Haralambos, U. (Eds.). (2004). Triangulation in social research: Qualitative and quantitative methods can really be mixed. In *Developments in Sociology*. Harlow: Causeway Press.

Parker, R. (2003). Building the foundations for the response for HIV/AIDS in Brazil: The development of HIV/AIDS policy, 1992–1996. *Divulgaçao em Saúde para Debate, 27*, 143–183.

Parkhurst, J. (2014). Structural approaches for prevention of sexually transmitted HIV in general populations: Definitions and an operational approach. *Journal of the International AIDS Society, 17*(1), 19052.

Piot, P. (2006). AIDS: From crisis to sustained response. *Lancet, 368*, 526–530.

Popay, J., & Graves, K. (2000). 'Narrative' in research on gender inequalities in health. In E. Annandale & K. Hunt (Eds.), *Gender Inequalities in Health* (pp. 64–89). Philadelphia: Open University Press.

Power, S. (2003). The AIDS Rebel. [online]. *The New Yorker*. Retrieved February 2, 2017, from http://www.newyorker.com/magazine/2003/05/19/the-aids-rebel

Preston-Whyte, E. (2003). Contexts of vulnerability: Sex, secrecy and HIV/AIDS. *African Journal of AIDS Research, 2*(2), 89–94.

Punpanich, W., Ungchusak, K., & Detels, R. (2004). Thailand's response to the HIV epidemic: Yesterday, today, and tomorrow. *AIDS Education and Prevention, 16*(Suppl. 3A), 119–136.

Rabe, M. (2003). Revisiting 'insiders' and 'outsiders' as social researchers. *African Sociological Review, 7*(2), 149–161.

Rawizza, H., Chan, C., Chaplin, B., Ahmed, I., Meloni, S., Oyebode, T., et al. (2015). Loss to follow-up within the prevention of mother-to-child transmission care cascade in a large ART program in Nigeria. *Current HIV Research, 13*(3), 201–209.

Richter, M. (2013). *Characteristics, sexual behaviour and access to health care services for sex workers in South Africa and Kenya.* Doctoral thesis, Ghent University.

Ritchie, J., & Lewis, J. (Eds.). (2012). *Qualitative Research Practice: A Guide for Social Science Students and Researchers* (2nd ed.). Thousand Oaks: Sage.

Robson, C. (1993). *Real World Research: A Resource for Social Scientists and Practitioner-Researchers.* Oxford: Blackwell.

Rosenberg, T. (2001). Drug companies are vincible. The AIDS crisis is solvable. *The New York Times Magazine.*

Scanlon, M. L., MacNaughton, G., & Sprague, C. (2017). Neglected disease, neglected right: Children living with HIV and their right to science. *Health & Human Rights Journal, 19*(2), 169–181.

Sen, A. (2004b). Health achievement and equity: External and internal perspectives. In S. Anand, F. Peter, & A. Sen (Eds.), *Public Health, Ethics, and Equity* (pp. 263–268). Oxford: Oxford University Press.

Sexual Violence Research Initiative. (2015). *Guidelines for the Prevention and Management of Vicarious Trauma Among Researchers of Sexual and Intimate Partner v Violence.* Pretoria: Sexual Violence Research Initiative.

Shilts, R. (1988). *And the Band Played On.* New York: St. Martin's Press.

Shisana, O., Rehle, T., Simbayi, L., Zuma, K., Jooste, S., Zungu, N., et al. (2014). *South African National HIV Prevalence, Incidence and Behaviour Survey, 2012.* Cape Town: HSRC Press.

Sprague, C. (2009). *Cui Bono: A Capabilities Approach to Understanding HIV Prevention and Treatment for Pregnant Women and Children in South Africa.* Doctoral thesis, University of the Witwatersrand.

Sprague, C., Chersich, M., & Black, V. (2011). Health systems weaknesses constrain access to PMTCT and maternal HIV services in South Africa: A qualitative enquiry. *AIDS Research and Therapy, 8*, 10.

Sprague, C., Scanlon, M., & Pantalone, D. W. (2017b). Qualitative methods to advance research on health inequities among previously incarcerated women living with HIV in Alabama. *Health Education & Behavior, 44*(5), 716–727.

Sprague, C., & Woolman, S. (2006). Moral luck: Exploiting South Africa's policy environment for an effective national antiretroviral treatment programme. *South African Journal on Human Rights, 22*(3), 337–379.

Staton-Tindall, M. (n.d.). *Female Offender Drug Use and Related Issues*. [online]. Retrieved January 22, 2017, from http://www.nij.gov/topics/drugs/markets/adam/documents/staton-paper.pdf

Steinberg, J. (2008). *Three-Letter Plague. A Young Man's Journey Through a Great Epidemic*. Johannesburg: Jonathan Ball.

Tazreiter, C., Weber, L., Pickering, S., Segrave, M., & McKernan, H. (2016). *Fluid Security in the Asia Pacific: Transnational Lives, Human Rights and State Control*. London: Palgrave Macmillan.

Teixeira, P. (2003). Universal access to AIDS medicines: The Brazilian experience. *Divulgaçao em Saúde para Debate, 27*, 184–191.

Tinker, A. (2000). Women's health: The unfinished agenda. *International Journal of Gynecology and Obstetrics, 70*, 149–158.

Tuhiwai Smith, L. (1999). *Decolonizing Methodologies*. New York: Zed Books.

UNAIDS. (2005). *Epidemiological Fact Sheets on HIV/AIDS and Sexually Transmitted Infections, 2005 Update (South Africa)*. Geneva: UNAIDS.

UNAIDS/WHO. (2008). *Sub-Saharan Africa AIDS Epidemic Update Regional Summary*. Geneva: UNAIDS/WHO.

Vearey, J. (2010). *The persistent urban challenges of migration and informal settlements in the context of HIV*. Doctoral thesis, University of the Witwatersrand, Johannesburg, South Africa.

Walensky, R., Paltiel, A., & Losina, E. (2006). The survival benefits of AIDS treatment in the United States. *Journal of Infectious Diseases, 194*(1), 11–19.

Wang, C., & Geale, S. (2015). The power of story: Narrative inquiry as a methodology in nursing research. *International Journal of Nursing Sciences, 2*, 195–198.

Wolffers, I. (2000). Biomedical and development paradigms in AIDS prevention. *Bulletin of the World Health Organization, 78*(2), 267–273.

Woolman, S. (2008). *Constitutional Law of South Africa* (2nd ed.). Cape Town: Juta Press.

WHO. (2014b). *World Health Statistics, 2014*. Geneva: WHO.

6

Capabilities for Women Living with HIV: Linking Health Systems to Social Structure

Hlabisa district, KwaZulu-Natal, September 1992

A Zulu woman carries groceries back to her village in the Hlabisa District of KwaZulu-Natal after walking more than 7 km. Source: Mendel, 2001, image 1/35. Reprinted with permission

C. Sprague, *Gender and HIV in South Africa*, Global Research in Gender, Sexuality and Health, https://doi.org/10.1057/978-1-137-55997-5_6

Before presenting details of the findings emerging from the empirical research conducted, I highlight regional demographic differences between the two provinces and additional socio-demographic characteristics of the population (Arber & Cooper, 2000; Boserup, 2007; Tinker, 2000). Factors such as participation in the workforce and a stable income (or the converse, poverty) affect women's control over aspects of their material and physical environment, including dynamics within intimate relationships in the household (Farmer, Connors, & Simmons, 2011). These factors also play a role in influencing women's ability to access HIV care provision and their accompanying health behaviours. They, ultimately, affect women's HIV outcomes over the long-term, including their linkage to HIV care, medication adherence, quality of life, co-morbidities and mortality (Uthman, Magidson, Safren, & Nachega, 2014; WHO, 2006a, 2006b).

Women's internal lived experiences were probed during extensive in-depth interviews over two time periods. Greater detail on the research methods, rationale, procedures and challenges are communicated in the methodology chapter. Here the dominant themes and influential factors characterising the narratives of women living with HIV across the sample are presented in the findings section (Charmaz, 1999). The external perspective (Sen, 2004b) on factors affecting women's health and their capabilities, including enabling policies, is brought forth in supplementary interviews conducted with health providers in the same clinical settings, and with expert key informants. I present the findings from each group in turn and then tether the main themes to implications for women's capabilities. All interview excerpts are taken from the later, more recent set of interviews (from 2014 to 2016) so as to reflect current realities and trends.

Socio-Demographics by Province

Gauteng

In mid-year 2016, Gauteng captured the largest share of South African residents across the nine provinces, at 24% (Stats SA, 2016a). Official unemployment in that year increased to 29.5% from 23% in 2009 (Stats SA, 2016b, p. xiv). The majority of residents, 78%, remained reliant on the public health system (Gauteng Provincial Department of Health, 2009). The poverty headcount, at 4.6%, was lower compared to other provinces, with 10.8% of households in Gauteng indicating they had skipped a meal in the preceding 12 months. This was lower than the national average of 13.3% (Stats SA, 2016c). This could suggest that Gauteng is capitalising on developmental benefits of urbanisation and serving as a concentrated centre of employment nationally. The proportion of households with access to electricity and piped water was one of the highest in the country, at 97.4%, although a notable share, 17.7%, reported living in informal dwellings, suggesting that access to piped water and stable electricity might be constrained for some (Stats SA, 2016c). Estimated provincial HIV prevalence in Gauteng, at 12.4%, was slightly higher than the national average of 11.2% (Shisana et al., 2014). Estimated life expectancy for women in the province, at 65.8 years in 2016, demonstrated a marked increase from the 2011 estimate of 61.5 years (Stats SA, 2016a).

Eastern Cape

In contrast to Gauteng, 12.6% of all South African residents reside in the Eastern Cape (Stats SA, 2016a). There was 28.6% unemployment in the province, a decrease from 30% in 2009 (Stats SA, 2016b), with an estimated 94% of residents seeking care in the public health system (Eastern Cape Provincial Department of Health, 2008). The poverty headcount was 12.7%, with 17.6% of Eastern Cape households indicating they had skipped a meal in the previous 12 months (Stats SA, 2016c). The Eastern Cape had the lowest proportion of households reporting access to piped water nationally at 75.1%. Only 42.6% of households reported access to electricity, with the highest number of households across the country, 26.6%, reporting they lived in traditional dwellings (structures, such as a *rondavel*, made of traditional materials) (Stats SA, 2016c). Provincial HIV prevalence was 11.6% in the last national survey (Shisana et al.,

2014), and estimated life expectancy for women in the Eastern Cape was 58.9%, a notable increase from 51.9% in 2011 but still far lower than for women in Gauteng and nationally (Stats SA, 2016a, p. 11).

Below I summarise the latest data on employment participation, including the proportion of black South African women by type of occupation. These are classified as skilled, semi-skilled or low-skilled (Stats SA, 2016b). Note that the study population, pregnant and postpartum women, were most likely to report being unemployed at the time of interviews due to pregnancy and child care following delivery and discharge from hospital. Nonetheless, this offers a snapshot of, not only black women's participation in the economy at present, but the occupations black women would be most likely to move into, if women were change their employment status following the period of maternity.

Employment Participation: South African Women

More than two decades into a democratic South Africa, a significantly large share of black South African women still held low-skilled occupations (comprising domestic work or elementary work) in mid-2016 (43.1%), with a large proportion represented in semi-skilled occupations (clerk, sales, services, agriculture, crafts, trade, plant and machine operators) (38.5%), and considerably fewer represented in skilled occupations (professional, technical, managerial roles) (18.3%) (Stats SA, 2016b, p. x). A higher proportion of coloured women held low-skilled occupations (28.5%) but they are over-represented in semi-skilled employment (49%), and under-represented in skilled professions (22.5%). By contrast, the share of white women in low-skilled occupations is notably low (1.1%), with some concentrated in semi-skilled professions (40.7%) and the majority (58.2%) in skilled occupations (Stats SA, 2016b, p. x). The share of Indian/Asian women occupying low-skilled employment is also comparatively low (5.2%), with most represented in either semi-skilled (49.3%) or skilled employment (45.5%) (2016b, p. x).

Socioeconomic Characteristics of South African Pregnant and Postnatal Women Living with HIV

The study population comprised HIV positive pregnant or postpartum women, aged 18 to 50, seeking HIV services (cART and PMTCT) in the public health system, across the two provinces. All women (100%) self-reported as black. The majority (93%) self-reported as being formally unemployed. Some communicated informal work in crafts or sales of goods as informal sellers. The remainder had jobs in the formal sector in some of the large companies, such as Pick n Pay.

Part 1. Findings

HIV Positive Women Participants in Clinical Health Settings—The Internal

Theme 1. Autonomy in health decision making and HIV disclosure constrained by lack of decision making power in households and economic dependence

Across the two locations, the majority of women were living with a partner or other family member (e.g., sister, mother or brother). In urban Gauteng, women were more likely to be living with a partner or on their own. They had greater health decision making autonomy compared to the rural Eastern Cape women interviewed. Yet with less autonomy to make health decisions than black South African men, who were uniformly viewed as key decision makers in the household. This will become more evident in the women's narratives. In the more rural Eastern Cape, women were more likely to be younger and to live with their parents.

In terms of women's decision making about their bodily health, when I, or a translator, asked women a standard question: Who makes the decisions about your health: is it you, or do you consult with someone—a husband, mother or sister? women would typically respond, 'I do' (participant #1) or 'It's just me' (#40), or 'Me' (#81). When probing their experiences further in IDIs, however, it became clear that these participants engaged in different types of negotiation strategies concerning health decision making generally and HIV specifically. They described exploring whether or not they could safely disclose their HIV status to their husbands without negative implications. Men's responses (reported by women participants) could be positioned on a spectrum from excellent to partial support, judgement, blame, denial, violence and abandonment, as captured in the excerpts below.

Control over Bodily Health Through Careful Management of HIV Disclosure

This narrative exemplifies one woman's careful management of the process of HIV disclosure but is illustrative of many respondents' stories.

> Interviewer: When you went home, did you decide you would disclose to anyone or not?
>
> Participant: At first I didn't [disclose], but then as the time goes on, I felt the guilty conscious [sic] within me, and I said 'how can I do this?' 'I know my status and then why do I let somebody else suffer because of me?'

This participant is expressing worry over the potential transmission of the virus to her husband whose HIV status was unknown. She uses some language that suggests self-blame, and potentially self-stigmatisation due to her HIV status. She decides to broach the topic of HIV to gauge his response:

> When I'm with my husband, we'll talk about HIV and AIDS [to] see how he's responded…he's that kind of a person who doesn't believe [in] this HIV and AIDS…but then I have to paint a picture for him to see the reality, that this…thing [exists]…[we] don't have to lie to each other.

This same respondent communicates her belief that, even in the absence of a cure, she may not necessarily die. She expresses how she came to reveal her status to her husband, over time, by gaining feedback and managing HIV disclosure carefully:

> As they've said…there is no cure. But that doesn't mean that…I'm going to death. It took a long time [to tell him] because I just had to see his emotions and everything…and find the right time to tell him.

After she disclosed, her husband ended up being very supportive. She states: 'He said, 'I'm here for you and we can see what we can do. We will deal with this thing."

In the next breath, she remarks: 'Then I find out the child is negative and he was happy as ever.' This seamless reference to the child's health was uppermost in women's minds and is worth emphasising. It was a principal concern that would figure in women's other actions and choices and will resurface later.

The supportive partner's response just cited was not necessarily shared by all women. Reports of abandonment were documented, and are discussed further below. Women's experiences of support, following HIV disclosure, were varied. What was uniform was women's fear and anxiety over the reactions by family and friends if they revealed their HIV status.

One participant shared her decision to disclose her HIV positive test result—which she had kept secret for some time—with her husband. She notes:

> I decided I'm not gonna leave [keep] secrets… [from] my husband, and we talked. I showed him the [positive test result]. I said 'Look, my results are HIV positive. And you don't say you want to go with me [to be tested and learn his status].' That's when he reacted badly. He throwed them away [the test results]…My husband doesn't support me.

These examples highlight a degree of complexity being managed by HIV positive women during their pregnancy and thereafter. Their HIV status was connected to concerns over their own emotional and economic welfare and security, and especially by a desire to protect their children from HIV infection.

At the superficial level, women communicated that they made health decisions concerning their bodily health on their own. Nevertheless, on digging deeper, we begin to glimpse that women are in fact highly influenced by the perceived and actual reactions of their partners, and they seek to gauge their behaviours accordingly. They deploy agentic behaviours within a set of parameters that they are exploring and negotiating.

Given women's minimal income and employment, their worries concerning how they would manage if their partners abandoned them were unmistakable in interviews, and were justified. Here one participant describes how her partner left her after she disclosed: an experience shared by an estimated 10% of the respondents who self-reported experiences of abandonment:

> After coming to test, when I found out I'm positive, I talked to him [partner]. I said, 'Even you must come to the clinic, so you can know your status'... He said 'No, never! There is no HIV! Why are you going on [about this]?'

After a pause, she notes that:

> [After that] 'My husband, he...ran away.'

One participant recalled her husband as supportive. Nevertheless, she makes a point of stressing the number of HIV positive women she had come to know over the months of antenatal care visits. She explained what she viewed as occupying women's minds most:

> [For] most of the women, the main problem [they face] is their partners [and being able to disclose and receive support]. You hear the women say, 'I never told my husband about my status.' Some say, 'I'm afraid of telling him 'cause he might walk away'... they are afraid of losing their partners.

In summary, the first dominant theme that was manifest across the sample demonstrates women's agentic actions to assess whether they could safely disclose their HIV status to their partner or not. Women's deepest aspirations seemed to be for support and freedom from fear and anxiety. The full exercise of their agency was circumscribed, and they were navigating and seeking to cross a divide, which could at times be seen as a crevasse. This was dangerous, fear-provoking terrain. At the centre of their journey to the other side, which could likely represent safety, is consideration of how their partners, who held the power in the household, including economic and decision making power, would respond. Their insecurity is directly connected to their lower socioeconomic status and their economic dependence, but also to complex concerns over the potential loss of love and support from their intimate partners, and anxiety over the welfare of their children (Hunter, 2010; Jewkes, Levin & Penn-Kekana, 2002, 2003). If women were bringing in income from informal trading, this could shift the balance of power in the household. However, many women reported that they had elected to forego employment, including informal work, during the perinatal period, which would seem to render them more economically vulnerable at that life stage compared to others.

Theme 2. Women enact agency to mediate psychosocial distress by seeking support, health care and establishing social ties

A second theme communicated by participants across the narratives was the importance of the health system as a site, not only for HIV treatment and medical care, but for psychosocial support. This was particularly due to women's reported fears surrounding HIV disclosure. Fear, anxiety and depression were communicated by approximately 68% of participants across Gauteng and the Eastern Cape. I interviewed many women soon after they first learnt of their seropositivity. Most individuals living with HIV typically require time to come to terms with and accept their HIV status, prior to sharing it with others. The time to disclose ranges but research indicates that HIV positive women report needing and seeking more social support than men. In one global survey conducted among HIV positive women in 94 countries, 82% of participants reported having depression symptoms following their HIV diagnosis, with a 3.5-fold increase in mental distress (Orza et al., 2015; see also Uthman et al., 2014). Note also that it is seen as socially acceptable for women to seek support for emotional needs, whereas men's socialisation into masculinities, while heterogeneous, would make them less inclined to do so as it could be seen as a 'sign of weakness' (Cooper, 2017). Much of the literature describes HIV positive women's needs for psychosocial support but not how women address those needs. What is communicated by participants here is not only their initial thoughts on learning they were HIV positive but the agentic actions participants took to mediate the psychosocial effects, i.e., their agency in seeking support. From the narratives, what emerges is support from different sources: from health providers and from other women. One participant's experience is illustrative of many narratives.

Recounting her response to her HIV positive status and her interaction with a lay HIV counsellor, she remarks:

> It was very touching [noting the HIV counsellor was a caring person]. But then I was still traumatised…distraught. She can say those words to comfort you, but they are just like going on and off.

The participant is communicating her sense of shock, which was likely disabling her from absorbing what the counsellor was saying. She then describes having to sit in hospital to process her HIV status, recalling her psychological state:

> I was about to leave the hospital [but instead she had] to sit about two hours in those silver chairs trying to have a start for me to go home and tell it all. It was…very very difficult.

Next, she recollects what transpired when she came across another visibly pregnant woman who she learnt was also HIV positive:

> On my way to the taxi, I was sitting so exhausted. Here comes another lady [from the same hospital]. I can see she was kind. I just assume we're in the same boat 'cause she was also pregnant. Then I started to question her… She said 'Yes [affirming she was living with HIV] and I don't know how I'm going to tell it [disclose] to my husband.' So we exchanged numbers. She was the first person to give me a motivation speaker [motivational talk] 'cause she was in the same boat. We just spoke over the phone for quite a long time…But then I said, 'no, let me be strong.'

Like this participant, women described utilising and mobilising resources informally, though still linked to the health system. She continues her narrative, noting that she confided in her friend before doing so with other friends she had known much longer. This excerpt is emblematic in reinforcing the importance to women of ensuring sufficient trust, prior to imparting information about their HIV status and related:

> Every time when we come to the [clinic, we] sit together, we'll discuss the issues, even before I admit it to my [other] friends.

The above participant stayed in touch with her friend by mobile phone. Such engagement between women stood out markedly across the interviews. Women described waiting in queues for hours, striking up conversations and establishing bonds of friendship. Thus the pattern that became visible was women's cultivation of social ties with other women living with HIV. This was possible because the health system was a place that women could visit without raising suspicion by their partners or other family members. It thus served as a safe space, and most pregnant women (over 92%) would attend their antenatal care appointments in public clinics and hospitals.

Selective disclosure, evident in theme one, was also dominant in theme two. This reflects how important it was for women to maintain control over this aspect of their lives because HIV represented a source of vulnerability. This caution also underscores an underlying threat of HIV stigma and discrimination over which women were trying to exert agentic control (Link & Phelan, 2001). This becomes more conspicuous in the next excerpt.

One woman indicated she had not disclosed to her sister who was also HIV positive. This participant appears to be anticipating HIV discrimination:

> My younger sister, she is HIV positive but...she doesn't know that I'm HIV positive...People are discriminating about people who are HIV positive...you don't know what...the world will bring.

A different participant said she had only disclosed to one trusted friend who was also HIV positive:

Interviewer (I):	have you disclosed to anyone?
Participant (P):	Yes.
I:	Who?
P:	It's my friend.
I:	And is she the only one?
P:	Yes. she [is the] only one, and she's also positive.
I:	So you share your stories?
P:	Yeah and questions 'cause she has been taking meds a long time. I ask her many things.

In addition to the peer support that women established, they sought the advice of lay counsellors or nurses for HIV education, management, and—particularly in instances where women failed to receive sufficient support at home—they seemed to actively turn to and embrace health providers as a bulwark against distress.

One woman mentioned her engagement with the nurses and lay counsellors as paramount due to her husband's unwillingness to attend her appointments with her or to discuss HIV:

> We won't even bring it up. He doesn't want to hear about [HIV] counselling. He won't go with me even [to] a scan [during pregnancy]. He's just like left me in the cold you know.

In this way, the role of health providers in providing not only care but also social support was prominent across the interviews. Women would emphasise seeking out particular HIV lay counsellors when they went to their ANC appointments, underscoring the importance of these relationships, 'When I come [to ANC], I always go to my counsellor [name omitted]. She helps me a lot.'

One participant tells how she sought the assistance of the lay counsellor for support in dealing with difficulties at home after she disclosed to her husband:

> He reacted in a violent [way]. Life was hell at home…He flushed [her ARVs] down [the toilet]… [Now, after the counsellor advised me] I throw away the boxes…I can call her [for support] anytime.

Notably, some participants described themselves as initially reticent to engage with health providers. Nurses in particular were described as bossy and overbearing at times, a theme supported by some of the literature from South Africa and other settings (Jewkes, Abrahams, & Mvo, 1998). (A relevant, telling expression in the US is that nurses in clinical health settings are known to 'eat their young'—referring to training younger nurses and developing their toughness). Thus some South African women participants characterised themselves as slow to trust, with some women communicating greater affinity for the lay counsellors who did not have the same power and authority as the nurses in the occupational hierarchy. Nurses appeared to recognise the power they held over their patients, and that they needed to be 'invited into' this intimate, vulnerable space. This group of nurses (interviewed) seemed to understand this invitation was not automatic but had to be earned. One nurse I interviewed referred to the counselling between the health provider and patient as hinging on trust in a manner that is reciprocal:

> Yeah, it's a lot of work [counselling women]. I must have trust in you, you have trust in me. We talk together. That is counselling.

What resounded across the narratives was that, through these engagements, as women living with HIV came back for a second or third ANC appointment, they began to shed their caution, as if removing a layer of clothing, perhaps worn as psychological protection. Participants, particularly in Gauteng, frequently mentioned being able to call their lay counsellors, and sometimes their nurses, at any time. In IDIs, women would often produce their mobile phones from their handbags and scroll through the contacts, or take up their phone and glance at it during the interview, as a sort of proof that the health providers were one touch away. This was done as one reaches for and fingers one's wallet to make sure it is safe, and the contents available, as a form of security. The relationship between women and their health providers thus seemed to hold a form of psychological symbolism for women that was palpable.

In sum, emerging from participant narratives was women's mediation of psychological distress through trust and active support-seeking in the health system by linking to peers and providers. Notable among participant accounts was the location of counselling within the health system—its presence and absence. The majority of reports of formal counselling, for example, were clustered among ANC participants, with far fewer respondents describing these encounters postpartum. Indeed, through participant observation, I observed that health providers were more present and likely to be available in antenatal care wards (especially lay counsellors and nurses), but less likely to be found in labour, delivery and postnatal care wards. This situation was exacerbated in the poorer-resourced Eastern Cape. I return to the location and availability of psychological care later in the chapter.

Theme 3. Patient-provider encounters shape women's positive health behaviours

In theme three, the focus shifts to the encounter between women patients, their health providers (nurses and HIV lay counsellors), and the nature of those interactions which seemed to hold deep significance for the study population. Core aspects of HIV treatment and prevention that informed women's health behaviours move to the fore. Women were gaining foundational knowledge about HIV management through contact with and guidance from their health providers. Here the role of health providers in imparting key health information and education in ways that were health promoting for women with HIV comes into focus more clearly.

Education About cART and PMTCT

One woman references her initial fears about taking HIV medication, anticipating side effects or worse, i.e., the presentation of clinical symptoms representative of AIDS. Because she initiated cART in hospital, she felt reassured that if anything went wrong, she was in in a system of care (in hospital) and would be looked after:

I: Before you went on ARVs, what were your thoughts about the medicine?
P: I was so scared because, you see, they said that I'm going to feel so bad. Maybe [it will be]...true. [But] since I started the medicine here at the

> hospital, if something is going to happen, the doctors are here. The nurses are here. Because I started here after I was admitted here [to hospital name omitted]...[and] they started the drugs and then... nothing [happened]. *[Participant starts laughing with relief because she did not have side effects or problems, contrary to what she had expected.]*

The comment above is indicative of a kind of compact that women were choosing to make in order to connect to HIV care and support services. This was an agentic choice to trust health providers.

A respondent relays her experience of pre- and post-test HIV counselling in ANC. She emphasises the educational benefit of speaking with the lay counsellor, while also making reference to its psychological value:

> It was very helpful 'cause they tell you what happens if you find out that you're positive... the kind of medication, the kind of food. What happens if you find out that you're negative...And it's a great thing to also speak to the counsellors 'cause you're channeling your prayers.

The 'myth busting' role of the nurse, counsellor and some doctors was emphasised by participants as indispensable in untangling the complex aspects of cART and PMTCT. Women mentioned learning for the first time about prevention of HIV transmission to the child during pregnancy, labour and delivery. They also described receiving vital information about HIV risks associated with breast versus bottle feeding (safe feeding of infants as part of PMTCT programmes), and enacting strategies for doing so in households when mothers-in-law or husbands might disagree with or judge women's choices and actions, and with an attendant fear of gossip (about women's HIV status and feeding choices) within families or communities, which women had to manage.

That women could ask providers questions directly and gain answers seemed to have a calming effect, giving them greater confidence about managing HIV and their health, their child's health and their options for health promotion. Over time, as women gained more information, they described how these new-found resources and the encounter with health providers also appeared to lift some of the psychological burdens they were carrying, seeming to give them more self-efficacy.

This participant mentions that prior to counselling she did not believe that HIV transmission to her child could be prevented. But this view was altered, once she received counselling:

> Before you go for counselling people say all sorts of things. So when you are counselled, everything changes 'cause you know you're talking to someone who already knows what she's talking about...[then] everything changes [after]...counselling [meaning she felt informed].

In the next exchanges presented, there is a shift taking place. We see health providers characterised by participants as more vocal and persuasive in order to exact behaviour changes in HIV positive women patients. Providers are winning the trust from participants in order to alter women's thinking and their actions. One respondent recalls how she was not taking her HIV medication regularly until a lay counsellor she met put the situation in stark terms:

> when I went to [facility name omitted], I saw a second counsellor [who] made a bigger impact [than the first]...She told me what could happen to my baby. Counsellor said... 'did you know that a baby can contract the HIV virus... during pregnancy? He can contract HIV during delivery. A baby can contract the HIV during breastfeeding.'

This interaction with the health provider created a new awareness for the woman in relation to the implications of her health behaviour for her child:

> She said to me, 'You've been for counselling, you've had enough time to digest. What are you doing? Are you killing your child?' I said 'No, I'm not killing my child!' She says, 'Yes you are, by not taking medication.' I cried. It was a wake-up call.

The woman stresses that she recognised her behaviour was potentially harmful (in relation to mother-to-child HIV transmission), and began to take her medication regularly. She describes doing so for the sake of her children:

> All that scared me and I was like I don't want...the baby to suffer from any consequences... The baby hasn't done anything wrong. He's innocent. So that's when I decided No. Whether he [husband] supports me or not, I'm in this alone. I'm doing it for my baby. That's when I started taking them all [ARVs]...I got two other children and have to be a responsible parent.

I then asked her about the notion of taking ARVs to support her own health, not solely for the health of her children:

> Interviewer: What about being healthy for yourself? Does that feature?
>
> Participant: Yes it does because if I'm not healthy, if I'm not well, how can I work? How can I cook dinner for my kids?

As is evident, the primary impetus for her positive health behaviour is being a caring mother, in keeping with this sociocultural norm in South Africa and other settings (Soman, 1997). It is worth noting that the nurse is emphasising the respondent's maternal role as a way to effect positive health behaviour change. The respondent became adherent to her medication as a result.

In this way, a gendered role (being a caring mother) was being reinforced by the health provider. Note that from this exchange it is unclear whether the health provider did so primarily for the child's welfare, or because she was genuinely concerned for her patient's health, or both. It cannot be assumed that the nurse would always elevate concern for the infant over the mother; she could be doing so for multiple reasons. Participants routinely described such direct exchanges, e.g., sharp warnings or promptings from health providers, as shaping their actions.

Regardless of whether their emphasis was on child or women's health, providers who gained the confidence of women were marshalling this trust to ensure that women patients were taking the necessary steps to promote and manage their health and that of their infants.

Theme 4. Some health providers act to reinforce women's choices and rights, reconstructing gender

The External

In theme four, the ways in which health providers were positioned to observe and assess factors influencing the health of their patients, and their own explanations for provider actions, becomes clearer. To probe how providers viewed gender norms, hierarchies and related factors that influence women's health, including HIV risk and management, I asked their views on some of these concerns in this research, and in previous research conducted with colleagues in some of these clinical settings in Johannesburg (Sprague, Hatcher, Woollett, & Black, 2015, Sprague, Hatcher, Woollett, Sommers, & Black, 2016a; Sprague, Woollett, Parpart, Hatcher, Sommers, Brown, & Black, 2016b).

I begin by querying the role of women patients in taking decisions about their own health and making choices that support their wellbeing. This is the same question asked of patients, only this time it was directed at nurses, social workers and doctors who provide care. The scope of inquiry shifts to providers' actions in clinical settings in response to gendered aspects associated with the health and health decision making of their women patients. Here providers share their observations. Note that in interviews some providers make references to women patients that they routinely see, HIV negative women and HIV positive women, who experience abuse.

Gender and Constraints to Health Decision Making

I asked a social worker whether women would seek support from providers in cases where men might insist on actions that conflicted with women's desires, and whether women spoke to social workers about those instances. A social worker seems to be communicating that health professionals do not shy away from such difficult cases. She states:

> In the hospital, we treat all of our patients equally. To us, when people have problems, they have problems. When we don't give them preparation or [HIV] treatment, we try and help them.

It soon becomes evident that the social worker is referring to women who experience abuse. She notes that social workers must address women's holistic health needs:

> Because we are in a hospital, if they come saying 'I am being assaulted by my partner' in the hospital, we cannot say 'go outside'. If they go outside, what if their partner is waiting at the gate? So, I don't think we have a choice in that matter.

In the social worker's statement, she seems to be indicating abuse exists and providers don't shy away from dealing with this. Note that she seems slightly defensive. This may be because there is no protocol to guide health providers on how to address abuse in their patients in the public health system (Sprague et al., 2015a). She may be concerned about reporting this aspect of her work in an interview.

In an interview with a different health provider in the same health facility, a nurse cites a patient's lack of autonomy over the termination of her pregnancy as an issue that is fairly common:

> Sometimes they [women patients] will come up here saying...that my husband doesn't want me to do this abortion. And...he's starting to be violent or whatever. [But after drawing out the realities, it turns out]...she will come and say [admit], 'I want to keep the child, but my husband says no.'

This provider is pointing to women's lack of choice and accompanying violence as a challenge facing her patients. Similarly, one physician in the same ward recalled her interaction with a woman patient who did not want to terminate her pregnancy but was being forced to do so by her husband. The doctor began to actively coach the woman about her options:

> I asked her 'did you go to see the social worker?'...She said no, because her husband was there and she didn't want her husband to see [her speaking to the social worker].

The physician continues:

> And she was already in tears, so I'd already separated her from [her family members] so I could do the history by myself. [The doctor] brought in the sister to make sure she goes to the social worker first…because she didn't want to do it [terminate the pregnancy]. She said she was being forced to do it by her husband.

In the situation just described, the doctor stepped in to allow the woman time to reflect on her agentic intentions and to reinforce to her that it is the woman's decision to terminate:

> I said 'well we can't do it then if someone else is forcing you to do it. It's your decision. If you want to do it then we can do it…but, if not, then it's your decision and no one can tell you what you must or must not do. And we can go to the social worker and we can either go for couples counselling, marriage counselling, or find a way to leave him whichever is your option.'

This physician indicates that the woman was so afraid of her husband that she didn't have time to wait for the social worker. The patient asked to go ahead with the termination of pregnancy, in spite of her desire to have the child.

Coming through in the provider narratives is a set of constraints restricting women's autonomy in health decision making, and the persistence of violence in women's lives.

In research conducted with my colleagues in these same health facilities, we documented the role of health providers to guide their patients in a manner that would protect or promote their health in these clinics through instruction or guidance. The next two quotations are drawn from that study. Here a nurse insists on condom use for a patient with HIV:

> I said to her you don't owe nobody [an] explanation …. Don't be afraid of other people who don't know their status…. If you[r] partner says he can't [use a condom], he should know that you are going to use a condom because you are a positive. Use a condom to protect yourself! (Sprague et al., 2015, p. 9)

Note that the suggestion of condom use, well intended by the nurse, may not be feasible for the patient. Thus, some experts suggest that adopting a problem-solving approach to negotiate these concerns is preferred (Cooper, 2017).

Similarly, in a different clinic, a nurse who had experienced intimate partner violence herself, described how she counselled her patients and referred them to social workers. This quote is illustrative of the concern providers have about the health consequences for their patients who experience violence:

> Usually I advise them [patients experiencing partner violence], why don't you go to [the] police? At least do something. Because one day, [he says] 'I will kill you, I will kill you'—[he] will end up killing you. So I usually advise them with police [matters], and will refer them to the social worker. (Sprague et al., 2015, p. 9)

A different nurse highlights the role of the health system vis-à-vis abuse, suggesting there should be more direct and concerted action to address violence against women, regardless of HIV status, particularly in pregnancy:

> It's not enough. It should be more. Actually, they...should have at least some health workers who are dealing strictly with abused women [in the health system]. Because this is happening every day. Those two, now as we are sitting now [making reference to two abused women in the queue], maybe many women are being beaten up, being pregnant.

Provider Perceptions of Gender Relations and Norms

These next extracts highlight providers' observations about gender norms that affect their patients. A nurse articulated her perceptions that men make health decisions for women. She shares her observations about gender relations and hierarchies, citing men's ownership of women as typical:

> They [the men partners think they] own you. Now you can't do anything. 'You are my thing.' She continues to reinforce her perception of a sociocultural norm in which men have the ability to exert control over women:

> We [women] are not allowed to do anything. They [men] will tell you [what you must do]. They dictate. They want to tell you what to do…and then after that, they want seriously to [dictate]….everything.

She is highlighting women's restricted agency and the ways in which she views men's preferences and verbal abuse as influencing women patients. Conspicuous in her statement just above is the seamless shift to 'we', indicating the nurse identifies with this norm. The nurse continues below, emphasising men's strategies to diminish women:

> there is nothing that you can do. You are not good. You don't look beautiful today…you know, demoralising [women].

Socialisation into the Gender Hierarchy: Cultural Customs and Harmful Masculinities

One nurse suggests that, owing to the cultural custom of *lobola* (in which a 'bride price' is paid by the groom or his family in exchange for the bride) is seen by women and men as a purchase that is equated with ownership. Thus women feel compelled to remain in abusive situations:

> Because you are held in those relationships because of *lobola*, because they [men] are providing for you—you feel you are obliged to stay in those relationships.

She continues, describing the role of gender socialisation in constructing gender relations and hierarchies:

> Women are socialised when they are growing up that they must respect men. I think those things escalate violence.

A provider in a different health facility, when asked about the health decisions of patients she sees, comments on women who choose men that demonstrate harmful masculinities:

> Sometimes it also depends on the personality of the person. Once they [women] get used to this violence it's not easy. They always tend to choose these men who are overpowering them. They want somebody to be in charge. They are never in charge. If a man is not taking control of her life, it's not a *real man*.

She shares her view that women may enable abuse, and that women may be complicit in establishing adverse gender norms, both masculinities and femininities. This notion of blaming women for the abuse they experience is routinely captured across the literature on VAW in South Africa (Jewkes, Penn-Kekana, & Rose-Junius, 2005; Human Rights Watch, 1995). A different nurse in a different facility observes that women are not able to leave violent relationships. She attributes this to economic dependence on their partners:

> [Women] stay in such relationships where there is [abuse] because they won't be able to support themselves [financially] if they leave.

One health provider describes men's use of power in situations where conflict in relationships is being managed:

> Men use power as defence and this power can come in different ways, sometimes it can be silence; he doesn't talk to you, he doesn't provide.

A different health provider also refers to the relationship dynamics within abusive partnerships. She identifies women's lack of economic autonomy as an explanatory factor underlying abuse:

> Because they are not working, so they depend on men to support them and if the man doesn't want…[to] then they beat them and they tell them, 'I won't give you my money, go and work like other women.'

She then highlights the tactic men employ to justify abuse, which she labels 'emotional blackmail':

> [He will say] 'but I love you and I beat you yesterday because you didn't [do what I wanted].' You know it's a blackmail thing, an emotional thing, 'I beat you because my food wasn't ready.' The man justifies the violence and blames the woman in that way. It is emotional blackmail.

This nurse continues, noting her perception of women's fears of reporting abuse to the police and why they refrain from doing so:

> [Women believe] that if they report [abuse to the police]…the man will hear that, and then he will get more aggressive [and] beat them. They also think that it is normal, like we discussed before.

In this way, health providers described other factors they perceived as exacerbating abuse of women. One nurse took care to emphasise the situation for rural women, whom she perceived as being at greatest risk of abuse:

> If such awareness campaigns [gender-based violence] can be done more often, even in the rural…areas where most women are submissive, and you know they are not financially independent, they are so dependent on these men.

She accentuates the role of education, skills and economic empowerment in breaking the cycle of abuse:

> I think it would help if more women would be empowered, in terms of… educating them, giving them skills so that they don't become dependent on a man.

In sum, from these accounts presented, what emerges is the role of the health system and health providers in observing threats to women's health. Some providers were directly engaged in upholding women's rights and choices. In particular, the health providers identified lack of agentic autonomy and choice as significant impediments to women's health. The narratives also illustrate that providers see women's health holistically. They appear to recognise structural determinants that undermine their patients' health, such as harmful masculinities, socialisation into gender hierarchies, adverse cultural norms of gender, and economic dependence (Sen, Östlin, & George, 2007). As with the participants quoted above, many of the providers interviewed spoke of their actions or their willingness to challenge adverse gender norms, and potentially with men as well.

Key Informants in Policy, Academia and Health Systems

Key informants offer a perspective into institutional (schools, universities, workplaces, the health system) and policy environments that affect women's health and capabilities. Respondents were drawn from sectors comprising gender, health and human rights law, HIV and violence against women (see Table 5.1). The focus here is on drawing out analytical insights from these experts to shed light on the research concern, particularly the enabling environment for HIV and women's health to be supported in law and policies that span the health system and the structural environment.

The Policy Environment for Women's Health in South Africa: Highly Progressive in the 1990s

Respondents noted that a coalition of progressive feminist women's health advocates in the late 1980s and early 1990s were quite successful in influencing health policy of the incoming African National Congress. One participant described the effort to integrate 'gendered concerns and rights concerns' at the time of the 1994 International Conference on Population and Development in Cairo when 'global norms were shifting and consolidating around women's reproductive right and population control.' Debates were taking place, nationally and globally (see Cooper et al., 2004; Tinker, 2000).

> The Women's Health Project [eventually housed at the Wits Centre for Health Policy] led this effort and was pushing 'the policy agenda before and

after democracy,' she noted. These ideas were already being integrated into the women's health policies of the ANC before it came into power. This effort succeeded in organising an influential women's health conference in 1993–1994.

One key informant notes:

It [the Women's Health Project] ended up consulting hundreds and hundreds of women at the conference. It was seen as easy because of the pre-existing relationships at the time—as some of the people who went into the state were feminists.

She emphasises the dynamics at play and the momentum achieved during this period. She also makes reference to how this was later lost:

It was really this sort of feminis inclusive attempt to workshop women's health policies with women on the ground. Cervical cancer…termination of pregnancy…contraception…the Women's Health Conference was the one that consolidated a lot of those policies. And of course this [was a] kind of golden age…

She stresses that issues of gender were located within state policy and reforms at the time:

in the 90s…women did put their [own] interests in the state. I think we lost after that…but… in significant areas [success was achieved], and I think health is one of them…

She highlights the evolution and contributions made:

there was a huge amount of work by NGOs and progressive feminists and academics going in to developing the policy frameworks and the laws, and in many instances it's based on quite grounded research about women's experience…And that, to some extent, is a success story… NGOs are involved in helping designate facilities and help train midwives and become involved in developing support groups for midwives and health workers.

The Reproductive Rights Alliance published the Barometer, which monitored reproductive rights and they helped the Portfolio Committee on Health organise two oversight hearings. She highlights the lack of rights' sensitisation of South African women as an issue, saying that 'a big problem [was] lack of knowledge of women of their rights.'

She references some research on health worker attitudes and social stigma, 'particularly against young women'. She notes that this 'depends on the leadership in particular hospitals as to whether service is provided and how well it's provided.' She states that

> we're a conservative country, and if people are resistant to providing terminations [of pregnancy], then they either don't happen or they happen...in a very limited way...women are turned away and not told where they can go so they're not told about their rights. So there's all kinds of barriers like that.

She remarks that the shift to implementation was more difficult:

> people also were beginning to think...this is the work that government must do, not NGOs...There was the kind of easy stuff, though it wasn't easy, but the easy stuff in terms of national frameworks and constitutions and policies, and implementation becomes a lot more difficult. I also think as the kind of relationship between those in government and civil society widens, your ability to influence becomes a whole lot less.

People who were involved also went on to do other things instead, she notes. She emphasises the reduction of services and burnout of health providers:

> We've witnessed a shrinkage as well. A kind of shrinkage in designated facilities, a shrinkage in availability, and a shrinkage in health workers because I think the health workers themselves through lack of support and stigma have really become exhausted and overburdened. There's a real struggle to implement at provincial level particularly.

The AIDS Movement Should Take on Gender—Or the Feminist Movement Should Take on AIDS?

This burnout and shrinkage became magnified, according to key informants, as the extent of HIV and TB co-infection became evident. One respondent noted that the TAC PMTCT case was criticised by feminists for binding women in the traditional role as bearers of children. She states:

> [They were] perpetuating this notion of women as mothers which…was very prevalent in the ANC and the ANC Women's League.

Nevertheless, it was acknowledged that the TAC case was simply a stepping stone towards universal access to HIV treatment for all South Africans (Albertyn & Meer, 2005). To summarise the view, TAC brought a case to court and won the case on the argument that the South African government must provide services to prevent mother-to-child HIV transmission. The rationale was that it would be easier to win the case on behalf of children in the country, as there was more likely to be sympathy on the part of the courts (and the public) to saving children's lives. This was seen as the most winnable, strategic approach to take, though it was part of a larger strategy to rollout access to cART for all (Heywood, 2009). TAC's approach was disparaged by some gender activists as succumbing to societal norms that see children as innocent victims of the HIV epidemic, whose lives were more valuable than those of women living with HIV (Albertyn & Meer, 2005; Cooper, 2017).

One prominent leader of the civil society mobilisation for treatment access asked the feminists: 'Why aren't you taking on gender?' To which the feminists replied, she recalls:

> It's not up to the women's movement to take it on. And if you think about AIDS, the women's movement is already taking on the issue because it's about gender-based violence and choice and all of these things… so the AIDS movement globally and locally wasn't taking women on at all… these are [the] core issues.

She observes the paradox:

> The AIDS movement here really thought that women should take on AIDS rather than [that the] AIDS [movement] should take on women.

She points to the gendered expectations, while also highlighting women's agency:

> There is absolutely gendered norms and stereotypes about roles and expectations and your place in the world [as a woman]. Women are...also agents that try and do a whole lot with their circumstances.

She highlights the gendered aspects of these problems:

> In the early days, there were people who understood that kind of patriarchy...was acting as a barrier to implementing those [policy] frameworks, and therefore they were able to articulate the problems as not just being ordinary problems of resources and capacity but sort of very gendered problems of attitudes and stereotypes.

Reflecting on the loss of that capability within government, she notes:

> But I think that ability...has disappeared to a large extent from government. So you'll have...these very well-meaning people who understand the basic need for something like abortion, for example, and will argue it and defend it...but, who aren't equipped to fight it in the more sophisticated manner that it needs to be fought [and] don't have that kind of capacity to engage with patriarchy.

The good work of the current Minister of Basic Education in successfully driving enabling policies for girls' education was commended, indicating there are locations of positive policy change in key government sectors:

> I do think there is a concern with the education of girls...in the Department of Education. I... think Angie Motshekga [current education minister] is a feminist. She believes strongly in the education of girls...that might translate into some policies around sexual harassment and safety at schools and all of that. [In contrast] I don't think there's too much around employment. My sense is that there was very little gender [specific focus] in there.

Conservatism

One key informant enunciates the absence of integration of reproductive health services with HIV services as problematic, noting that the very concept of sexual reproductive health and rights is 'tenuous'. It exists in law only, 'with little integration'. She notes that the women's health movement is 'very demobilised at the moment' with the focus on treatment, maternal health and things like MOM Connect [funded by UNICEF, it sends pregnant women reminders about appointments and other information through mobile phone text messaging], which only starts at 20 weeks of pregnancy. She states:

> HIV funding has come from a conservative space. And some funding is tied to conservative groups with little integration of HIV and SRHR.

A respondent highlights that focusing on mothers is socially acceptable, saying 'They are the most vulnerable and most accessible.' She suggests that groups like sex workers, for example, would be less 'politically acceptable' as a targeted group for funding and support by the Department of Health and the donor community.

One key informant remarks that while the leadership within the Ministry of Health has introduced some laudable initiatives, including 'the campaign to have all school girls immunised against HPV', that on the other hand, 'the leadership of Zuma has reinforced the conservative, traditional patriarchal side of our politics and society'.

On this theme, a respondent remarked:

> The sexual harassment case…the head of the ANC in the Cape…He's been accused. He's a friend of Zuma's…This is the head of state. This is the role model. They [ANC] are brushing it aside. The women who actually lay charges are attacked.

Pointing to leadership structures that fail to champion women's role and rights in society and the health sector as a mirror of that, one key informant observes:

> If you look at what is happening within the ANC Women's League [at the moment], they are…cheerleaders for Zuma…the general status of women

as…perceived by traditional patriarchal structures in society…are reflected in the health sector.

On leadership in the Department of Health, one key informant stresses that there has not been the internal leadership in the department to take women's health forward:

My sense is that gender has never really been driven coherently from within the Department of Health. That it's been pushed from outside by really good sort of feminist health programmers—because the health sector, the women's health sector and the NGO sector, were strong and good in this country [historically].

She notes:

[But now] it's very fragmented and very ad hoc because it depends if you can successfully push something through and then, and then get attended to the policy and the question is whether the policy is even implemented.

HIV and Gender-Based Violence

One key informant highlighted the problem of gender-based violence as a health and human rights concern that remains insufficiently recognised:

I think human rights lawyers still frame it [gender-based violence] as [a] health [concern]…We use the word pandemic [to describe gender-based violence], but I do think that we have to understand it equally as a violation of one's civil and political rights.

She highlights a recent example of intimate partner violence that was fatal:

[When Reeva Steenkamp] was tragically murdered, and it captured the country's attention… a lot of people in the women's rights movement were like, 'Please. This happens all the time. Why are you suddenly concerned about this?' I was quite delighted that the country took the position it took. It was a resounding 'this is not ok'. Does it bother me that it doesn't happen in response to every rape and death and act of violence against women? Sure. Am I glad that it at least got a reaction in this particular—and the country gave a loud message, 'No, this is not what we are.' Yes [affirming the importance of this message].

She mentions her work with an NGO focused on stopping abuse and its prevalence among young people:

[Initially] I was focused just on adults being hurt, and over 60–70% of our cases are kids in school being hurt by their educators…we are looking at 9, 10, 11 and 12 year olds. And [a] huge…intersection between early [abuse] and victimisation.

She highlights three life events she characterises as fraught with risk:

there are three things in this country that are some of the most dangerous things to do…ever. One is go to school, the second is get married and the third is have a baby.

She elaborates:

Getting to and from school, the travel involved [alluding to the possibility of rape perpetration]. One. Two: being at school exposes you to incredible rates of violence by the educator. And you have to be in school, and the state is turning away from this…you're punished when you're pregnant, you punished at every turn.…we had a case come out that we couldn't take forward because the learners refused.

She explains the case and the notion of 'sexually transmitted marks' (see Jewkes et al., 2003):

Twenty learners came out saying that the science teacher required them to perform sexual activity with him in order to get their grades. You know there is this phrase, STM?…Sexually transmitted marks. And the phenomenon of sexual marks is so rife…You have to provide sex if you want to catch a taxi. And they [girls] divvy it up, they share it…they'll say "this week it's your turn to give the taxi driver a blow job so we can go to school and so that we can drive to rather than walk to school and all be raped." It's just, so dangerous, right?

She continues to highlight the pernicious effects of IPV, particularly for women in pregnancy:

> And then you live with a man, and we know what the statistics are there regarding intimate partner violence. You are going to be beaten. It's one of the most dangerous things you can do [get married]. And then there is maternal mortality, which is [what] we are busy [fighting]...And of course it triggers the most terminal, life threatening form of violence is when you seek help or get pregnant... is one that is replete with...danger.

She further casts the threats to women's health and wellbeing at particular life stages into sharp relief:

> The aspiration of a happy family unit is filled with danger. The aspiration of exercising your reproductive rights is filled with danger. These are things we are trying to protect, and yet, in protecting them we are exposing people to danger. Women to danger. And then we are not even getting into the realm of equal pay for equal work. We aren't even getting into the realm of institutional sexism or the combination of sexism and racism.

She continues, communicating how this has informed conversations about HIV and GBV:

> It also led to a lot of discussions by campaigners and...movements, like the HIV movement, like the trade labour movement, to say 'Look. Why can't we get a movement around GBV? Can we... find 20 people in this country who are prepared to be public and high profile about their violence based on sex?' And that's assuming all sorts of things. That's assuming that they are wealthy enough. That's assuming that they have enough support. That's assuming that it's not same sex.

She notes recent discussions and differences between the movements for HIV and AIDS and for GBV:

> I remember speaking with someone who was very very high up in the trade union movement who called a meeting to decide he's getting involved now... He's going to sort out GBV. And, he called in a group of people and

> I happened to be there and he was like 'why haven't we got a movement on this. Where's the movement?' I was like, well, with tact, and with HIV, the brilliance of that movement was that it addressed, to some extent, the stigma…you never escape your status of living with HIV… but you…deal with that stigma. But with rape, or domestic violence, what are you going to do? Go out into the street with a placard saying 'my uncle raped me, my father raped me, my husband raped me' and go back home?

She emphasises her perception that HIV can be solved with medication [ARVs] but GBV cannot:

> Because it's not just the stigma of coming out with the reality of this, but it's also that HIV has a solution, it's called an antiretroviral, and thank God we have that solution! Thank goodness, right? But there is some solution to it. What's your solution for GBV? What are they gonna say? Arrest the guy? Most survivors don't want him arrested, they just want it to stop.

The counterview to this, however, is that, as seen earlier in this chapter and in Chap. 2, there are multi-level factors that may render the uptake of or adherence to cART impossible for some women; or, pose great challenges to continuous HIV care.

The Biomedical vs. the Social Model

One respondent suggests the need to go beyond HIV and to remember that health is rooted in social structure. She recalls the historical trajectory of the epidemic and the social response in South Africa:

> I think we should go beyond HIV… Health is embedded in social structure. There is no question. Obviously biology plays a part. HIV/AIDS put health on the public agenda…[A]lso funding came in, so there were people paid to work on AIDS.

She elaborates:

> There is an interesting type of chronology of the power play between the biomedical model and the social model…there was a virus that needed to

> be curbed. And I'm speaking on purpose in medical language. A virus we fight. We find treatment. We find a vaccine. Nothing happened [there was no treatment for many years]. That was the discourse.

She continues to highlight the evolution of the epidemic in South Africa:

> First came prevention. So condoms came in. [with a] straight focus on the individual. So that was the dominant model. When the model did not achieve what it was meant to achieve—treatment was not coming [not yet available, nationally]. Prevention was not successful. Vaccine was not being successfully launched. Slowly, social sciences voices began to arrive. The social voices were coming up and the medical establishment was taking cognisance of the social [science] voices.

She describes being part of an initiative to investigate a potential school of public health in South Africa (at a time when there were none):

> At that stage there was a doctor running it, and she said, you know what? AIDS is not my problem. AIDS is your problem. It's a social problem. That was back in '94. I had been arguing for a long time that AIDS is a social problem...and Jonathan Mann...the first director of [the global AIDS programme at] WHO...was saying we had to look at the three epidemics: the viral epidemic, AIDS (medical condition) and the social epidemic.

She traces the arc of history:

> Unfortunately, he [Mann] was killed in Halifax, but in those years that actually gave...rise to the social aspects...Now that we have treatment that is effective, in the developing countries AIDS is becoming...a rather chronic condition, but we still have the structural issues of risk for young women in societies like South Africa.

She emphasises women's continuing social vulnerability as a factor underpinning HIV risk, particularly among young African women. She then points to remarks at the opening of the July 2016 International

AIDS Society conference in Durban to underscore the low status of black women, linked to rising HIV incidence, as problematic:

> Did you hear Charlize Theron?...[the South African-born Hollywood actress]. Somebody briefed her. She was arguing [at the international AIDS 2016 conference in Durban], 'I'm not happy to be here [discussing the need to prevent new HIV infections in black South African women and girls].' Basically she was arguing that their [black women's] lives don't matter. If you're a black woman, your life matters less.

Part 2. Discussion

Applying the Capabilities Approach to the Findings

In this section, I elaborate the themes (see summary Table 6.1). My objective is to apply the capabilities approach to the findings to investigate what these women participants are able to do and be, using two broad questions as a guide: *What do the findings tell us about the health and capabilities of the study population within South African social context? Do these South African women living with HIV meet the threshold level of capabilities?*

The analysis in the discussion section lays the groundwork for the subsequent chapter, which focuses on gender-transformative interventions to address some of the concerns identified.

Commonality and differences (Nussbaum and Sen). In the Capabilities Approach, Sen (1999) and Nussbaum (2000) both give concerted attention to women's human development and to considerations of gender but their conceptualisations of the CA differ in distinct ways, as noted in Chap. 3. Nussbaum, for example, identifies 10 specific capability domains, suggesting that these ten central capabilities create an account of *indivisible* capabilities that are a pre-requisite to human functioning (Nussbaum, 2002, p. 131). In her view, the larger project of the CA is to pursue capability for each individual, treating each person as an end. The social goal is getting every person above the capability threshold to fulfil the requirements of justice (Nussbaum, 2011). Nussbaum envisages constitutional law as the main vehicle that would address shortfalls in capabilities (2003, 2011). In contrast, Sen spurns the idea of generating a

Table 6.1 Summary of findings from IDIs with participants and health providers

Women's self-reported experiences—the internal
Theme 1: Women's agentic autonomy in health decision making and HIV disclosure constrained by lack of decision making power in households and economic dependence
• Self-reports of autonomy in decision making high but women moderate their behaviours to mitigate economic and health vulnerabilities (physical and psychosocial) that radiate from the household sphere
• Women gauge partner responses, while carefully managing HIV disclosure
Theme 2: Women enact agency to mediate psychosocial distress by seeking formal social support and establishing informal social ties in the health system
• Women actively seek to address lack of partner support
• Health system as first line of defence:
– women link to health providers for formal social support
– women cultivate social ties with other HIV positive women building informal support
• Mental health structures are few and counselling opportunities exist primarily in antenatal care with few to none reported in postnatal period
Theme 3: Patient-provider encounters shape women's positive health behaviours
• Women report education about cART and PMTCT crucial in establishing HIV knowledge and health behaviours
• Health providers reportedly play 'myth busting' role with women patients
• Health providers produce women's health behaviour changes to protect and promote women and child health:
– employing reported tactics of direct prompting, stark warnings of negative effects, reinforcing traditional gender roles (e.g., women as good mothers)
Health providers' experiences with women patients—the external
Theme 4: Some health providers act to reinforce women's choices and rights, reconstructing gender
• Providers view gender hierarchies negatively as affecting patient
– citing gender socialisation, cultural customs reinforcing gender norms and harmful masculinities
• Providers inform and instruct women in key health and human rights' domains: termination of pregnancy, HIV medication adherence, condom use
• Providers express willingness to reconstruct adverse gender norms in relation to women's health and decision making

definitive list of capabilities. His CA is under-theorised and under-formulated by design. He cites the importance of democratic deliberation in determining the nature of the social evaluation process. And suggests that assessment of capabilities, including their weighting and valuation, is to be based on 'reasoned consensus' (Sen, 1999, pp. 78–79; see also Nussbaum's interpretation of Sen, 2011, pp. 69–76).

I capture the rich diversity evident in Sen and Nussbaum's respective formulations by drawing on elements of each, though my analysis in this section engages more carefully with Nussbaum's central capabilities. I assess seven of the ten domains that Nussbaum puts forward. Due to insufficient data from participant interviews to generate a robust analysis along these capabilities, I don't address: *other species; play; or control over one's political environment* (see Nussbaum, 2000, pp. 78–80). I also engage with several chief aspects within Sen's conception, including agency, process and opportunity freedoms and participation. I pay particular attention to the multiple ways that these HIV positive women enact agency in their lives, in order to mediate and navigate structural constraints they face in relation to their own health and HIV care, as well as that of their infants. I also consider how health providers demonstrate agency in ways that take the contestation over gender norms and hierarchies affecting this population into the health system itself.

Bodily health, bodily integrity and control over one's material environment are part of the 10 central capabilities within Nussbaum's treatment of the CA. (For the full list, see Nussbaum, 2000, pp. 78–80.) For Nussbaum, *bodily health* means being able to have good health, which embraces reproductive health, adequate nutrition and shelter (Nussbaum, 2000). *Bodily integrity* entails freedom from violent assault, choice in matters of sexual and reproductive health and sexual satisfaction; while *control over one's material environment* refers to holding property and goods, seeking employment and being able to work, and engaging in meaningful relationships with others in the world of work (Nussbaum, 2000, 2011). In theme 1, this trio of concerns is not only connected in women's lives, they appear to be correlated, as I will show. I thus group them together to explore the nature of those associations.

Theme one captures HIV positive women's reported perceptions of their control over their health, and their autonomy in health decision making. Women stated in IDIs that they themselves made the decisions about their health. Yet, on unspooling the threads of women's stories, through probes and clarifications, a more complex reality emerges. Women gave examples in which their agentic autonomy over their health and wellbeing was constrained in ways that affected them profoundly. For instance, participants consistently cited anxiety, fear and reluctance about disclosing their HIV status because they anticipated partners' angry reactions: a theme also found in other South African studies (Gourlay, Birdthistle, Mburu, Iorpenda, & Wringe, 2013; Hatcher et al., 2014). In a second, dominant example, women reported that they were forced to terminate their pregnancies due to the preferences of their partners. Forced termination went against the deepest fertility intentions of the women cited, also posing a violation of their right to bodily integrity in South African law, i.e., freedom and security of the person (Section 12), and their right to bodily health (Section 27) (Government of South Africa, 1996). These patterns illustrate the ways in which women deferred to men on matters concerning their own bodies. They indicate the manner by which men's preferences constrained women's agentic desires and behaviours in ways that indelibly affected women's physical and mental health. Notably, the perceptions and experiences described by women and captured in the findings were not just cited by the participants. They were confirmed by health providers, highlighted in theme four. Hence, these participants described enacting agency within their circumstances—yet their agentic preferences and behaviours were located within a social system governed largely by harmful gender norms.

Socio-demographic characteristics. The women in the sample were almost uniformly of low socioeconomic status, low social position, and they lacked employment. These characteristics are social stratifiers, and thus play a role in increasing women's exposure and vulnerability to disease, injury and poor health outcomes (Diderichsen, Evans, & Whitehead, 2001). These characteristics, it should be noted, are roughly similar for most black women in South Africa who are living with HIV, and would thus be relevant for women beyond the sample. Although women reported that they typically had sufficient housing and food, it was clear that this was a challenge for some. Indeed, in many cases, women described their situations as precarious. Women's SES, social position and lack of employment help explain why this population describes having reduced agency in the household.

Men's greater power to make key decisions in the household aligns with gender norms in South Africa and other settings (Soman, 1997). Mills wrote in her study of household headship that 'social norms reverberate within constructs of the 'household' in South Africa' (2004, p. 99). In this vein, increasing research points to factors that determine women's range of influence in decision making processes in the home. These include control of assets and income, level of education and age at marriage (UNICEF, 2007). Decisions made within households, UNICEF notes, are negotiated through a bargaining process and one that typically favours men over women, across a range of countries (2007). Along UNICEF's criteria, the South African study population generally lacked control of income and assets, were unemployed and had a secondary level education.

A key point that emerges from the findings is that men's control and decision making—a demonstration of the gender order and women's place within the hierarchy—was not limited to the household domain. Rather, the findings reveal that clinical settings are a location where men seek to extend their sphere of influence and control over women's bodily health and bodily integrity. Women described how their intentions were trumped by men's, and their sexual desires blunted. Similarly, Mills found that South African women participants in her study 'rarely contradicted their husbands' claims to be heads and were for the most part in concurrence that male household headship was a cultural phenomenon' (2004, p. 99). Mills seems to suggest that this gender hierarchy is fairly fixed. However, she observes that 'they [women participants] were keen to challenge other male cultural prerogatives, such as domestic violence' (2004, p. 99). By implication, interventions that address domestic or intimate partner violence (I use the terms interchangeably here) may create an entry point to challenge longstanding gender relations, particularly if women are likely to welcome them. There is a continuum of possible locations in which interventions could be positioned, and these sites within the gender order are connected. How does mediation of one site (e.g., the health system or employment) affect the other (the household)?

The findings, depicted in theme two, highlight women's agentic strategies. Their low income, low employment and low SES generated dual economic and health vulnerabilities they sought to mitigate. Their reported fear of abuse and abandonment linked to being HIV positive was indicative. Women were responding to those vulnerabilities by asserting agentic control over their HIV status, so that they could manage any conflicts that might arise with their partners. Here participants were acting to minimise stress, and seeking to cope with a new HIV diagnosis that had inducted many into a grave new world. Stress seemed most acute for women with the lowest incomes and the most unstable partner relations due to the frequent reports of threatened and actual abuse. Indeed, the high prevalence of IPV in South Africa has been documented in other studies (Dunkle et al., 2004; Hoque & Kader, 2009; Human Rights Watch, 1995), as discussed in previous chapters.

Lower SES has been associated with poorer health for less advantaged groups in different settings. In South Africa, this together with low social position and HIV disclosure to an abusive partner introduce the potential for increased exposure and vulnerability to intimate partner violence in this population. When women experience IPV, there are dire health consequences (Campbell, 2002; Ellsberg et al., 2008), and the real possibility for loss of life: a statistical fact borne out by the South African MRC's statistics on femicide (reviewed in Chap. 2; Abrahams, Mathews, Jewkes, Martin, & Lombard, 2012). Nussbaum defines the capability to life as 'being able to live to the end of a human life of normal length; not dying prematurely, or before one's life is so reduced as to be not worth living' (2000, p. 78). Routine cases of femicide take place in South Africa. This national problem was elevated to the international stage by the news media when Oscar Pistorius, dubbed the Olympian 'Blade Runner' for his use of prosthetic legs, was accused of killing his partner, Reeva Steenkamp. Pistorius was later convicted of culpable homicide (Woolman & Sprague, 2015). One key informant, cited earlier in the chapter, communicated the importance of the Steenkamp case as a litmus test of the country's tolerance for gender-based violence. I take up the capability of life in greater detail shortly.

Given these grounded realities, it becomes difficult for women to engage their imaginations in more pleasurable pursuits or endeavours associated with *senses, imagination and thought*, a capability that Nussbaum describes as 'being able to use imagination and thought in connection with experiencing and producing works and events of one's own choice, religious, literary, musical, and so forth' (2007, pp. 22–24). When women live in anticipation of abandonment, violence or abuse, they are thrust into survival mode, with all of the bodily responses heightened by fear and survival. When abuse remains an impending threat hanging over women like the sword of Damocles, as it seemed to do with this population, their capabilities related to emotions and practical reason contract severely. *Emotions* in Nussbaum's central capabilities entail 'not having one's emotional development blighted by fear and anxiety' (2006, p. 172). *Practical reason* is the capability to formulate desires and accompanying plans, as part of notions of the 'good life' which Nussbaum refers to as the ability 'to form a conception of the good and to engage in critical reflection about the planning of one's life' (2007, pp. 22–24). In these circumstances, women's ability to envisage the good life and to engage in practical reason, to think and to dream, diminishes considerably.

Moreover, women's physical (bodily) and emotional health may be impaired in ways that are difficult to estimate because such abuse is often recurrent. García-Moreno emphasises that 'without intervention, the violence usually escalates in frequency and severity resulting in repeat visits to the healthcare system' (2002, p. 1509; see Rand & Saltzman, 2003). Noting the South African Constitutional Court's recognition of domestic violence as a crime, Meyersfeld writes about its repetitive nature as a distinguishing feature, quoting *State v. Godfrey Baloyi* 2000:

> The South African Constitutional Court has stated that what distinguishes domestic violence from other crimes is its hidden, repetitive character and its immeasurable ripple effects on our society, and in particular, on family life. (2008, p. 72)

In themes three and four, health providers highlighted economic dependence and gender relations as factors enabling women's vulnerability to violence and abuse among their patients. They cited socialisation of women into the gender hierarchy and gender norms, including women's acquiescence to men's insistence on dry sex and lack of condom use, as placing them at risk of HIV. The findings underline the ways that women cannot fully access the sexual satisfaction associated with the capability of bodily integrity. Instead, sexual desires in this population seemed to be ignored so that men could realise theirs (as discussed in Chap. 2). The overall picture drawn is one in which HIV and IPV are correlates: relational threats for women that are deeply enmeshed within the South African context and the gender system. They are part of the fabric of women's every day moral experience and their local worlds (Kleinman, 2004). These two interact to diminish women's agency, erode their human dignity, puncture women's semblance of security, while impairing their human development (Meyersfeld, 2003, 2008).

Process and opportunity freedoms. For Sen, a crucial capability question for women is freedom. Freedom in Sen's CA has an opportunity aspect and a process aspect. For HIV positive women, the opportunity aspect pertains to women's ability to exercise choice in converting their desires into reality, e.g., if a woman wanted to take her ARVs or terminate her pregnancy, the emphasis is on whether she has the opportunity to execute that choice. It does not matter whether she actualises the choice (or indeed, what choice she makes): the focus is on her *opportunity* to do so, as a marker for a set of creative possibilities that allow women agentic power to design their futures. The process aspect is the other side of the coin. It concerns women's ability to exercise agency in ways that influence processes that affect women within society, communities, households and families. The accent is on whether women execute and actualise preferences within their lives (Sen, 1999). These data indicate that in manifold ways, women's opportunity freedoms and their process freedoms, especially related to their bodily integrity, were blocked. Worryingly, this translates into reduced functionings along the entire vector of women's capabilities. It demonstrates the multiple ways that women's human development was impeded (Alkire, 2004).

Affiliation is a capability that includes engaging in social interaction, showing concern for others, having the 'social bases of self-respect' and 'being able to be treated as a dignified being' as well as 'non-discrimination' (Nussbaum, 2007, pp. 22–24). In theme two, the health system as an affiliative location for both medical and psychosocial care (formal and informal), becomes illumined more readily. HIV positive women's reliance on each other was a dominant current coursing through the interviews. Women described the trust and solidarity that came from knowing that other women were going through the same challenges. This illustrates the crucial peer interaction within the community of people living with HIV that has become a signature aspect of the epidemic, seemingly regardless of context (UNAIDS, 2004). It demonstrates how important peers can be in offering positive role modelling and coping, documented in other South African institutional settings such as workplaces (Dickinson, 2009). The health system offers yet another setting where social ties and networks are established. Here the findings contribute to the literature by emphasising the agentic behaviours of women in forging these relationships among themselves. At the same time, the role of the health system in enabling a space for a majority of women to feel non-discrimination, respect and care in their encounters with health providers shifts into clearer focus.

Mental Health

An additional layer is worthy of note: pregnancy. Pregnancy introduces a host of health and psychosocial considerations for women to manage, again affixed to women's biological and social vulnerabilities. These participants voiced concerns over their infants' health and welfare, and their own. Low-income women in low- and middle-income countries have been shown to be at high risk of depression during both antenatal and postnatal periods (Bennett, Einarson, Taddio, Koren, & Einarson, 2004). Two studies of South African women in different locations found 40–50% of women experience depression during the perinatal period, regardless of HIV status (Hartley et al., 2011; Rochat, Bland, Tomlinson, & Stein, 2011). Globally, 82% of women living with HIV report depression symptoms (Orza et al., 2015), and these are likely to increase during the perinatal period (Nachega et al., 2012; WHO, n.d.). Studies have documented that HIV stigma is particularly associated with depressive symptoms; and that HIV stigma and social support are inter-related, suggesting that support helps mediate the negative effects of anticipated, experienced, self-stigma (or internalised stigma) (Brittain et al., 2017; Helms et al., 2016; HSRC, 2015). Multiple studies from sub-Saharan Africa generally and South Africa specifically have focused on associations between depression and poor adherence among HIV positive women (Hodgson et al., 2014). There is, however, an absence of literature on how women in African health systems seek to gain psychosocial support over the entire HIV care continuum as active agents rather than as more passive recipients.

The findings here contribute to filling this gap in the extant literature. They indicate that women actively mediate their distress by relying on the support they find within the health system or linked to it; and they point to a possible void. Access to psychosocial support and resources was reported by women primarily during pregnancy, and through formal structures in antenatal care. Few women spoke of mental health support in postnatal care, which suggests that there might be a vacuum in facilities at that stage as much of the policy emphasis in South Africa has focused on antenatal care in order to minimise the potential for HIV transmission to the child. The extant literature indicates that women are lost to follow up in the postnatal period. This phenomenon, termed the 'postpartum cliff' by Psaros et al. (2015) suggests that there are limited data on the postpartum period, with few data on retention of women in long-term care. In short, factors such as mobility may help explain why women patients seem to vanish from the health system, becoming lost to follow up. But the findings also suggest that there could be socioeconomic or psychosocial factors underlying these patterns, as studies in other settings have shown (Lindau et al., 2006). Data are sufficient to demonstrate the critical importance of attending to psycho-social dimensions HIV positive women face, through greater investments in formal mental health structures or informal support mechanisms. The findings also lend further support to calls by SANAC for electronic data, better data capture and reporting, and shorter release times of data, in order to understand phenomena on HIV care linkage, lapses and adherence to optimise the health of women and their infants (2014).

Given these patterns, there are at least two distinguishing features associated with the South African context that raise the stakes, and thus the urgency, of disrupting patterns of men's dominance, especially over women's health and decision making, while better attending to factors that stratify social opportunities that influence women's health. First, unlike some countries, women's sexual and reproductive health and rights in

South Africa, the legal right to choose to terminate their pregnancies, or not to terminate, are enshrined in the Bill of Rights and the basic law, along with women's right to substantive equality (Albertyn, 2007; Government of South Africa, 1996). That women were unable to make choices affecting their sexual and reproductive health is then a clear infringement of their rights. This is a point that holds for all women, whether or not they are HIV positive. These data thus highlight the gap that exists between the legal framework and women's ability to benefit from it in their daily lives.

Second, women in the sample are indeed living with HIV. HIV could be managed as a chronic condition with the appropriate treatment, care and support. Studies have found HIV disclosure to be important in fostering medication adherence for those who are HIV positive (Gourlay et al., 2013). In a qualitative study among South African pregnant women accessing PMTCT services, for example, colleagues Hatcher et al. (2014) found that women's non-disclosure of their HIV status to partners, primarily due to fear of violence, led to barriers in terms of visiting health clinics for services and to adhering to medication, as these activities might accidentally disclose their status. Similarly, in a systematic review of barriers to cART uptake for women in sub-Saharan Africa accessing PMTCT programmes, women reported fear of disclosure of their HIV status to partners, family and community members as a major barrier to care (Gourlay et al., 2013). Achieving continuous care and adherence are crucial to the achievement of optimal HIV outcomes for women and their children (Gardner, McLees, Steiner, Del Rio, & Burman, 2011; McNairy & El-Sadr, 2012; Wettstein et al., 2012), and to reduce the possibility of multiple morbidities and premature HIV-related deaths from opportunistic infections (WHO, 2006a).

These data suggest that South African women living with HIV are not able to access the full gamut of existing resources that should be available to them, both in the law and in health care settings. Moreover, this is not because health providers are failing women, or because women lack legal rights, the impediments can be attributed to gender norms that subvert women's agentic power and control.

Women's Inability to Access Employment as a Capability

A measure of capability within Sen's CA is *participation*. Participation can refer to community life, relationships, the household and working life (Alkire, 2004). While women were able to participate in various structures, such as the family and church life, the extent of their control was described as curtailed. Many women in the sample were unable to partake in a core aspect of wellbeing, gainful employment. Stable employment can serve as a route out of structural poverty (Boserup, 2007). Employment has extrinsic benefits of regular, reliable pay and retirement, typically associated with the skilled professions. These tangibles include accumulated earnings, greater economic security as people age, and in turn, more secure lives. Economic benefits also offer a stream of future possibilities for accessing opportunities for individuals to construct lives they have reason to value (Sen, 1999), in accordance with their desires and choices. Employment can also confer important intrinsic benefits, such as a sense of fulfilment, self-esteem or purpose, and possibilities to become part of a community of like-minded colleagues. The benefits attributed to employment represent important quality of life dimensions (WHO Quality of Life, 2012).

That the capability of employment participation remains out of reach for these women living with HIV, and black South African women generally, more than 14 years after the introduction of democracy is troubling. This places emphasis on the role of employment and education as essential building blocks that support human development along the life course (Kuh, Ben-Schlomo, Lynch, Hallqvist, & Power, 2003). *Life* is regarded as a core capability by Sen (2002), Nussbaum (2000) and Ruger (2006). All three make explicit mention of the deleterious effects of HIV on the capability of life. Each stresses that HIV is *preventable and treatable*, and *HIV-related deaths are avoidable*. Sen emphasises the importance of the 'particularly pernicious influence of deaths that could be avoided due to preventable and treatable diseases, like HIV' (1999). Along the capability of life, the study population has a shorter lifespan compared to their white or Indian counterparts. They are more likely to acquire HIV and to die prematurely from HIV-related illnesses than women of other race groups in South Africa. Chapter 2 reviewed the robust body of evidence demonstrating black South African women's increased exposure and vulnerability to HIV via various mechanisms. Nevertheless, there is some support and protection of the study population's capabilities in terms of life, bodily health and bodily integrity. Much of this comes from the health system. An avalanche of published data reaffirm cART's primary role as a lifesaving intervention for people living with HIV (Walensky, Paltiel, & Losina, 2006; UNAIDS, 2014b). Therefore, these participants were describing access to cART, prevention and health care, which was supporting life and bodily health in crucial ways. Concerted attempts were also being made by providers to protect and support women's bodily integrity.

Strikingly, themes three and four place the health encounters between participants and their health providers into sharper relief. By establishing trust and guiding women, health providers were assisting women to establish an essential base of HIV knowledge such that women could manage HIV as a chronic condition, assisting in improving—not just their health—but their wellbeing, through access to lifelong HIV care and psychosocial support. The participants recalled their direct promptings by health providers on specific aspects of HIV, telling women how to change their health behaviours to protect or to promote the woman's health or the child's. These health encounters were characterised by HIV positive women as highly influential and generally positive, though poor care and some judgemental or rude health providers were cited by participants, particularly in the labour and maternity wards. In those instances, women communicated their tendency to 're-route', i.e., they would go around those individuals, like obstacles on an obstacle course, and instead seek out the friendly, caring providers.

While the focus has been on HIV positive women as the protagonists of the story thus far, in theme four the dominant frame shifts from patients to providers of health care. Health providers offering care to the study population move onto centre stage. Emerging from provider interviews are the ways this group is positioned to observe and address gender and health in their patients. They describe resorting to specific tactics to change health behaviours in their patients, with a view to protecting women's health, life and bodily integrity as capabilities. Providers expressed seeing gender norms and expectations that affect women's human rights in particular domains. They communicated strong negative views on the role of gender hierarchies. Providers' comments demonstrate how health threats and abuse in their patients are a distinct motif that appears in providers' daily interactions with women.

Underlying their narratives is an unmistakable pattern. These health providers questioned pernicious social constructions of gender and how they affect women's health. They appear to identify adverse gender norms as a crucial impediment to their patients' health that they are willing to keep in check, a pattern found in other studies (Joyner & Mash, 2012; Kim & Motsei, 2002). This offers another dimension. It illustrates the power of the health system as an important social institution that can be transformative in women's lives. These descriptions from the stewards of health care indicate the potential to reshape gender norms that is yet unexploited (see also Sprague et al., 2015; Woolman & Sprague, 2015). We begin to see how the health system as an institution of care can be located within both the broader framework of society (reflecting gender norms) and within women's daily experience (Kleinman, 2004).

These findings suggest, overall, that while some women living with HIV in the sample do meet threshold levels of capability, the majority do not. Rather, as a group they experience capability deprivation in the following particular domains: life, bodily health, bodily integrity and control over their material environment. These deprivations cascade to undermine other capabilities in the domains of emotions, practical reason, and senses, imagination and thought. In analysing the data underlying these findings, it can be observed that the health care system and social-structural determinants (i.e., income, employment and SES) are not only tightly bound in influencing women's health and wellbeing, these forces act in a web-like pattern and are inseparable (Solar & Irwin, 2007; Sen et al., 2007). In this setting where HIV and IPV prevalence are both high due to the prevailing social structure, access to continuous health and HIV care fundamentally affects black South African women's life chances and full range of capabilities: what women are able to be and do (Campbell, 2003; Ellsberg et al., 2008; Meyersfeld, 2003, 2008). While women's capabilities in terms of life and bodily health are supported by cART and by their contact with health providers and women in the health system, these gains might diminish as they lose more regular exposure to the health system following delivery. Although 89 women is a relatively small sample, the characteristics of the sample are indeed shared by many HIV positive pregnant and postpartum women across the country, and therefore the findings are relevant outside of the Eastern Cape and Gauteng.

References

Abrahams, N., Mathews, S., Jewkes, R., Martin, L., & Lombard, C. (2012). *Every Eight Hours: Intimate Femicide in South Africa 10 Years Later!* [online]. Tygerberg: South African Medical Research Council. Retrieved November 1, 2016, from http://www.mrc.ac.za/policybriefs/everyeighthours.pdf

Albertyn, C. (2007). Substantive equality and transformation in South Africa. *South African Journal on Human Rights, 23*(2), 253–276.

Albertyn, C., & Meer, S. (2005). Citizens or mothers? The marginalisation of women's reproductive rights in the struggle for access to health care for HIV positive pregnant women in South Africa. In M. Mukhopadhyay & S. Meer (Eds.), *Gender, Rights and Development: A Global Sourcebook* (pp. 26–56). Amsterdam: The Royal Tropical Institute.

Alkire, S. (2004, September). *The Capability Approach and Human Development Presentation*. Oxford University, 1–15.

Arber, S., & Cooper, H. (2000). Gender and inequalities in health across the lifecourse. In E. Annandale & K. Hunt (Eds.), *Gender Inequalities in Health* (pp. 123–149). Philadelphia: Open University Press.

Bennett, H., Einarson, A., Taddio, A., Koren, G., & Einarson, T. (2004). Prevalence of depression during pregnancy: Systematic review. *Obstetrics and Gynecology, 103*(4), 698–709.

Boserup, E. (2007). *Women's Role in Economic Development*. New York: Earthscan.

Brittain, K., Mellins, C. A., Phillips, T., Zerbe, A., Abrams, E. J., Myer, L., & Remien, R. H. (2017). Social support, stigma and antenatal depression among HIV-infected pregnant women in South Africa. *AIDS & Behavior, 21*(1), 274–282.

Campbell, C. (2003). *Letting Them Die: Why HIV/AIDS Prevention Programmes Fail*. Bloomington: Indiana University Press.

Campbell, J. (2002). Intimate partner violence and physical health consequences. *Archives of Internal Medicine, 162*(10), 1157–1163.

Charmaz, K. (1999). Stories of suffering: Subjective tales and research narratives. *Qualitative Health Research, 9*(3), 362–382.

Cooper, D. (2017). Email communication with the author, 30 May.

Cooper, D., Morroni, C., Orner, P., Moodley, J., Harries, J., Cullingworth, L., et al. (2004). Ten years of democracy in South Africa: Documenting transformation in reproductive health policy and status. *Reproductive Health Matters, 12*(24), 70–85.

Dickinson, D. (2009). *Changing the Course of AIDS: Peer Education in South Africa and Its Lessons for the Global Crisis.* Ithaca, NY: Cornell University Press.

Diderichsen, F., Evans, T., & Whitehead, M. (2001). The social disparities in health. In T. Evans, M. Whitehead, F. Diderichsen, A. Bhuiya, & M. Wirth (Eds.), *Challenging Inequities to Health: From Ethics to Action* (pp. 12–23). Oxford: Oxford University Press.

Dunkle, K., Jewkes, R., Brown, H., Gray, G., McIntyre, J., & Harlow, S. (2004). Transactional sex among women in Soweto, South Africa: Prevalence, risk factors and associations with HIV infection. *Social Science & Medicine, 59*(8), 1581–1592.

Eastern Cape Department of Health, Government of South Africa. (2008). *HIV, AIDS & STIs 2007–2008 Business Plan.* Bisho: Eastern Cape Department of Health.

Ellsberg, M., Jansen, H., Heise, L., Watts, C., García-Moreno, C., & WHO Multi-Country Study on Women's Health and Domestic Violence Against Women Study Team. (2008). Intimate partner violence and women's physical and mental health in the WHO multi-country study on women's health and domestic violence: An observational study. *Lancet, 371*(9619), 1165–1172.

Farmer, P., Connors, M., & Simmons, J. (2011). *Women, Poverty, and AIDS.* Monroe: Common Courage Press.

García-Moreno, C. (2002). Dilemmas and opportunities for an appropriate health-service response to violence against women. *Lancet, 359*(9316), 1509–1514.

Gardner, E., McLees, M., Steiner, J., Del Rio, C., & Burman, W. (2011). The spectrum of engagement in HIV care and its relevance to test-and-treat strategies for prevention of HIV infection. *Clinical Infectious Diseases, 52*(6), 793–800.

Gauteng Provincial Department of Health, Government of South Africa. (2009). *Annual Performance Plan 2009*. Pretoria: Gauteng Department of Health.

Gourlay, A., Birdthistle, I., Mburu, G., Iorpenda, K., & Wringe, A. (2013). Barriers and facilitating factors to the uptake of antiretroviral drugs for prevention of mother-to-child transmission of HIV in sub-Saharan Africa: A systematic review. *Journal of the International AIDS Society, 16*, 18588.

Government of South Africa. (1996). The Constitution of the Republic of South Africa, Act No. 108 of 1996. Cape Town: South Africa.

Hartley, M., Tomlinson, M., Greco, E., Comulada, W., Stewart, J., Roux, I., et al. (2011). Depressed mood in pregnancy: Prevalence and correlates in two Cape Town peri-urban settlements. *Reproductive Health, 8*, 9.

Hatcher, A., Woollett, N., Pallitto, C., Mokoatle, K., Stockl, H., MacPhail, C., et al. (2014). Bidirectional links between HIV and intimate partner violence in pregnancy: Implications for prevention of mother-to-child transmission. *Journal of the International AIDS Society, 17*, 19233.

Helms, C. B., Turan, J. M., Atkins, G., Kempf, M. C., Clay, O. J., Raper, J. L., et al. (2016). Interpersonal mechanisms contributing to the association between HIV-related internalized stigma and medication adherence. *AIDS and Behavior, 21*(1), 238–247.

Heywood, M. (2009). South Africa's Treatment Action Campaign: Combining law and social mobilization to realize the right to health. *Journal of Human Rights Practice, 1*(1), 14–36.

Hodgson, I., Plummer, M., Konopka, S., Colvin, C., Jonas, E., Albertini, J., et al. (2014). A systematic review of individual and contextual factors affecting ART initiation, adherence, and retention for HIV-infected pregnant and postpartum women. *PLoS ONE, 9*(11), e111421.

Hoque, M., & Kader, S. (2009). Prevalence and experience of domestic violence among rural pregnant women in KwaZulu-Natal, South Africa. *South African Journal of Epidemiology and Infection, 24*(4), 34–37.

Human Rights Watch. (1995). *Violence Against Women in South Africa: The State Response to Domestic Violence and Rape*. New York: Human Rights Watch.

Human Sciences Research Council. (2015). *The People Living with HIV Stigma Index: South Africa 2014*. Pretoria: HSRC, South African National AIDS Council, and UNAIDS.

Hunter, M. (2010). *Love in the Time of AIDS. Inequality, Gender and Right in South Africa*. Durban: University of KwaZulu-Natal Press.

Jewkes, R., Abrahams, N., & Mvo, Z. (1998). Why do nurses abuse patients? Reflections from South African obstetric services. *Social Science & Medicine, 47*(11), 1781–1795.

Jewkes, R., Levin, J., & Penn-Kekana, L. (2002). Risk factors for domestic violence: Findings from a South African cross-sectional study. *Social Science & Medicine, 55*, 1603–1617.

Jewkes, R., Levin, J., & Penn-Kekana, L. (2003). Gender inequalities, intimate partner violence and HIV preventive practices: Findings of a South African cross-sectional study. *Social Science & Medicine, 56*, 125–134.

Jewkes, R., Penn-Kekana, L., & Rose-Junius, H. (2005). "If they rape me, I can't blame them": Reflections on gender in the social context of rape in South Africa and Namibia. *Social Science & Medicine, 61*, 1809–1820.

Joyner, K., & Mash, B. (2012). A comprehensive model for intimate partner violence in South African primary care: Action research. *BMC Health Services Research, 12*, 399.

Kim, J., & Motsei, M. (2002). "Women enjoy punishment": Attitudes and experiences of gender-based violence among PHC nurses in rural South Africa. *Social Science & Medicine, 54*, 1243–1254.

Kleinman, A. (2004). Ethics and experience: An anthropological approach to health equity. In P. Anand, F. Peter, & A. Sen (Eds.), *Public Health, Ethics, and Equity* (pp. 269–282). Oxford: Oxford University Press.

Kuh, D., Ben-Schlomo, Y., Lynch, J., Hallqvist, J., & Power, C. (2003). Life course epidemiology. *Journal of Epidemiology & Community Health, 57*, 778–783.

Lindau, S., Jerome, J., Miller, K., Monk, E., Garcia, P., & Cohen, M. (2006). Mothers on the margins: Implications for eradicating perinatal HIV. *Social Science & Medicine, 62*(1), 59–69.

Link, B., & Phelan, J. (2001). Conceptualizing stigma. *Annual Review of Sociology, 27*, 363–385.

McNairy, M., & El-Sadr, W. (2012). The HIV care continuum: No partial credit given. *AIDS, 26*(14), 1735–1738.

Mendel, G. (2001). *A Broken Landscape: HIV/AIDS in Africa*. London: Blume.

Meyersfeld, B. (2003). Reconceptualizing domestic violence in international law. *Albany Law Review, 67*, 371–426.

Meyersfeld, B. (2008). Domestic violence, health and international law. *Emory International Law Review, 22*, 61–112.

Mills, S. (2004). *Housing the household: Gender and empowerment in South Africa*. PhD thesis. London: London School of Economics, Department of Geography and Environment.
Nachega, J., Uthman, O., Anderson, J., Peltzer, K., Wampold, S., Cotton, M., et al. (2012). Adherence to antiretroviral therapy during and after pregnancy in low-income, middle-income, and high-income countries: A systematic review and meta analysis. *AIDS, 26*(16), 2039–2052.
Nussbaum, M. (2000). *Women and Human Development: The Capabilities Approach*. Cambridge: Cambridge University Press.
Nussbaum, M. (2002). Capabilities and social justice. *International Studies Review, 4*(2), 123–135.
Nussbaum, M. (2003). Capabilities as fundamental entitlements: Sen and social justice. *Feminist Economics, 9*(2–3), 33–59.
Nussbaum, M. (2006). Women's bodies: Violence, security, capabilities. *Journal of Human Development, 6*(2), 167–183. Published online 17 August.
Nussbaum, M. (2007). Human rights and human capabilities: Twentieth century reflections. *Harvard Human Rights Journal, 20*, 21–24.
Nussbaum, M. (2011). *Creating Capabilities*. Cambridge: Harvard University Press.
Orza, L., Bewley, S., Logie, C. H., Crone, E. T., Moroz, S., Strachan, S., et al. (2015). How does living with HIV impact on women's mental health? Voices from a global survey. *Journal of the International AIDS Society, 18*(Suppl. 5), 20289.
Psaros, C., Remmert, J., Bangsberg, D., Safren, S., & Smit, J. (2015). Adherence to HIV care after pregnancy among women in sub-Saharan Africa: Falling off the cliff of the treatment cascade. *Current HIV/AIDS Reports, 12*(1), 1–5.
Rand, M., & Saltzman, L. (2003). The nature and extent of recurring intimate partner violence against women in the United States. *Journal of Comparative Family Studies, 34*, 137–149.
Rochat, T., Bland, R., Tomlinson, M., & Stein, A. (2011). The prevalence and clinical presentation of antenatal depression in rural South Africa. *Journal of Affective Disorders, 135*, 362–373.
Ruger, J. (2006). Ethics and governance of global health inequalities. *Journal of Epidemiological and Community Health, 60*, 998–1003.
Sen, A. (1999). *Development as Freedom*. New York: Random House.
Sen, A. (2002). Why health equity? *Health Economics, 11*, 659–666.

Sen, A. (2004b). Health achievement and equity: External and internal perspectives. In S. Anand, F. Peter, & A. Sen (Eds.), *Public Health, Ethics, and Equity* (pp. 263–268). Oxford: Oxford University Press.

Sen, A. (2009). *The Idea of Justice*. Cambridge: Harvard University Press.

Sen, G., Östlin, P., & George, A. (2007). Unequal, unfair, ineffective and inefficient gender inequity in health: Why it exists and how we can change it. In *Report of the Women and Gender Equity Knowledge Network of the Commission on Social Determinants of Health, Final Report to the Commission on Social Determinants of Health*. Geneva: WHO.

Shisana, O., Rehle, T., Simbayi, L., Zuma, K., Jooste, S., Zungu, N., et al. (2014). *South African National HIV Prevalence, Incidence and Behaviour Survey, 2012*. Cape Town: HSRC Press.

Soman, K. (1997). Picture of Women's Health: Three stories. *Economic and Political Weekly, 32*(8), 396–398.

Solar, O., & Irwin, A. (2007). *A Conceptual Framework for Action on the Social Determinants of Health*. Discussion paper for the Commission on Social Determinants of Health (April). Geneva: WHO.

South African National AIDS Council (SANAC). (2014). *Progress Report on the National Strategic Plan for HIV, TB and STIs 2012–2016*. Pretoria: South African National AIDS Council.

Sprague, C., Hatcher, A., Woollett, N., & Black, V. (2015). How nurses in Johannesburg address intimate partner violence in female patients: Understanding IPV responses in low and middle-income country health systems. *Journal of Interpersonal Violence, 32*(11), 1591–1619.

Sprague, C., Hatcher, A., Woollett, N., Sommers, T., & Black, V. (2016a). They can't report abuse; they can't move out. They are at the mercy of these men: Exploring connections between intimate partner violence, gender and HIV in South African clinical settings. *Culture, Health & Sexuality, 18*(5), 567–581. Epub, 2016.

Sprague, C., Woollett, N., Parpart, J., Hatcher, A., Sommers, T., Brown, S., et al. (2016b). When nurses are also patients: Intimate partner violence and the health system as an enabler of women's health and institutional agency in Johannesburg. *Global Public Health, 11*(1–2), 169–183, Epub 2015.

Stats SA. (2016a). *Mid-Year Population Estimates 2016, Statistical Release P0302*. Pretoria: Statistics South Africa.

Stats SA. (2016b). *Labour-Force Survey, Quarter 2*. Pretoria: Statistics South Africa.

Stats SA. (2016c). *Community Survey 2016*. Pretoria: Statistics South Africa.

Tinker, A. (2000). Women's health: The unfinished agenda. *International Journal of Gynecology and Obstetrics, 70*, 149–158.

UNAIDS. (2004). *Greater Involvement of People Living with HIV and AIDS Policy Brief.* [online]. New York: UNAIDS. Retrieved February 2, 2016, from http://data.unaids.org/pub/BriefingNote/2007/jc1299_policy_brief_gipa.pdf

UNAIDS. (2014b). *The Gap Report.* Geneva: UNAIDS.

UNICEF. (2007). *State of the World's Children.* New York: UNICEF.

Uthman, O., Magidson, J., Safren, S., & Nachega, J. (2014). Depression and adherence to antiretroviral therapy in low-, middle- and high-income countries: A systematic review and meta-analysis. *Current HIV/AIDS Reports, 11*(3), 291–307.

Walensky, R., Paltiel, A., & Losina, E. (2006). The survival benefits of AIDS treatment in the United States. *Journal of Infectious Diseases, 194*(1), 11–19.

Wettstein, C., Mugglin, C., Egger, M., Blaser, N., Vizcaya, L. S., Estill, J., et al. (2012). Missed opportunities to prevent mother-to-child-transmission: Systematic review and meta-analysis. *AIDS, 26*(18), 2361–2373.

Woolman, S., & Sprague, C. (2015). Nowhere to run, nowhere to hide: The absence of public policy as to how health care professionals should address intimate partner violence constitutes a breach of the rights to health and bodily integrity under the South African Constitution. *Cardozo Journal of Law & Gender, 22*(1), 29–74.

WHO. (2006a). *Sexual and Reproductive Health for Women Living with HIV/AIDS: Guidelines on Care, Treatment and Support for Women Living with HIV/AIDS and Their Children in Resource-Constrained Settings.* Geneva: WHO.

WHO. (2006b). *Defining Sexual Health: Report of a Technical Consultation on Sexual Health.* Geneva: WHO.

WHO Quality of Life (WHOQOL). (2012). *WHOQOL BREF Instrument.* Geneva: WHO.

WHO. (n.d.). Maternal and perinatal health. Retrieved June 30, 2017, from http://www.who.int/maternal_child_adolescent/topics/maternal/maternal_perinatal/en/

Part III

Moving from Evidence to Action

7

Gender-Transformative Structural Interventions to Advance South African Women's Capabilities

In the previous chapter, I applied the Capabilities Approach to the findings from the empirical research conducted among 89 women living with HIV. This yielded insights concerning the health, wellbeing and capabilities of the study population of women living with HIV. That analysis allowed for a clearer depiction of those capabilities that are being undermined and rights infringed in the study population. In this chapter, my aim is to sharpen the analytical focus on structure to investigate how selected interventions might protect women from HIV, as part of the capability of bodily health, and from IPV, as part of the capability of bodily integrity. I review the published literature, using these questions as a guide: What are examples of interventions that hold the most promise of engaging with structural and social factors that underlie women's risk of HIV? What are the criteria, i.e., the essential elements, comprising such interventions? What is the evidence of their effectiveness? What do the results tell us about their potential role in advancing the capabilities of bodily health and bodily integrity in women and girls?

To answer the questions, I conduct a thematic review of the extant research literature, with an emphasis on published journal articles (limited to the last five to twelve years) that have gone through a process of double blind peer review. I use the results from this review and synthesis

C. Sprague, *Gender and HIV in South Africa*, Global Research in Gender, Sexuality and Health, https://doi.org/10.1057/978-1-137-55997-5_7

of the literature to construct a set of criteria—a mix of elements that emerge from the findings and analyses within the published studies. Based on the results of the review, I present two case studies that meet the criteria, have been implemented in South Africa (and in other countries) and evaluated, with fruitful results: The Stepping Stones empowerment programme; and the Intervention with Microfinance for AIDS and Gender Equity (IMAGE), a microfinance, gender and HIV education programme. I tease out the insights that can be drawn from those experiences, and reflect on their core strengths in advancing key capabilities for South African women living with and at risk of HIV acquisition. I close the chapter with brief discussion of continuing debates and challenges.

Evolving Concepts and Evidence

> There has been a definite shift in the international public and political rhetoric on HIV/AIDS over the last two years. The dominant discourse now reflects an increased acknowledgement of the role that gender plays in fuelling the epidemic. (Gupta, 2000, p. 7)

In the health sciences, interventions can be defined as actions, typically directed by health experts, to address a disease or risk of disease acquisition (Blankenship, Friedman, Dworkin, & Mantell, 2006) (see Chap. 2 for an explanation of the concept of risk and the risk environment in South Africa). Interventions tend to occur in groups, as in a 'family' of clustered activities that engage different factors or dimensions as part of the whole. Structural interventions refer to those activities that advance health by altering the structural context 'within which health is produced and reproduced' (Blankenship et al., 2006, p. 59). Structural interventions are distinguished from other public health interventions that seek to promote or protect health because they locate 'the cause of public health problems in contextual or environmental factors that shape determinants of infection or morbidities' rather than in characteristics of individuals (Blankenship et al., 2006, p. 59).

A two-fold set of assumptions underpins the relatively recent focus on GTIs pitched at structural level change—that have been developed to respond to high HIV risk among women in particular settings—such as

Southern Africa. First, the interventions are premised on the notion, described earlier, that a social basis undergirds ongoing HIV risk in women and girls, and that these social factors are capable of being modified through clusters of targeted activities (Gupta, Parkhurst, Ogden, Aggleton, & Mahal, 2008). The results of the structural interventions implemented in South Africa point to what factors are modifiable, while offering evidence to guide policy. Second, the emphasis on structure as a target of interventions is a path-breaking shift that explicitly recognises the role of gender as a structural determinant of health in relation to women's risk of IPV and HIV acquisition.

The introduction of the term gender-transformative interventions, vis-à-vis HIV and AIDS, is largely attributed to research and related contributions by Geeta Rao Gupta. In July 2000, Gupta made a powerful plenary address at the Durban XIIIth International AIDS Conference. She called on scholars, programmers, government officials, donors and health providers to reflect on the ways that gender norms, roles and relations contribute to fostering the HIV epidemic (Gupta, 2000). She asked the audience:

> How is one to overcome these seemingly insurmountable barriers of gender and sexual inequality? How can we change the cultural norms that create these damaging, even fatal, gender disparities and roles?

Gupta then went on to highlight key aspects of gender-transformative programmes conducted in different locales, including in South Africa. At the time, a *frisson* of electrical energy lit up the conference hall, igniting the HIV community's efforts and ushering in a new chapter of the global HIV response, whereby gender relations and gendered power in HIV transmission moved from the margins to take up a more central role.

Notably, this change occurred on the back of an evidence base of interventions that had largely failed to prevent new HIV infections, particularly in sub-Saharan Africa. The primary focus had historically been on individual behaviour, with a neglect of structural factors and other social determinants of health. Parkhurst stresses the importance of this shift:

> For three decades, the HIV prevention community has struggled to reduce the spread of HIV through sexual risk behaviours with limited success, but

> equally with limited engagement with the lessons…learned about the social realities shaping patterns of sexual practice. (2014, p. 1; see Auerbach, Caceres, & Parkhurst, 2011)

Since then, significant contributions to knowledge have shaped the terrain in which gender, health inequalities and HIV can be located. These have occurred along a historical trajectory with stark differences by region and country that accord with national responses to the continuing problems of HIV and violence against women and girls (VAWG).

Within the developing body of evidence—spanning social and gender inequalities in health, HIV, intimate partner violence, and VAWG, gendered health behaviours and social constructions of gender—intervention approaches have been giving careful attention to supporting and protecting women who are at risk of HIV infection, and at risk of intimate partner violence. Indeed, the literature demonstrates a growing recognition of HIV and VAWG as dual threats (Chaps. 2–3). However, measures, including health measures, to address dimensions of both violence and HIV are still developing. While there are some debates and differences, there is convergence on a set of factors or essential elements that must be in place for GTIs to generate changes at the structural level.

Core Elements Within Effective Gender-Transformative Interventions

A first element among the essentials is, then, that interventions must be tailored to the specific social context as, crucially, the relation of structural factors to HIV risk is complex and variable, as is the interaction of HIV with other endemic and epidemic factors (e.g., TB or other STIs) (Dworkin, Hatcher, Colvin, & Peacock, 2013; Dworkin, Treves-Kagan, & Lippman, 2013; Gupta et al., 2008). The nature of evidence and its contextual relevance may differ by country, and responses must align with the needs of key affected populations. This is true particularly for those most vulnerable and marginalised, who carry the weight of social disadvantage and social stigma, and for whom social position in the social hierarchy and gender order influences their agentic desires, and whether—and to what extent—they can be realised. In acknowledging the key importance of social context, UNAIDS has adopted the approach to HIV prevention programming titled, *Know your epidemic, know your response* to locate epidemic responses within their respective social settings (Buse, Dickinson & Sidibe, 2008). Accordingly, in this chapter, I select concepts, debates and interventions that have typically been implemented in the South African context, with its particular social, cultural norms (reviewed in Chap. 2) and political dispensation; and its high prevalence of HIV and IPV, as well as other types of structural violence.

There is recognition, too, that interventions must conceptualise and then address social or structural factors underlying women's risk of HIV and IPV. There is a lack of definition and consensus on what these factors comprise, however. UNAIDS, for example, refers to factors underpinning HIV risk as both structural and social factors. A working group called the 'social drivers group AIDS' notes that there is no uniform or agreed definition (Auerbach et al., 2011). UNAIDS, they write, refers to these as 'the social and structural factors, such as poverty, gender inequality, and human rights violations, that are not easily measured that increase people's vulnerability to HIV infection' (Auerbach et al., 2011, p. 2). Gibbs, Willan, Misselhorn, and Mangoma march boldly into the muddied terrain to underscore that there are two chief structural factors that are associated with HIV risk in Southern Africa, namely, 'gender inequalities...and livelihood insecurity' (2012, p. 2). They suggest a focus on structural interventions: 'on how these two factors intersect', with the guiding premise that such interventions will engage and modify these factors (Gibbs et al., 2012, p. 2). Much of the literature identifies three structural factors underpinning HIV and IPV: (1) poverty and economic inequality; (2) gender inequality and social norms that condone violence; and (3) the social constructions of gender, specifically femininities and masculinities (see Adimora & Auerbach, 2010; Auerbach et al., 2011; Dworkin, Hatcher,et al., 2013; Dworkin, Treves-Kagan, et al., 2013; Jewkes, Dunkle, Nduna, & Shai, 2010; Jewkes et al., 2006a, 2006, 2014; Jewkes, Flood, & Lang, 2015; Jewkes, Levin, & Penn-Kekana, 2002a; Jewkes, Martin, & Penn-Kekana, 2002b; Jewkes, Penn-Kekana, & Rose-Junius, 2005).

A first point of entry into unravelling elements of the GTIs that appear to work well, then, is to look at how they conceptualise structural factors, and how they engage with and seek to modify these dynamic factors within the social structure and the gender order within it. Structure remains a slippery concept. It is not some alien thing 'out there'—an amorphous abstraction on which blame can be apportioned. Nor is it an unyielding monolith, as in reference to 'the patriarchy' in casual conversations among colleagues and friends, both in the tone of '*ack, shame man!*' with a throwing up of hands in dread, and the relinquishing of possibility, and perhaps responsibility, for change. Structure is not static but dynamic (Vaughan, 2001). While it can be difficult to modify, it is in fact both changing and changeable (Morrell, 2001; Moynihan, 1998). At the social level, one look at the alteration of South Africa's social order from apartheid to democracy attests to this reality. Within the GTI literature, a distinguishing feature that underpins the conceptualisations of structural factors is the use of social theory to conceptualise the structural factors to be addressed within the respective context.

Structure and Social Theory

Social theory, particularly the work of the sociologists, has given us points of departure to engage with structure. Parkhurst notes that structural factors in interventions pay attention to the 'recognition of the locally specific and dynamic ways in which they influence behaviour are strongly rooted in sociological theory about how human actions and choices are related to broader influences'. Moreover, he emphasises, 'Understanding this complex linkage has never been easy' (2014, p. 3). Gibbs and colleagues pick up the line of thinking in sociological theory, casting it towards a better understanding of how structures limit or influence the behaviours of the groups in question. This, they argue, is the premise underlying theory:

> sociological theory…argues human behaviour is not simply rational volition, which can be reshaped by providing knowledge and information, but rather is shaped by structures that constrain what appropriate and achievable behaviours are. (2012, p. 2)

Gibbs and co-authors note that the design of the intervention incorporates this assumption and thus seeks to 'reshape these structures' (2012, p. 2). Thus, theory is not just part of the design and approach, theory makes fundamental assumptions about the social world and the social patterning of ill health: how and where change can be understood to affect the factors or variables they target. These assumptions are built into the process. There is not one structural approach in social or other theories, however. Theorists' notions of structure reflect developments in different disciplines and their ways of engaging with social problems, which have evolved over the ages. This traverses structuralism, functionalism, structuration and post-structuralism, Parkhurst reminds us (2014, p. 3).

In engaging with structure, Sewell cautions that 'those features of social existence denominated as structures tend to be reified and treated as primary, hard, and immutable, like the girders of a building' (1992, p. 2). What tends to get lost in the language of structure, he argues, is the 'efficacy of human action—or agency' (1992, p. 2). Sewell posits that the social scientists adopted the notion of inflexibility of structure from the natural scientists and how they viewed the world, tracing it to the study of botany in the seventeenth century (1992, p. 2; Foucault, 1994, pp. 132–138). Giddens, however, saw structure and agency as 'mutually implicated in and constituted by the same event—social practices' (quoted in Vaughan, 2001). In structuration theory, Giddens sought to reclaim agency and to give it greater import in the social world, recognising that agents have considerable power (1984). In this vein, the GTI cases tend to take up Gidden and Sewell's notions that structure in the gender order is malleable. Like Goffman, who highlighted the quintessential role of agentic behaviours in recreating the social world through daily interactions (1967), these GTIs see the daily interactions of people as the canvas on which gender can be reconstituted and redrawn. The GTIs view the socialisation of individuals into gender norms and hierarchies at the local level as a crucial point of engagement. They also recognise the agency of multiple actors involved in the social process of constructing the gender order.

Giddens viewed the duality of structure as the 'medium and the outcome of the practices which constitute social systems' (1981, p. 27). Sewell highlights that structure, cast in the role of causal determinism is inaccurate (1992; Vaughan, 2001). He builds on Giddens' conceptualisation of structure to stress that structure provides the conditions for action but is itself the outcome of action and is always open to the possibility of transformation (Sewell, 1992, p. 2). The two case studies seem to embed Giddens's and Sewell's assumptions of the dynamic interaction between agency and structure. The GTIs recognise the social transformation that is necessary to redress the balance between black women's agency and structure, and to move the prevailing paradigm from health disabling to promoting. This is not a theoretical exercise. These intervention case studies have a laser-like focus on a set of structured activities that seek, ultimately, to reconfigure gender relations and reach towards the possibility of gender transformation within larger South African society.

In South Africa, transformation has long referred to the project of social transformation, principally an inclusive nonracial democracy seeking to fundamentally overturn the systemic injustices of the past to create a new social order. It is used in the policy literature to refer to whole-scale reform of specific sectors, like the education sector, the mining or the health sector. Sectoral transformation is part of that process and these are inter-linked aspects of large-scale social change. Here the use of the word transformation is deliberate, in line with the vision of social change, referenced by key informants in the last chapter, who were integrally involved in shaping policies towards women's health, and advancing women's equality. That effort was not only a project to overturn racial injustice, but all forms and types of injustice, including gender injustice (Hassim, 2006). Transforming gender, observes Butler 'requires staying on the edge of what we know, questioning our own certainties.' She adds that 'creating openness to risk permits 'another way of knowing and living in the world'—one that expands 'our capacity to imagine the human' (2004, p. 228). Advancing human capabilities in South Africa can only be achieved through a participant-centred approach to and vision of social transformation in which South Africans themselves reimagine and reconceive the gender order. The GTIs give us a great deal of evidence to demonstrate what is possible.

A central question underpinning the gender-transformative interventions implemented is: How can structure yield to change to become enabling and supportive of women's health and capabilities rather than disabling? Like Giddens, the GTIs recognise that structure could be oppressive but it could also be enabling, thereby overturning the apple cart and challenging the dominant view (1981). Notably this recognition of structure as facilitating positive change and agency, or the converse, i.e., disabling agency, is also a criterion within structural interventions that are gender transformative, i.e., they should be conceptualised as enablers or disablers. To gain traction on how to modify aspects that underpin the gender order, the body of research on GTIs agrees that structural interventions must be geared towards shifting harmful social norms, mobilising sociopolitical changes, and 'empowering communities and groups' (Adimora & Auerbach, 2010, p. S132). Dworkin et al. place particular emphasis on activities that seek to make norms of masculinity 'more gender equitable' (2013b, p. 2845). A focus should be on socialisation into gender, daily interactions, and engaging boys and men, girls and women (Carlson et al., 2015). This means addressing the assumptions that underpin the gender order by addressing routine interactions within the *mundanal ruido*: the daily exchanges that punctuate gender relations and our larger human existence.

Jewkes et al. and others stress that such interventions should engage with, not just norms and behaviours, but masculinities and ideals of manhood (2015; Dworkin, Fleming, & Colvin, 2015; Fulu & Kerr-Wilson, 2015) Thus, a signature aspect of GTIs is that they do not just focus on women, they engage men and boys. As Dworkin et al. emphasise, 'modifying norms of masculinity is one approach to attain reduced rates of violence, decreased levels of unsafe sex, and improvements in inequitable gender relations' (2013b, p. 2857).

An additional criterion of successful GTIs is a focus on including a gender equality framework (GEF). VAWG interventions have long recognised the critical significance of wrestling with structure by emphasising GEFs, as well as using legal mechanisms to support and protect women's wellbeing in the domestic, so-called 'private' sphere, for example. These have been much less present in the HIV literature (Heise & McGrory, 2016). The research shows that protection against HIV infection is supported by strengthening GEFs that also address VAW and target women's subordinate position in society. They do this by engaging the private (historically called 'domestic') and public spheres, by emphasising legal protections. Write Carlson et al:

> A gender equality framework applied to violence prevention argues that because gender inequality operates in the public sector as well as [in]

> individual relationships, work with men must also actively challenge and change larger unequal systems within society, rather than limiting the focus to workshops and community education. (2015, p. 1421)

GEFs should ideally be linked to the national legal framework, which in countries like South Africa, seeks to advance and support women's substantive equality and protect women from IPV, thereby offering legal recourse and protections from abuse. Whether or not they work (e.g., police compliance with the law or effectiveness of protection orders) has been debated (see Government of South Africa, 2009; Woolman & Sprague, 2015).[1] Another assumption that undergirds use of GEFs in interventions is that, without government involvement and support, interventions are less likely to be socially responsive, relevant and be aligned with key national gender, health and social development objectives and frameworks.

A key domain identified as crucial for effective GTIs is *engagement with economic barriers for women*. How this is done remains a source of debate. GTIs must *engage economic poverty* and *address women's lack of economic power* in the household, via initiatives that enhance women's agency through greater economic participation in the formal economy. A long-term aim could be to improve the proportion of black women in the skilled professions, as discussed in Chap. 6 (see challenges highlighted at end of this chapter). Fulu and Kerr-Wilson stress the need for economic interventions in violence prevention against women and girls and the types of interventions to be levelled (caveats are spelt out later in the chapter):

> Interventions to increase productive assets and build gender equality typically seek to:
>
> (i) *build women's economic resources*, particularly in terms of *assets and income*; and (ii) *empower women* or transform gender relationships in their lives through a variety of approaches. (2015, p. 12)

Experts contend that GTIs must target multi-levels in the change process, for example, the family and the community. Cohen and Swift describe one approach, the spectrum of prevention, which is a multi-level approach to injury prevention, comprising six inter-related levels:

> (1) strengthening individual knowledge and skills, (2) promoting community education, (3) educating providers, (4) fostering coalitions and networks, (5) changing organizational practices, and (6) influencing policy and legislation. Activities at each of these levels have the potential to support each other and promote overall community health and safety. (1999, p. 203)

Intervention experts also emphasise that elements of interventions should be mutually reinforcing across the levels.

Another crucial dimension of GTIs is skill building and opportunities to practise using those skills. Such skills include sex and relationship communication, including negotiation and resolution of conflicts between couples that can lead to violence or abuse, as noted; skills could be in relation to parenting, encompassing listening skills, empathy and problem-solving; or adolescents or young people dealing with their first relationships (Jewkes, 2016).

An essential criterion for GTIs is for them to evaluate and measure the interventions at multiple time points, using both qualitative and quantitative methods. Researchers argue that evaluation of the intervention is essential, particularly process evaluation. Gupta and colleagues underscore the importance of process evaluations, particularly to isolate variables and how these operate under the influence of the intervention. They contend that 'the mechanisms by which an action or intervention works must be studied while the action is done' (2008, p. 772).

Structural change evaluations typically measure factors along the causal pathway, the authors emphasise, to validate the causal pathway hypothesis and 'assess which changes resulted in changes in HIV risk and vulnerability' note Gupta et al. (2008, p. 772). By implication, the authors warn that only measuring at the end of the causal chain, or the beginning, does not yield information as to the mechanism or the effect. Neither does it assist with quality assurance during implementation, adaptation to other locations or generalisability (2008). At the same time, qualitative evaluative methods are regarded as an essential counterpart to quantitative methods, to extract the experiences, attitudes and perceptions of participants. Researchers thus call for both quantitative and qualitative methods in the evaluation. I discussed the importance of both qualitative and quantitative methods and the differing knowledge paradigms and assumptions they introduce in Chap. 5.

Notably, the evaluation must also inform the theory. In this regard Gupta et al. note that approaches to assessments that 'rigorously measure key health outcomes of an activity or intervention, but do not provide and test any theory or model' fail to help researchers understand by what mechanism the outcome was achieved (2008, p. 772). Gupta and colleagues also call for additional techniques of assessment to be developed (2008). Further debates are summarised later in the chapter. Other points of emphasis in the published research are to be flexible with the timeframe. It may be necessary to continue the intervention beyond the initial timeline or to make adjustments.

The main criteria that emerge from the published literature are synthesised and the results from interventions presented in Table 7.1. However, it is critical to note that this remains contested terrain. There is no 'one size fits all' approach endorsed in the literature nor am I endorsing such

Table 7.1 Summary of GTI criteria

1.	Be rooted in and tailored to the specific social context
2.	Conceptualise factors as structural drivers or facilitators/barriers
3.	Address the three structural drivers of HIV and IPV: gender inequality and social norms that condone violence; social constructions of gender; and poverty/economic inequality
4.	Incorporate a social theory underpinning the intervention and align the theory with the evaluation
5.	Target multiple levels of influence for impact and be mutually reinforcing, e.g., household and community
6.	Implement a gender equality framework that links to national policy and legislative frameworks
7.	Address social gender roles and norms, including hierarchies and social constructions of gender: masculinities and femininities. This includes the following distinct components, as part of the GTI: (a) involve boys and girls, men and women (b) target daily relationships to foster greater gender equity (c) consider the gender socialisation process
8.	Address economic barriers and impediments related to poverty
9.	Evaluate and measure GTIs at different time points using quantitative and qualitative methods (a) include multiple health outcomes
10.	Be flexible with the time frame

Source: Sprague (2018). Constructed from a synthesis of the literature an approach here. I am suggesting that a set of criteria have emerged from the South African context that have had promising results, which would also advance the capabilities of women living with or at risk of HIV and IPV in South Africa. In moving considerations about HIV and women's health to the forefront of priority social concerns, we must try to leverage what is known as there is now sufficient evidence to inform future policy and interventions even if some uncertainty prevails.

GTI Case Studies

In this section I present excerpts of the two GTI case studies.

Stepping Stones Aims and History

Stepping Stones is a structural intervention that targets HIV prevention by seeking to build more gender equitable and stronger relationships. Alice Welbourn first developed Stepping Stones in the early to mid-1990s for use in small, rural communities in Uganda. The goal of Stepping Stones is to improve sexual health, HIV prevention and violence prevention by 'building stronger, more gender equitable relationships with better communication between partners' (Jewkes et al., 2006b, p. 5). The intervention does this by educating participants on sexual health and creating opportunities for participants to reflect on the motivations for their behaviours (Jewkes et al., 2006). In particular, Stepping Stones aims to engage community peers of young adults and teens through this intervention (Shai & Sikweyiya, 2015). 'The package was designed in response to the vulnerability of most women, men and young people in decision making regarding sexual behaviour, through men's gendered patriarchal domination of women and older people's generally repressive attitudes towards youth' note Welbourn and Bollinger (2015, p. 1). In 1998, Rachel Jewkes, who leads the South African MRC's Gender and Health Unit, adapted Welbourn's Uganda Stepping Stones intervention to the South African context (Jewkes & Cornwall, 1998). Then, drawing on the four years of experience from the first edition, in

2002, Jewkes and colleagues adapted another edition of the South Africa Stepping Stones for implementation (Jewkes et al., 2006). In total, the Stepping Stones intervention has been adapted and used in over 40 countries (Jewkes & Morell, 2010, p. 8).

Core Activities and Approach

Stepping Stones takes a community-based, participatory approach, involving participants in a series of workshops 'designed to promote sexual health, improve psychological well-being and prevent HIV' (Shai & Sikweyiya, 2015, p. 34). The workshops use adult education methods, which include critical reflection, drama, role-playing, group discussions and related exercises, to engage participants in an interactive manner (Jewkes et al., 2006). The Stepping Stones programme is led by a trained facilitator who matches the gender of the participants in each workshop series they lead and implements the intervention as instructed in the Stepping Stones manual (Jewkes et al., 2006, p. 5).

There are 13 main sessions of the programme. Each of the sessions averages three hours and covers issues such as: 'reflecting on love, sexual health joys and problems, body mapping, menstruation, contraception and conception (including infertility), sexual problems, unwanted pregnancy, HIV, STDs, safer sex, gender-based violence, motivations for sexual behaviour, and dealing with grief and loss' (Jewkes et al., 2006, p. 5; Jewkes, Sikweyiya, Nduna, Jama-Shai, & Dunkle, 2012). Participants are divided into peer groups based on gender and age to work separately, initially. Later the groups are combined and collaborate over a three to four month period to build a collective knowledge base and encourage cross-gender and cross-generational dialogue (Skevington, Sovetkina, & Gillison, 2013). The goal of having participants engage within the small groups first is to gain as much as possible from their interactions, allowing time for reflection (Skevington et al., 2013). At the end of the entire intervention, a community meeting is held in which 'each peer group presents its own 'special request' to the community outlining its most important problem or need' that should be addressed in the community (Skevington et al., 2013, p. 1026). This aligns with models historically rooted in African culture as processes for community social dialogue, such as the *lekgotla* method, *indaba* and *imbizo*, which have been adopted for more popular use but have traditional antecedents (Bojer, Mckay, & Roehl, 2006).

In the Eastern Cape implementation of Stepping Stones, the intervention was conducted through a partnership with the Planned Parenthood Association (Eastern Cape Branch). They employed, supervised and trained the project staff who facilitated Stepping Stones (Jewkes et al., 2006, p. 14; Jewkes et al., 2008, p. 2). The National Institute for Communicable Diseases provided assistance with quality control, testing, and storage of specimens (Jewkes et al., 2008, p. 10). This implementation involved 2776 participants enrolled at baseline, with '1360 men and 1416 women aged 15–26 years, who were mostly attending schools' (Jewkes et al., 2008, p. 1).

After presenting the second case study, I provide an assessment of the respective strengths, innovations and limitations of each case.

IMAGE Aims and History

The IMAGE combines a microfinance initiative with a gender training and health awareness initiative, with the aim of preventing HIV and IPV (Hargreaves et al., 2009, p. 2). IMAGE was a partnership between academic institutions in South Africa (Wits School of Public Health) and the United Kingdom (London School of Hygiene and Tropical Medicine). This combination intervention originated from the recognition that women's economic vulnerability increases their HIV vulnerability by reducing their choices and options 'in relation to male partners' (Mathews, 2010, p. 176). In fact, poverty and HIV are recognised as correlates since 'poverty fuels HIV transmission, and HIV/AIDS deepens poverty', as noted by Pronyk et al. (2005, p. 26). This is especially relevant since women who are poor or are in relationships of economic dependence are more likely to experience violence (Mathews, 2010).

A main goal of IMAGE is 'to improve the poorest women's economic wellbeing, social capital, and empowerment and thus reduce IPV and

HIV incidence' (Mathews, 2010, p. 176). IMAGE aims to do this by creating 'an enabling environment for behaviour change that engages poverty and gender-based inequalities as key structural factors driving the HIV epidemic' (Pronyk et al., 2005, p. 29). As a result, IMAGE sought to change particular gender and social norms that can lead to sexual violence and GBV and thus potentially, HIV (Mathews, 2010, p. 176). While a focus of IMAGE was on preventing VAW by empowering women, the intervention also had ambitions at creating *community-level change* by focusing on the importance of the structural environment for both violence prevention and HIV incidence (Gender Links, 2009).

IMAGE was initially conducted for roughly four years in the rural area of Sekhukhuneland in Limpopo province. The intervention involved an estimated 860 women enrolled in the programme (Pronyk et al., 2006). A South African microfinance institution led the microfinance component of IMAGE, and an HIV research and training programme led the gender and health training component (Pronyk et al., 2005). IMAGE was first piloted from 1998 to 2000, and then fully implemented from 2001 to 2005 (Pronyk et al., 2005, 2006). From the existing literature, IMAGE had a scale up from 2005 to 2007 that stretched to surrounding districts (Hargreaves et al., 2010; Jan et al., 2011). However, aside from the scale up, IMAGE seems to have been implemented predominantly in villages in the Limpopo Province (Hargreaves et al., 2010, p. 30). Replication trials of IMAGE are also currently being conducted in Peru, Kenya, Tanzania, and Zimbabwe (Lufuno, 2016).

Core Activities and Approach

Structured activities included microfinance, gender and HIV training/education. Importantly, prior to the intervention, 'no village [involved in the intervention] had significant access to microfinance services, and the penetration of HIV education had been low' (Pronyk et al., 2005, p. 30).

The Small Enterprise Foundation (SEF), a South African not-for-profit organisation, implemented the microfinance part of the programme. SEF, established in 1992, operates today with a base in the Limpopo Province, one of the poorest provinces (SEF, 2016). The participants were all women, 18 years of age or older, who either received loans or were part of the study's control group. These women were identified using SEF's 'participatory wealth-ranking criteria' which 'identifies and recruits the most economically disadvantaged members within a target area' (Pronyk et al., 2005, p. 29). This led to the identification of women participants from each participating village. The microfinance component of IMAGE adapted the Grameen Bank model of group lending: 'While businesses are run by individual women, groups of five women act to guarantee each other's loans' (Pronyk et al., 2005, p. 29). Additionally, all five women had to repay their loans before the group could qualify for additional credit. About 40 women (eight groups of five) comprised each loan centre, and they met every two weeks to apply for more credit, repay loans, or discuss plans for future business (Kim et al., 2007).

The gender and health education component of IMAGE was called the Sisters-for-Life programme, a participatory learning programme developed by the Rural AIDS and Development Action Research Programme (RADAR) at the Wits School of Public Health, in collaboration with a local domestic violence NGO (the NGO is not identified in the literature) (Hargreaves et al., 2010, p. 28; Kim et al., 2007, p. 1976). RADAR initially managed the Sisters-for-Life part of the intervention (Hargreaves et al., 2010, p. 28). Sisters-for-Life was delivered at the loan centres' bi-weekly meetings by a team of trainers working in the village over a period of 12 months (Kim et al., 2007; Pronyk et al., 2006). Sisters-for-Life had two phases. 'Phase 1 consisted of ten 1-hour training sessions and covered topics including gender roles, cultural beliefs, relationships, communication, domestic violence, and HIV infection; and aimed to strengthen communication skills, critical thinking, and leadership' (Kim et al., 2007, p. 1796). It lasted for about six months (Pronyk et al., 2006). Phase 2 was more open-ended. It involved community mobilisation and seems to be the only part of the intervention that directly aimed to engage men from the communities, both youth and adults, in the programme. Phase 2 is discussed more fully in the last section of the chapter.)

Table 7.2 offers a snapshot of the two interventions along the identified criteria.

Table 7.2 GTI criteria applied to Stepping Stones and IMAGE

Criteria	Stepping Stones	IMAGE
Be tailored to the specific *social context*	Adapts design and application to the South African context, though implemented in many other contexts	Design and activities shaped by and respond to the South African context, with a focus on rural women's agentic constraints due to economic dependence and gender norms in households; also implemented in other countries.
Conceptualise factors as structural drivers/facilitators and barriers	Conceptualises structural factors as both drivers/ facilitators and barriers. Drivers in the intervention are high risk behaviour, and the facilitators/ barriers are the nature of communication in relationships	Conceptualises structural factors as both drivers and facilitators/barriers. Drivers include high risk behaviour, and the facilitators/barriers include women's economic status and level of empowerment
Include a social theory to underpin the interventions	Uses education theory, social learning theory, Freire on role of reflection and dialogue for learning	Participatory learning and action principles, group-based learning, and the relationship between poverty/empowerment and health
Address main structural drivers of HIV and IPV	Targets primarily two structural drivers of HIV and IPV: gender inequality and social norms that condone violence; and the social constructions of gender, specifically femininity and masculinity	Focuses on all three of the structural drivers of HIV and IPV: poverty and economic inequality; gender inequality and social norms that condone violence; and the social constructions of gender, specifically femininity and masculinity
Target multiple levels for impact and mutually reinforcing	Aims to implement individual, family and community levels	Aims to influence individual, family and community levels. Also aims to address women's economic status

(*continued*)

Table 7.2 (continued)

Criteria	Stepping Stones	IMAGE
Implement gender equality framework	Implements GEF by engaging both sexes at the individual and community levels	Implements GEF by promoting the empowerment of women and by engaging both sexes through its community mobilisation component
Address gender roles/ norms	Aims to promote healthy behaviour and communication by educating its participants about the relationship among gender norms, gender roles, and gender equity, including a focus on masculinities	Aims to change the gender and social norms that can lead to violence against women and IPV and thus potentially to HIV
Involve men/boys and women/girls	Involves men, women, boys, girls in sessions separately and together	Community mobilisation component, where women participants engage with their larger communities (of men, women and youth)
Engage with daily relationships	Focus is to change the nature of people's relationships so that they are stronger and more gender equitable	Aims to improve relationship between intimate partners to become more equitable. Additionally, aims to improve the sex/health communication between adults/parents and youth regarding the risks and dangers related to unsafe sex
Engage with the *socialisation process*	Targets knowledge they already have about gender norms/roles/ equity and then focuses on education and dismantling misinformation	By focusing on gender norms and social norms and by focusing on the communication between parents and children so parents can transfer the knowledge they learn

(continued)

Table 7.2 (continued)

Criteria	Stepping Stones	IMAGE
Address economic barriers and impediments related to poverty	No explicit economic empowerment component in initial programme. However, MRC intervention in the Eastern Cape targeted those most affected by poverty. The livelihood intervention, Creating Futures, was initiated later (in 2012)	Aims to address economic empowerment and poverty through its combined intervention involving a microfinance component
Add skill building components and *opportunities to practise* them	Offers skills in communication viz. relationships, HIV, sex and conflict resolution	Teaches participants micro-lending and microfinance. Develops communication skills on sex, HIV, relationships
Evaluate and measure GTIs at multiple time points, using qualitative and quantitative methods	Evaluations occurred three times over two years, using quantitative and qualitative methods	Assessments at baseline and after two years. Uses quantitative and qualitative methods
Measure and evaluate health GTIs by focusing on multiple health outcomes at different time points	Measures multiple health outcomes, including incidence of herpes, engagement in transactional sex and mental health	Measures multiple health outcomes, including women's empowerment, condom use, and sexual education/communication
Be flexible with the timeframe	Intervention for two to three months. Evaluations with participants conducted over two years	RCT initially ran for four years (2001–2005). Scale-up phase lasted from 2005–2007

Source: Sprague (2018)

Assessment: Evidence of Effectiveness, Strengths and Limitations

Both GTIs have demonstrated positive results overall. The two case studies illustrate that the two capabilities of bodily health and bodily integrity are directly enhanced by the intervention activities. The most visible evidence of Stepping Stones' effectiveness was a randomised controlled trial in rural South Africa, which demonstrated a 33% reduction in herpes simplex type 2 incidence among both women and men; a lower proportion of men reporting IPV perpetration after the two years; less reported transactional sex; and less problem drinking after a 12-month period (Jewkes et al., 2008).

After two years, IMAGE participants experienced a 55% reduction in IPV compared to participants in the control groups. Youth participants reported more HIV-related communication, HIV testing, and more condom use with (non-spousal) partners (Kim et al., 2009). The dropout rate for loan centres involved with IMAGE was much lower, compared to the average loan centre (Pronyk et al., 2005). One weakness of the evaluations of these interventions is that in most cases the architects and implementers appear to be involved to some degree in assessing the interventions they implemented. It is highly probable that the evaluations would never be completed without the involvement of these individuals, however. Nonetheless, it raises questions about how subjective views and bias would be controlled for, since these issues are not mentioned in the evaluations. At the same time, given the results captured in the published evidence, both Stepping Stones and IMAGE should be pursued as GTIs to prevent HIV infection and to reduce the incidence of IPV to support the capabilities of women's bodily health and their bodily integrity most directly, along with additional capabilities, highlighted in the next section.

Themes and Relevance for Supporting Women's Capabilities

Across the two case studies, the interventions display distinct (some similar and some different) features that underpin their ability to be effective at creating structural level change and enhancing capabilities, particularly for women, but in some cases also for men.

Working with men, women, boys and girls, to transform relationships to advance gender equality

As per the review of the extant literature on GTIs, presented in Table 7.1, the most effective interventions appear to be 'group based' (Dworkin et al., 2015). Stepping Stones demonstrates the importance of working within families and engaging entire communities in order to reach its gender-transformative goals. If a programme aims to generate changes in society that deal with socialisation processes, accepted norms of behaviour on the basis of gender, and social constructions of masculinity and femininity that undergird the gender order, to do so, it needs to engage men and women, as well as boys and girls within family and social settings. This engagement is most pronounced within Stepping Stones (Jewkes et al., 2015). IMAGE also included a group-based approach in its scale up (phase 2), and it seems to have done so in its replication outside of South Africa.

A specific focus of these two GTIs is on *transforming relationships* in order to address fundamental gender inequalities. This takes the location of 'struggle' into families and communities, which is where norms and values are profoundly shaped on a daily basis. (By this, I do not mean to suggest that the intervention facilitators went into family homes; rather, that the intervention was conducted in the community as a social setting but the learnings were then tried out by participants in their homes.) A foundational principle of both interventions is the importance of *better communication* in contributing to the building of *stronger relationships*, for power sharing and sensitising participants about norms that are harmful. This recognises that underlying these adverse gender norms is the use of violence and abuse to resolve conflicts. This quote from a man who participated in the IMAGE intervention is indicative: 'I have noticed how easy it is for people to say 'it is our culture' that I should beat my wife. Health talks have shown me that it is wrong for any man to beat up his wife,' (Kim et al., 2007, p. 1801). In this manner, the interventions are taking on fundamental assumptions about gender norms that accept abuse of South African women (Boonzaier, 2005). They seek to reconstitute gender relations and social constructions of masculinities, thereby targeting IPV and HIV prevention. The intervention activities focus on teaching people ways of resolving discord without resorting to violence—

a pattern underlying partner abuse (Heise & McGrory, 2016). An IMAGE participant stated: 'Now we know how to talk to our husbands about sexual matters, but before they would beat you when talking about those things' (Kim et al., 2007, 1801). A different participant stated, 'I also find it easier to talk to my partner about his other affairs without being angry and shouting at him—and I found that I make a difference because he listens' (Kim et al., 2007, p. 1799). A Stepping Stone participant, Mthobisi, reflected on what was most important for him, saying, 'The communication part. It was important to talk to your woman so that everything can go well. I never used to talk. I would get angry and walk away, but now I can talk about it and then all goes well' (Gibbs, Jewkes, Sikweyiya, & Willan, 2015, p. 213). This emphasis on communication also addresses the gender socialisation process, which is part of norm setting. The intervention curricula encourage participants to engage with underlying values about treating others with dignity and respect, as equals. One Stepping Stones participant, Gwedi, reflected on what he learnt, saying that, 'When I listened to what they were saying at the intervention, I realised that it was informative…A man should respect himself and others, not think that his power entitles him to do otherwise' (Gibbs et al., 2015, p. 216). Improved communication skills among partners and norm-setting predicated on gender equality have onward positive effects of reducing IPV in women and improving negotiation of condom use to promote safe sex. There would potentially be additional benefits for children and the family as a whole, e.g., in transferring relationship skills to participants' parental roles and modelling positive behaviours for children.

A Participant-Centred and Community-Based Approach to Social Change

Both interventions engage communities, and perhaps the distinction is not that they do so but how they do so. This is most evident in the last part of the Stepping Stones intervention, which involves peer groups making presentations to their larger communities and educating them about the problems in society that need to be addressed. This matches historical approaches to solving challenges within African communities, through the *lekgotla* and other methods. This roots change within culturally appropriate methods and it likely enhances the familiarity and acceptability of participants with these methods of discussion and problem solving. In this regard, whereas other GTIs tend to focus more on the intervention's direct participants, the Stepping Stones model (in its most recent iteration) appears to go one step further. It utilises the intervention's participants to act as a bridge between Stepping Stones and the community. IMAGE also seems to incorporate this in phase 2. In this way, these interventions are adopting a community-based approach to social change, which is able to capitalise on innovation that may emerge naturally from the intervention activities. It thus serves as a generator of change and empowerment that could have multiple, positive spin-offs for families and communities.

The participant-centred approach to change and to human development and capability (Sen, 1999) represents a major strength of the designs and implementation. It also poses a major challenge. A pre-requisite to achieving successful results of Stepping Stones and effectively implementing this intervention rests heavily on successful mobilisation of communities and gaining community support for the intervention (Jewkes et al., 2006, p. 6). This is as it should be—though it is neither simple nor easy.

In terms of capabilities, the emphasis on altering the dynamics of communication, socialisation and power within relationships, and to establish changed norms and patterns of behaviour serves to support what women are able to do and to be by *expanding* women's choices, *their opportunity and process freedoms*, and their *agency*. Addressing the familial, intimate relationships in women's lives has the most direct relevance for supporting the capability of *bodily integrity* by potentially allowing them to be free from violent assault or the threat of it, which also supports their bodily health. This is effected by working with men to inform their dominant perceptions and attitudes as well as their means of resolving conflicts through listening and effective communication. It also engages with the capability of *affiliation*, which entails how individuals live with and towards others showing concern and respect. Notably, these interventions are supporting the capabilities for women and men in terms of the capability of *emotions* by teaching couples how to deal with anger, frustration and confusion in safe, healthy ways in their relationships. The support of these capabilities may have effects for other capabilities but these are the capabilities likely to be most directly enhanced.

Additional Debates and Key Challenges

Addressing the Economic Inequalities and Poverty Underpinning IPV and HIV Risk

IMAGE takes an innovative and critically important approach to HIV and IPV prevention by targeting economic, gender and health concerns, and their inter-relationships. The distinctive aspect and strength of IMAGE, relative to other GTIs, is its effort to tackle HIV, IPV and economic empowerment in a context of relative poverty for women. Pronyk et al. note that, 'lack of economic opportunities for both sexes, and entrenched inequalities in the distribution of power, resources, and responsibilities between men and women (gender inequalities)...create a risk environment' and this environment 'supports high levels of both HIV infection and intimate partner violence. GTIs seek to affect these circumstances that create risk environments for HIV and IPV' (2006, see p. 1973). By recognising that economic inequalities can lead women to become more vulnerable to IPV and HIV, IMAGE seeks to engage with HIV and IPV prevention through a microlending initiative. This approach also allows IMAGE to have access to a vulnerable population, poorer women in rural areas—over a longer duration—than it would without the component. This renders IMAGE a quintessentially structural intervention at multiple levels because it aims to affect both gender relations and women's economic and livelihood status. Compared to those interventions that only address gender, IMAGE takes a more holistic approach to gender transformation, and is able to generate impact at multiple levels. Caveats about follow just below, however.

Role of Economic Interventions in Increasing IPV

There is a debate about the effectiveness of economic interventions in decreasing VAW. Some studies have found that changes in economic status and social status can in fact lead to an increase in IPV in certain contexts. (For a nationally representative study in Bangladesh, see Murshid, Akincigil, & Zippay, 2016.) Methods of generating employment for women largely centre on microfinance. However, there are debates about its use because giving women credit cannot guarantee their control over the money's use in the household. Additionally, the pressure on women to pay back loans can be an extremely heavy responsibility, particularly for women who are already poor (Kim et al., 2007). This could even lead women to try to 'pay back loans' by giving sexual favours to loan officers, which could put them in further danger of GBV or contracting HIV (Kim et al., 2007, p. 1795). Additionally, evidence has shown that changes in a woman's social or economic standing could potentially lead to an increase in violence in some settings. Subsequently, and importantly, Kim et al. note that 'the question of whether women's empowerment more broadly, and participation in microfinance in particular, contributes to reductions in violence has remained an unresolved research question of central policy importance' (2007, p. 1795). In contrast, other recent studies have found that microfinance in specific settings can lead to a reduction in IPV (Orton et al., 2016).

Options other than a microfinance component could include an economic component that involves schools, workplace programmes, conditional cash transfers or other incentive-based programmes to promote certain health behaviours (Pronyk et al., 2008, p. 1664). Note again that the most effective approaches are ones used in combination and that target multiple levels. An economic intervention on its own is thus likely to be ineffective, and potentially even harmful.

Psychological and Behavioural Factors

There was some attention to these in the interventions but additional emphasis is needed. Increasing evidence demonstrates the importance of childhood factors (including early abuse), in patterning psychological responses, behaviours and in shaping the risk pathway for IPV, HIV and other forms of violent victimisation. Thus additional research and interventions could address exposure to childhood abuse and its psycho-social effects (including untreated trauma), while emphasising earlier intervention in the life course (Heise & McGrory, 2016; Sprague, Scanlon, & Pantalone, 2017b).

Sustainability, Type of Models and Organisations Working in Partnership

The model type used for the organisations involved in interventions such as IMAGE remains another topic of debate. There are three prototypes IMAGE reports that it could have used: a model in which the two involved organisations work in parallel to each other (which is the model IMAGE started out using); a linked model in which the two organisations work together (which is the approach IMAGE took later); or a unified model in which 'one person delivered both credit and education', (Hargreaves et al., 2010, pp. 37–38). IMAGE used both the parallel and linked models. However, there was no one institution prepared to take on 'management' (Hargreaves et al., 2010, p. 38). Further research is needed to assess the sustainability and effectiveness of using such models for interventions (Hargreaves et al., 2010).

The Timeline for Social Change

A primary issue of debate in the literature is the timeline needed to shift fundamental sociocultural norms. Skevington and colleagues argue that gender beliefs and social norms are linked to high risk behaviours which are 'deeply rooted cultural beliefs and traditions' (2013, p. 1037). As a result, it can be extremely difficult to address such norms through a series of workshops. It is a long-term proposition to change beliefs and norms that are entrenched in society. This speaks to the need for interventions that have effects over a longer duration of time. As part of the same concern, interventions are typically funded for a short time span of two to three years but structural change takes longer (Dworkin et al., 2015). How would modifications in relationship dynamics and behavioural changes continue to be reinforced when the intervention has concluded? This remains unclear.

Aligning with Processes of Social Transformation: Capitalising on NGOs as Agents of Social Change

What seems missing or under-emphasised in the research literature and the documentation of the GTIs is closer alignment between national goals of social transformation, including gender, and the activities taking place in the intervention. At the centre of the social change process is a set of actors, communities and community-based NGOs. These local actors play a crucial role, including at the local level, in being able to establish new gender norms and diffuse those norms after the intervention ceases. They could be engaged to do this in ways that focus more strongly on human development or social development. However, this is not automatic. It would require reconsideration by intervention specialists, by the state and by donors.

Perhaps GTIs could make even more impact if they were to align themselves with larger goals of social transformation—of which gender is a critical part—while engaging in encouraging human development in the community. This could be done by offering community members particular types of skills, education, or training, along with sensitisation and workshops on changing gender norms. This could involve deeper, long-term partnerships with NGOs that would, ideally, be able to carry on the work in communities after the initial interventions cease. This might allow NGOs to be agents of change that also facilitate agency and capability for communities. This would then become a community initiative which could ideally be funded by the Government and donors who would be investing in gender equality, HIV prevention and reduction of IPV, but might also be targeting youth workforce development, education and employment generation, for example. While this might make the HIV and IPV prevention activities part of a larger cluster of activities, with a risk that these become secondary, it might also create possibilities for greater community ownership and sustainability, align GTIs with national health and development frameworks, while establishing a longer time horizon for implementation and for change to be realised.

To conclude this chapter, the use of the term gender transformative by health and social scientists recognises how gender inequalities shape HIV and IPV risk, incidence and health outcomes for women with HIV in social context, while fundamentally curtailing women's agentic desires and their capabilities. Based on the extant literature, a set of core criteria emerges with associated activities and practices that appear to underpin effective GTIs—GTIs that could enhance the capabilities of women, especially, as well as men in South Africa. The interventions investigated, Stepping Stones and IMAGE, match these criteria. The results reveal that they are responsive to the South African context of high HIV and IPV prevalence and its social acceptance of VAWG. They give attention to both the problem of HIV and violence against women as synergistic correlates. Their design and activities engage with and ascertain the specific social mechanisms that influence risk of injury or disease acquisition, with a view to mediating and changing them. Moreover, the evidence of their effectiveness is compelling: the two case studies demonstrate success in reducing incidence of sexually transmitted infections, including HIV, reducing IPV perpetration by partners, reducing transactional sex among men, increasing condom use, increasing communication about sex and HIV among partners, imparting new skills, reconstituting adverse gender norms and reshaping social constructions of gender in families and communities. In some cases, the interventions go further than national policy and related frameworks. The interventions have limitations but they illustrate promise and possibility.

Newer interventions recently underway and not yet evaluated, such as the PEPFAR-funded DREAMS initiative and others, could take cognisance of these case studies and their lessons learnt. There is not one formula for effective structural interventions but a series of preconditions that would increase the likelihood for supporting change processes that would advance women's capabilities, while having benefits for families, communities and society. These alone are insufficient, but coupled with protective social policies and other national responses to VAWG and HIV, they could support a human development pathway for South African women and girls.

Note

1. A large study of VAW in South Africa by Human Rights Watch (1995), for example, documented that South African women failed to seek legal remedies due to factors spanning mistrust of the law enforcement system, economic dependence, fear of retaliation, shame, stigma, self-blame and love (see also Harrison 2008; Hunter 2010; Jewkes & Morrell 2012; Woolman & Sprague, 2015).

References

Adimora, A., & Auerbach, J. (2010). Structural interventions for HIV prevention in the United States. *Journal of Acquired Immune Deficiency Syndromes, 55*(Suppl. 2), S132–S135.

Auerbach, J., Caceres, C., & Parkhurst, J. (2011). Addressing social drivers of HIV/AIDS for the long-term response: Conceptual and methodological considerations. *Global Public Health, 6*(Suppl 3), S293–309.

Blankenship, K., Friedman, S., Dworkin, S., & Mantell, J. (2006). Structural interventions: Concepts, challenges, and opportunities for research. *Journal of Urban Health, 83*(1), 59–72.

Bojer, M., Mckay, E., & Roehl, H. (2006). *Mapping Dialogue: A Research Project Profiling Dialogue Tools and Processes for Social Change*. Johannesburg: Pioneers of Change.

Boonzaier, F. (2005). Woman abuse in South Africa: A brief contextual analysis. *Feminism & Psychology, 15*(1), 99–103.

Buse, K., Dickinson, C., & Sidibe, M. (2008). HIV: Know your epidemic: Act on its politics. *Journal of the Royal Society of Medicine, 101*(12), 572–573.

Butler, J. (2004). *Undoing Gender*. New York: Routledge.

Carlson, J., Casey, E., Edleson, J., Tolman, R., Neugut, T., & Kimball, E. (2015). Strategies to engage men and boys in violence prevention: A global organizational perspective. *Violence Against Women, 21*(11), 1406–1425.

Cohen, L., & Swift, S. (1999). The spectrum of prevention: Developing a comprehensive approach to injury prevention. *Injury Prevention, 5*(3), 203–207.

Dworkin, S., Fleming, P., & Colvin, C. (2015). The promises and limitations of gender-transformative health programming with men: Critical reflections from the field. *Culture, Health & Sexuality, 17*(Suppl. 2), 128–143.

Dworkin, S., Hatcher, A., Colvin, C., & Peacock, D. (2013). Impact of a gender-transformative HIV and antiviolence program on gender ideologies and masculinities in two rural, South African communities. *Men and Masculinities, 16*(2), 181–202.

Dworkin, S., Treves-Kagan, S., & Lippman, S. (2013). Gender-transformative interventions to reduce HIV risks and violence with heterosexually-active men: A review of the global evidence. *AIDS and Behavior, 17*(9), 2845–2863.

Foucault, M. (1994). *The Order of Things: An Archaeology of the Human Sciences*. New York: Vintage.

Fulu, E., & Kerr-Wilson, A. (2015). *What Works to Prevent Violence Against Women and Girls Evidence Reviews—Paper 2: Interventions to Prevent Violence Against Women and Girls*. [online]. London: UKAID. Retrieved July 1, 2016, from https://www.whatworks.co.za/documents/publications/35-global-evidence-reviews-paper-2-interventions-to-prevent-violence-against-women-and-girls-sep-2015/file

Gender Links. (2009). *IMAGE Study*. [online]. Johannesburg: Gender Links. Retrieved February 24, 2017, from http://genderlinks.org.za/programme-web-menu/image-study-2009-06-16/

Gibbs, A., Jewkes, R., Sikweyiya, Y., & Willan, S. (2015). Reconstructing masculinity? A qualitative evaluation of the stepping stones and creating futures interventions in urban informal settlements in South Africa. *Culture, Health & Sexuality, 17*(2), 208–222.

Gibbs, A., Willan, S., Misselhorn, A., & Mangoma, J. (2012). Combined structural interventions for gender equality and livelihood security: A critical review of the evidence from Southern and Eastern Africa and the implications for young people. *Journal of the International AIDS Society, 15*(Suppl. 1), 1–10.

Giddens, A. (1981). *A Contemporary Critique of Historical Materialism. Vol. 1., Power, Property and the State*. London: Macmillan.

Giddens, A. (1984). *The Constitution of Society*. Cambridge: Polity Press.

Goffman, E. (1967). *Interaction Ritual: Essays on Face to Face Behavior*. New York: Anchor Books.

Government of South Africa. (2009). *A Study of the Factors Contributing to SAPS Non-Compliance with the Domestic Violence Act*. [online]. Pretoria: National Department of Health. Retrieved January 1, 2016, from http://govza.gcis.gov.za/tn/node/521070

Gupta, G. (2000). Gender, sexuality and HIV/AIDS: The what, the why and the how. Plenary address at the XIII international AIDS conference. [online].

In *XIII International AIDS Conference*. Durban, South Africa: International AIDS Society. Retrieved February 23, 2017, from http://siteresources.worldbank.org/EXTAFRREGTOPGENDER/Resources/durban_speech.pdf

Gupta, G., Parkhurst, J., Ogden, J., Aggleton, P., & Mahal, A. (2008). Structural approaches to HIV prevention. *Lancet, 372*, 764–775.

Hargreaves, J., Hatcher, A., Strange, V., Phetla, G., Busza, J., Kim, J., et al. (2009). Group-microfinance and health promotion among the poor: Six-year process evaluation of the Intervention with Microfinance for AIDS and Gender Equity (IMAGE) in rural South Africa. [online]. Retrieved February 7, 2017, from http://www.sef.co.za/files/02%20%20Hargreaves%20IMAGE%20Process%20Evaluation%20working%20paper%202009.pdf

Hargreaves, J., Hatcher, A., Strange, V., Phetla, G., Busza, J., Kim, J., et al. (2010). Process evaluation of the Intervention with Microfinance for AIDS and Gender Equity (IMAGE) in rural South Africa. *Health Education Research, 25*(1), 27–40.

Harrison, A. (2008). Hidden love: Sexual ideologies and relationship ideals among rural South African adolescents in the context of HIV/AIDS. *Culture, Health and Sexuality, 10*, 175–189.

Hassim, S. (2006). *Women's Organizations and Democracy in South Africa*. Madison: University of Wisconsin Press.

Heise, L., & McGrory, E. (2016). *Greentree II: Violence Against Women and Girls, and HIV—Report on a High-Level Consultation on the Evidence and Implications*. Greentree Estate, NY: STRIVE.

Human Rights Watch. (1995). *Violence Against Women in South Africa: The State Response to Domestic Violence and Rape*. New York: Human Rights Watch.

Hunter, M. (2010). *Love in the Time of AIDS. Inequality, Gender and Right in South Africa*. Durban: University of KwaZulu-Natal Press.

Jan, S., Ferrari, G., Watts, C., Hargreaves, J., Kim, J., Phetla, G., et al. (2011). Economic evaluation of a combined microfinance and gender training intervention for the prevention of intimate partner violence in rural South Africa. *Health Policy and Planning, 26*, 366–372.

Jewkes, R. (2016). What works to prevent VAWG. [online]. Retrieved February 4, 2017, from http://www.svri.org/sites/default/files/attachments/2016-07-05/Jewkes%20R%20presentation%20for%20UNFPA%20and%20SVRI%20.pdf

Jewkes, R., & Cornwall, A. (1998). *Stepping Stones: A Training Manual for Sexual and Reproductive Health Communication and Relationship Skills*. [online]. London: Institute for Development Studies. Retrieved February 7, 2017, from http://www.participatorymethods.org/resource/stepping-stones-training-manual-sexual-and-reproductive-health-communication-and

Jewkes, R., Dunkle, K., Koss, M., Levin, J., Nduna, M., Jama, N., et al. (2006). Rape perpetration by young, rural South African men: Prevalence, patterns and risk factors. *Social Science & Medicine, 63*(11), 2949–2961.

Jewkes, R., Dunkle, K., Nduna, M., & Shai, N. (2010). Intimate partner violence, relationship power inequity, and incidence of HIV infection in young women in South Africa: A cohort study. *Lancet, 376*(9734), 41–48.

Jewkes, R., Flood, M., & Lang, J. (2015). From work with men and boys to changes of social norms and reduction of inequities in gender relations: A conceptual shift in prevention of violence against women and girls. *Lancet, 385*, 1580–1589.

Jewkes, R., Gibbs, A., Jama-Shai, N., Willan, S., Misselhorn, A., Mushinga, M., et al. (2014). Stepping stones and creating futures intervention: Shortened interrupted time series evaluation of a behavioral and structural health promotion and violence prevention intervention for young people in informal settlements in Durban, South Africa. *BMC Public Health, 14*, 1325.

Jewkes, R., Levin, J., & Penn-Kekana, L. (2002a). Risk factors for domestic violence: Findings from a South African cross-sectional study. *Social Science & Medicine, 55*, 1603–1617.

Jewkes, R., Martin, L., & Penn-Kekana, L. (2002b). Correspondence: The virgin cleansing myth: Cases of child rape are not exotic. *Lancet, 359*, 711.

Jewkes, R., & Morrell, R. (2010). Gender and sexuality: Emerging perspectives from the heterosexual epidemic in South Africa and implications for HIV risk and prevention. *Journal of the International AIDS Society, 13*(1), 6.

Jewkes, R., & Morrell, R. (2012). Sexuality and the limits of agency among South African teenage women: Theorising femininities and their connections to HIV risk practices. *Social Science & Medicine, 74*, 1729–1737.

Jewkes, R., Nduna, M., Levin, J., Jama, N., Dunkle, K., Khuzwayo, N., et al. (2006). A cluster randomized-controlled trial to determine the effectiveness of Stepping Stones in preventing HIV infections and promoting safer sexual behaviour amongst youth in the rural Eastern Cape, South Africa: Trial design, methods and baseline findings. *Tropical Medicine and International Health, 11*(1), 3–16.

Jewkes, R., Nduna, M., Levin, J., Jama, N., Dunkle, K., Puren, A., et al. (2008). Impact of stepping stones on incidence of HIV and HSV-2 and sexual behaviour in rural South Africa: Cluster randomised controlled trial. *BMJ, 337*, a506.

Jewkes, R., Penn-Kekana, L., & Rose-Junius, H. (2005). "If they rape me, I can't blame them": Reflections on gender in the social context of rape in South Africa and Namibia. *Social Science & Medicine, 61*, 1809–1820.

Jewkes, R., Sikweyiya, Y., Nduna, M., Jama-Shai, N., & Dunkle, K. (2012). Motivations for, and perceptions and experiences of participating in, a cluster randomised controlled trial of a HIV-behavioural intervention in rural South Africa. *Culture, Health & Sexuality, 14*(10), 1167–1182.

Kim, J., Ferrari, G., Abramsky, T., Watts, C., Hargreaves, J., Morison, L., et al. (2009). Assessing the incremental effects of combining economic and health interventions: The IMAGE study in South Africa. *Bulletin of the World Health Organization, 87*(11), 824–832.

Kim, J., Watts, C., Hargreaves, J., Ndhlovu, L., Phetla, G., Morison, L. A., et al. (2007). Understanding the impact of a microfinance-based intervention on women's empowerment and the reduction of intimate partner violence in South Africa. *American Journal of Public Health, 97*(10), 1794–1802.

Lufuno, M. (2016). *The IMAGE Programme: Empowering Women Through Microfinance and Community Action to Reduce Violence Against Women.* [online]. Johannesburg: SVRI. Retrieved February 7, 2017, from http://www.svri.org/sites/default/files/attachments/2016-07-05/IMAGE%20UNFPA%20VAW%20scaling%20up%20lessons%20%20.pdf

Mathews, C. (2010). Reducing sexual risk behaviors: Theory and research, successes and challenges. In S. Abdool Karim & Q. Abdool Karim (Eds.), *HIV/AIDS in South Africa* (2nd ed., pp. 157–183). Cambridge: Cambridge University Press.

Morrell, R. (Ed.). (2001). *Changing Men in Southern Africa.* Pietermaritzburg: University of KwaZulu-Natal and Zed Press.

Moynihan, C. (1998). Theories in health care and research: Theories of masculinity. *BMJ, 317*, 1072–1075.

Murshid, N., Akincigil, A., & Zippay, A. (2016). Microfinance participation and domestic violence in Bangladesh: Results from a nationally representative survey. *Journal of Interpersonal Violence, 31*(9), 1579–1596.

Orton, L., Pennington, A., Nayak, S., Sowden, A., White, M., & Whitehead, M. (2016). Group-based microfinance for collective empowerment: A systematic review of health impacts. *Bulletin of the World Health Organization, 94*(9), 694–704A.

Parkhurst, J. (2014). Structural approaches for prevention of sexually transmitted HIV in general populations: Definitions and an operational approach. *Journal of the International AIDS Society, 17*(1), 19052.

Pronyk, P., Hargreaves, J., Kim, J., Morison, L., Phetla, G., Watts, C., et al. (2006). Effect of a structural intervention for the prevention of intimate partner violence and HIV in rural South Africa: A cluster randomised trial. *Lancet, 368*, 1973–1983.

Pronyk, P., Kim, J., Abramsky, T., Phetla, G., Hargreaves, J., Morison, L., et al. (2008). A combined microfinance and training intervention can reduce HIV risk behavior in young female participants. *AIDS, 22*, 1659–1665.

Pronyk, P., Kim, J., Hargreaves, J., Makhubele, M., Morison, L., Watts, C., et al. (2005). Microfinance and HIV prevention—Emerging lessons from rural South Africa. *Small Enterprise Development, 16*(3), 26–38.

Sen, A. (1999). *Development as Freedom*. New York: Random House.

Sewell, W. (1992). A theory of structure: Duality, agency and transformation. *The American Journal of Sociology, 98*(1), 1–29.

Shai, N., & Sikweyiya, Y. (2015). Programmes for change: Addressing sexual and intimate partner violence in South Africa. *South Africa Crime Quarterly, 51*, 31–41.

Skevington, S., Sovetkina, E., & Gillison, F. (2013). A systematic review to quantitatively evaluate 'Stepping Stones': A participatory community-based HIV/AIDS prevention intervention. *AIDS and Behavior, 17*(3), 1025–1039.

Small Enterprise Foundation. (2016). About Small Enterprise Foundation. [online]. Retrieved January 2, 2017, from http://www.sef.co.za/about-sef

Sprague, C., Scanlon, M., & Pantalone, D. W. (2017b). Qualitative methods to advance research on health inequities among previously incarcerated women living with HIV in Alabama. *Health Education & Behavior, 44*(5), 716–727.

Vaughan, B. (2001). Handle with care: On the use of structuration theory within criminology. *British Journal of Criminology, 41*(1), 185–200.

Welbourn, A., & Bollinger, A. (2015). The original Stepping Stones—What is it? The Stepping Stones Feedback Project. [online]. Retrieved February 16, 2017, from http://www.steppingstonesfeedback.org/index.php/About/What_is_it/gb

Woolman, S., & Sprague, C. (2015). Nowhere to run, nowhere to hide: The absence of public policy as to how health care professionals should address intimate partner violence constitutes a breach of the rights to health and bodily integrity under the South African Constitution. *Cardozo Journal of Law & Gender, 22*(1), 29–74.

8

Assessing Equity in Health and Women's Opportunities to Be Healthy

Each chapter of this work can be seen as comprising a distinct location or vantage point on a larger journey of investigation into key dimensions of this problem of HIV in black women and the factors and processes that underpin it. Use of multiple approaches, interdisciplinary methods, and various sites, e.g., research in clinical settings (Chaps. 3 and 6) and community settings (Chap. 7) yielded distinct perspectives. Indeed, together they offer supplementary views and insights that strengthen and deepen the analysis of the nature and extent of the problem of HIV for black South African women. The aim of this chapter is to take the analysis further, to determine what this investigation yields in terms of this population's opportunities to be healthy, and what more, if anything, justice might demand of the South African government in response. First, I conduct an assessment of whether this problem rises to the level of a health inequity in this population by reviewing the results of the quantitative and qualitative data and other sources against the key definitions and criteria outlined below. Then I consider the implications, possible objections by the State and the way forward.

C. Sprague, *Gender and HIV in South Africa*, Global Research in Gender, Sexuality and Health, https://doi.org/10.1057/978-1-137-55997-5_8

Assessing Inequities in Health: Definitions and Guiding Criteria

Making an assessment of whether a health difference constitutes a health inequity requires that judgments be made based on a set of specified assessment criteria that then guide the evaluation (Sen, 2001). Such judgments recognise that health is shaped by, and subject to, multiple influences and determinants, and that health is not simply a biological norm but 'the product of complex social and biological valuations' (Peter & Evans, 2001, p. 26). To that end, what is distinctive with regard to HIV in black South African women, and must be captured in the assessment, is the role of gendered structural health determinants and how they operate and interact with other social processes within the larger gender order.

Capturing such multi-level processes in the assessment necessitates reliance on inter-disciplinary methods and approaches, while avoiding dependency on a single indicator or type of evidence (such as life expectancy, or even health outcomes, alone) (Sen, 2004a, 2004b). It also requires locating the potential inequity in health within the respective social context. It needs to be noted, at the outset, that this is not an easy ride akin to mounting a horse and galloping effortlessly off into the sunset. Rather, it is a messy, winding labyrinthine journey by foot through a dark, scraggly wood, with a nod to Dante Alighieri (1984). Noting the focus here is on LMIC settings, and there is no easy roadmap to follow when it comes to health equity assessments. The South African setting is a complex terrain with pitfalls that threaten to ensnare weary travellers. Sen's comment on the evaluation processes that can be used to assess economic and social policies to support capabilities has relevance here. He writes that Euclid is reported to have told Ptolemy that there was no 'royal road' to geometry. Sen remarks: 'It is not clear that there is any royal road to evaluation' (1999, p. 85). Let it be emphasised that there is no royal road to assessing health inequities or capabilities in this population of women. Indeed, there is only an emerging path. The poet David Whyte beseechs the traveller, 'don't leave the old road for a new one' (1994, p. 190). This suggests that the problem of HIV in South African women must be located within the unfolding post-apartheid sociohistorical context, on the larger journey towards social transformation begun in earnest during the transition to democracy. Any social accounting of the health of a particular group in South Africa must then locate black South African women's health along a larger trajectory of the envisaged 'good life' for South Africans—in line with the country's Final 1996 Constitution and the road travelled thus far. This is the 'long walk to freedom' characterised by Madiba in his work of the same name, and I do not make this reference lightly. Mandela was positioning his own life history within the nation's trajectory to independence and beyond, as indeed those paths are inextricably bound (1995). And so must this problem be anchored within this longer journey. The emerging path to advance HIV positive women's substantive freedoms, through greater equity in health, has some formidable and distressing features. If it is not at times, harrowing, even wrenching, then I have not accurately represented the on-the-ground realities and considerations that emanated from the narratives of these black South African women living with HIV. In assessing whether this situation rises to the level of a health inequity for black South African women, I draw particularly on the work of other scholars, both philosophers and public health specialists who will serve as a composite 'Virgil' to this Dantean quest: Braveman (2006); Sen (2004a, 2004b); Peter (2004); Pogge (2004); Evans, Whitehead, Diderichsen, Bhuiya, and Wirth (2001); Diderichsen, Evans, and Whitehead (2001); Whitehead (1992); and Alighieri (1984).

The criteria and evidence being used to generate the health equity assessment include the four questions below. In the section which follows, they are discussed and summarised in turn, and a final composite assessment is rendered thereafter.

1. Is there evidence of systematic health differences that are also linked to social disadvantage?
2. Is there evidence of avoidability?
3. Are there relational justice considerations, i.e., how is society related to the health condition that is experienced by this population?
4. Are key opportunities/capabilities for women to be healthy compromised?

To answer the questions, I am mobilising the foundational materials (data, evidence and analysis) from previous chapters to erect and undergird the scaffolding, the very structure of the analysis, that is presented here as part of this investigation. The working definition I am applying to guide the assessment has been developed primarily by Whitehead (1990, 1992) in the European context; and extended to other contexts by Evans et al. (2001), Braveman and Gruskin (2003) and others (Leppo et al., 2013). To constitute a health inequity, a disparity or difference in health:

> Must be systematically associated with social disadvantage (e.g., there is a social basis to ill health) that is frequent, substantial and persistent, not random or occasional. (Braveman & Gruskin, 2003; Whitehead, 1990)

And noting: Health differences must be *strongly associated with unjust social structures*, such that *socially-created structures are* then *systematically putting socially disadvantaged groups at greater disadvantage*—at increased risk of ill health, *thus compounding the social and economic consequences of ill health* (Braveman & Gruskin, 2003; Whitehead, 1990).[1]

1. *Does this group of black South African women experience health differences that are linked to systematic social disadvantage?*

Three main health differences are evident in this population, relative to other groups of South African women: the large burden of HIV disease; and the effects of HIV on these women's health outcomes in terms of reduced life expectancy; and increased maternal mortality.

Differences in HIV prevalence and incidence. These data, reviewed in Chap. 2, underscore that black South African women exhibit sustained high HIV risk and prevalence as a long-term trend (Shisana et al., 2014). In contrast, South African women of all other race groups have much lower HIV prevalence, even as black South African men have lower HIV prevalence across all age brackets, relative to black South African women, up to age 59 (Shisana et al., 2005, 2009, 2014; see Chap. 2, Tables 2.1 and 2.2). Data on HIV incidence indicate that young women (aged 15–24) have the highest incidence among all age groups, an estimated 2.83%, which compares with lower HIV incidence, an estimated 0.82%, in young men (SANAC, 2014).

Social disadvantage. Black South African women exhibit systematic differences in HIV disease and in accompanying poor health outcomes compared to women of other race groups. Black women are officially designated by the South African government as 'historically disadvantaged' (as are black South African men)—a classification that is enshrined in law and policy in order to recognise and redress the systematic ills they experienced at the hands of the apartheid regime (Gutto, 2002; Woolman, 2008). Moreover, black women have the lowest social position, the lowest participation in the skilled professions and low SES relative to other race groups of South African women and men (Stats SA, 2016b).

Differences in life expectancy. Latest available data indicate that in 2015 black South African women's life expectancy was 65 years (Stats SA, 2016a): an improvement from a low of 52 years in 2005. Lower life expectancy in this population, relative to South African women of other race groups (an estimated nine fewer years) and in other African countries (an estimated 20 years), is largely attributed to HIV and AIDS (Stats SA, 2016a). In the absence of AIDS, for example, women's life expectancy in 2015 was projected to be 73 years (for modelling assumptions, see Stats SA, 2015). By 2015, substantial gains for black women were achieved, through cART interventions which reduced mortality in this population to some extent. However, as noted, continued improvements are not assured (see Stats SA, 2015, p. 1).

Differences in maternal mortality. Black South African women have higher maternal mortality than other groups of South African women, and these premature deaths in black women in the perinatal period are again primarily associated with HIV-related diseases (Msemburi et al., 2016). Maternal mortality is estimated by two main sources with different review periods and durations. In one estimate, non-pregnancy related infections—primarily deaths in pregnant women with HIV—contributed to 34.7% of maternal deaths (from 2011 to 2013). (This is based on the sixth report on confidential enquiries into maternal deaths in South Africa, see Government of South Africa, 2015b.) In the second (MRC) estimate, indirect maternal factors associated with TB and HIV were responsible for 39.9% of maternal deaths over the 2008–2012 period (see Msemburi et al., 2016). These data suggest that the contribution of HIV to maternal mortality—ranging from a low of approximately 35% to a high of 40% based on the two sources—remains significant.

To sum up section one of the assessment, a comparative view of HIV prevalence and incidence data across the South African population indicates that HIV disease is not distributed evenly. Relative to men and to other groups of women, black South African women carry a disproportionate risk and burden of HIV infection. Black women have reduced life expectancy and increased maternal mortality, relative to other groups of women, and these differences are substantial and persistent in this population, while being consistent over time. These health differences also correspond with their race and lower social position, whereby it is black women who experience social disadvantage and accompanying poorer health outcomes, compared to other groups of women.

2. *Is there evidence of avoidability?*

Health equity is concerned with differences in health outcomes that are unnecessary, unfair and avoidable (Whitehead, 1990, 1992; Peter & Evans, 2001). There seem to be some debates about the role of avoidability in health equity assessments (Braveman, 2006; Venkatapuram, 2011; Whitehead, 1992). However, Peter and Evans make a strong case that when illness or premature deaths are 'unavoidable, judgments of fairness and justice do not apply' (2001, p. 28). For example, if events of illness or disability are unavoidable, they can still be horrible—even tragic—but that does not make them unjust (Peter & Evans, 2001). This is because the concern of equity in health is with patterning of poor heath in particular groups: systematic, persistent, and substantial differences associated with social disadvantage, not random or *ad hoc* events (Braveman & Gruskin, 2003).

The question of avoidability could be applied at two different time points: in terms of whether HIV could be prevented in women in the first instance (i.e. preventing new HIV infections); and whether premature deaths, once women contract the virus, could be avoided. Each raises a set of different and important considerations. I discuss avoidability of new HIV infections in the section further below. Regarding premature maternal deaths in women living with HIV, we know that HIV prevalence in pregnant women is an estimated 30% (Government of South Africa, 2013a, 2015b), thus there is a large burden of HIV infection in pregnant women, and significant numbers of maternal deaths are attributed to HIV, as discussed above (Msemburi et al., 2016; Government of South Africa, 2015b). While the intervention of cART before, during or after labour may safeguard women's health and survival, other factors may play a role, including underlying conditions and obstetric complications, as well as mediating and protective factors. The *South Africa Every Death Counts Writing Group* investigated maternal deaths in women, regardless of HIV status, finding that 44% of maternal deaths had a modifiable factor related to family/community action—e.g., inadequate or no antenatal care, while 32% of maternal deaths had a modifiable factor related to administrator action—e.g., absence of blood for transfusion, and no transport between health institutions (2008a, 2008b). Additionally, 54% of maternal deaths had a modifiable factor related to health care provider action at the primary facility level; 48% at secondary level; and 37% at tertiary level, e.g., non-adherence to standard protocols (2008a, p. 1299). Note that these data refer to the period of reporting that precedes the current one. While some of these gaps may have closed, the longstanding trends in maternal mortality remain intact. Given that non-pregnancy related infections, such as HIV and TB—infections that are preventable and treatable—are responsible for 35–40% of maternal deaths, this leads to a conclusion that premature maternal deaths due to HIV remain avoidable to some degree.

How reliable are these data? This is an important question to ask in all settings, and particularly in LMICs that struggle to establish data systems and reporting. The trends in HIV prevalence, life expectancy and maternal mortality are based on routine statistical data from reliable sources that produce national, well accepted high quality data that are used by the Government and scientific community (particularly the HSRC, MRC and StatsSA).

In concluding section two of the assessment: there is strong evidence that this group of black South African women experiences systematic health differences that are frequent, substantial and persistent (in acquiring HIV and in reduced life expectancy and increased maternal mortality attributed to HIV). These health differences are associated with the social disadvantage experienced by this population, which correlates with their race as black women, and with their lower social position within the gender and the social hierarchy.

3. *Are there relational justice considerations?*

In assessing inequities in health, it is necessary to move beyond the measures of health outcomes just reviewed to look to underlying social processes, and how those influence, or do not influence, systematic health differences between groups. Indeed, what renders such systematic health differences unjust is the influence of unjust social arrangements (Peter & Evans, 2001). The focus must not only be on the outcome but the *process* by which outcomes were achieved, note Sen (2001) and Pogge (2004). This shift represents a more active approach to justice in health, and it reflects a number of developments (Pogge, 2004).

This shift to recognise process also recognises the social role and obligation in social patterning of ill health for some members of society, against a background where individual behaviours and individual responsibility for health have dominated (see Pogge, 2004). Here Pogge captures the same shift to embrace approaches to combination HIV prevention, highlighted in Chap. 7, as part of gender-transformative interventions that look to mediate the role of structural drivers in HIV risk and transmission specifically. This shift represents a marked change from the focus on individual risk factors and behaviours which had long dominated public health efforts until the more recent embrace of structural drivers (Coates, Richter, & Caceres, 2008; Gupta, Parkhurst, Ogden, Aggleton, & Mahal, 2008). This shift also reflects greater awareness of linkages between social determinants of health, social causation and equity in health, and more normative commitments to social justice at global and national levels, through the dialogue taking place at national and transnational (UN) levels, including through the SDGs. Making this shift requires re-engaging with Pogge's relational justice considerations in this chapter (2004). I also make brief reference to Rawls' requirement for justice in social arrangements (1993), which has relevance.

Recall that relational justice considerations concern how society is related to the health condition that causes the affected group, black South African women living with HIV in this instance, to experience ill health (Pogge, 2004). The question to be answered follows from the initial guiding definition and questions: *Are these health differences strongly associated with unjust social structures, such that socially-created structures are then systematically putting socially disadvantaged groups at greater disadvantage—at increased risk of ill health, thus compounding the social and economic consequences of ill health?*

The data and evidence relied upon to answer this question are elaborated in detail in Chap. 2, as part of the review of the thick literature emerging from South and Southern Africa that identifies an array of social-level factors that facilitate HIV risk and acquisition in this population of women. These are summarised in Fig. 2.2 in Chap. 2. They encompass three main structural drivers (elaborated in the discussion of GTIs in Chap. 7): gender inequality and social norms that condone violence; social constructions of gender (masculinities and femininities); and poverty/economic inequality. These drivers are part of the gendered structural determinants of health that are situated within a gender system that influences how power is distributed according to members of the social hierarchy. Social processes encompass the social attitudes, norms and beliefs about gender equality documented. Social, gendered processes also govern health and HIV risk, vulnerability and exposure—i.e., who is vulnerable to HIV, who is HIV-exposed, who becomes ill. Because gender equality and health equity are 'socially governed' (i.e., governed by society), they are therefore viewed as 'actionable' by agents of the State (Sen, Östlin, & George, 2007, p. xii).

Rawls avoided any discussion of health in his theory of justice as fairness (1993; Peter, 2004). However, Peter applies an indirect approach to health equity to infer that for Rawls the role of social institutions and how they function is more important than the health outcomes that are produced (i.e., whether there is just distribution in health outcomes, such as with the fair innings argument reviewed in Chap. 2). For Rawls, if the basic structure of society produces inequalities in health, then social arrangements are playing an important role in generating a health inequity in ways that are unjust (1993; see also Peter, 2004, pp. 102–103).

My analysis therefore supports a conclusion that a social basis is perpetuating HIV acquisition in this population and that basic social arrangements are playing a key role in generating HIV risk and transmission, which underpins poor health achievements in this population.

Moreover, there is wide agreement from the growing evidence base that gender norms and factors affecting HIV transmission can be modified over the long term through targeted policies and selected interventions, and that both HIV and IPV can be avoided to some degree through prevention efforts, as demonstrated through the IMAGE and Stepping Stones evaluations. This affirms that while it is neither simple nor easily achievable, new HIV infections are avoidable. Indeed, this sizeable evidence base on gender-transformative interventions (reviewed in Chap. 7) demonstrates where interventions can be located to engage with, and potentially alter, these structural drivers.

In sum, relational considerations of health as social justice recognise the social role and responsibility in the production of ill health. In the South African context, social factors and drivers of HIV risk and infection are well documented. That there would be a social obligation to address the relational justice considerations associated with this problem have been under-emphasised. There are a number of implications discussed shortly.

4. *Are key opportunities/capabilities for women to be healthy compromised?*

One final section of the assessment remains. While the quantitative indicators reviewed shed light on systematic health differences for women, they offer virtually no insight into HIV positive women's wellbeing in the day to day, namely, the nature of their lived experience. Qualitative data thus had to be generated to fill this gap using the research design and methodology described in Chap. 5. By investigating what women living with HIV are able to do and be, their agency, opportunity and process freedoms, it was possible to generate a more robust portrait of this population's opportunities to be healthy, while also utilising these data to inform the health equity assessment undertaken here. I now return to the findings from the empirical research and take the analysis further to see what the results yield in terms of HIV positive women's capabilities.

Sen notes that, within any assessment of health inequities, it is imperative to specify the informational base, i.e., is the assessment relying on external views of the population, or internal views by the affected population whose health is being assessed (Sen, 2001)? Recall that both external and internal views were solicited and drawn upon to offer independent data sources thereby assisting in minimising bias and allowing for triangulation (Ritchie & Lewis, 2012; Anfara, Brown, & Mangione, 2002; Denzin & Lincoln, 2011). The internal perspectives enabled a view of women's capabilities by drawing on their own reported experiences along the ten central domains (Nussbaum, 2000), and in terms of women's agency, process and opportunity freedoms (Sen, 1999) by emphasising women's lived experiences. This was supplemented by external perspectives from health providers who treat these women and further enhanced by seeking the expert views of key informants in women's health, HIV, gender and law who contributed perspectives on the enabling environment towards HIV positive women and women at risk of acquiring the virus. Note that I am also drawing from the base of published evidence to put forth further conclusions.

Capabilities and Rights: Deprivations and Infringements

Results from the study conducted among the 89 women living with HIV in the two provinces indicated that the majority of the study population expressed particular deprivations in the following four capability domains: bodily integrity, bodily health, life, and control over one's material environment (for the full list of central capabilities, see Nussbaum, 2007, pp. 22–24). Very significantly, some elements to protect and enable the first three of these capabilities are in place as part of the progressive constitutional law and policy framework (shown in Table 8.1). If the correlation between the South African Constitution and capabilities surprises readers, this is because Nussbaum holds up capabilities as political entitlements and constitutions as a mechanism for redress (for reference to the South African Constitution, see Nussbaum, 2011, pp. 105, 114 and 166). Table 8.1 outlines the capabilities that are diminished in the study population and the rights that correspond with those capabilities.

Table 8.1 Capability deprivations and rights infringements for the study population of black South African women living with HIV

Nussbaum's central capabilities	South Africa's Final 1996 Constitution
Bodily Integrity. Being able to move freely from place to place; to be secure against violent assault, including sexual assault and domestic violence; having opportunities for sexual satisfaction and for choice in matters of reproduction.	*Section 12*. (1) Everyone has the *right to freedom and security of the person*, which includes *the right—(c) to be free from all forms of violence from either public or private sources;* (2) Everyone has the *right to bodily and psychological integrity*, which includes *the right: (a) to make decisions concerning reproduction; (b) to security in and control over their body;* *The Domestic Violence Act of 1998* further spells out the State's responsibility concerning domestic, or intimate partner, violence.
Bodily Health. Being able to have good health, including reproductive health; to be adequately nourished; to have adequate shelter.	*Section 27*. Everyone has the *right to health care, food, water and social security: (a) health care services,* including *reproductive health care*.
Life. Being able to live to the end of a human life of normal length; not dying prematurely, or before one's life is so reduced as to be not worth living.	*Section 11*. Everyone has the *right to life*.

Source: Adapted from Government of South Africa 1996, pp. 5–11; Nussbaum, 2000

On the Right to Freedom and Security of the Person (Bodily Integrity) (Section 12)

The first right and capability that women, their health providers, key informants, as well as the published literature, have affirmed as being inaccessible for black South African women living with HIV was that of bodily integrity, which has its mirror in Section 12 of the Bill of Rights in the Constitution. Section 12 affords each person the right to freedom and security of the person, while protecting and promoting bodily and psychological integrity. Additionally, the Domestic Violence Act 116 of 1998 makes IPV unlawful (Government of South Africa, 1998), and specifies further actions and protections available to women who experience partner abuse.

The majority of the women in the sample of 89 could not fully exercise this right and capability for reasons that were attributed to the very same social factors and structural drivers that foster HIV risk in this population, as discussed above. Namely, women's agency, their process and opportunity freedoms were constrained by the triumvirate of gender-related factors that work in lockstep: gender inequality and social norms that condone violence; social constructions of gender (masculinities and femininities); and poverty/economic inequality. Among this cluster of hazards, a principal threat was intimate partner violence. As indicated, IPV is typically defined as physical, sexual, or psychological abuse, attempted or completed, by a current or former partner (see Government of South Africa, 1998; WHO, 2013b). Many South African women experience IPV, and the statistical and qualitative evidence indicates it is indeed widespread across race groups (Human Rights Watch, 1995). However, there are at least two key aspects that must be emphasised with regard to this population of South African women relative to other South African women who experience IPV.

First the women studied were HIV positive. Second, they were pregnant or had given birth within the last four months. Together, those realities introduced a set of distinct health risks that generate significant psychological and physical vulnerabilities for this population. Published estimates of IPV prevalence in HIV positive women, at 31–55%, are high (Dunkle et al., 2004; Gass, Stein, Williams, & Seedat, 2010). In one seminal study conducted among 1395 pregnant women in South Africa, 30% of participants reported being sexually or physically assaulted in the last 12 months by a male partner and 55.5% of participants reported being sexually and/or physically assaulted by a male partner at least once over the course of their lives. In that study, after adjusting for age, current relationship status and women's risk behaviours, IPV was significantly associated with HIV positivity, and with high levels of male control in a woman's current relationship (Dunkle et al., 2004). Studies of South African women living with HIV found that they experience higher rates of IPV preceding and during pregnancy (see Hoque & Kader, 2009; Mbokota & Moodley, 2003; Dunkle et al., 2004). The postpartum period appears to be somewhat protective in terms of violence exposure, for reasons that might be associated with women's mobility, i.e., travel to traditional homes following delivery, but require further study.

Additionally, and significantly, studies have found that women who experience violence also have a decreased ability to effectively engage in HIV testing and treatment, which demonstrates the likely effect on services uptake (WHO, 2013c), and underscores the complex multi-faceted interrelationship between HIV and IPV. There is growing literature on the pathways linking the two (Dunkle & Decker, 2013; Kouyoumdjian et al., 2013) and WHO concludes that further research is needed to understand the link between IPV and HIV, and between IPV, HIV and other health outcomes, including reproductive and child health, mental health (particularly depression and anxiety) and injuries (WHO, 2013b). Figure 3.3 in Chap. 3 specifies the likely effect on health and HIV services uptake. Alongside this, three systematic reviews of sub-Saharan African studies, which include South African studies, found links between disclosure of HIV status, violence and access to and adherence to cART (Hodgson et al., 2014; Gourlay, Birdthistle, Mburu, Iorpenda, & Wringe, 2013; Wettstein et al., 2012) (further details are located in Chap. 3) (see also Campbell et al., 2008). A qualitative South African study demonstrated a link between disclosure of HIV status, partner violence and access and adherence to HIV treatment (Hatcher et al., 2014). Much of this association seems to revolve around women's management of HIV stigma in order to safely disclose their HIV status to partners (or families), which is a pre-requisite to optimal cART initiation and adherence in continuous lifelong HIV care. This was visible in the empirical research undertaken (Chap. 6), where HIV positive women's narratives repeatedly highlighted the manner in which women shouldered deep anxieties over whether or not to disclose their HIV status to partners and others.

Stigma can be anticipated, experienced, self-stigma—or a combination of these (Link & Phelan, 2001; Goffman, 1963). It is a social process that is linked to loss of esteem, i.e., HIV stigma 'discredits' and 'devalues' individuals, and can very often result in women being abandoned by partners or experiencing IPV. HIV stigma can have profound physiological and moral consequences in other populations in ways that have a bearing on this population as well. Women in the perinatal period who become HIV positive often experience anticipated losses along a number of key dimensions, including an anticipated loss of esteem, where esteem is part of each person's valued social identity. Stigma thus has significant psychological consequences.

Yang et al. (2007) note that stigma also affects the moral experience, or what is 'most at stake' for individuals who are devalued. This was most visible when black South African women exercised their agency to control, negotiate and ascertain whether or not they could safely disclose to partners, and to family members. Their efforts served as an agentic way of protecting their psychological integrity from the discrediting that is expected, or that takes place, once women are categorised as being HIV positive. This process of black South African women's response to stigma offers a window onto the mechanisms of the social construction of stigma and 're-identifying', as Goffman (1963) called it (i.e., reidentifying as HIV positive persons), as well as how women sought to resist or stave off this categorisation by controlling who had access to knowledge about their HIV status. (Foucault, 1977 locates this social process within knowledge systems of control and dominance in societies, which perpetuate inequalities).

Stigma also has moral-emotional and moral-somatic consequences, note Yang et al., referring to values and processes that are linked to emotional states and physical health states (2007). A palpable and visceral object of HIV positive women's agentic negotiation and actions was in managing HIV disclosure, in terms of avoiding IPV and/or abandonment and averting other multi-centric concerns. Here the reality of black South African women's vulnerability to the experience or the threat of abuse was influenced by their economic dependence on their partners (and sometimes other family members), but also by intertwined motivations, such as their basic needs for love, care, support and other agentic desires, including for increased social status, esteem and/or material or other intangible benefits which they saw as attainable through their partnerships with men (Hunter, 2010; Leclerc-Madlala, 2008a, 2008b; Jewkes, Penn-Kekana, & Rose-Junius, 2005; Wood, Maforah, & Jewkes, 1998). Women's lack of decision making power in households, as part of the capability of control over one's material environment, underpinned these calculations. This is because it reduced women's autonomy, control over the circumstances that affected them and their agentic options in defraying the social, psychological, physical and other costs of losing these benefits, while elevating their stress and anxiety, with potential consequences for their mental and physical health.

In sum, HIV stigma, IPV, and women's economic vulnerability were part of women's gendered experiences of living with HIV. Gender-associated factors continue to affect, and limit, women's opportunities to be healthy in distinct ways that are different for men, and for different groups of women of higher social standing and socio-economic status. While these multi-factors work in tandem, the consistency and frequency of IPV for HIV positive women signifies that the capability of bodily integrity, and its counterpart—the right to freedom and security of the person—is compromised.

On the Right to Health Care Including Reproductive Health Services (Section 27), the Capability of Bodily Health, the Right to Life (Section 11) and the Capability of Life

The capability of bodily health is matched closely by Section 27 of the South African Constitution which entitles each person the right to access health care, including the reproductive health and HIV services that are freely available in the South African public health system. Above, I have already drawn out some implications for HIV positive women's bodily and mental health when bodily integrity is inaccessible. The focus in South African law and policy is also on access to health care services. Additionally, the right to life is protected and enabled by Section 11, and matches the capability of the same name (i.e., life). One of the most protective and important measures to advance HIV positive women's capabilities along these two dimensions is through cART. However, significant numbers of HIV positive women in this study, and in other published studies, report difficulties adhering to HIV medication because adherence is strongly associated with disclosing their HIV status, and women are reluctant to disclose to their partners for fear of IPV and stigma—as discussed above—including the stigma of IPV (see Sprague et al., 2016b). The cyclicality of these factors is ever-present. Over the long-term lack of access or adherence to cART negatively affects women's HIV outcomes.

Thus the domino effect of diminished capability in the sphere of bodily integrity, and the interactive factors of gender and stigma, reduce women's access to and enjoyment of the right to health and HIV care. This interferes with women's ability to achieve optimal HIV and related health outcomes. In the perinatal period, this equates to a need for earlier cART initiation and adherence in pregnancy to capitalise on the benefits of cART for their own health, and PMTCT programmes to avert paediatric HIV in their infants (Chersich, 2007; Sprague, 2009; McNairy & El-Sadr, 2012). In short, HIV positive women's ability to exercise their right to health and HIV care in section 27 is undercut by social factors and norms. The eroded capability and right to access HIV and health care rebounds to undermine women's capability to, and right to, life (section 11), as the inability to benefit from cART places women at higher risk of dying prematurely from HIV by compromising their survival benefits from cART. Additionally, the diminished capability of bodily integrity, and ongoing concerns over IPV, also reverberates to undermine women's right to make decisions concerning reproduction—for example, to elect not to terminate their pregnancies (the choice of their partners) and to elect to use condoms to prevent HIV re-infection and other STIs.

There is an additional capability deprivation that women experience, which does not appear to have a direct counterpart in South African law: women are experiencing deprivation in the capability to exercise control over their material environment (Nussbaum, 2007, pp. 22–24). That skilled employment remains largely inaccessible to these women living with HIV, and black South African women generally, more than 12 years after the introduction of democracy warrants special notice. This capability deprivation places emphasis on the role of employment and education as components that can be located along a life course pathway of women's human development to address women's underlying social and economic disadvantage as part of social stratification processes (Sen et al., 2007; Kuh, Ben-Schlomo, Lynch, Hallqvist, & Power, 2003).

In summary, in multiple ways, gender-related factors most grievously manifest in partner abuse, or the impending threat of it, but also gender norms, expectations, social constructions and economic inequalities. These rebound to generate specific capability deprivations for this population, most visibly seen in their reduced ability to exercise the capability of and the right to bodily integrity, but also their ability to access the capabilities of bodily health and life, including HIV and reproductive care and services, while generating a domino effect on some other capabilities. Capabilities are indivisible and inter-dependent, thus deprivations in the four domains of capability have a negative effect on the exercise of some of the other central capabilities. This includes undermining the capabilities of emotions, of practical reason, and the capability of senses, imagination and thought. This would vary by person, degree and timing. The continuing role of intimate partner violence as a catalyst that introduces a range of unfreedoms could not be starker, however. While the pathway linking exposures to violence to adverse health outcomes in women is complex and might be mediated, this suggests that important opportunities to be healthy—that have been made available in keeping with the NSP, with policies in the health system to promote the health of women living with HIV and to extend their lives—are out of reach.

In short, this reality strongly suggests a further conclusion that the very social factors or structural drivers that facilitate HIV infection and intimate partner violence against women in the first instance, also limit women's capabilities of bodily integrity, health and life, once they contract HIV. In the South African context, with its high HIV prevalence—an estimated 29–30% in pregnant women—this is affecting a sizable number of South African women (Government of South Africa, 2013a). The full lack of access women have to HIV services and reproductive health care in South Africa, unlike other settings internationally, poses infringements on women's human rights. The inability to enjoy these rights as they were intended by the Government in the basic law as capabilities constrains women's human development, reduces their wellbeing, diminishes their process and opportunity freedoms and thus fundamentally undermines what black South African women are able to be and do.

Final Assessment vis-à-vis Health Equity

Based on the review of the published literature, combined with the original research undertaken, I conclude that black South African women do experience health inequities, relative to South African women of other race groups. These are systematic differences in health: in terms of acquiring HIV, life expectancy and maternal mortality. Health differences in this population are tied to women's social disadvantage as black women. Black women occupy a role in the gender system that is subordinate to other groups. The particular features of the South African social context are playing a key role in generating social stratification and related processes that produce ill health in this population. The social patterning of ill health in black women can be attributed largely to gendered structural health determinants. The evidence also indicates that such social factors are modifiable. This suggests that there are unexploited opportunities for the State or State parties to do more to address these gaps. Additionally, key capabilities are not fully accessible due to the structural factors, drivers and processes elaborated. Society plays a role in facilitating increased HIV risk, reduced opportunities and capabilities in the basic social structure, for black women.

I thus complete this assessment by concluding that: (a) this problem does constitute a health inequity that is modifiable; (b) four central capabilities are undermined and these have direct counterparts in sections 11, 12 and 27 of the South African 1996 Final Constitution; (c) the current Government response to HIV in South African women is insufficient because it fails to attend to the social factors that foster HIV risk and transmission in women; (d) relational factors associated with the basic social structure are contributing to HIV in this population; (e) this problem can be socially governed, which generates an obligation by agents of the State to take further action to ameliorate HIV in women and to facilitate the enjoyment of their rights. Moreover, the Government and SANAC are aware of these structural drivers and other social factors but have failed thus far to address them fully in the NSP.

Implications

The clearest rationale for action to address health inequities and capability deprivations for these South African women is located in the South African government's commitments, enshrined in the Bill of Rights (Government of South Africa, Final Constitution, 1996, pp. 5–11) and spelt out in Table 8.1. The normative basis and claim for further action is reflected in the State's obligation to ensure that those rights are promoted and protected.

Social Evaluation Process: A Social and Moral Accounting

Where to from here? The normative social justice framework that undergirds the Capabilities Approach offers a rope that can be tied securely to South African women's rights in the Constitution. This tethers capabilities to constitutional rights that comprise legal entitlements in South Africa. Significantly, the fact that specific social arrangements in South Africa are contributing to diminished capability for women thrusts the State's obligation to do more to protect and promote health and wellbeing for this population into the spotlight (Ruger, 2006, 2010). Justice requires more of the South African state in response to HIV in black South African women, both in the CA and in the law.

From a CA perspective, Sen is ever-mindful of diverse considerations; never prescriptive. He throws the process of determining social action, in response to capability deprivation, onto the back of governments and related decision making bodies. He also recognises the differences in social values and political priorities which makes certain outcomes tolerable or intolerable, according to the country or region. This seems to explain his reluctance to elevate capabilities to become political entitlements as Nussbaum does, as I return to below. When it comes to social evaluation of health inequities for this population, while it may be true that—to use Sen's metaphor—there is no 'royal road' that announces itself in all its glory, there is an emerging pathway that takes us to a new threshold in the trajectory of social transformation and the location of black South African women within it. Sen notes that 'A variety of considerations that call for attention are involved, and evaluations have to be done with sensitivity to these concerns' (1999, p. 85).

Objections

The State could argue that it has done the work of protecting women's bodily integrity, their reproductive health and right to health care, and even to life because it has laws to this effect. I take up discussion of this below and suggest that the legal analysis could be deepened and extended. The Constitution requires the State to make good on the rights outlined in Table 8.1, subject to 'reasonable legislative and other means', 'available resources' and 'progressive realisation' which place a limit on remedies by the courts. The multi-pronged test that must be met, constructed by colleague Woolman (Woolman & Sprague, 2015, see pp. 39–41), is as follows:

1. Has the State adopted a reasonable plan for all affected parties?
2. Has the State taken steps to progressively realise the access to a particular good within available resources?
3. Is the State's duty to progressively realise the right reflected in a reasonable plan?

The State could argue that it fulfils points 1 and 2 above because there is a multi-sectoral National Strategic Plan governing the epidemic response, which has inputs and responsibilities from each sector. And, because it makes HIV services freely available in the public health system (see Chaps. 3 and 6), the State could further argue that it has come up with a reasonable plan to ensure the right to access health care, which addresses point 3. The question is whether the NSP and related services meet the following requirements.

1. Is it a comprehensive, coordinated plan that engages all spheres of government?
2. Does the plan ensure that appropriate financial and human resources are available?
3. *Is the plan capable of facilitating the realisation of the right?*
4. Is the plan reasonable in conception and implementation?
5. *Does the plan attend to crises?*
6. Is the plan conceived in a manner that does not exclude a significant segment of the affected population?
7. *Does the plan respond to the urgent needs of those in desperate situations?*

The State could reasonably answer yes to questions 1 and 2 just above. However, HIV positive women's right to access health services, their right to life and their right to freedom and security of the person/bodily integrity are other rights that remain unaddressed by this plan, and those rights and capabilities remain compromised. The NSP fails to facilitate the realisation of this range of rights, as outlined in Table 8.1. Neither the provision of HIV services nor the Domestic Violence Act are facilitating the realisation of these rights in ways that would meet the requirements above because of structural impediments that restrict women's enjoyment. Note that it is unclear what constitutes crises and desperate situations, and those would need to be further specified. The evidence does indicate that locating the response within the health system is failing to meet the requirements of justice in this population, in terms of point 3.

State obligation. In at least two primary ways, the State is failing in its response and is obliged to do more. First, the NSP fails to sufficiently protect black women who are HIV negative from new HIV infections, which suggests that the health of black women known to be at high risk of HIV is not receiving sufficient attention. The health system response has been characterised by the rollout of cART and has increasingly moved to a model of test and treat (UNAIDS, 2014a). Thus, the response focuses on keeping people alive after they have contracted the virus, rather than averting new HIV infections, even though the basic structure is facilitating risk in this population, as indicated.

Second, as discussed in detail above, once women contract the virus, their opportunities to be healthy are reduced, including their access to cART and other programmes, as part of their right to access health care, and as part of their right to life, due to the gender-related aspects that undermine their agency and process freedoms and disable them from actualising their choices to be healthy, including preferences associated with their fertility intentions. This suggests that there are real impediments to women's substantive freedoms that breach the laws in place to protect their health, wellbeing, freedom and security of the person, and that prohibit their realisation of these rights. Moreover, these social drivers of HIV have been recognised by State agents responsible for mounting the HIV response at the national level, namely the Department of Health and SANAC.

The latest SANAC report points to two gaps in the NSP: they are structural drivers of HIV and human rights. SANAC stresses that while 'strong emphasis is placed on structural drivers…social drivers…are not included as clearly articulated goals or indicators' (2016, p. 36). The SANAC report recommended a consensus workshop to identify lead entities to do this, which demonstrates acknowledgment and awareness by Government and other actors of social factors that foster HIV acquisition in women, but this appears not to have gone further. However, the excerpt just cited evinces an ongoing inability to take action on structural factors associated with gender that have been pushed to the outer edges of the response, and a continued delay in protecting and advancing the human rights of those living with HIV. It also reveals a mismatch between the focus of the HIV response and the drivers of the HIV epidemic. It is all too easy to continue as is—by focusing on locating the epidemic response within health systems where it has been situated since the ARV rollout in 2004. In the last year, the Department of Health has been making a big push to reach the 90–90–90 treatment target set by UNAIDS. While this is laudable, this approach is treatment-centred and focused on people who have already acquired the virus. Furthermore, it does not address the factors that preclude women from taking advantage of health and HIV services that are in place to improve their health and wellbeing.

Altering the HIV response to engage with structural determinants and drivers would require a new vision for women's health and their capabilities: for considering what women are able to be in South Africa. That guiding vision could occur through greater public discussion. Civil society pushed the Government to initiate the national HIV response, through social mobilisation in communities. In this new phase, it may be that civil society can stimulate Government action by taking back the fight. It is in communities where fundamental changes could make the most impact, as evidenced by the GTIs reviewed here. I have suggested in Chap. 7 how communities and local NGOs could play a role. There must be leadership across key areas of government and within SANAC to do so, as part of an inter-sectoral effort. It calls for shifts at virtually every level and across levels and sectors. The NSP leads this process and the urgency of the situation could not be greater.

Finally, per Wikler's earlier note, 'We also need a moral account, a compelling argument that health inequalities represent or constitute an injustice that places a claim on society's resources' (2004, p. 114). The State is not recognising the moral implications of the systematic health differences experience by black South African women documented here.[2] South Africa currently represents 18% of the world population living with HIV (UNAIDS, 2014b). Over 51% of those living with HIV in South Africa are black women and this is likely to increase, given current projections. Recall that South Africa leads the world in new HIV infections in women aged 15–24 years and HIV prevalence among women of other age groups remains consistently high (UNAIDS, 2016a, 2016b). Indeed, black women remain at risk of acquiring HIV over their entire life course (Shisana et al., 2014). The deleterious effects of HIV on black women's health outcomes are clear, and should compel the State to act of its own volition. Moreover, these stark health differences are coupled with unmistakable infringements of black women's rights to bodily integrity, health care and life. These infringements are an affront to women's human dignity and to their substantive equality. And they are being borne by the women least able to overturn the very social and structural complex of factors that are facilitating their risk of acquiring HIV due to their lower position in the social hierarchy.

Notes

1. Italicised emphases are mine.
2. Note that in political philosophy, the moral and the ethical are most often used interchangeably to refer to what is right, just and good and I am applying this same convention here. Where distinctions are made, particularly in law and business, morality tends to be viewed as located from 'within' the individual person and ethics is imposed from 'without' by the government, society or the profession to guide right conduct. Both revolve around social values and norms in keeping with the good life in a given society.

References

Alighieri, D. (1984). *The Divine Comedy. Volume 1: Inferno* (Mark Musa, Trans.). New York: Penguin Books.

Anfara, V., Brown, K., & Mangione, T. (2002). Qualitative analysis on stage: Making the research process more public. *Educational Researcher, 31*(7), 28–38.

Braveman, P. (2006). Health disparities and health equity: Concepts and measurement. *Annual Review of Public Health, 27*, 167–194.

Braveman, P., & Gruskin, S. (2003). Defining equity in health. *Journal of Epidemiology and Community Health, 57*(4), 254–258.

Campbell, J., Baty, M., Ghandour, R., Stockman, J., Francisco, L., & Wagman, J. (2008). The intersection of intimate partner violence and HIV/AIDS: A review. *The International Journal of Injury Control and Safety Promotion, 15*(4), 222–231.

Chersich, M. (2007). *Preventing HIV in Infants in Eastern and Southern Africa by Improving Access to HIV Testing, Maternal Health and Quality Services.* Doctoral thesis, Ghent University.

Coates, T., Richter, L., & Caceres, C. (2008). Behavioural strategies to reduce HIV transmission: How to make them work better. *Lancet, 372*(9639), 669–684.

Denzin, N., & Lincoln, Y. (2011). *Handbook of Qualitative Research.* Thousand Oaks: Sage.

Diderichsen, F., Evans, T., & Whitehead, M. (2001). The social disparities in health. In T. Evans, M. Whitehead, F. Diderichsen, A. Bhuiya, & M. Wirth (Eds.), *Challenging Inequities to Health: From Ethics to Action* (pp. 12–23). Oxford: Oxford University Press.

Dunkle, K., & Decker, M. (2013). Gender-based violence and HIV: Reviewing the evidence for links and causal pathways in the general population and high risk groups. *American Journal of Reproductive Immunology, 69*(Suppl. 1), 20–26.

Dunkle, K., Jewkes, R., Brown, H., Gray, G., McIntyre, J., & Harlow, S. (2004). Transactional sex among women in Soweto, South Africa: Prevalence, risk factors and associations with HIV infection. *Social Science & Medicine, 59*(8), 1581–1592.

Evans, T., Whitehead, M., Diderichsen, F., Bhuiya, A., & Wirth, M. (Eds.). (2001). *Challenging Inequities to Health: From Ethics to Action.* Oxford: Oxford University Press.

Foucault, M. (1977). *Discipline and Punish: The Birth of the Prison.* New York: Vintage.

Gass, J., Stein, D., Williams, D., & Seedat, S. (2010). Intimate partner violence, health behaviours, and chronic physical illness among South African women. *South African Medical Journal, 100*(9), 582–585.

Goffman, E. (1963). *Stigma: Notes on the Management of Spoiled Identity.* Englewood Cliffs: Prentice-Hall.

Gourlay, A., Birdthistle, I., Mburu, G., Iorpenda, K., & Wringe, A. (2013). Barriers and facilitating factors to the uptake of antiretroviral drugs for prevention of mother-to-child transmission of HIV in sub-Saharan Africa: A systematic review. *Journal of the International AIDS Society, 16*, 18588.

Government of South Africa. (1996). The Constitution of the Republic of South Africa, Act No. 108 of 1996. Cape Town: South Africa.

Government of South Africa. (1998). Domestic Violence Act 116 of 1998. Cape Town: South Africa.

Government of South Africa. (2013a). *The 2012 National Antenatal Sentinel HIV and Herpes Simplex Type-2 Prevalence Survey, South Africa*. Pretoria: National Department of Health.

Government of South Africa. (2015b). *Saving Mothers 2011–2013: Sixth Report on the Confidential Enquiries into Maternal Deaths in South Africa*. Pretoria: National Department of Health.

Gupta, G., Parkhurst, J., Ogden, J., Aggleton, P., & Mahal, A. (2008). Structural approaches to HIV prevention. *Lancet, 372*, 764–775.

Gutto, S. (2002). *Equality and Non-discrimination in South Africa: The Political Economy of Law*. Wynberg: David Philip Publishers.

Hatcher, A., Woollett, N., Pallitto, C., Mokoatle, K., Stockl, H., MacPhail, C., et al. (2014). Bidirectional links between HIV and intimate partner violence in pregnancy: Implications for prevention of mother-to-child transmission. *Journal of the International AIDS Society, 17*, 19233.

Hodgson, I., Plummer, M., Konopka, S., Colvin, C., Jonas, E., Albertini, J., et al. (2014). A systematic review of individual and contextual factors affecting ART initiation, adherence, and retention for HIV-infected pregnant and postpartum women. *PLoS ONE, 9*(11), e111421.

Hoque, M., & Kader, S. (2009). Prevalence and experience of domestic violence among rural pregnant women in KwaZulu-Natal, South Africa. *South African Journal of Epidemiology and Infection, 24*(4), 34–37.

Human Rights Watch. (1995). *Violence Against Women in South Africa: The State Response to Domestic Violence and Rape*. New York: Human Rights Watch.

Hunter, M. (2010). *Love in the Time of AIDS. Inequality, Gender and Right in South Africa*. Durban: University of KwaZulu-Natal Press.

Jewkes, R., Penn-Kekana, L., & Rose-Junius, H. (2005). "If they rape me, I can't blame them": Reflections on gender in the social context of rape in South Africa and Namibia. *Social Science & Medicine, 61*, 1809–1820.

Kouyoumdjian, F. G., Findlay, N., Schwandt, M., & Calzavara, L. M. (2013). A systematic review of the relationships between intimate partner violence and HIV/AIDS. *PloS One, 8*(11), e81044.

Kuh, D., Ben-Schlomo, Y., Lynch, J., Hallqvist, J., & Power, C. (2003). Life course epidemiology. *Journal of Epidemiology & Community Health, 57*, 778–783.

Leclerc-Madlala, S. (2008a). Age-disparate and intergenerational sex in Southern Africa: The dynamics of hypervulnerability. *AIDS, 22*(Suppl. 4), S17–S25.

Leclerc-Madlala, S. (2008b). Intergenerational/age-disparate sex and young women's vulnerability in Southern Africa. In *UNAIDS Technical Meeting on Young Women in HIV Hyper-Endemic Countries of Southern Africa.* Muldersdrift, South Africa: UNAIDS.

Leppo, K., Ollla, E., Pena, S., Wismar, M., & Cook, S. (2013). *Health in All Policies: Seizing Opportunities, Implementing Policies.* Helsinki: Finland Ministry of Social Affairs and Health.

Link, B., & Phelan, J. (2001). Conceptualizing stigma. *Annual Review of Sociology, 27*, 363–385.

Mbokota, M., & Moodley, J. (2003). Domestic abuse—An antenatal survey at King Edward VIII Hospital, Durban. *South African Medical Journal, 93*(6), 455–457.

McNairy, M., & El-Sadr, W. (2012). The HIV care continuum: No partial credit given. *AIDS, 26*(14), 1735–1738.

Msemburi, W., Pillay-van Wyk, V., Dorrington, R., Neethling, I., Nannan, N., Groenewald, P., et al. (2016). *Second National Burden of Disease Study for South Africa: Cause-of-Death Profile for South Africa, 1997–2012.* Cape Town: South African Medical Research Council.

Nussbaum, M. (2000). *Women and Human Development: The Capabilities Approach.* Cambridge: Cambridge University Press.

Nussbaum, M. (2007). Human rights and human capabilities: Twentieth century reflections. *Harvard Human Rights Journal, 20*, 21–24.

Nussbaum, M. (2011). *Creating Capabilities.* Cambridge: Harvard University Press.

Peter, F. (2004). Health equity and social justice. In S. Anand, F. Peter, & A. Sen (Eds.), *Public Health, Ethics, and Equity* (pp. 93–106). Oxford: Oxford University Press.

Peter, F., & Evans, T. (2001). Ethical dimensions of health equity. In T. Evans, M. Whitehead, F. Diderichsen, A. Bhuiya, & M. Wirth (Eds.), *Challenging Inequities to Health: From Ethics to Action* (pp. 25–33). Oxford: Oxford University Press.

Pogge, T. (2004). Relational conceptions of justice: Responsibilities for health outcomes. In S. Anand, F. Peter, & A. Sen (Eds.), *Public Health, Ethics, and Equity* (pp. 135–161). Oxford: Oxford University Press.

Rawls, J. (1993). *Political Liberalism*. New York: Columbia University Press.
Ritchie, J., & Lewis, J. (Eds.). (2012). *Qualitative Research Practice: A Guide for Social Science Students and Researchers* (2nd ed.). Thousand Oaks: Sage.
Ruger, J. (2006). Ethics and governance of global health inequalities. *Journal of Epidemiological and Community Health, 60*, 998–1003.
Ruger, J. (2010). *Health and Social Justice*. Oxford: Oxford University Press.
Sen, A. (1999). *Development as Freedom*. New York: Random House.
Sen, A. (2001). Health equity, perspectives, measurability and criteria. In T. Evans, M. Whitehead, F. Diderichsen, A. Bhuiya, & M. Wirth (Eds.), *Challenging Inequities to Health: From Ethics to Action* (pp. 69–75). Oxford: Oxford University Press.
Sen, A. (2004a). Why health equity? In S. Anand, F. Peter, & A. Sen (Eds.), *Public Health, Ethics, and Equity* (pp. 21–34). Oxford: Oxford University Press.
Sen, A. (2004b). Health achievement and equity: External and internal perspectives. In S. Anand, F. Peter, & A. Sen (Eds.), *Public Health, Ethics, and Equity* (pp. 263–268). Oxford: Oxford University Press.
Sen, G., Östlin, P., & George, A. (2007). Unequal, unfair, ineffective and inefficient gender inequity in health: Why it exists and how we can change it. In *Report of the Women and Gender Equity Knowledge Network of the Commission on Social Determinants of Health, Final Report to the Commission on Social Determinants of Health*. Geneva: WHO.
Shisana, O., Rehle, T., Simbayi, L., Parker, W., Zuma, K., Bhana, A., et al. (2005). *South African National HIV Prevalence, Incidence and Communication Survey*. Cape Town: HSRC Press.
Shisana, O., Rehle, T., Simbayi, L., Zuma, K., Jooste, S., Pillay-van Wyk, V., et al. (2009). *South African National HIV Prevalence, Incidence and Communication Survey, 2008. A Turning Tide Among Teenagers?* Cape Town: HSRC Press.
Shisana, O., Rehle, T., Simbayi, L., Zuma, K., Jooste, S., Zungu, N., et al. (2014). *South African National HIV Prevalence, Incidence and Behaviour Survey, 2012*. Cape Town: HSRC Press.
South Africa Every Death Counts Writing Group. (2008a). Every death counts: Use of mortality audit data for decision making to save the lives of mothers, babies, and children in South Africa. *Lancet, 371*, 1294–1304.
South Africa Every Death Counts Writing Group. (2008b). *Every Death Counts: Saving the Lives of Mothers, Babies, and Children in South Africa*. Cape Town: National Department of Health, Medical Research Council, University of Pretoria, Save the Children and UNICEF.

South African National AIDS Council (SANAC). (2014). *Progress Report on the National Strategic Plan for HIV, TB and STIs 2012–2016*. Pretoria: South African National AIDS Council.

South African National AIDS Council (SANAC). (2016). *Enhanced Progress Report, National Strategic Plan for HIV, TB and STIs 2012–2016*. Pretoria: SANAC.

Sprague, C. (2009). *Cui Bono: A Capabilities Approach to Understanding HIV Prevention and Treatment for Pregnant Women and Children in South Africa*. Doctoral thesis, University of the Witwatersrand.

Sprague, C., Woollett, N., Parpart, J., Hatcher, A., Sommers, T., Brown, S., et al. (2016b). When nurses are also patients: Intimate partner violence and the health system as an enabler of women's health and institutional agency in Johannesburg. *Global Public Health, 11*(1–2), 169–183, Epub 2015.

Statistics South Africa (Stats SA). (2015). *Mid-Year Population Estimates 2015, Statistical Release P0302*. Pretoria: South Africa.

Stats SA. (2016a). *Mid-Year Population Estimates 2016, Statistical Release P0302*. Pretoria: Statistics South Africa.

Stats SA. (2016b). *Labour-Force Survey, Quarter 2*. Pretoria: Statistics South Africa.

UNAIDS. (2014a). *90-90-90: An Ambitious Treatment Target to Help End the AIDS Epidemic*. Geneva: UNAIDS.

UNAIDS. (2014b). *The Gap Report*. Geneva: UNAIDS.

UNAIDS. (2016a). *UNAIDS 2016 Estimates*. [online]. Geneva: UNAIDS. Retrieved February 8, 2017, from http://www.unaids.org/en/resources/documents/2016/HIV_estimates_with_uncertainty_bounds_1990-2015

UNAIDS. (2016b). *UNAIDS 2016 Guidance: HIV Prevention Among Adolescent Girls and Young Women. Putting HIV Prevention Among Adolescent Girls and Young Women on the Fast-Track and Engaging Men and Boys*. [online]. Geneva: UNAIDS. Retrieved February 8, 2017, from http://www.unaids.org/sites/default/files/media_asset/UNAIDS_HIV_prevention_among_adolescent_girls_and_young_women.pdf

Venkatapuram, S. (2011). *Health Justice*. Cambridge: Polity Press.

Wettstein, C., Mugglin, C., Egger, M., Blaser, N., Vizcaya, L. S., Estill, J., et al. (2012). Missed opportunities to prevent mother-to-child-transmission: Systematic review and meta-analysis. *AIDS, 26*(18), 2361–2373.

Whitehead, M. (1990). *The Concepts and Principles of Equity in Health*. Copenhagen: WHO Regional Office for Europe.

Whitehead, M. (1992). The concepts and principles of equity in health. *International Journal of Health Services, 22*(3), 429–435.

WHO. (2013b). *Global and Regional Estimates of Violence Against Women: Prevalence and Health Effects of Intimate Partner Violence and Non-Partner Sexual Violence*. Geneva: WHO.

WHO. (2013c). *16 Ideas for Addressing Violence Against Women in the Context of the HIV Epidemic a Programming Tool*. Geneva: WHO.

Whyte, D. (1994). *The Heart Aroused*. New York: Doubleday.

Wikler, D. (2004). Personal and social responsibility for health. In S. Anand, F. Peter, & A. Sen (Eds.), *Public Health, Ethics, and Equity* (pp. 109–134). Oxford: Oxford University Press.

Wood, K., Maforah, F., & Jewkes, R. (1998). 'He forced me to love him': Putting violence on the adolescent sexual health agenda. *Social Science & Medicine, 47*, 233–242.

Woolman, S. (2008). *Constitutional Law of South Africa* (2nd ed.). Cape Town: Juta Press.

Woolman, S., & Sprague, C. (2015). Nowhere to run, nowhere to hide: The absence of public policy as to how health care professionals should address intimate partner violence constitutes a breach of the rights to health and bodily integrity under the South African Constitution. *Cardozo Journal of Law & Gender, 22*(1), 29–74.

Yang, L. H., Kleinman, A., Link, B. G., Phelan, J. C., Lee, S., & Good, B. (2007). Culture and stigma: Adding moral experience to stigma theory. *Social Science & Medicine, 64*(7), 1524–1535.

9

Concluding Reflections: From Research to Policy and Practice

In a set of final observations, I highlight the particular strengths of the Capabilities Approach in response to complex health, gender and social justice problems, taking into account both its distinguishing strengths and limitations. I then offer a set of concluding reflections and close by identifying selected areas for research, policy and practice in relation to the core concerns engaged in this work.

On Capabilities as a Conceptual Approach: Utility, Strengths and Limitations

Whereas other scholars have discussed varied dimensions of the CA with an emphasis on developing the conceptual foundations of health capabilities (Ruger, 2010; Venkatapuram, 2011), here I reflect on its application to the research problem—HIV in women—in ways that also elucidate how the CA deftly probes the intersection of gender inequality and health inequity. The goal is to extract insights into the CA's novel features and shortcomings to assist in informing theory and theory-to-practice in response to complex health and social justice problems like this one. The questions can be posed: In what ways is the Capabilities Approach

C. Sprague, *Gender and HIV in South Africa*, Global Research in Gender, Sexuality and Health, https://doi.org/10.1057/978-1-137-55997-5_9

particularly responsive to health and social justice considerations, and what are its limitations?

A first distinguishing strength of the CA is its thickness as a conceptual framework. This is revealed in the CA's ability to produce a rich depiction of health as a construct—one that is socially and biologically determined—but also one that embraces health as a concern for social justice. Some of the CA's robustness comes from initial choices made by Sen (1999) and Nussbaum (2000) in its formulation. For example, the core assumption of the CA is that freedom is both the principal end and primary means by which development is achieved; it is by expanding the real freedoms people have that the 'good life' can be realised for individuals and society (Sen, 1999, pp. 35–53). Sen and Nussbaum root assessments of wellbeing in the essential capabilities question: 'What are individuals able to do and be?' Predicating wellbeing on this question recalls the origins, the Aristotelian foundations, of the CA as an approach to human development. That these architects have formulated the CA to link health explicitly with human development and with other social processes proves crucial for generating enhanced understanding of the social basis that undergirds ill health in this population. The CA therefore recognises that health and human development are connected, dynamic processes. Notably, neither Sen nor Nussbaum elevates health above other human development concerns. Paradoxically, this seems to be why the CA seems to be highly skilful in peeling away these multi-level layers and processes to ascertain how social factors and processes affect HIV positive women's opportunities to be healthy. This assumption of breaking the 'health as a silo' approach might seem counter-intuitive, and even heretical to public health specialists. Yet it is this assumption that allows for capturing the complexity and heterogeneity of multi-level determinants that influence health and wellbeing over the life course for these black South African women, with relevance for other women. The CA recognises that capabilities can expand in one sphere or stage and contract at another; and that particular life stages are important in human development: just as the life course approach and pathway models recognise that early 'critical life periods' and subsequent exposures influence later health trajectories (Kuh, Ben-Schlomo, Lynch, Hallqvist, & Power, 2003).

Using a life course or life cycle approach to HIV, an infant might avoid HIV infection through PMTCT at birth. However, given the data on HIV incidence, taking the long view of opportunities to be healthy for black women over the lifespan is essential in elucidating wellbeing for this population. Because influential health determinants are web-like and operate on multiple levels to affect the wellbeing of this population, the CA allows for probing these dynamics in ways that are not only useful; they offer greater understanding of the circuitry of social patterning of disease that is linked to unjust social structures. Thus the robust aspects of the CA make it particularly responsive to complex health problems, and this can be attributed to its formulation as a theory of human development rather than a health theory.

An additional, distinctive feature of the CA is its dexterity in unwinding the multiple, knotted threads of HIV positive women's gendered health concerns. These characteristics make it not only atypical in social justice frameworks (rightly noted by Nussbaum) but highly relevant and even innovative. Being responsive to gender means embracing the asymmetries of power that are experienced by this population (and others) in ways that untangle gender as a structural health determinant. Power dimensions are made visible in women's economic inequalities; the expected social roles and behaviours that determine what women are expected to do and be; their reduced social opportunities; and their unequal power in health and household decision making. Sen fully acknowledges these realities for women in social context. He devotes a chapter in his 1999 work to *Women's Agency and Social Change* (pp. 189–203). This is followed by a chapter in which he briefly discusses the empowerment of young women viz. reproductive and property rights, education, earning independent incomes and social standing (1999, pp. 210–226).

The CA recognises that gendered concerns fundamentally influence the real freedoms that women have to construct a life they have reason to value (Nussbaum, 2000; Sen, 1999). Capturing agency, opportunity and process freedoms sharpens the research lens by illuminating the role of social context in producing social stratification along the lines of gender and race in South Africa. This social stratification effectively reduces opportunities for women to be healthy by determining black women's position and limiting their opportunities within the social hierarchy.

The CA assists in illustrating that prevailing gender roles and norms depicted by women and their health providers in South Africa serve to socially enable men's preferences to dominate women's. Application of the CA proved fruitful in determining how these sociocultural norms precluded some women from taking decisions about fertility and contraception, thereby limiting their agentic desires and autonomy, and reducing both their opportunity and process freedoms. Yes, South African women retained some agency but they could not, as individuals, disassemble the entire edifice of the gendered social order in which they were located. These examples, elaborated in Chap. 6, illustrate the span of connected concerns. These comprise a multiplex of locations that shape health, and particularly the gendered factors that remain at the forefront of the HIV epidemic in black South African women living with HIV, and in women in other settings.

Moreover, these social mechanisms, including women's lower social position and their expected social roles and norms, introduce differential and elevated exposure, risk and vulnerability to HIV and abuse, relative to other women (Diderichsen, Evans, & Whitehead, 2001). While women still retained degrees of agency, they made choices and took agentic actions within circumscribed parameters. This reinforces that the CA can deliver on its promise of accommodating the role of gender as a structural determinant that influences health and development, and at a level of sophistication that is absent in many other approaches.

Building on the strength of engaging with gender, a notable aspect of the CA is its ability to produce insight into women's lived experience within their social context in ways that connect the moral, social experience of individuals or groups to a normative social evaluation, with ethical dimensions. Use of the CA allowed for the texture of HIV positive women's daily lived experience to be located on a larger canvas of human development (Sen, 1999). When the lived experience of socially marginalised groups is characterised by capability deprivations, the CA acknowledges these have moral implications. These are nimbly brought forth in what Kleinman (2004) terms the moral dimension of social experience and the ethics of the everyday. The equity and ethical underpinnings of the CA allow for a more muscular analysis of the ways in which basic social arrangements that affect individuals' health then propel inequities, while allowing for probing the social factors that generate capability deprivations.

The CA gives health moral value and standing. Capabilities are moral entitlements; Nussbaum (2000) also views them as political entitlements, and in South Africa most of these capabilities are indeed moral and political entitlements that have a counterpart in rights obligations safeguarded in the basic law. Asserting that health has moral content is part of very many countries' social values rooted in their constitutional law and human rights frameworks. The contribution of the CA is to elevate this focus; and to establish that these capabilities assert a moral claim that capabilities should be developed in cases of deprivation. This is unusual in health and wellbeing frameworks that so often (and helpfully) direct action to *where* intervention is needed but do not specify *why* by providing a normative rationale. Powerful frameworks and theories, spanning the socio-ecological (Kaufman, Cornish, Zimmerman, & Johnson, 2014; WHO, 2017), life course (Elder, 1998; Kuh et al., 2003), intersectionalities (Crenshaw, 1989) and syndemics theories (Meyer, Springer, & Altice, 2011), though highly useful, lack the normative rationale, which provides the necessary gravitas to underpin policy change and intervention. For policy change is determined, not by health researchers, but by government officials who are faced with competing budgetary resources and pressures. This policy influence is made possible, too, because of the CA's close connection to human rights and constitutional law. But the CA goes further. It ties possible capability deprivations to a process of public deliberation and social evaluation. Built into the CA is a connection between the assessment of 'what people are able to do and to be'—and a process to take this forward if deprivations are identified. The CA thus offers the *where*, the *why* and the initial beginnings of the *how*.

The CA tethers the moral sanction that capabilities should be supported to the South African state's duty to create the conditions for the 'good life' that is enshrined in the basic law. In this way, the CA yields richer analyses of justice in health (health as a consideration for social justice) than utilitarian theories, which tend to focus on utilities, preferences and choices in health care decision making. It also generates thicker analyses than those of egalitarian theories which typically emphasise the distribution of certain goods such as health care (Daniels, 1981, 2008). By taking the site of investigation beyond health care, and engaging with women's choices, freedoms (and unfreedoms), it also becomes clear in the South African context that health care is only one site for women to be healthy, for their capabilities to be protected and supported, among a series of locations that are connected. Here, the focus on access to health care is relational with other opportunities that affect human development. The analysis in this work indicated that while there are gaps to plug in HIV care, more and better HIV care is not going to address mediating factors that could modify the HIV risk environment, or engage with—let alone, overturn—structural, gender-related factors that facilitate HIV infection in South African women in the first instance.

Another marked feature of the CA that sets it apart from other frameworks is its ability to be both empirical and normative. While robust frameworks, such as the socio-ecological and life course approaches also pay attention to multi-factorial considerations that connect health with human development, and helpfully serve to pinpoint interventions in response to health problems, they are not so amenable to normative considerations. In contrast, the CA can be used to gather empirical data and to make normative arguments from the data collected. Not only does it give in-depth treatment to both types of considerations, it can slide along a trajectory to better link theoretical conceptualisations of health as social justice to evidence on poor health in ways that are more likely to produce intervention and change than those that are only empirical or only normative. Regarding the empirical aspect, the Capabilities Approach enables a comparative quality of life assessment that can offer data to view capabilities along specified variables between groups in the same society. Using Nussbaum's central capabilities (2000) as I have done in Chap. 6, produces a view of women's wellbeing along those ten dimensions; Sen's (1999) agency, process and opportunity freedoms supplement and take the analysis deeper. Nevertheless, it is Nussbaum that most enables the CA to be empirical because she devises metrics in the form of the ten central capabilities. Without these specified, this task, already a complex, time-consuming, demanding (and vexing) one, would have been much more difficult. The key message is that—in the absence of metrics to guide the assessment, which Sen suggests is possible but does not provide himself—they would need to be created. Metrics are required to be able to render quality of life and health inequity assessments. This seems to explain why Nussbaum, having foreseen this problem, stepped into the breach, though she admits that she has not completely solved the problem. Nussbaum addresses this head on, stating that the CA appears to 'have one disadvantage, in comparison to some other approaches: it seems difficulty [sic] to measure human capabilities' (2002, p. 135). She mentions the perplexing task of doing so in relation to her own list of central capabilities, recognising that 'we know, however, that anything worth measuring, in human quality of life, is difficult to measure' (2002, p. 135). Thus, while the ten central capabilities are far from perfect, they do offer a powerful way forward.

Limitations

Several limitations are apparent in the CA. I highlight three principal ones that became evident. The synergy between human rights and capabilities which is present in the CA offers an invaluable tool of analysis because capabilities are mirrored so closely by the South African state's obligation in the basic law. However, this might not serve as effective a lever in countries where human rights and legal protections are not assured, thereby potentially limiting the applicability of the CA.

Additionally, Nussbaum's writing evinces a lack of clarity regarding the threshold level of her central capabilities. She maintains that 'when a given capability has been recognised as a fundamental entitlement in a nation's constitution… much more work needs to be done…[and] the capability will need further elaboration or specification, and the threshold will have to be correctly set' (2011, p. 170).

There is also a lack of specificity concerning remedies, in cases of capability deprivation. For instance, Sen acknowledges that social arrangements play a decisive role in influencing capabilities. He recognises these factors as a crucial groundwork and discusses them in different ways: as social opportunities (for education and health care); as economic facilities (participation in the economy); protective security (i.e., social welfare policies);

and political freedoms (1999, pp. 36–49). Nonetheless, in cases of capability deprivation, he leaves remedies associated with social arrangements up to reasoned consensus (1999) and does not offer a clear indication of how redress would be achieved. In this vein, Nussbaum writes that 'Sen's work…makes little reference to law and to institutional structures within democracy' (2011, p. 166). Sen's style is subtle and allusive. Clearly, ideas of justice cannot be considered in the absence of social arrangements; but Sen remains reluctant to specify further. Conceptual work on remedies within the CA thus seem to be nascent. This vagueness can lead to much hand wringing. Despite considerable limitations, the Capabilities Approach takes us far along a pathway of understanding what women can 'do and be', and what they cannot, their opportunities to be healthy, and the accompanying constraints.

Reflections on Health Equity Assessments

Across settings, it is necessary to recognise the complexity of evaluations of health inequities; that there is a social valuation attached to health, and that justice in health is going to engage with social processes: both in how poor health is produced, through social stratification, and in how poor health is then to be remedied. I have four reflections.

First, the mobilisation of long-term health data to inform health equity plans is necessary, and is still lacking in LMIC settings. A common theme in the research undertaken as part of this work was the dearth of data systems, indicators and reporting. Improved timely, quality electronic data systems are also paramount. This encompasses systems and processes to capture and report data, and to release data more rapidly to the public for use. A number of data indicators for monitoring are sorely needed, particularly for IPV and GBV (WHO, 2015, 2016a). A key point coming through in the literature is that health equity assessments, especially in LMICs, need to work to integrate gender-related concerns.

Second, social values of equity are essential in addressing inequities in health. Based on the SDH and health justice/health equity literature, and the protracted wrestling with this problem of HIV in black women in South Africa, the analysis reveals that greater action on health inequities is indeed hindered or advanced by prevailing social values, across settings.

Some experts have suggested that moving from evidence to action requires gaining clarity on social values, in terms of placing a value on social equity, and health equity particularly (2001). Indeed, values clarification vis-à-vis equity and health are essential underpinnings for advancing social change, particularly in societies like the US, where there is no right to health or to health care (MacNaughton, Haigh, McGill, Koutsioumpas, & Sprague, 2015). Such social values are a prerequisite for achieving greater health equity.

Social equity is part of the social contract in South Africa. Policies across sectors have quite comprehensively sought to redress the inequities of apartheid, in character and in content: through protective social welfare policies and reforms of all sectors, higher education, labour, social and economic development. These were given effect in the RDP and other governing policies, and then drafted into protective socioeconomic policies. Socioeconomic rights also reflect the acknowledgement of some interdependency between health and the role of other socioeconomic rights: e.g., housing, water, electricity. An integrated socio-economic rights based approach is crucial. Nonetheless, a commitment to social equity in law and policy does not equate to gender equality; nor to good health, which ties into the next observation.

Third, normative values that espouse principles of equity pose an important starting point but they are insufficient unless they are accompanied by other means: this places emphasis on the political and social determinants of health (Ottersen et al., 2014). To move from research to policy action, just social institutions and actors are necessary. It is not enough to have equity in policy. When these social values and principles of equity, given their content in human rights, are infringed and put to the test, as they are for black women with HIV, there is an indispensable role played by social justice actors and institutions. Actors like South African civil society, including the academic community, are critical; as are the institutions that review claims to justice and uphold law and justice in society. These actors and institutions are the monitors and enforcers of equity. Without the force of law, however, institutions and actors that can hold states to account on health inequities, 'equality in some space' (to use Sen's phrasing) (1999), supported by health indicators and analyses, may not be fully actionable. This suggests several possibilities to push the frontier of knowledge to policy translation, to effect action. And it makes a case for strengthening research in social-health science for improved public policy—with special attention to the social bases of social health inequalities, and to deepening transdisciplinary fields, such as health and human rights, to maximise the strengths of sub-fields.

On the Gender Order

While much is known about the nexus linking gender and HIV, the capability lens generates deeper insight into black South African women's opportunities to be healthy by peeling back the layers of the gender system in which women are located and offering some insight into how it operates. The interface between the gender system and structural processes (i.e., processes made possible by social actors, institutions and social relations) comprise the gendered structural determinants of health (Sen, Östlin, & George, 2007). The extant literature, together with the original research findings, demonstrate how basic social arrangements allow for social stratification and socially produced gender norms, hierarchies, values and practices effectively structure social and economic opportunities in ways that have important, pernicious health consequences for black South African women. Drawing from the Diderichsen et al. model (Fig. 2.2 in Chap. 2) (2001, see p. 15), the arrow linking social context to social process represents the social stratification taking place. Women's lower social position, their gender and economic inequality work together to introduce differences in HIV exposure and vulnerability for women—exacerbated to some extent by women's physiology, but to a much larger extent made possible by social drivers. Black women thus have differential exposure to, risk and acquisition of HIV.

Living with HIV generates additional adverse social and economic implications for this population of HIV positive women, while reducing their opportunities to be healthy. Unless the policy context can engage with the social drivers of HIV, the existing range of policy interventions will miss the essential conditions which are continuing to generate elevated HIV vulnerability and exposure in this population.

What determines the pace of change in the gender order? The analysis strongly suggests that structural locations, like the home, and social institutions, such as the health system, are part of a continuum of locations that shape women's capabilities and reflect accepted dominant norms and social constructions of gender in this context. Dominant in the HIV literature is a propensity either to engage with health care within health systems, or to engage with social determinants of health outside of health systems, i.e., in community settings. This work exemplifies that those locations need to be unified. These are relational spaces: researchers need to look at integrating the home, the health system, and the workplace as sites or opportunities for women to be healthy across these locations. Similarly, it remains crucial to take a life course perspective, in order to recognise the dynamism that takes place in health and human development—health needs, risks, and mediating factors—at different life stages and during critical life periods.

On Protective Factors that Support Women's Agency and Capabilities

Based on the empirical research, the harmful and pervasive health threats and trends in this population were obvious. However, a number of key bulwarks appear to offer potential for women to gain information, resources and support in ways that may be protective, and that radiate from the health system. By protective, I mean this in a broad sense of shielding them from further negative physical or psychological consequences (including by mediating stress and distress), but also in promoting growth, development, coping and resilience. Here the emphasis is on the ones that were clearly depicted in clinical settings.

The Health System as a Transformative Social System

Paradoxically, the health system is a microcosm of larger society but the research indicates that its role in and potential for engaging with structure is virtually ignored. While the emphasis on delivering cART is needed, the structural processes that are hindering women from taking advantage of treatment are being neglected. The Department of Health is not taking advantage of the opportunities that exist to address these within the health system itself, by training and guiding health providers and other stakeholders in this regard, including through human rights education, sensitisation and monitoring. As such, the South African health system remains an important yet neglected location in which gender hierarchies are being challenged and women's rights affirmed 'from below' by health providers in ways that are spontaneous and unsanctioned by the government (Sprague, Hatcher, Woollett, & Black, 2015; Sprague, Hatcher, Woollett, Sommers, & Black 2016a; Woolman & Sprague, 2015). This suggests that the direction and perhaps the pace of change in the gender system may come from less obvious quarters, and from women themselves.

As part of this, an important protective factor women identified was health providers and other health staff: nurses, doctors, lay counsellors and social workers. While a few women had negative experiences with their providers, on the whole, the South African health system was serving as a transformative social system for women to link to care, receive counselling, psychosocial support and crucial information about HIV treatment and PMTCT. Much research has looked at the health system in South Africa and elsewhere in relation to health system strengthening to improve HIV care specifically (Sprague, 2009; Sprague, Chersich, & Black, 2011). The emphasis has historically been on barriers to cART and PMTCT for women (see Chap. 3), and more recently on enablers: the focus of several recent systematic reviews (Colvin et al., 2014; Gourlay, Birdthistle, Mburu, Iorpenda, & Wringe, 2013; Hodgson et al., 2014). This has included perceptions of health providers in care provision, and attention to dynamics affecting women's disclosure, including some of the same issues documented here (e.g., fear of partner violence and economic insecurity). These have undoubtedly enriched the knowledge base. What seems to be missing, and what this research adds, is a focus on women's agency, and the dynamic social process that takes place in clinical settings between patients and providers. These dimensions are fundamentally important in understanding how to further advance HIV positive women's capabilities. Social theory to explain 'what is' and to consider social change, with the health system a micro portrait of wider society's macrocosm has been largely absent, however. The findings indicate that health systems weaknesses can be overcome for women to access treatment and prevention, and that the health system in South Africa has made remarkable advances. The research strongly suggests that structural barriers, particularly gender hierarchies and exposure to violence, are highest in negatively shaping women's health and wellbeing and their opportunities to be healthy. As indicated in Chap. 3, there is less research on how structure influences HIV care and decision making, which points to a needed area for research. And, the health system and social structure (what happens in community or family settings) seem to be divorced from each other both in the research literature and in interventions.

The health system is showing itself to be a highly complex social system. It serves as a source of institutional agency: with health providers in South Africa acting in dynamic ways to buttress the agency of their patients (see Sprague et al., 2016b). On the whole, the narratives of women capture a vibrant reality taking place in these clinical settings, particularly between women patients and providers who are social workers, lay counsellors, nurses and doctors. Health providers are not only educating and sensitising women to particular ways of managing their health, they are in some cases giving women the tools to manage HIV as a chronic disease, some are socialising women to reconstitute gender norms. Their role can be somewhat subversive and those actions depict the health system as a critical site for gender and health.

Health providers are demonstrating their particular willingness and ability to reconstruct gender norms and to challenge men's decision-making authority in relation to women's reproductive health, HIV disclosure and more. But many health providers seem to be doing more than 'sustaining' social structure, they are instead destabilising it in some South African health settings, which warrants study in more rural and poorly resourced locations in the country. Providers seem to be getting involved because of the high stakes for their women patients. By reasserting women's rights and their choices, they are engaging in transforming the social structure. As Sewell writes:

> the same resourceful agency that sustains the reproduction of structures also makes possible their transformation by means of transpositions of schemas and remobilizations of resources that make the new structures recognizable as transformations of the old. (1992, p. 27)

What emerges here is the range of possibilities to address adverse gender norms and to strengthen a women's health paradigm in which women are at the centre. This can be effected by invoking the core expertise of health providers who are key agents of change whom women engage with on a routine basis. It needs to be noted that the largest cohort of health providers, the very source and skeletal structure of health care in South Africa, are nurses (see Marks, 1994; Kim & Motsei, 2002).

Additionally, HIV positive women actively cultivated social ties with other HIV positive women in the health system. This was seen in the health system and outside it. Social support ties included those forged with trusted family members, some of whom were themselves living with HIV. Notably, women could control who gained access to their social networks and therefore became knowledgeable about their HIV status, which enhanced their agency. The importance of social networks in reducing distress and bolstering self-efficacy among HIV positive populations has had attention in the research. Requiring emphasis here is that such support seemed to assist women in navigating HIV disclosure, HIV treatment demands, pregnancy and partner abuse, and at a critical period for these women's health in which many women learnt of their HIV status for the first time.

Connecting Research and Methods to Policy and Practice to Advance Gender Transformation

It seems obvious to note that gender transformation is not only about women. Gender transformation connotes enhanced wellbeing for other members of the gender order. The remainder of this conclusion identifies where additional attention in research, policy and practice is needed.

Masculinities and Changing Men

Locating men and diverse masculinities within a changing gender order—one that eschews adverse gender norms—requires taking cognisance of men's realities (Morrell, 2001; Ouzgane & Morrell, 2005). This requires locating South African men within structural processes that are fettered to the economic, political, social, demographic and health transitions underway in South and Southern Africa (Coovadia, Jewkes, Barron, Sanders, & McIntyre, 2009; Gennrich, 2013). These transitions have introduced changes and pressures to men's identities and sense of security at multiple levels. Individual men must then be positioned within the frame of structural processes as well. Engaging with multiple masculinities necessitates recognition of a divisive past. This past was one in which most black men faced structural violence, systematic oppression, and a range of restrictions on what they could be and do until quite recently, and in ways that have shaped and constrained them. The lived experience of black men in the social order has and continues to influence how they view expanded economic or employment opportunities for women (Jewkes & Morrell, 2012; Morrell, 2001). Colleagues have noted that more nuanced understandings of masculinities in South Africa must investigate the role of SES and class (Levon, Milani, & Kitis, 2017). Men typically experience social pressures to conform to gender expectations, and men continue to sanction gender-related practices and behaviours that they deem socially acceptable. 'Undoing' gender, or reconstructing it, means grappling with the push-pull factors that mitigate against men's changing identities to embrace gender equality, sometimes through resistance to change by other men and by women (Butler, 2004). Hence, as colleagues have observed, reconstructing gender requires making men stakeholders in the process of social change (Morrell, 2001; Moynihan, 1998). Perhaps researchers and policy makers might work to assist men to better grasp how their own health and wellbeing is eroded by harmful masculinities (Dworkin, Treves-Kagan, & Lippman, 2013). The Government has launched a needed focus on men's health which seems to have lost momentum. The evidence for improved men's health resulting from the GTI case studies is compelling. They reduced the incidence of herpes simplex type-2 in men and women;

reduced transactional sex and problem drinking among men (Gibbs, Jewkes, Sikweyiya, & Willan, 2015, p. 210; Jewkes et al., 2014); and built men and women's skills—the negotiation and conflict resolution skills between couples that can so often lead to violence or abuse and which assist in rendering relationships more gender-equitable (Jewkes, 2016). Improved listening and communication skills can build empathy and problem solving. At the same time, the evaluations of GTIs indicated that HIV-related communication between partners can improve, HIV testing can increase, as can condom use, which promotes HIV prevention among couples (Kim et al., 2009).

What seems crucial is to move understandings of gender transformation to a more participant-centred vision by men of their own capabilities, while fostering more holistic conceptualisations of men's wellbeing that also incorporate mental health. An equally powerful, compelling vision of changing masculinities that can offer an enriched understanding of what men can be and do, as part of gender transformation, is needed by and for men. To that end, the CA might offer fertile ground in which to develop conceptions of masculinities and men's opportunities for improved health and human development, given the CA's emphasis on agency, process and opportunity freedoms. This could be conceived with particular attention to men and masculinities that are marginalised, including sexual minorities who tend to face social exclusion and have poorer health. Research could investigate how South African men's agency could be enabled to capture the benefits of transforming gender in ways that enhance their choices and their wellbeing.

The GTI chapter illustrated, with thoughtful quotes from men who participated, the powerful effects on men's relationship dynamics. The self-realisation and new possibilities captured by those men's voices cannot be over-emphasised as a beginning point on a larger potential trajectory of change in their gendered identities. How are those initial changes then sustained once the interventions, typically running two to three years, come to their end? The locations for continuing to support such change might be varied and the NSP could foster research and interventions that bring different sectors (education, social development) together, to identify skill building and other programmes. This could potentially be effected through government partnerships with CBOs, and men working with other men, through organisations like Sonke Gender Justice and campaigns like 'One Man Can' (Dworkin et al., 2013; Dworkin, Fleming, & Colvin, 2015).

Communities are an obvious site for bottom-up approaches to norm setting, changing beliefs and changing practices. The GTIs illustrated how interventions take the struggle for gender equality into the communities, with the potential to yield important bottom-up strategies for sensitising men and women, boys and girls, on gender. If such initiatives could be situated within communities to become led by local, South African CBOs, and run as community mobilisation initiatives, while also being located within national policy frameworks, these shifts might enable greater sustainability of activities that promote education, life skills, gender socialisation, norm setting and a full set of other beneficial programmes responsive to people's needs. The NSP and the gender equality framework are two obvious national policy frameworks that allow responses to be State-supported. It seems most appropriate that these initiatives shift from being academic interventions that show effectiveness in RCTs to become community-based programmes that work well in people's daily lives and enable human flourishing. Ultimately, such interventions can only be continued over the long term if they are re-envisaged in ways that address structural drivers of HIV and IPV, and that facilitate at least partial State ownership to secure financial and programmatic sustainability.

Neglected Women and Key Populations

Chapter 3 brought to bear the latest available research on women's ability to access and benefit from HIV medication, with the original research findings presented in Chap. 6, and the implications for women's capabilities and rights communicated in Chap. 8. Groups of women were notably absent or poorly represented in the extant HIV literature, including migrants, women incarcerated in jails, prisons or detention centres, sex workers, women with disabilities, and older women, aged 50 and above. Young African women often face judgement and discrimination by many stakeholders, including health providers. All of these population groups have distinct health and HIV risk factors and exposures, and gender-specific pressures and barriers to health and HIV care that accord with particular life stages (UNAIDS, 2014b). Notably, transgender individuals living with HIV are a key population, globally. UNAIDS estimates that they are *49 times more likely to be living with HIV* compared to their cisgender counterparts (2016c). Transgender and intersex persons often seek employment through sex work, and face multiple types of discrimination and stigma that reduce their opportunities for wellbeing and elevate their risk of harm, particularly through laws and policies that criminalise these groups (Baral et al., 2013; Sen et al., 2007). To affirm that key populations need greater attention in research and policy agendas is stating the obvious. Figuring out how to elevate research attention to engage with groups that are pushed to the social margins poses a key opportunity and challenge for researchers, CBOs, health and human rights programmers to find ways to protect and promote their dignity, health and safety, using responsive human rights frameworks and interventions (Baral et al., 2013; see *Journal of the International AIDS Society* 2016 special supplement, 'HIV epidemics among transgender populations: the importance of a trans-inclusive response' 19(Suppl 2), 1193).

Agency, Women's Sexuality and Wellbeing

An area of wellbeing that I was unable to sufficiently probe in this research was the sexuality and sexual desires of black South African women living with HIV. While this work engaged with the sexual vulnerability and sexual agency of women and captured the limits of their sexual and reproductive rights, conversations about sexual desire for women living with HIV were about placating men's desires (Correa, Petchesky, & Parker, 2008). So often women described their aspirations being thwarted or ignored, including sexual desires and expressions. Sexual identity was not even raised for discussion, as the many layers of anxiety, concerns, stress surrounding managing HIV and other anticipated threats, consumed our conversations, thus precluding other topics. While there is excellent research on sexual transactions and partnerships in South Africa (Harrison, 2008; Hunter, 2010; Jewkes & Morrell, 2012; Leclerc-Madlala; Wood, Maforah, & Jewkes, 1998), there is greater scope for advancing conceptualisations of agency for HIV positive women that consider the shifting landscape of women's sexuality, including sexual desires and aspirations tied to their sense of wellbeing. Research is needed on different stages of the life course, including how women's sexuality might evolve over time as women become more comfortable living positively with HIV and as they age. Potentially such investigations could locate and explore changing experiences of HIV stigma within it. HIV stigma threatens desire, self-expression and wellbeing, psychologically and physically, including sexually.

HIV-IPV Links and Pathways

A chief theme in this work has been the HIV-IPV linkages that affect South African women's HIV risk, disclosure, connection to and adherence in HIV care, and social experience of being HIV positive. A recent systematic review on the association between IPV and HIV included 101 studies, 45 of which were from sub-Saharan Africa. The review found that most studies showed a positive link between IPV and HIV. The authors of the review pose four key areas for future research on IPV and HIV: (1) what types of IPV are most relevant to HIV infection; (2) what is the most important period of exposure to IPV and HIV infection (e.g., lifetime exposure, recent exposure, etc.); (3) what instruments should we use to most accurately measure IPV and its sub-types; and, (4) longitudinal data investigating potential mechanisms of IPV and HIV are needed to assess causality (Kouyoumdjian et al., 2013). These offer crucial avenues for future research.

A National Strategic Plan on Gender-Based Violence

One of the obvious policy gaps continues to be the lack of a national strategic plan on gender-based violence. South Africa's NSP specifically addresses gender equality, noting that 'Acknowledging the fact that gender inequality hinders social and economic development, the achievement of gender equality remains one of the critical components of the transformation agenda… South Africa is grappling with high levels of violence against women, with sexual assault and intimate partner violence contributing to increased risks for HIV infection' (2012, p. 35).

The NSP calls for a comprehensive approach to address GBV. In 2015, South African civil society called on South African President Jacob Zuma to develop a national strategic plan on GBV, noted below:

> The Zuma administration must follow through on its promises to create a National Strategic Plan for GBV: Beginning in December 2012, Government committed to creating the country's first NSP on Gender-Based Violence. The process was begun, but has been stalled, undermined and suspended over the last year. Civil society has thus taken to the streets over the last 16 days of activism campaign to challenge government to live up to its promises to develop and fully fund an NSP on GBV. (Gender Links, 2015)

The SANAC women's sector reaffirmed this call, stating:

> Gender based violence (GBV) is one of the biggest drivers of HIV in women and girls and South Africa has a significant and well publicised GBV problem. Yet there is still no national strategic plan to address it. (2015)

The time for such a plan is past due.

Routine GBV and IPV Data Indicators and Timely Release of Health Data

GBV and IPV data and indicators to monitor and collect routine data on IPV and gender-based violence in the health system are not available. These are essential. Improved monitoring and evaluation of routine health data is crucial to support existing health and HIV services, as is the timely release of data and findings to inform national reports and evolving policy (SANAC, 2014).

Addressing VAWG in the Health System

The WHO recognises that HIV services are key entry points to identify and address various factors related to violence against women (WHO,

2013a, 2013b). The 2013 report outlines a more detailed conceptual pathway linking gender inequality more broadly as a driver of both violence against women and HIV and makes clear how it affects health care services, as discussed in Chap. 3 (WHO, 2013a). There is an evolving literature on the association between violence and HIV risk among women, but there is significantly less literature focused on VAW living with HIV and how violence impacts women's care, behaviours and long-term treatment outcomes along the HIV care continuum. Gender inequality is dominant in much of the data. It is evident particularly in studies on IPV (and other forms of gender-based violence) and mental health. However, the manner by which it should be addressed within the health system has not been engaged, and there is insufficient evidence cited (WHO, 2013b). While interventions in South Africa have been limited, and thus far not shown to be effective in introducing screening for IPV in antenatal care, there is a minimum level of training that health providers are meant to have to address violence in women patients, in line with WHO standards (WHO, 2013b). South Africa does not meet the minimum requirements and currently has no policy or protocol to direct health providers in engaging with intimate partner violence (Sprague et al., 2015). This is a glaring gap that needs attention, as the research shows that the health system is the first, and often the only, location where women seek support, following partner abuse (WHO, 2013a).

Normative Frameworks, Indicators and Monitoring to Protect and Promote Human Rights

South Africa is distinguished by its progressive embrace of socioeconomic rights. Law is an essential vehicle for advancing wellbeing yet better integration of human rights standards and norms into sexual and reproductive health and HIV services is needed. Rights sensitisation of individuals, both in communities, and in the health system, is critical. This could focus on sensitising women, men, boys and girls to gender equality including rights to bodily integrity, reproductive choice and other human rights that inhere in each person, regardless of gender identification, race or sexual orientation (Gupta, 2000). Methodologies and indicators for monitoring human rights standards are needed in the health system but in other sectors and settings as well. There has been attention to human rights based approaches (HRBAs) (MacNaughton et al., 2015), but they are typically very firmly tied to health care and services. As this research indicates, in LMICs, social and structural determinants and rights infringements in those domains are important to engage as multi-factorial determinants and structures that influence women's human development.

Theorising the HIV Care Continuum

In African health systems, theoretical frameworks, including those that would conceptualise women's agency and linkage to HIV care, dropout and lapses for pregnant and non-pregnant women, are not well formulated and are needed. These could explore and explain how women move through the system (from the perspective of women) in ways that are theoretically grounded in order to link women's behaviour to their lived experiences, their available choices, desires and agency within social context.

Postpartum/postnatal care. There are specific knowledge gaps associated with postnatal care for HIV positive women in South Africa which are reflected in the literature on women living with HIV seeking care in other African health systems. While treatment has become more available and accessible over time in the South African health system, the overall HIV care continuum for pregnant women can be characterised as discontinuous and fragmented with frequent LTFU and drop out among women post-partum. The trends suggest that the post-partum portion of care and the transition to adult cART is problematic but data on this phenomenon are largely absent. Psaros, Remmert, Bangsberg, Safren, and Smit (2015) term this the postpartum 'cliff'. This 'frontloading' of so many HIV services, with a heavy emphasis on ANC reflects the design of PMTCT programmes, efforts to avert paediatric HIV and the international policy and funding attention to reduce maternal mortality, including through MDG 5. However, the strength of ANC service delivery lies in sharp contrast with weaker service availability for postpartum women, revealing inattention to women's full spectrum of health needs in the perinatal period. The drop off that can be seen in HIV care linkage, manifest as LTFU and poor adherence, documented in the literature and NSP, seems to mimic the drop off in services that are tailored and directed to women as they move from ANC to postnatal care in the HIV care continuum, and requires additional research and intervention. Lapses in care are likely to be associated with the structural factors documented in this work. Of note, this finding might also have a bearing on non-pregnant women who have much less dedicated attention to their health needs, compared to pregnant women, and fewer visits before they initiate cART, with a less formalised HIV care continuum.

Mental Health and Care

Very significantly, in conceptions of health and capabilities in particular, insufficient attention is given to integrating bodily and mental health in ways that reflect the actuality of this inter-relationship, particularly for those living with HIV, and for those who also experience IPV. A better account of mental health is needed in policy priorities, as mental health is typically underfunded in South Africa. In terms of psychological needs for women with HIV, studies have documented the key role played by lay counsellors, nurses and social workers in offering counselling and guidance to HIV positive women. Yet comparisons of where and when in the HIV care continuum women have highest reported need and unmet need for psychosocial support appear to be lacking in the literature, and require further study. Differentiation between psychosocial support needs and strategies in rural versus urban settings appear to be absent and are also needed. Clearly, women living with HIV demonstrate psychological vulnerability and their needs for psycho-social support come out frequently, consistently and powerfully. In a global survey conducted by Orza et al. (2015), respondents advocated for increased psychological and mental health counselling for women living with HIV, as well as for peer support in relation to gender-based violence and human rights interventions. Mental health remains one of the largest, persistent gaps in health and HIV care in South Africa.

Research Methods: Making Normative Commitments to Advance Social Justice

Engaging gender, health and inequality as a nexus requires research engagement with tools that can uncover structural factors and mechanisms that foster power imbalances through social institutions, with skill and care. Qualitative research methods continue to have an essential role to play in this pursuit, particularly in health equity research that must wrestle with multifactorial health determinants. Qualitative research does this in three ways that might be particularly relevant to junior scholars and PhD students electing and fashioning the tools they will use on their research paths in a globalising world.

First, while qualitative research does not engage with the causal pathway that connects social with biological and other factors, it can document timing, sequence, temporal and other factors in women's lives that predispose or place them on trajectories of poor health (Meyer et al., 2011). Qualitative research skilfully captures complex social worlds, enabling probing of processes and determinants across multiple, intersecting levels.

Additionally, qualitative methods make possible the documentation and the witnessing of the everyday experience that comprises the moral ground of people's lives (Kleinman, 2004). Gaining such an account will only result from protracted, in-depth engagement with people who most often experience injustice: the socially excluded and disadvantaged. If the moral and ethical are to be, as Kleinman suggests, 'at the heart of efforts on behalf of health equity', then researchers need to locate ourselves to some extent in 'the local moral condition of real people' (2004, p. 271). For, as Kleinman notes, it is vulnerable or marginalised groups in society 'who experience the systematic injustices of higher rates of ill health and fewer health care resources owing to their positioning in local social structures of power' (2004, p. 271). This is the crucial groundwork of equity research: how people live, how they experience illness, how they rise. In South Africa, this is taking place on the razed foundations of apartheid and is being shaped in multiple spaces and locations—schools, workplaces, homes, health clinics and communities. The possibility of greater gender equality and greater equity in health lie within, and it is qualitative research that can plumb these depths. As such, it offers a necessary and essential complement to quantitative research.

To make my second point, I wish to flip the lens which is typically trained on research populations (participants) such that the researcher enters the frame and becomes part of the social phenomena under investigation. Qualitative research methods recognise that the researcher is indeed in the frame as a 'positioned subject'. The core assumption, then, is that a dynamic, fully social interaction is taking place between researchers and participants. Stern has highlighted that the acknowledgment of such a social co-creation is leading to changes in the 'classical mode of science' (2013) as a result. Embracing social co-creation suggests greater possibilities for making commitments to normative social justice research methods that can be transformative, both for research participants and for researchers.

Indeed, there are new possibilities for transdisciplinary approaches to overcome the silos of academic disciplines to give us greater traction in tackling structural inequalities. The 'transformative' or 'emancipatory' paradigm contends that the advancement of social good occurs through engagement and interaction with individuals or groups who are marginalised or socially excluded (Dankwa-Mullan et al., 2010; Mertens, 2011; Tazreiter, Weber, Pickering, Segrave, & McKernan, 2016).

The benefits for both researchers and participants may, in part, be attributed to the phenomenon of intersubjectivity. Intersubjectivity can be seen as subjective experience being brought forth through an engagement between participants and researchers—primarily through interview dialogue (neurobiology also offers a neural explanation for intersubjectivity's process and effect due to mirror neurons firing in the brain of the researcher that mimics the participants) (Stern, 2013). Intersubjectivity and accompanying social experience introduce greater possibility for achieving enhanced understanding between individuals who can be divided by race, class, education and social experience. Rather than erecting walls, it suggests a 'bridge' that can transport and transcend these traditional divisions. Qualitative methods foster intersubjective dialogue, largely through interviews. Dialogue fosters the human connection to one another that is at the very centre of real social change. This is the new world, and even the new South Africa, which we have all seen from time to time. It is one that recognises *ubuntu*, our humanity, is what binds us to one another, and to a common, shared future. Such qualitative research methods, including intersubjectivity, allow us to bridge our local worlds and to forge shared connection so that we can see that the lived values that are at stake are those that we share.

Third, the qualitative research engagement has been shown to have important benefits for participants (Disch, 2001), as co-authors and I have documented elsewhere (Sprague, Scanlon, & Pantalone, 2017b). Use of methods like life course narratives afford participants the space and attention to reflect on key events and their meaning (Stern & Cooper, 2014; Wang & Geale, 2015). These methods endow agency and power to participants in telling their life stories, while offering a form of social support and voice that is typically denied marginalised individuals (Charmaz, 1999).

In these ways, method can allow the research community to use research tools to assist social transformation as a social goal, with researchers gaining the ability to locate themselves within those institutional structures that enable people's capabilities to expand or to contract. Researchers, through their research methods, can find themselves within the larger social fabric and very social structure that we seek to alter. Social injustice calls us to account for how we are part of the very social hierarchy that we study, and how we choose to contribute to more equitable local, national and globalising worlds.

Standing on a New Threshold

Earlier in this work I outlined the ways in which rising HIV prevalence in South Africa crystallised social justice and human rights concerns over access to essential antiretroviral medicines. Health and human rights as a dual pursuit was embedded within wider global health considerations about the need to value health as a public good and to advance health as a social justice claim, particularly in the developing world where 80% of the global population resides. The health as social justice discourse was being generated by multiple country experiences in the LMICs with burgeoning HIV epidemics and little hope of treatment on the horizon. Brazil's bold government leadership to introduce the first large-scale, universal national ARV programme, predicated on the domestic manufacture of active pharmaceutical ingredients to ensure a sustainable supply of ARVs for its population living with HIV, was path breaking. This was done in the face of steep opposition from international actors such as the World Bank and great scepticism about HIV adherence in LMIC settings (Parker, 2003).

Brazil ultimately achieved highly significant health gains for its population (Marins et al., 2003), and succeeded in enlarging the health equity frame to be more inclusive and responsive to global health epidemics, while placing 'health as social justice' at the centre instead of on the margins (Rosenberg, 2001; Teixeira, 2003). South African civil society fearlessly followed Brazil's lead in shattering conventional approaches to public health epidemics. The urgency of HIV as an increasingly social epidemic, where an estimated 330,000 South Africans died as the Government dithered on treatment (Chigwedere, Seage, Gruskin, Lee, & Essex, 2008), shaped not only the response but also the methodological research tools we used at the time of the ARV rollout. Not only does this example reveal the innovative approach to 'health as social justice' emerging out of the Global South, it underscores that these same LMIC settings are in a position to lead the paradigm shift on gender and HIV that is so crucial now. This is the new threshold on which the HIV epidemic response currently stands.

Throughout this work, I have suggested that differing disciplinary perspectives and varied sources open up enhanced possibilities for viewing dimensions of the problem of HIV in black South African women, and marshalling the evidence base for action in response. Life expectancy, maternal mortality, HIV prevalence data, and social drivers of HIV risk shed light on particular constraints to women's health and wellbeing. Relational justice considerations, women's capabilities and the health equity assessment together widen and deepen understanding of the problem of HIV in women as a dual problem of public health and social justice. All of this brings us to a new threshold 'where past and future are gathered' (Eliot, 1971, p. 15). The new world where women are able to fully access substantive equality and enjoy their rights is an outgrowth of the old one. It is the same path being trodden, whether it is called Sen's 'development as freedom' or Mandela's 'long walk'. They were speaking of a similar path to a new world where those denied the good life would have access to its fruits in ways that would allow them to flourish. The past has a firm historical arc, and HIV in South Africa has had a grand social justice narrative of victorious access to essential medicines for the treatment of HIV. Yet, the work of the HIV response remains incomplete, even as the future remains to be written. Advancing the health and human development needs of black South African women is going to require a break with the existing paradigm to embrace structural health determinants, notably gender, that limit women's capabilities, while ensuring needed HIV care in health systems. This pathway, one that protects and enables the human development and the health of women and girls, is evolving. Making this pathway possible will necessitate a fundamental shift in the directions of the epidemic response. It requires a new vision for protecting women's capabilities: their opportunities to be healthy. While this work has suggested shifts and changes, this vision can only be generated from within, and must be nurtured and cultivated by South Africans themselves. This has always been the reality.

Genuine transformation is born in struggle, through a slow scorching fire that threatens to clear everything in its path to make way for a new and fertile ground. I suggest this problem of HIV in women is presenting a crucible moment for South Africa. Perhaps other countries will find this to be true as well. The current situation, the ongoing HIV prevalence, the increasing HIV incidence, reduced life expectancy and elevated HIV-related mortality in black South African women forces everyone—members of government and civil society—to the mirror. Jonathan Mann, a founder of the field of health and human rights, asked 'what are the transformative possibilities of the AIDS pandemic?' (1999).

Mann observed that the epidemic forced us all to confront 'unexamined beliefs, prejudices…our ways of oversimplifying the world…and how we all fear abandonment and isolation' (1999, p. 171). The costs of continuing as is are made visible in women's compromised health outcomes and capabilities, their reduced human dignity and diminished wellbeing. This problem, a health inequity for black women, calls us all to confront what remains undone in the larger struggle for and journey towards freedom and equality for all. Structural health determinants associated with gender have limited what black South African women are able to do and to be, while restricting women's agency to realise the good life for far too long (Albertyn & Meer, 2005; Hassim, 2006). The way forward is emergent. There is a pathway that protects and promotes women's health and human development; one that calls for greater protection of women's bodily integrity and their substantive equality, in keeping with women's rights in the basic law and the promise of social transformation within the new South Africa.

References

Albertyn, C., & Meer, S. (2005). Citizens or mothers? The marginalisation of women's reproductive rights in the struggle for access to health care for HIV positive pregnant women in South Africa. In M. Mukhopadhyay & S. Meer (Eds.), *Gender, Rights and Development: A Global Sourcebook* (pp. 26–56). Amsterdam: The Royal Tropical Institute.

Baral, S., Poteat, T., Stromdahl, S., Wirtz, A., Guadamuz, T., & Beyrer, C. (2013). Worldwide burden of HIV in transgender women: A systematic review and meta-analysis. *Lancet Infectious Diseases, 13*(3), 214–222.

Butler, J. (2004). *Undoing Gender*. New York: Routledge.

Charmaz, K. (1999). Stories of suffering: Subjective tales and research narratives. *Qualitative Health Research, 9*(3), 362–382.

Chigwedere, P., Seage, G., Gruskin, S., Lee, T., & Essex, M. (2008). Estimating the lost benefits of antiretroviral drug use in South Africa. *Journal of Acquired Immune Deficiency Syndrome, 49*(4), 410–415.

Colvin, C., Konopka, S., Chalker, J., Jonas, E., Albertini, J., Amzel, A., et al. (2014). A systematic review of health system barriers and enablers for antiretroviral therapy for HIV-infected pregnant and postpartum women. *PLoS ONE, 9*(10), e108150.

Coovadia, H., Jewkes, R., Barron, P., Sanders, D., & McIntyre, D. (2009). The health and health system of South Africa: Historical roots of current public health challenges. *Lancet, 374*(9692), 817–834.

Correa, S., Petchesky, R., & Parker, R. (2008). *Sexuality, Health and Human Rights*. New York: Routledge.

Crenshaw, K. (1989). Demarginalizing the intersection of race and sex: A black feminist critique of antidiscrimination doctrine, feminist theory and antiracist politics. *The University of Chicago Legal Forum, 140*, 139–167.

Daniels, N. (1981). Health care needs and distributive justice. *Philosophy and Public Affairs, 10*(2), 146–179.

Daniels, N. (2008). *Just Health: Meeting Health Needs Fairly*. Cambridge: Cambridge University Press.

Dankwa-Mullan, I., Rhee, K., Stoff, D., Pohlhaus, J., Sy, F., Stinson, N., et al. (2010). Moving toward paradigm-shifting research in health disparities through translational, transformational, and transdisciplinary approaches. *American Journal of Public Health, 100*(Suppl. 1), S19–S24.

Diderichsen, F., Evans, T., & Whitehead, M. (2001). The social disparities in health. In T. Evans, M. Whitehead, F. Diderichsen, A. Bhuiya, & M. Wirth (Eds.), *Challenging Inequities to Health: From Ethics to Action* (pp. 12–23). Oxford: Oxford University Press.

Disch, E. (2001). Research as clinical practice: Creating a positive research experience for survivors of sexual abuse by professionals. *Sociological Practice: A Journal of Clinical and Applied Sociology, 3*(3), 221–239.

Dworkin, S., Fleming, P., & Colvin, C. (2015). The promises and limitations of gender-transformative health programming with men: Critical reflections from the field. *Culture, Health & Sexuality, 17*(Suppl. 2), 128–143.

Dworkin, S., Treves-Kagan, S., & Lippman, S. (2013). Gender-transformative interventions to reduce HIV risks and violence with heterosexually-active men: A review of the global evidence. *AIDS and Behavior, 17*(9), 2845–2863.

Elder, G. (1998). The life course as developmental theory. *Child Development, 69*(1), 1–12.

Eliot, T. (1971). *Four Quartets*. New York: Houghton Mifflin Harcourt.

Gender Links. (2015). *South Africa: Zuma Must Commit to a National Plan to End GBV!* [online]. Johannesburg: Gender Links. Retrieved February 24, 2017, from http://genderlinks.org.za/programme-web-menu/south-africa-zuma-must-commit-to-a-national-plan-to-end-gbv-2015-02-12/

Gennrich, D. (2013). *Men and Masculinities in South Africa: Men Making a Difference*. Pietermaritzburg: ACSA/Sonke Gender Justice.

Gibbs, A., Jewkes, R., Sikweyiya, Y., & Willan, S. (2015). Reconstructing masculinity? A qualitative evaluation of the stepping stones and creating futures interventions in urban informal settlements in South Africa. *Culture, Health & Sexuality, 17*(2), 208–222.

Gourlay, A., Birdthistle, I., Mburu, G., Iorpenda, K., & Wringe, A. (2013). Barriers and facilitating factors to the uptake of antiretroviral drugs for prevention of mother-to-child transmission of HIV in sub-Saharan Africa: A systematic review. *Journal of the International AIDS Society, 16*, 18588.

Gupta, G. (2000). Gender, sexuality and HIV/AIDS: The what, the why and the how. Plenary address at the XIII international AIDS conference. [online]. In *XIII International AIDS Conference*. Durban, South Africa: International AIDS Society. Retrieved February 23, 2017, from http://siteresources.worldbank.org/EXTAFRREGTOPGENDER/Resources/durban_speech.pdf

Harrison, A. (2008). Hidden love: Sexual ideologies and relationship ideals among rural South African adolescents in the context of HIV/AIDS. *Culture, Health and Sexuality, 10*, 175–189.

Hassim, S. (2006). *Women's Organizations and Democracy in South Africa*. Madison: University of Wisconsin Press.

Hodgson, I., Plummer, M., Konopka, S., Colvin, C., Jonas, E., Albertini, J., et al. (2014). A systematic review of individual and contextual factors affecting ART initiation, adherence, and retention for HIV-infected pregnant and postpartum women. *PLoS ONE, 9*(11), e111421.

Hunter, M. (2010). *Love in the Time of AIDS. Inequality, Gender and Right in South Africa*. Durban: University of KwaZulu-Natal Press.

Jewkes, R. (2016). What works to prevent VAWG. [online]. Retrieved February 4, 2017, from http://www.svri.org/sites/default/files/attachments/2016-07-05/Jewkes%20R%20presentation%20for%20UNFPA%20and%20SVRI%20.pdf

Jewkes, R., Gibbs, A., Jama-Shai, N., Willan, S., Misselhorn, A., Mushinga, M., et al. (2014). Stepping stones and creating futures intervention: Shortened interrupted time series evaluation of a behavioral and structural health promotion and violence prevention intervention for young people in informal settlements in Durban, South Africa. *BMC Public Health, 14*, 1325.

Jewkes, R., & Morrell, R. (2012). Sexuality and the limits of agency among South African teenage women: Theorising femininities and their connections to HIV risk practices. *Social Science & Medicine, 74*, 1729–1737.

Journal of the International AIDS Society 2016 Special supplement, HIV epidemics among transgender populations: The importance of a trans-inclusive response. *19*(Suppl. 2), 1193.

Kaufman, M., Cornish, F., Zimmerman, R., & Johnson, B. (2014). Health behavior change models for HIV prevention and AIDS care: Practical recommendations for a multi-level approach. *Journal of Acquired Immune Deficiency Syndromes, 66*(Suppl. 3), S250–S258.

Kim, J., & Motsei, M. (2002). "Women enjoy punishment": Attitudes and experiences of gender-based violence among PHC nurses in rural South Africa. *Social Science & Medicine, 54*, 1243–1254.

Kim, J., Ferrari, G., Abramsky, T., Watts, C., Hargreaves, J., Morison, L., et al. (2009). Assessing the incremental effects of combining economic and health interventions: The IMAGE study in South Africa. *Bulletin of the World Health Organization, 87*(11), 824–832.

Kleinman, A. (2004). Ethics and experience: An anthropological approach to health equity. In P. Anand, F. Peter, & A. Sen (Eds.), *Public Health, Ethics, and Equity* (pp. 269–282). Oxford: Oxford University Press.

Kouyoumdjian, F. G., Findlay, N., Schwandt, M., & Calzavara, L. M. (2013). A systematic review of the relationships between intimate partner violence and HIV/AIDS. *PloS One, 8*(11), e81044.

Kuh, D., Ben-Schlomo, Y., Lynch, J., Hallqvist, J., & Power, C. (2003). Life course epidemiology. *Journal of Epidemiology & Community Health, 57*, 778–783.

Levon, E., Milani, T. M., & Kitis, E. D. (2017). The topography of masculine normativities in South Africa. *Critical Discourse Studies*, 1–18 (epub ahead of print).

MacNaughton, G., Haigh, F., McGill, M., Koutsioumpas, K., & Sprague, C. (2015). The impact of human rights on universalizing health care in Vermont, USA. *Health & Human Rights Journal, 17*(2), 83–95.

Mann, J. (1999). The transformative potential of the HIV/AIDS pandemic—Access to reproductive health: A question of distributive justice. *Reproductive Health Matters, 7*(14), 164–172.

Marins, J., Jamal, L., Chen, S., Marilisa, B., Hudes, E., Barbosa, A., et al. (2003). Dramatic improvement in survival among adult Brazilian AIDS patients. *AIDS, 17*, 1675–1682.

Marks, S. (1994). *Divided Sisterhood: Race, Class and Gender in the South African Nursing Profession*. New York: St. Martin's Press.

Mertens, D. (2011). Mixed methods as tools for social change. *Journal of Mixed Methods Research, 5*(3), 195–197.

Meyer, J., Springer, S., & Altice, F. (2011). Substance abuse, violence, and HIV in women: A literature review of the syndemic. *Journal of Women's Health, 20*, 991–1006.

Morrell, R. (Ed.). (2001). *Changing Men in Southern Africa*. Pietermaritzburg: University of KwaZulu-Natal and Zed Press.

Moynihan, C. (1998). Theories in health care and research: Theories of masculinity. *BMJ, 317*, 1072–1075.

Nussbaum, M. (2000). *Women and Human Development: The Capabilities Approach*. Cambridge: Cambridge University Press.

Nussbaum, M. (2002). Capabilities and social justice. *International Studies Review, 4*(2), 123–135.

Nussbaum, M. (2011). *Creating Capabilities*. Cambridge: Harvard University Press.

Orza, L., Bewley, S., Logie, C. H., Crone, E. T., Moroz, S., Strachan, S., et al. (2015). How does living with HIV impact on women's mental health? Voices from a global survey. *Journal of the International AIDS Society, 18*(Suppl. 5), 20289.

Ottersen, O., Dasgupta, J., Blouin, C., Buss, P., Chongsuvivatwong, V., Frenk, J., et al. (2014). The political origins of health inequity: Prospects for change. *Lancet, 383*(9917), 630–667.

Ouzgane, L., & Morrell, R. (Eds.). (2005). *African Masculinities: Men in Africa from the Late Nineteenth Century to the Present*. New York: Palgrave.

Parker, R. (2003). Building the foundations for the response for HIV/AIDS in Brazil: The development of HIV/AIDS policy, 1992–1996. *Divulgaçao em Saúde para Debate, 27*, 143–183.

Psaros, C., Remmert, J., Bangsberg, D., Safren, S., & Smit, J. (2015). Adherence to HIV care after pregnancy among women in sub-Saharan Africa: Falling off the cliff of the treatment cascade. *Current HIV/AIDS Reports, 12*(1), 1–5.

Rosenberg, T. (2001). Drug companies are vincible. The AIDS crisis is solvable. *The New York Times Magazine*.

Ruger, J. (2010). *Health and Social Justice*. Oxford: Oxford University Press.

Sen, A. (1999). *Development as Freedom*. New York: Random House.

Sen, A. (2009). *The Idea of Justice*. Cambridge: Harvard University Press.

Sen, G., Östlin, P., & George, A. (2007). Unequal, unfair, ineffective and inefficient gender inequity in health: Why it exists and how we can change it. In *Report of the Women and Gender Equity Knowledge Network of the Commission on Social Determinants of Health, Final Report to the Commission on Social Determinants of Health*. Geneva: WHO.

Sewell, W. (1992). A theory of structure: Duality, agency and transformation. *The American Journal of Sociology, 98*(1), 1–29.

South African National AIDS Council (SANAC). (2014). *Progress Report on the National Strategic Plan for HIV, TB and STIs 2012–2016*. Pretoria: South African National AIDS Council.

SANAC Women's Sector. (2015). Make a plan to stop GBV. [online]. Retrieved February 24, 2017, from http://sanacws.org.za/make-a-plan-to-stop-gbv/

Sprague, C. (2009). *Cui Bono: A Capabilities Approach to Understanding HIV Prevention and Treatment for Pregnant Women and Children in South Africa*. Doctoral thesis, University of the Witwatersrand.

Sprague, C., Chersich, M., & Black, V. (2011). Health systems weaknesses constrain access to PMTCT and maternal HIV services in South Africa: A qualitative enquiry. *AIDS Research and Therapy, 8*, 10.

Sprague, C., Hatcher, A., Woollett, N., & Black, V. (2015). How nurses in Johannesburg address intimate partner violence in female patients: Understanding IPV responses in low and middle-income country health systems. *Journal of Interpersonal Violence, 32*(11), 1591–1619.

Sprague, C., Hatcher, A., Woollett, N., Sommers, T., & Black, V. (2016a). "They can't report abuse; they can't move out. They are at the mercy of these men." Exploring connections between intimate partner violence, gender and HIV in South African clinical settings. *Culture, Health & Sexuality, 27*, 1–15, Epub 2015.

Sprague, C., Woollett, N., Parpart, J., Hatcher, A., Sommers, T., Brown, S., et al. (2016b). When nurses are also patients: Intimate partner violence and the health system as an enabler of women's health and institutional agency in Johannesburg. *Global Public Health, 11*(1–2), 169–183, Epub 2015.

Sprague, C., Scanlon, M., & Pantalone, D. W. (2017b). Qualitative methods to advance research on health inequities among previously incarcerated women living with HIV in Alabama. *Health Education & Behavior, 44*(5), 716–727.

Stern, D. (2013). Intersubjectivity. In E. Person, A. Cooper, & G. Gabbard (Eds.), *The American Psychiatric Publishing Text—Book of Psychoanalysis* (pp. 77–92). Arlington, TX: American Psychiatric Publishing.

Stern, E., & Cooper, D. (2014). Experiences and conceptualizations of sexual debut from the narratives of South African men and women in the context of HIV/AIDS. *African Journal of AIDS Research, 13*(2), 121–131.

Tazreiter, C., Weber, L., Pickering, S., Segrave, M., & McKernan, H. (2016). *Fluid Security in the Asia Pacific: Transnational Lives, Human Rights and State Control*. London: Palgrave Macmillan.

Teixeira, P. (2003). Universal access to AIDS medicines: The Brazilian experience. *Divulgaçao em Saúde para Debate, 27*, 184–191.

UNAIDS. (2014b). *The Gap Report*. Geneva: UNAIDS.

UNAIDS. (2016c). *Global AIDS Update 2016c*. Geneva: UNAIDS.

Venkatapuram, S. (2011). *Health Justice*. Cambridge: Polity Press.

Wang, C., & Geale, S. (2015). The power of story: Narrative inquiry as a methodology in nursing research. *International Journal of Nursing Sciences, 2*, 195–198.

Wood, K., Maforah, F., & Jewkes, R. (1998). 'He forced me to love him': Putting violence on the adolescent sexual health agenda. *Social Science & Medicine, 47*, 233–242.

Woolman, S., & Sprague, C. (2015). Nowhere to run, nowhere to hide: The absence of public policy as to how health care professionals should address intimate partner violence constitutes a breach of the rights to health and bodily integrity under the South African Constitution. *Cardozo Journal of Law & Gender, 22*(1), 29–74.

WHO. (2013a). *Responding to Intimate Partner Violence and Sexual Violence Against Women, WHO Clinical and Policy Guidelines*. Geneva: WHO.

WHO. (2013b). *Global and Regional Estimates of Violence Against Women: Prevalence and Health Effects of Intimate Partner Violence and Non-Partner Sexual Violence*. Geneva: WHO.

WHO. (2015). *Global Health Observatory Data*. [online]. Geneva: WHO. Retrieved January 14, 2017, from http://www.who.int/gho/database/en/

WHO. (2016a). *World Health Statistics 2016: Monitoring Health for the SDGs*. Geneva: WHO.

WHO. (2017). *The Ecological Framework*. [online]. Geneva: WHO. Retrieved June 15, 2017, from http://www.who.int/violenceprevention/approach/ecology/en/

References

Abdool Karim, S., & Abdool Karim, Q. (Eds.). (2005). *HIV/AIDS in South Africa*. Cambridge: Cambridge University Press.

Abdool Karim, S., & Baxter, C. (2010). Microbicides and their implications in HIV prevention. *Indian Journal of Medical Research, 132*(6), 656–659.

Abrahams, N., Mathews, S., Jewkes, R., Martin, L., & Lombard, C. (2012). *Every Eight Hours: Intimate Femicide in South Africa 10 Years Later!* [online]. Tygerberg: South African Medical Research Council. Retrieved January 15, 2018, from http://www.mrc.ac.za/policybriefs/everyeighthours.pdf

Ackermann, L., & de Klerk, G. (2002). Social factors that make South African women vulnerable to HIV infection. *Health Care for Women International, 23*(2), 163–172.

Adimora, A., & Auerbach, J. (2010). Structural interventions for HIV prevention in the United States. *Journal of Acquired Immune Deficiency Syndromes, 55*(Suppl. 2), S132–S135.

Akullian, A., Bershteyn, A., Klein, D., Vandormael, A., Bärnighausen, T., & Tanser, F. (2017). Sexual partnership age pairings and risk of HIV acquisition in rural South Africa. *AIDS, 31*(12), 1755–1764.

Albertyn, C. (2007). Substantive equality and transformation in South Africa. *South African Journal on Human Rights, 23*(2), 253–276.

Albertyn, C. (2009). 'The stubborn persistence of patriarchy'? Gender equality and diversity in South Africa. *Constitutional Court Review, 2*(1), 165–208.

C. Sprague, *Gender and HIV in South Africa*, Global Research in Gender, Sexuality and Health, https://doi.org/10.1057/978-1-137-55997-5

Albertyn, C., & Meer, S. (2005). Citizens or mothers? The marginalisation of women's reproductive rights in the struggle for access to health care for HIV positive pregnant women in South Africa. In M. Mukhopadhyay & S. Meer (Eds.), *Gender, Rights and Development: A Global Sourcebook* (pp. 26–56). Amsterdam: The Royal Tropical Institute.

Alcoff, L. (1994). The problem of speaking for others. In S. Weisser & J. Fleischner (Eds.), *Feminist Nightmares: Women at Odds: Feminism and the Problem of Sisterhood* (pp. 285–309). New York: New York University Press.

Alighieri, D. (1984). *The Divine Comedy. Volume 1: Inferno* (Mark Musa, Trans.). New York: Penguin Books.

Alkire, S. (2003). *The Capability Approach as a Development Paradigm?* Document part of training course preceding the 3rd International Conference on the Capability Approach, Pavia, Italy, 7 September.

Alkire, S. (2004, September). *The Capability Approach and Human Development Presentation*. Oxford University, 1–15.

Alkire, S. (2005). Why the capability approach? *Journal of Human Development, 6*(1), 115–135.

Alma-Ata Declaration. (1978). Retrieved January 15, 2018, from http://www.who.int/publications/almaata_declaration_en.pdf

Anand, S. (2004). The concern for equity in health. In S. Anand, F. Peter, & A. Sen (Eds.), *Public Health, Ethics, and Equity* (pp. 15–20). Oxford: Oxford University Press.

Anand, S., Peter, F., & Sen, A. (Eds.). (2004). *Public Health, Ethics, and Equity*. Oxford: Oxford University Press.

Anfara, V., Brown, K., & Mangione, T. (2002). Qualitative analysis on stage: Making the research process more public. *Educational Researcher, 31*(7), 28–38.

Annandale, E., & Hunt, K. (2000). Gender inequalities in health: Research at the crossroads. In E. Annandale & K. Hunt (Eds.), *Gender Inequalities in Health* (pp. 1–35). Philadelphia: Open University Press.

Arber, S., & Cooper, H. (2000). Gender and inequalities in health across the lifecourse. In E. Annandale & K. Hunt (Eds.), *Gender Inequalities in Health* (pp. 123–149). Philadelphia: Open University Press.

Ardington, C., Barnighausen, T., Case, A., & Menendez, A. (2014). The economic consequences of AIDS mortality in South Africa. *Journal of Development Economics, 111*, 48–60.

Aristotle. (1998). *The Nicomachean Ethics* (C. Taylor, Trans.). Oxford: Oxford University Press.

Arras, J., Fenton, E., & Kukla, R. (2015). *The Routledge Companion to Bioethics*. New York: Routledge.

Auerbach, J., Caceres, C., & Parkhurst, J. (2011). Addressing social drivers of HIV/AIDS for the long-term response: Conceptual and methodological considerations. *Global Public Health, 6*(Suppl 3), S293–S309.

Badsha, O. (Ed.). (1986). *South Africa, the Cordoned Heart: Essays by Twenty South African Photographers*. Cape Town: The Gallery Press.

Baral, S., Poteat, T., Stromdahl, S., Wirtz, A., Guadamuz, T., & Beyrer, C. (2013). Worldwide burden of HIV in transgender women: A systematic review and meta-analysis. *Lancet Infectious Diseases, 13*(3), 214–222.

Barker, D. (Ed.). (1992). *Fetal and Infant Origins of Adult Disease*. London: BMJ Books.

Bartley, M. (2017). *Health Inequality: An Introduction to Concepts, Theories and Methods* (2nd ed.). Cambridge: Polity.

Bayer, R., & Oppenheimer, G. (2000). *AIDS Doctors. Voices from the Epidemic: An Oral History*. New York: Oxford University Press.

Bennett, H., Einarson, A., Taddio, A., Koren, G., & Einarson, T. (2004). Prevalence of depression during pregnancy: Systematic review. *Obstetrics and Gynecology, 103*(4), 698–709.

Bertaux, D. (Ed.). (1981). *Biography and Society: The Life History Approach in the Social Sciences*. Beverly Hills, CA: Sage.

Bilchitz, D. (2006). The right to health. In S. Woolman & M. Bishop (Eds.), *Constitutional Law of South Africa* (2nd ed.). Cape Town: Juta Press, Chapter 56A.

Bilchitz, D. (2008). *Poverty and Fundamental Rights: The Justification and Enforcement of Socio-Economic Rights*. Oxford: Oxford University Press.

Blaauw, D., & Penn-Kekana, L. (2010). Maternal health. In S. Fonn & A. Padarath (Eds.), *South African Health Review 2010* (pp. 3–11). Durban: Health Systems Trust.

Black, D., Morris, J., Smith, C., & Townsend, P. (1980). *Inequalities in Health: Report of a Research Working Group*. London: Department of Health and Social Security.

Black, V., Black, A., Rees, H., Guidozzi, F., Scorgie, F., & Chersich, M. (2016). Increased access to antiretroviral therapy is associated with reduced maternal mortality in Johannesburg, South Africa: An audit from 2003–2012. *PLoS ONE, 11*(12), e0168199.

Black, V., Hoffman, R., Sugar, C., Menon, P., Venter, F., Currier, J., et al. (2008). Safety and efficacy of initiating highly active antiretroviral therapy in an integrated antenatal and HIV clinic in Johannesburg, South Africa. *Journal of Acquired Immune Deficiency Syndrome, 49*(3), 276–281.

Blair, J., Paxton, L., & Kamb, M. (2012). HIV and AIDS in women. In M. Goldman, R. Troisi, & K. Rexrode (Eds.), *Women and Health* (2nd ed., pp. 505–522). Boston: Academic Press.

Blankenship, K., Friedman, S., Dworkin, S., & Mantell, J. (2006). Structural interventions: Concepts, challenges, and opportunities for research. *Journal of Urban Health, 83*(1), 59–72.

Bogdan, R., & Biklen, S. (2006). *Qualitative Research in Education: An Introduction to Theory and Methods.* New York: Allyn & Bacon.

Boily, M., Baggaley, R., Wang, L., Masse, B., White, R., Hayes, R., et al. (2009). Heterosexual risk of HIV-1 infection per sexual act: A systematic review and meta-analysis of observational studies. *Lancet Infectious Diseases, 9*(2), 118–129.

Bojer, M., Mckay, E., & Roehl, H. (2006). *Mapping Dialogue: A Research Project Profiling Dialogue Tools and Processes for Social Change.* Johannesburg: Pioneers of Change.

Boonzaier, F. (2005). Woman abuse in South Africa: A brief contextual analysis. *Feminism & Psychology, 15*(1), 99–103.

Boserup, E. (2007). *Women's Role in Economic Development.* New York: Earthscan.

Bozzoli, B., & Nkotsoe, M. (1991). *Women of Phokeng: Consciousness, Life Strategy, and Migrancy in South Africa, 1900–1983: Social History of Africa.* London: Heinemann.

Bradshaw, D., & Nannan, N. (2005). Mortality and morbidity among women and children. In *South African Health Review 2006* (pp. 127–150). Health Systems Trust: Durban.

Bradshaw, D., & Nannan, N. (2006). Mortality and morbidity among women and children. In *South African Health Review 2006* (pp. 127–150). Durban: Health Systems Trust.

Braveman, P. (2006). Health disparities and health equity: Concepts and measurement. *Annual Review of Public Health, 27*, 167–194.

Braveman, P., & Gruskin, S. (2003). Defining equity in health. *Journal of Epidemiology and Community Health, 57*(4), 254–258.

Brittain, K., Mellins, C. A., Phillips, T., Zerbe, A., Abrams, E. J., Myer, L., & Remien, R. H. (2017). Social support, stigma and antenatal depression among HIV-infected pregnant women in South Africa. *AIDS & Behavior, 21*(1), 274–282.

Broder, S. (2010). The development of antiretroviral therapy and its impact on HIV-1/AIDS pandemic. *Antiviral Research, 85*(1), 1–38.

Bronfenbrenner, U. (1979). *The Ecology of Human Development: Experiments by Nature and Design*. Cambridge: Harvard University Press.

Buchmann, E., Mnyani, C., Frank, K., Chersich, M., & McIntyre, J. (2015). Declining maternal mortality in the face of persistently high HIV prevalence in a middle-income country. *BJOG, 122*(2), 220–227.

Burton, R. (2013). Maternal health: There is cause for optimism. *South African Medical Journal, 103*(8), 520–521.

Buse, K., Dickinson, C., & Sidibe, M. (2008). HIV: Know your epidemic: Act on its politics. *Journal of the Royal Society of Medicine, 101*(12), 572–573.

Butler, J. (2004). *Undoing Gender*. New York: Routledge.

Campbell, C. (2003). *Letting Them Die: Why HIV/AIDS Prevention Programmes Fail*. Bloomington: Indiana University Press.

Campbell, C., & Mannell, J. (2016). Conceptualising the agency of highly marginalized women: Intimate partner violence in extreme settings. *Global Public Health, 11*(1–2), 1–16.

Campbell, J. (2002). Intimate partner violence and physical health consequences. *Archives of Internal Medicine, 162*(10), 1157–1163.

Campbell, J., Baty, M., Ghandour, R., Stockman, J., Francisco, L., & Wagman, J. (2008). The intersection of intimate partner violence and HIV/AIDS: A review. *The International Journal of Injury Control and Safety Promotion, 15*(4), 222–231.

Canguilhem, G. (1991). *On the Normal and the Pathological*. New York: Zone Books.

Carlson, J., Casey, E., Edleson, J., Tolman, R., Neugut, T., & Kimball, E. (2015). Strategies to engage men and boys in violence prevention: A global organizational perspective. *Violence Against Women, 21*(11), 1406–1425.

Carpenter, M. (2000). Reinforcing the pillars: Rethinking gender, social divisions and health. In E. Annandale & K. Hunt (Eds.), *Gender Inequalities in Health* (pp. 36–63). Buckingham: Open University Press.

Carrotte, E., Vella, A., Bowring, A., Douglass, C., Hellard, M., & Lim, M. (2016). 'I am yet to encounter any survey that actually reflects my life': A qualitative study of inclusivity in sexual health research. *BMC Medical Research Methodology, 16*(1), 86.

Casale, M., Rogan, M., Hynie, M., Flicker, S., Nixon, S., & Rubincam, C. (2011). Gendered perceptions of HIV risk among young women and men in a high-HIV-prevalence setting. *African Journal of AIDS Research, 10*(1), 301–310.

Castor, D., Cook, S., Leclerc-Madlala, S., & Shelton, J. (2010). Intimate partner violence and HIV in South African women. *Lancet, 376*(9748), 1219–1220.

Centers for Disease Control and Prevention (CDC). (1998). HIV prevention through early detection and treatment of other sexually transmitted diseases—United States. *Morbidity and Mortality Weekly Report, 47*(12), 1–24.

CDC. (2017). *Selected National HIV Prevention and Care Outcomes in the United States*. [online]. Atlanta: CDC. Retrieved January 5, 2018, from https://www.cdc.gov/hiv/pdf/library/factsheets/cdc-hiv-national-hiv-care-outcomes.pdf

CDC. (2017a). *Selected National HIV Prevention and Care Outcomes in the United States*. [online]. Atlanta: CDC. Retrieved January 5, 2018, from https://www.cdc.gov/hiv/pdf/library/factsheets/cdc-hiv-national-hiv-care-outcomes.pdf

CDC. (2017b). *HIV Among Women*. [online]. Atlanta: CDC. Retrieved January 15, 2018, from http://www.cdc.gov/hiv/group/gender/women/

CDC. (2018). *HIV and AIDS in the United States by Geographic Distribution*. [online]. Atlanta: CDC. Retrieved January 15, 2018, from https://www.cdc.gov/hiv/statistics/overview/geographicdistribution.html

Charlesworth, H. (2000). Martha Nussbaum's feminist internationalism. *Ethics, 111*(1), 64–78.

Charmaz, K. (1991). *Good Days, Bad Days: The Self in Chronic Illness and Time*. New Brunswick: Rutgers University Press.

Charmaz, K. (1999). Stories of suffering: Subjective tales and research narratives. *Qualitative Health Research, 9*(3), 362–382.

Chersich, M. (2007). *Preventing HIV in Infants in Eastern and Southern Africa by Improving Access to HIV Testing, Maternal Health and Quality Services*. Doctoral thesis, Ghent University.

Chersich, M., & Rees, H. (2008). Vulnerability of women in Southern Africa to infection with HIV: Biologic determinants and priority health sector interventions. *AIDS, 22*(Suppl. 4), S27–S40.

Chigwedere, P., Seage, G., Gruskin, S., Lee, T., & Essex, M. (2008). Estimating the lost benefits of antiretroviral drug use in South Africa. *Journal of Acquired Immune Deficiency Syndrome, 49*(4), 410–415.

Cicero, M. (2013). *On the Republic and On the Laws* (D. Fott, Trans.). Ithaca, NY: Cornell University Press.

Clark, D. (2005). *The Capability Approach: Its Development, Critiques and Recent Advances*. [online]. Manchester: University of Manchester. Retrieved January 5, 2018, from http://www.gprg.org/pubs/workingpapers/pdfs/gprg-wps-032.pdf

Clouse, K., Schwartz, S., Van Rie, A., Bassett, J., Yende, N., & Pettifor, A. (2014). 'What they wanted was to give birth; nothing else': Barriers to retention in option B+ HIV care among postpartum women in South Africa. *Journal of Acquired Immune Deficiency Syndromes, 67*(1), e12–e18.

Cluver, L., Boyes, M., Orkin, M., Pantelic, M., Molwena, T., & Sherr, L. (2013). Child-focused state cash transfers and adolescent risk of HIV infection in South Africa: A propensity-score-matched case-control study. *Lancet Global Health, 1*(6), e362–e370.

Coates, T., Richter, L., & Caceres, C. (2008). Behavioural strategies to reduce HIV transmission: How to make them work better. *Lancet, 372*(9639), 669–684.

Cohen, J. (2000). McIntyre and Gray have a will and a way. *Science, 288*(5474), 2163.

Cohen, L., & Swift, S. (1999). The spectrum of prevention: Developing a comprehensive approach to injury prevention. *Injury Prevention, 5*(3), 203–207.

Cohen, M., Chen, Y., McCauley, M., Gamble, T., Hosseinipour, M., Kumarasamy, N., et al. (2011). Prevention of HIV-1 infection with early antiretroviral therapy. *New England Journal of Medicine, 365*, 493–505.

Colvin, C., Konopka, S., Chalker, J., Jonas, E., Albertini, J., Amzel, A., et al. (2014). A systematic review of health system barriers and enablers for antiretroviral therapy for HIV-infected pregnant and postpartum women. *PLoS ONE, 9*(10), e108150.

Connell, R. (1987). *Gender and Power: Society, the Person and Sexual Politics*. Stanford: Stanford University Press.

Connell, R. (1995). *Masculinities*. Berkeley: University of California Press.

Connell, R., & Messerschmidt, J. (2005). Hegemonic masculinity: Rethinking the concept. *Gender Society, 19*(6), 829–859.

Connolly, C., Ramjee, G., Sturm, A., & Abdool Karim, S. (2002). Incidence of sexually transmitted infections among HIV positive sex workers in KwaZulu-Natal, South Africa. *Sexually Transmitted Diseases, 29*(11), 721–724.

Cooke, G., Tanser, F., Barnighausen, T., & Newell, M. (2010). Population uptake of antiretroviral treatment through primary care in rural South Africa. *BMC Public Health, 10*, 585.

Cooper, D., Harries, J., Moodley, J., Constant, D., Hodes, R., Mathews, C., et al. (2016). Coming of age? Women's sexual and reproductive health after twenty-one years of democracy in South Africa. *Reproductive Health Matters, 24*(48), 79–89.

Cooper, D., Morroni, C., Orner, P., Moodley, J., Harries, J., Cullingworth, L., et al. (2004). Ten years of democracy in South Africa: Documenting transformation in reproductive health policy and status. *Reproductive Health Matters, 12*(24), 70–85.

Coovadia, H., Jewkes, R., Barron, P., Sanders, D., & McIntyre, D. (2009). The health and health system of South Africa: Historical roots of current public health challenges. *Lancet, 374*(9692), 817–834.

Correa, S., Petchesky, R., & Parker, R. (2008). *Sexuality, Health and Human Rights*. New York: Routledge.

Cox, S., & McDonald, M. (2013). Ethics is for human subjects too: Participant perspectives on responsibility in health research. *Social Science & Medicine, 98*(C), 224–231.

Crenshaw, K. (1989). Demarginalizing the intersection of race and sex: A black feminist critique of antidiscrimination doctrine, feminist theory and antiracist politics. *The University of Chicago Legal Forum, 140*, 139–167.

Crespo, R. F. (2012). The capabilities approaches and Aristotelian practical reason. *Revista de Instituciones, Ideas y Mercados, 57*, 57–86.

Dahl, R. (1998). *On Democracy*. New Haven: Yale University Press.

Dahlgren, G., & Whitehead, M. (1992). *Policies and Strategies to Promote Equity in Health*. Copenhagen: World Health Organization Regional Office for Europe.

Dangarembga, T. (2008). *The Sharing Day (Film)*. Harare: Nyerai Films. Retrieved July 1, 2017, from http://tve.org/film/the-sharing-day/

Daniels, K., George, A., Howard, N., Koleva, G., et al. (2016). Fair publication of qualitative research in health systems: A call by health policy and systems researchers. *International Journal for Equity in Health, 15*(1), 98.

Daniels, N. (1981). Health care needs and distributive justice. *Philosophy and Public Affairs, 10*(2), 146–179.

Daniels, N. (2008). *Just Health: Meeting Health Needs Fairly*. Cambridge: Cambridge University Press.

Dankwa-Mullan, I., Rhee, K., Stoff, D., Pohlhaus, J., Sy, F., Stinson, N., et al. (2010). Moving toward paradigm-shifting research in health disparities through translational, transformational, and transdisciplinary approaches. *American Journal of Public Health, 100*(Suppl. 1), S19–S24.

Davis, R. (2017). HIV and TB: New government plan raises concerns over practicalities and politics. [online]. *Daily Maverick*. Retrieved January 15, 2017, from https://www.dailymaverick.co.za/article/2017-04-11-hiv-tb-new-government-plan-raises-concerns-over-practicalities-and-politics/#.WUKvwhPysYE

Decker, S., Naugle, A., Carter-Visscher, R., Bell, K., & Seifert, A. (2011). Ethical issues in research on sensitive topics: Participants' experiences of distress and benefit. *Journal of Empirical Research on Human Research Ethics, 6*(3), 55–64.

Denzin, N., & Lincoln, Y. (2011). *Handbook of Qualitative Research*. Thousand Oaks: Sage.

Department of Public Service and Administration, Government of South Africa. (1997). *Batho Pele—"People First." White Paper on Transforming Public Service Delivery*. [online]. Pretoria: Department of Public Service and Administration. Retrieved January 16, 2017, from http://www.dpsa.gov.za/dpsa2g/documents/acts&regulations/frameworks/white-papers/transform.pdf

Dickinson, D. (2009). *Changing the Course of AIDS: Peer Education in South Africa and Its Lessons for the Global Crisis*. Ithaca, NY: Cornell University Press.

Dickson-Swift, V., James, E., Kippen, S., & Liamputtong, P. (2007). Doing sensitive research: What challenges do qualitative researchers face? *Qualitative Research, 7*(3), 327–353.

Diderichsen, F., Evans, T., & Whitehead, M. (2001). The social disparities in health. In T. Evans, M. Whitehead, F. Diderichsen, A. Bhuiya, & M. Wirth (Eds.), *Challenging Inequities to Health: From Ethics to Action* (pp. 12–23). Oxford: Oxford University Press.

Disch, E. (2001). Research as clinical practice: Creating a positive research experience for survivors of sexual abuse by professionals. *Sociological Practice: A Journal of Clinical and Applied Sociology, 3*(3), 221–239.

Doggett, E., Lanham, M., Wilcher, R., Gafos, M., Karim, Q., & Heise, L. (2015). Optimizing HIV prevention for women: A review of evidence from microbicide studies and considerations for gender-sensitive microbicide introduction. *Journal of the International AIDS Society, 18*(1), 20536.

Doll, R. (1992). Health and the environment in the 1990s. *America Journal of Public Health, 82*(7), 933–941.

Doyal, L. (2006). How well are women worldwide? *Lancet, 367*(9526), 1893–1894.

Dubihlela, J., & Dubihlela, D. (2014). Social grants impact on poverty among the female-headed households in South Africa. *Mediterranean Journal of Social Sciences, 5*(8), 160–167.

Duff, P., Kipp, W., Wild, T., Rubaale, T., & Okech-Ojony, J. (2010). Barriers to accessing highly active antiretroviral therapy by HIV positive women attending an antenatal clinic in a regional hospital in western Uganda. *Journal of the International AIDS Society, 13*, 37.

Dunkle, K., & Decker, M. (2013). Gender-based violence and HIV: Reviewing the evidence for links and causal pathways in the general population and high risk groups. *American Journal of Reproductive Immunology, 69*(Suppl. 1), 20–26.

Dunkle, K., Jewkes, R., Brown, H., Gray, G., McIntyre, J., & Harlow, S. (2004). Transactional sex among women in Soweto, South Africa: Prevalence, risk factors and associations with HIV infection. *Social Science & Medicine, 59*(8), 1581–1592.

Durevall, D., & Lindskog, A. (2015). Intimate partner violence and HIV in ten sub-Saharan African countries: What do the Demographic and Health Surveys tell us? *Lancet Global Health, 3*(1), e34–e43.

Dworkin, S., Fleming, P., & Colvin, C. (2015). The promises and limitations of gender-transformative health programming with men: Critical reflections from the field. *Culture, Health & Sexuality, 17*(Suppl. 2), 128–143.

Dworkin, S., Hatcher, A., Colvin, C., & Peacock, D. (2013). Impact of a gender-transformative HIV and antiviolence program on gender ideologies and masculinities in two rural, South African communities. *Men and Masculinities, 16*(2), 181–202.

Dworkin, S., Treves-Kagan, S., & Lippman, S. (2013). Gender-transformative interventions to reduce HIV risks and violence with heterosexually-active men: A review of the global evidence. *AIDS and Behavior, 17*(9), 2845–2863.

Eastern Cape Department of Health, Government of South Africa. (2008). *HIV, AIDS & STIs 2007–2008 Business Plan*. Bisho: Eastern Cape Department of Health.

Elder, G. (1998). The life course as developmental theory. *Child Development, 69*(1), 1–12.

Eliot, T. (1971). *Four Quartets*. New York: Houghton Mifflin Harcourt.

Ellsberg, M., Jansen, H., Heise, L., Watts, C., García-Moreno, C., & WHO Multi-Country Study on Women's Health and Domestic Violence Against Women Study Team. (2008). Intimate partner violence and women's physical and mental health in the WHO multi-country study on women's health and domestic violence: An observational study. *Lancet, 371*(9619), 1165–1172.

Emerson, R. (2017). *The Conduct of Life*. North Charleston: CreateSpace Independent Publishing.

Evans, T., Whitehead, M., Diderichsen, F., Bhuiya, A., & Wirth, M. (Eds.). (2001). *Challenging Inequities to Health: From Ethics to Action*. Oxford: Oxford University Press.

Farmer, P. (1992). *AIDS & Accusation, Haiti and the Geography of Blame*. Berkeley: University of California Press.

Farmer, P., Connors, M., & Simmons, J. (2011). *Women, Poverty, and AIDS*. Monroe: Common Courage Press.

Fast, P., & Kaleebu, P. (2010). HIV vaccines: Current status worldwide and in Africa. *AIDS, 24*(Suppl. 4), S50–S60.

Fauci, A. (2008). Twenty-five years of HIV. *Nature, 453*, 289–290.

Feldman, S., & Gellert, P. (2003). Central capabilities and entitlements: A critique of Nussbaum's Ahistorical and Universalist Western Liberal Claims. In *Annual Meeting of the American Sociological Association*. Atlanta: American Sociological Association.

Ferguson, L., Grant, A., Watson-Jones, D., Kahawita, T., Ong'ech, J., & Ross, D. (2012). Linking women who test HIV positive in pregnancy-related services to long-term HIV care and treatment services: A systematic review. *Tropical Medicine and International Health, 17*(5), 564–580.

Foucault, M. (1977). *Discipline and Punish: The Birth of the Prison*. New York: Vintage.

Foucault, M. (1994). *The Order of Things: An Archaeology of the Human Sciences*. New York: Vintage.

Frankfort-Nacmias, C., Nacmias, D., & DeWaard, J. (2014). *Research Methods for the Social Sciences*. New York: Worth Publishers.

Freidson, E. (1970). *Profession of Medicine: A Study of the Sociology of Applied Knowledge*. New York: Harper & Row.

Frenk, J., Gomez-Dantas, O., & Chacon, F. (2011). Global health in transition. In R. Parker & M. Sommer (Eds.), *Handbook of Global Public Health* (pp. 11–17). London: Routledge.

Frenk, J., & Moon, S. (2013). Governance challenges in global health. *New England Journal of Medicine, 368*, 936–942.

Fried, L., Piot, P., Spencer, H., & Parker, R. (2012). The changing landscape of global public health. *Global Public Health, 7*(Suppl. 1), S1–S4.

Friedman, S., & McKnight, K. (2003). What is the role of structural interventions in HIV prevention? [online]. San Francisco: University of San Francisco. Retrieved June 20, 2017, from https://caps.ucsf.edu/uploads/pubs/FS/structural.php

Fulu, E., & Kerr-Wilson, A. (2015). *What Works to Prevent Violence Against Women and Girls Evidence Reviews—Paper 2: Interventions to Prevent Violence Against Women and Girls*. [online]. London: UKAID. Retrieved January 15, 2018, from https://www.whatworks.co.za/documents/publications/35-global-evidence-reviews-paper-2-interventions-to-prevent-violence-against-women-and-girls-sep-2015/file

Galvão, J. (2005). Brazil and access to HIV/AIDS drugs: A question of human rights and public health. *American Journal of Public Health, 95*(7), 1110–1115.

Gannon, M. (2016, February 5). Race is a social construct scientists argue. *Scientific American*. Retrieved October 25, 2017, from https://www.scientificamerican.com/article/race-is-a-social-construct-scientists-argue/

García-Moreno, C. (2002). Dilemmas and opportunities for an appropriate health-service response to violence against women. *Lancet, 359*(9316), 1509–1514.

Gardner, E., McLees, M., Steiner, J., Del Rio, C., & Burman, W. (2011). The spectrum of engagement in HIV care and its relevance to test-and-treat strategies for prevention of HIV infection. *Clinical Infectious Diseases, 52*(6), 793–800.

Garnett, G., & Røttingen, J. A. (2001). Measuring the risk of HIV transmission. *AIDS, 15*(5), 641–643.

Gasper, D. (2002). Is Sen's capability approach an adequate basis for considering human development? *Review of Political Economy, 14*(4), 435–446.

Gasper, D. (2007). What is the capability approach? Its core, rationale, partners and dangers. *Journal of Socio-Economics, 36*(3), 335–359.

Gass, J., Stein, D., Williams, D., & Seedat, S. (2010). Intimate partner violence, health behaviours, and chronic physical illness among South African women. *South African Medical Journal, 100*(9), 582–585.

Gauteng Provincial Department of Health, Government of South Africa. (2009). *Annual Performance Plan 2009*. Pretoria: Gauteng Department of Health.

Gender Links. (2009). *IMAGE Study*. [online]. Johannesburg: Gender Links. Retrieved February 24, 2017, from http://genderlinks.org.za/programme-web-menu/image-study-2009-06-16/

Gender Links. (2015). *South Africa: Zuma Must Commit to a National Plan to End GBV!* [online]. Johannesburg: Gender Links. Retrieved February 24, 2017, from http://genderlinks.org.za/programme-web-menu/south-africa-zuma-must-commit-to-a-national-plan-to-end-gbv-2015-02-12/

Gennrich, D. (2013). *Men and Masculinities in South Africa: Men Making a Difference*. Pietermaritzburg: ACSA/Sonke Gender Justice.

Gerntholtz, L., Gibbs, A., & Willan, S. (2011). The African women's protocol: Bringing attention to reproductive rights and the MDGs. *PLoS Medicine, 8*(4), 1–4.

Gibbs, A., Jewkes, R., Sikweyiya, Y., & Willan, S. (2015). Reconstructing masculinity? A qualitative evaluation of the stepping stones and creating futures interventions in urban informal settlements in South Africa. *Culture, Health & Sexuality, 17*(2), 208–222.

Gibbs, A., Willan, S., Misselhorn, A., & Mangoma, J. (2012). Combined structural interventions for gender equality and livelihood security: A critical review of the evidence from Southern and Eastern Africa and the implications for young people. *Journal of the International AIDS Society, 15*(Suppl. 1), 1–10.

Giddens, A. (1981). *A Contemporary Critique of Historical Materialism. Vol. 1., Power, Property and the State*. London: Macmillan.

Giddens, A. (1984). *The Constitution of Society*. Cambridge: Polity Press.

Gilbert, L. (1995). Sociology and the "New Public Health" in South Africa. *South African Journal of Sociology, 26*, 115–124.

Gilbert, L. (2012). 'Upstream/downstream'—Locating the 'social' in health promotion and HIV/AIDS in South Africa? *South African Review of Sociology, 43*(1), 62–77.

Gilbert, L., & Selikow, T. (2011). "The epidemic in this country has the face of a woman": Gender and HIV/AIDS in South Africa. *African Journal of AIDS Research, 10*(Suppl. 1), 325–334.

Gilbert, T., & Gilbert, L. (2004). Globalisation and local power: Influences on health matters in South Africa. *Health Policy, 67*(3), 245–255.

Gimbel, S., Rustagi, A., Robinson, J., Kouyate, S., Coutinho, J., Nduati, R., et al. (2016). Evaluation of a systems analysis and improvement approach to optimize prevention of mother-to-child transmission of HIV using the Consolidated Framework for Implementation Research. *Journal of Acquired Immune Deficiency Syndrome, 72*(Suppl. 2), S108–S116.

Glaser, B., & Strauss, A. (1965). *Awareness of Dying*. Chicago: Aldine Transaction.

Godoy-Ruiz, P., Cole, D., Lenters, L., & McKenzie, K. (2016). Developing collaborative approaches to international research: Perspectives of new global health researchers. *Global Public Health, 11*(3), 253–275.

Goffman, E. (1963). *Stigma: Notes on the Management of Spoiled Identity*. Englewood Cliffs: Prentice-Hall.

Goffman, E. (1967). *Interaction Ritual: Essays on Face to Face Behavior*. New York: Anchor Books.

Gostin, L. (2010). *Public Health Law and Ethics: A Reader*. Berkeley: University of California Press.

Gourlay, A., Birdthistle, I., Mburu, G., Iorpenda, K., & Wringe, A. (2013). Barriers and facilitating factors to the uptake of antiretroviral drugs for prevention of mother-to-child transmission of HIV in sub-Saharan Africa: A systematic review. *Journal of the International AIDS Society, 16*, 18588.

Gouws, E., & Abdool Karim, Q. (2005). HIV infection in South Africa: The evolving epidemic. In S. Abdool Karim & Q. Abdool Karim (Eds.), *HIV/AIDS in South Africa* (pp. 48–66). Cambridge: Cambridge University Press.

Government of South Africa. (1996). The Constitution of the Republic of South Africa, Act No. 108 of 1996. Cape Town: South Africa.

Government of South Africa. (1998). Domestic Violence Act 116 of 1998. Cape Town: South Africa.

Government of South Africa. (1999). *Saving Mothers Report on Confidential Enquiries into Maternal Deaths in South Africa*. Pretoria: National Department of Health.

Government of South Africa. (2009). *A Study of the Factors Contributing to SAPS Non-Compliance with the Domestic Violence Act*. [online]. Pretoria: National Department of Health. Retrieved January 1, 2016, from http://govza.gcis.gov.za/tn/node/521070

Government of South Africa. (2012). *National Strategic Plan on HIV, STIs and TB 2012–2016*. Pretoria: National Department of Health.

Government of South Africa. (2013a). *The 2012 National Antenatal Sentinel HIV and Herpes Simplex Type-2 Prevalence Survey, South Africa*. Pretoria: National Department of Health.

Government of South Africa. (2013b). *MDG Country Report: The South Africa I Know The Home I Understand*. Pretoria: Government of South Africa.

Government of South Africa. (2015a). *2013 National Antenatal HIV Prevalence Survey*. Pretoria: National Department of Health.

Government of South Africa. (2015b). *Saving Mothers 2011–2013: Sixth Report on the Confidential Enquiries into Maternal Deaths in South Africa*. Pretoria: National Department of Health.

Government of South Africa. (2015c). White paper on national health insurance (11 December). National health insurance for South Africa: Towards universal health coverage. Version 40. Government Gazette No. 39506. Pretoria: National Department of Health.

Greeff, M., Uys, L., Wantland, D., Makoae, L., Chirwa, M., Dlamini, P., et al. (2010). Perceived HIV stigma and life satisfaction among persons living with HIV infection in five African countries: A longitudinal study. *International Journal Nursing Studies, 47*(4), 475–486.

Greenhalgh, T., Annandale, E., Ashcroft, R., et al. (2016). An open letter to The BMJ editors on qualitative research. *BMJ, 352*, i563.

Gruskin, S., Mills, E., & Tarantola, D. (2007). History, principles, and practice of health and human rights. *Lancet, 370*(9585), 449–455.

Gupta, G. (2000). Gender, sexuality and HIV/AIDS: The what, the why and the how. Plenary address at the XIII international AIDS conference. [online]. In *XIII International AIDS Conference*. Durban, South Africa: International AIDS Society. Retrieved February 23, 2017, from http://siteresources.worldbank.org/EXTAFRREGTOPGENDER/Resources/durban_speech.pdf

Gupta, G., Parkhurst, J., Ogden, J., Aggleton, P., & Mahal, A. (2008). Structural approaches to HIV prevention. *Lancet, 372*, 764–775.

Gutto, S. (2002). *Equality and Non-discrimination in South Africa: The Political Economy of Law*. Wynberg: David Philip Publishers.

Habib, A., & Bentley, K. (2008). *Racial Redress and Citizenship in South Africa*. Cape Town: HSRC Press.

Hargreaves, J., & Glynn, J. (2002). Educational attainment and HIV-1 infection in developing countries: A systematic review. *Tropical Medicine & International Health, 7*(6), 489–498.

Hargreaves, J., Hatcher, A., Strange, V., Phetla, G., Busza, J., Kim, J., et al. (2009). Group-microfinance and health promotion among the poor: Six-year process evaluation of the Intervention with Microfinance for AIDS and Gender Equity (IMAGE) in rural South Africa. [online]. Retrieved February 7, 2017, from http://www.sef.co.za/files/02%20%20Hargreaves%20IMAGE%20Process%20Evaluation%20working%20paper%202009.pdf

Hargreaves, J., Hatcher, A., Strange, V., Phetla, G., Busza, J., Kim, J., et al. (2010). Process evaluation of the Intervention with Microfinance for AIDS and Gender Equity (IMAGE) in rural South Africa. *Health Education Research, 25*(1), 27–40.

Harling, G., Msisha, W., & Subramanian, S. (2010). No association between HIV and intimate partner violence among women in 10 developing countries. *PLoS ONE, 5*(12), e14257.

Harrison, A. (2008). Hidden love: Sexual ideologies and relationship ideals among rural South African adolescents in the context of HIV/AIDS. *Culture, Health and Sexuality, 10*, 175–189.

Harrison, A., O'Sullivan, L., Hoffman, S., Dolezal, C., & Morrell, R. (2006). Gender role and relationship norms among young adults in South Africa: Measuring the context of masculinity and HIV risk. *Journal of Urban Health: Bulletin of the New York Academy of Medicine, 83*(4), 709–722.

Hartley, M., Tomlinson, M., Greco, E., Comulada, W., Stewart, J., Roux, I., et al. (2011). Depressed mood in pregnancy: Prevalence and correlates in two Cape Town peri-urban settlements. *Reproductive Health, 8*, 9.

Hassim, S. (2006). *Women's Organizations and Democracy in South Africa*. Madison: University of Wisconsin Press.

Hassim, S. (2007). Social justice, gender and developmental social welfare in South Africa. In *Conference on Social Justice*. Johannesburg: University of the Witwatersrand.

Hatcher, A., Woollett, N., Pallitto, C., Mokoatle, K., Stockl, H., MacPhail, C., et al. (2014). Bidirectional links between HIV and intimate partner violence in pregnancy: Implications for prevention of mother-to-child transmission. *Journal of the International AIDS Society, 17*, 19233.

Hayes, R., Watson-Jones, D., Celum, C., van de Wijgert, J., & Wasserheit, J. (2010). Treatment of sexually transmitted infections for HIV prevention: End of the road or new beginning? *AIDS, 24*(Suppl. 4), S15–S26.

Health & Human Rights Journal. (2015). Special Issue 'Evidence of the impact of human rights-based approaches to health'. *17*(2). Retrieved June 1, 2017, from http://www.hhrjournal.org/

Health Resources and Services Administration, HIV/AIDS Bureau (HRSA) (US). (2006). *Linkage to HIV Care.* Rockville, MD: Health Resources and Services Administration.

Heimer, C. (2013). 'Wicked' ethics: Compliance work and the practice of ethics in HIV research. *Social Science & Medicine, 98*, 371–378.

Heise, L. (1998). Violence against women: An integrated, ecological framework. *Violence against Women, 4*(3), 262–290.

Heise, L., & McGrory, E. (2016). *Greentree II: Violence Against Women and Girls, and HIV—Report on a High-Level Consultation on the Evidence and Implications.* Greentree Estate, NY: STRIVE.

Helms, C. B., Turan, J. M., Atkins, G., Kempf, M. C., Clay, O. J., Raper, J. L., et al. (2016). Interpersonal mechanisms contributing to the association between HIV-related internalized stigma and medication adherence. *AIDS and Behavior, 21*(1), 238–247.

Hertzman, C. (1999). The biological embedding of early experience and its effects on health in adulthood. *Annals of the New York Academy of Sciences, 896*, 85–95.

Hertzman, C. (2010). Framework for the social determinants of early child development. In *Encyclopedia on Early Childhood Development.* Montreal: Université de Montréal.

Heywood, M. (2003). Preventing mother-to-child HIV transmission in South Africa: Background, strategies and outcomes of the Treatment Action Campaign case against the Minister of Health. *South African Journal of Human Rights, 19*, 278–280.

Heywood, M. (2009). South Africa's Treatment Action Campaign: Combining law and social mobilization to realize the right to health. *Journal of Human Rights Practice, 1*(1), 14–36.

Hodgson, I., Plummer, M., Konopka, S., Colvin, C., Jonas, E., Albertini, J., et al. (2014). A systematic review of individual and contextual factors affecting ART initiation, adherence, and retention for HIV-infected pregnant and postpartum women. *PLoS ONE, 9*(11), e111421.

Hogan, M., Foreman, K., Naghavi, M., Ahn, S., Wang, M., Makela, S., et al. (2010). Maternal mortality for 181 countries, 1980–2008: A systematic analysis of progress towards Millennium Development Goal 5. *Lancet, 375*(9726), 1609–1623.

Hoque, M., & Kader, S. (2009). Prevalence and experience of domestic violence among rural pregnant women in KwaZulu-Natal, South Africa. *South African Journal of Epidemiology and Infection, 24*(4), 34–37.

Horstmann, E., Brown, J., Islam, F., Buck, J., & Agins, B. D. (2010). Retaining HIV-infected patients in care: Where are we? Where do we go from here? *Clinical Infectious Diseases, 50*(5), 752–761.

Horwood, C., Butler, L., Haskins, L., Phakathi, S., & Rollins, N. (2013). HIV-infected adolescent mothers and their infants: Low coverage of HIV services and high risk of HIV transmission in KwaZulu-Natal, South Africa. *PLoS ONE, 8*(9), e74568.

Huerga, H., Van Cutsem, G., Ben Farhat, J., Reid, M., Bouhenia, M., Maman, D., et al. (2016). Who needs to be targeted for HIV testing and treatment in KwaZulu-Natal? Results from a population-based survey. *Journal of Acquired Immune Deficiency Syndromes, 73*(4), 411–418. https://doi.org/10.1097/QAI.0000000000001081

Human Rights Watch. (1995). *Violence Against Women in South Africa: The State Response to Domestic Violence and Rape*. New York: Human Rights Watch.

Human Sciences Research Council. (2015). *The People Living with HIV Stigma Index: South Africa 2014*. Pretoria: HSRC, South African National AIDS Council, and UNAIDS.

Hunter, M. (2002). The materiality of everyday sex: Thinking beyond prostitution. *African Studies, 61*(1), 99–120.

Hunter, M. (2010). *Love in the Time of AIDS. Inequality, Gender and Right in South Africa*. Durban: University of KwaZulu-Natal Press.

Islam, M. (2007). The safe motherhood initiative and beyond. *Bulletin of the World Health Organization, 85*(10), 735.

Jacobsen, K. (2012). *Introduction to Health Research Methods: A Practical Guide*. Sudbury: Jones & Bartlett.

Jamison, D., Feachem, R., Makgoba, M., Bos, E., Baingana, F., Hofman, K., et al. (Eds.). (2006). *Disease and Mortality in Sub-Saharan Africa* (2nd ed.). Washington, DC: World Bank.

Jan, S., Ferrari, G., Watts, C., Hargreaves, J., Kim, J., Phetla, G., et al. (2011). Economic evaluation of a combined microfinance and gender training intervention for the prevention of intimate partner violence in rural South Africa. *Health Policy and Planning, 26*, 366–372.

Jewkes, R. (2016). What works to prevent VAWG. [online]. Retrieved February 4, 2017, from http://www.svri.org/sites/default/files/attachments/2016-07-05/Jewkes%20R%20presentation%20for%20UNFPA%20and%20SVRI%20.pdf

Jewkes, R., & Abrahams, N. (2002). The epidemiology of rape and sexual coercion in South Africa: An overview. *Social Science & Medicine, 55*(7), 1231–1244.

Jewkes, R., Abrahams, N., Mathews, S., Seedat, M., Van Niekerk, A., Suffla, S., et al. (2009). Preventing rape and violence in South Africa: Call for leadership in a new agenda for action. In *MRC Policy Brief*. Pretoria: Medical Research Council.

Jewkes, R., Abrahams, N., & Mvo, Z. (1998). Why do nurses abuse patients? Reflections from South African obstetric services. *Social Science & Medicine, 47*(11), 1781–1795.

Jewkes, R., & Cornwall, A. (1998). *Stepping Stones: A Training Manual for Sexual and Reproductive Health Communication and Relationship Skills*. [online]. London: Institute for Development Studies. Retrieved February 7, 2017, from http://www.participatorymethods.org/resource/stepping-stones-training-manual-sexual-and-reproductive-health-communication-and

Jewkes, R., Dunkle, K., Koss, M., Levin, J., Nduna, M., Jama, N., et al. (2006a). Rape perpetration by young, rural South African men: Prevalence, patterns and risk factors. *Social Science & Medicine, 63*(11), 2949–2961.

Jewkes, R., Dunkle, K., Nduna, M., & Shai, N. (2010). Intimate partner violence, relationship power inequity, and incidence of HIV infection in young women in South Africa: A cohort study. *Lancet, 376*(9734), 41–48.

Jewkes, R., Flood, M., & Lang, J. (2015). From work with men and boys to changes of social norms and reduction of inequities in gender relations: A conceptual shift in prevention of violence against women and girls. *Lancet, 385*, 1580–1589.

Jewkes, R., Gibbs, A., Jama-Shai, N., Willan, S., Misselhorn, A., Mushinga, M., et al. (2014). Stepping stones and creating futures intervention: Shortened interrupted time series evaluation of a behavioral and structural health promotion and violence prevention intervention for young people in informal settlements in Durban, South Africa. *BMC Public Health, 14*, 1325.

Jewkes, R., Levin, J., & Penn-Kekana, L. (2002a). Risk factors for domestic violence: Findings from a South African cross-sectional study. *Social Science & Medicine, 55*, 1603–1617.

Jewkes, R., Levin, J., & Penn-Kekana, L. (2003). Gender inequalities, intimate partner violence and HIV preventive practices: Findings of a South African cross-sectional study. *Social Science & Medicine, 56*, 125–134.

Jewkes, R., Martin, L., & Penn-Kekana, L. (2002b). Correspondence: The virgin cleansing myth: Cases of child rape are not exotic. *Lancet, 359*, 711.

Jewkes, R., & Morrell, R. (2010). Gender and sexuality: Emerging perspectives from the heterosexual epidemic in South Africa and implications for HIV risk and prevention. *Journal of the International AIDS Society, 13*(1), 6.

Jewkes, R., & Morrell, R. (2012). Sexuality and the limits of agency among South African teenage women: Theorising femininities and their connections to HIV risk practices. *Social Science & Medicine, 74*, 1729–1737.

Jewkes, R., Nduna, M., Levin, J., Jama, N., Dunkle, K., Khuzwayo, N., et al. (2006b). A cluster randomized-controlled trial to determine the effectiveness of Stepping Stones in preventing HIV infections and promoting safer sexual behaviour amongst youth in the rural Eastern Cape, South Africa: Trial design, methods and baseline findings. *Tropical Medicine and International Health, 11*(1), 3–16.

Jewkes, R., Nduna, M., Levin, J., Jama, N., Dunkle, K., Puren, A., et al. (2008). Impact of stepping stones on incidence of HIV and HSV-2 and sexual behaviour in rural South Africa: Cluster randomised controlled trial. *BMJ, 337*, a506.

Jewkes, R., Penn-Kekana, L., & Rose-Junius, H. (2005). "If they rape me, I can't blame them": Reflections on gender in the social context of rape in South Africa and Namibia. *Social Science & Medicine, 61*, 1809–1820.

Jewkes, R., Sikweyiya, Y., Morrell, R., & Dunkle, K. (2011). Gender inequitable masculinity and sexual entitlement in rape perpetration in South Africa: Findings of a cross-sectional study. *PLoS ONE, 6*(12), e29590.

Jewkes, R., Sikweyiya, Y., Nduna, M., Jama-Shai, N., & Dunkle, K. (2012). Motivations for, and perceptions and experiences of participating in, a cluster randomised controlled trial of a HIV-behavioural intervention in rural South Africa. *Culture, Health & Sexuality, 14*(10), 1167–1182.

Jewkes, R., Vundule, C., Maforah, F., & Jordaan, E. (2001). Relationship dynamics and teenage pregnancy in South Africa. *Social Science & Medicine, 52*(5), 733–744.

Jong-wook, L. (2003). Global health improvement and WHO: Shaping the future. *Lancet, 362*, 2083–2088.

Journal of the International AIDS Society 2016 Special supplement, HIV epidemics among transgender populations: The importance of a trans-inclusive response. *19*(Suppl. 2), 1193.

Joyner, K., & Mash, B. (2012). A comprehensive model for intimate partner violence in South African primary care: Action research. *BMC Health Services Research, 12*, 399.

Kabira, W. M., Gachukia, E. W., & Matiangi, F. O. (1997). The effect of women's role on health: The paradox. *International Journal of Gynecology & Obstetrics, 58*, 23–34.

Kalanithi, P. (2016). *When Breath Becomes Air*. New York: Random House.

Karger, H., Midgely, J., & Brown, C. (2003). *Controversial Issues in Social Policy*. Boston: Allyn and Bacon.

Kassebaum, N., Bertozzi-Villa, A., Coggeshall, M., Shackelford, K., Steiner, C., Heuton, K., et al. (2014). Global, regional, and national levels and causes of maternal mortality during 1990–2013: A systematic analysis for the Global Burden of Disease Study 2013. *Lancet, 384*(9947), 980–1004.

Kaufman, C., & Stavrou Stavros, E. (2004). Bus fare please: The economics of sex and gifts among young people in urban South Africa. *Culture, Health and Sexuality, 6*(5), 377–391.

Kaufman, M., Cornish, F., Zimmerman, R., & Johnson, B. (2014). Health behavior change models for HIV prevention and AIDS care: Practical recommendations for a multi-level approach. *Journal of Acquired Immune Deficiency Syndromes, 66*(Suppl. 3), S250–S258.

Kim, J., Ferrari, G., Abramsky, T., Watts, C., Hargreaves, J., Morison, L., et al. (2009). Assessing the incremental effects of combining economic and health interventions: The IMAGE study in South Africa. *Bulletin of the World Health Organization, 87*(11), 824–832.

Kim, J., & Motsei, M. (2002). "Women enjoy punishment": Attitudes and experiences of gender-based violence among PHC nurses in rural South Africa. *Social Science & Medicine, 54*, 1243–1254.

Kim, J., Watts, C., Hargreaves, J., Ndhlovu, L., Phetla, G., Morison, L. A., et al. (2007). Understanding the impact of a microfinance-based intervention on women's empowerment and the reduction of intimate partner violence in South Africa. *American Journal of Public Health, 97*(10), 1794–1802.

Kingori, P. (2013). Experiencing everyday ethics in context: Frontline data collectors perspectives and practices of bioethics. *Social Science & Medicine, 98*, 361–370.

Klee, P. (1968). *The Diaries of Paul Klee 1898–1918*. Berkeley: University of California Press.

Kleinman, A. (2004). Ethics and experience: An anthropological approach to health equity. In P. Anand, F. Peter, & A. Sen (Eds.), *Public Health, Ethics, and Equity* (pp. 269–282). Oxford: Oxford University Press.

Klot, J., Auerbach, J., & Berry, M. (2013). Sexual violence and HIV risk. *American Journal of Reproductive Immunology, 69*(1), 5–19.

Koivusalo, M. (2010). The state of health in all policies (HiAP) in the European Union: Potential and pitfalls. *Journal of Epidemiology and Community Health, 64*(6), 500–503.

Kontis, V., Bennett, J., Mathers, C., Guangquan, L., Foreman, K., & Ezzati, M. (2017). Future life expectancy in 35 industrialised countries: Projections with a Bayesian model ensemble. *Lancet, 389*(10076), 1323–1335.

Koplan, J., Bond, T., Merson, M., Reddy, K., Henry, M., Sewankambo, N., et al. (2009). Towards a common definition of global health. *Lancet, 373*, 1993–1995.

Kouyoumdjian, F. G., Findlay, N., Schwandt, M., & Calzavara, L. M. (2013). A systematic review of the relationships between intimate partner violence and HIV/AIDS. *PloS One, 8*(11), e81044.

Krieger, N. (2001). Theories for social epidemiology in the 21st century: An ecosocial perspective. *International Journal of Epidemiology, 30*, 668–677.

Krieger, N., & Birn, A. (1998). A vision of social justice as the foundation of public health. *American Journal of Public Health, 88*(11), 1603–1606.

Krug, E. G., et al. (Eds.). (2002). *World Report on Violence and Health*. Geneva: World Health Organisation.

Kuehner, A., Ploder, A., & Langer, P. (2016). Introduction to the special issue: European contributions to reflexivity. *Qualitative Inquiry, 22*(9), 699–704.

Kuh, D., Ben-Schlomo, Y., Lynch, J., Hallqvist, J., & Power, C. (2003). Life course epidemiology. *Journal of Epidemiology & Community Health, 57*, 778–783.

Kumar, S., Gruskin, S., Khosla, R., & Narasimhan, M. (2015). Human rights and the sexual and reproductive health of women living with HIV—A literature review. *Journal of the International AIDS Society, 18*(Suppl. 5), 20290.

Laher, F., Cescon, A., Lazarus, E., Kaida, A., Makongoza, M., Hogg, R., et al. (2012). Conversations with mothers: Exploring reasons for prevention of mother-to-child transmission (PMTCT) failures in the era of programmatic scale-up in Soweto, South Africa. *AIDS and Behavior, 16*(1), 91–98.

Lancet Editorial. (2014). Women, children, and adolescents: The post-2015 agenda. *Lancet, 384*, 1159.

Langer, A., Meleis, A., Knaul, F., Atun, R., Aran, M., Arreola-Ornelas, H., et al. (2015). Women and health: The key for sustainable development. *Lancet, 386*(9999), 1165–1210.

Lawn, J., Rohde, J., Rifkin, S., Were, M., Vinod, P., & Chopra, M. (2008). Alma-Ata: Rebirth and revision Alma-Ata 30 years on: Revolutionary, relevant, and time to revitalize. *Lancet, 372*, 917–927.

Leclerc-Madlala, S. (2002). Youth HIV/AIDS and the importance of sexual culture and context. *Social Dynamics, 28*, 20–41.

Leclerc-Madlala, S. (2008a). Age-disparate and intergenerational sex in Southern Africa: The dynamics of hypervulnerability. *AIDS, 22*(Suppl. 4), S17–S25.

Leclerc-Madlala, S. (2008b). Intergenerational/age-disparate sex and young women's vulnerability in Southern Africa. In *UNAIDS Technical Meeting on Young Women in HIV Hyper-Endemic Countries of Southern Africa*. Muldersdrift, South Africa: UNAIDS.

Le Compte, M., & Schenoul, J. (1999). *Designing and Conducting Ethnographic Research*. Sausalito: AltaMira Press/Sage.

Leppo, K., Ollla, E., Pena, S., Wismar, M., & Cook, S. (2013). *Health in All Policies: Seizing Opportunities, Implementing Policies*. Helsinki: Finland Ministry of Social Affairs and Health.

Levon, E., Milani, T. M., & Kitis, E. D. (2017). The topography of masculine normativities in South Africa. *Critical Discourse Studies*, 1–18 (epub ahead of print).

Levy, J. (2009). Women's expectations of treatment and care after an antenatal HIV diagnosis in Lilongwe, Malawi. *Reproductive Health Matters, 17*(33), 152–161.

Liamputtong, P. (2006). *Researching the Vulnerable: A Guide to Sensitive Research Methods*. Thousand Oaks: Sage.

Lima, N. (2007). Public health and social ideas in modern Brazil. *American Journal of Public Health, 97*, 1168–1177.

Lincoln, Y., & Guba, E. (1985). *Naturalistic Inquiry*. Thousand Oaks: Sage.

Lindau, S., Jerome, J., Miller, K., Monk, E., Garcia, P., & Cohen, M. (2006). Mothers on the margins: Implications for eradicating perinatal HIV. *Social Science & Medicine, 62*(1), 59–69.

Link, B., & Phelan, J. (2001). Conceptualizing stigma. *Annual Review of Sociology, 27*, 363–385.

Lippman, S. A., Shade, S. B., El Ayadi, A. M., Gilvydis, J. M., Grignon, J. S., Liegler, T., et al. (2016). Attrition and opportunities along the HIV care continuum: Findings from a population-based sample, North West Province, South Africa. *Journal of Acquired Immune Deficiency Syndromes, 73*(1), 91–99. https://doi.org/10.1097/QAI.0000000000001026

Loder, E. (2016). Qualitative research and *The BMJ*: A response to Greenhalgh and colleagues' appeal for more. *BMJ, 352*, i641.

Looker, K. J., Elmes, J. A. R., Gottlieb, S. L., Schiffer, J. T., Vicker, P., Turner, K. M. E., et al. (2017, August 23). Effect of HSV-2 infection on subsequent HIV acquisition: An updated systematic review and meta-analysis. *Lancet Infectious Diseases* (online). https://doi.org/10.1016/S1473-3099(17)30405-X

Lufuno, M. (2016). *The IMAGE Programme: Empowering Women Through Microfinance and Community Action to Reduce Violence Against Women.* [online]. Johannesburg: SVRI. Retrieved February 7, 2017, from http://www.svri.org/sites/default/files/attachments/2016-07-05/IMAGE%20UNFPA%20VAW%20scaling%20up%20lessons%20%20.pdf

MacCarthy, S., Rasanathan, J., Ferguson, L., & Gruskin, S. (2012). The pregnancy decisions of HIV positive women: The state of knowledge and way forward. *Reproductive Health Matters, 20*(Suppl. 39), 119–140.

MacNaughton, G., Haigh, F., McGill, M., Koutsioumpas, K., & Sprague, C. (2015). The impact of human rights on universalizing health care in Vermont, USA. *Health & Human Rights Journal, 17*(2), 83–95.

Mann, J. (1997). Medicine and public health, ethics and human rights. *The Hastings Centre Report, 27*(3), 6–13.

Mann, J. (1999). The transformative potential of the HIV/AIDS pandemic—Access to reproductive health: A question of distributive justice. *Reproductive Health Matters, 7*(14), 164–172.

Marins, J., Jamal, L., Chen, S., Marilisa, B., Hudes, E., Barbosa, A., et al. (2003). Dramatic improvement in survival among adult Brazilian AIDS patients. *AIDS, 17*, 1675–1682.

Marks, S. (1994). *Divided Sisterhood: Race, Class and Gender in the South African Nursing Profession*. New York: St. Martin's Press.

Marmot, M. (1998). Improvement of social environment to improve health. *Lancet, 351*, 57–60.

Marmot, M. (2015). *The Health Gap: The Challenge of an Unequal World.* London: Bloomsbury.

Marmot, M., Friel, S., Bell, R., Houweling, T., & Taylor, S. (2008). Closing the gap in a generation: Health equity through action on the social determinants of health. *Lancet, 372*(9659), 1661–1669.

Marmot, M., & Shipley, M. (2006). Do socioeconomic differences in mortality persist after retirement? 25 year follow up of civil servants from the first Whitehall study. *British Medical Journal, 313*, 1177–1180.

Marti, T., & Mertens, D. (2014). Mixed methods research with groups at risk: New developments and key ideas. *Journal of Mixed Methods Research, 8*(3), 207–211.

Martin, S., Li, Y., Casanuevam, C., Harris-Britt, A., Kupper, L., & Cloutier, S. (2006). Intimate partner violence and women's depression before and during pregnancy. *Violence Against Women, 12*(3), 221–239.

Mathews, C. (2005). Reducing sexual risk behaviours: Theory and research, successes and challenges. In S. Abdool Karim & Q. Abdool Karim (Eds.), *HIV/AIDS in South Africa*. Cambridge: Cambridge University Press.

Mathews, C. (2010). Reducing sexual risk behaviors: Theory and research, successes and challenges. In S. Abdool Karim & Q. Abdool Karim (Eds.), *HIV/AIDS in South Africa* (2nd ed., pp. 157–183). Cambridge: Cambridge University Press.

Mbokota, M., & Moodley, J. (2003). Domestic abuse—An antenatal survey at King Edward VIII Hospital, Durban. *South African Medical Journal, 93*(6), 455–457.

McCann, L., & Pearlman, L. (1989). Vicarious traumatization: A framework for understanding the psychological effects of working with victims. *Journal of Traumatic Stress, 3*, 131–149.

McNairy, M., & El-Sadr, W. (2012). The HIV care continuum: No partial credit given. *AIDS, 26*(14), 1735–1738.

Mendel, G. (2001). *A Broken Landscape: HIV/AIDS in Africa*. London: Blume.

Merson, M., Black, R., & Mills, A. (2011). *Global Health: Diseases, Programs, Systems and Policies* (3rd ed.). Burlington: Jones & Bartlett.

Mertens, D. (2007). Transformative paradigm: Mixed methods and social justice. *Journal of Mixed Methods Research, 1*(3), 215–225.

Mertens, D. (2011). Mixed methods as tools for social change. *Journal of Mixed Methods Research, 5*(3), 195–197.

Meyer, J., Springer, S., & Altice, F. (2011). Substance abuse, violence, and HIV in women: A literature review of the syndemic. *Journal of Women's Health, 20*, 991–1006.

Meyersfeld, B. (2003). Reconceptualizing domestic violence in international law. *Albany Law Review, 67*, 371–426.

Meyersfeld, B. (2008). Domestic violence, health and international law. *Emory International Law Review, 22*, 61–112.

Mills, S. (2004). *Housing the household: Gender and empowerment in South Africa*. PhD thesis. London: London School of Economics, Department of Geography and Environment.

Mkandawire, T. (2001). *Social Policy in a Development Context.* Geneva: United Nations Research Institute for Social Development.

Moodley, J., Cooper, D., Mantell, J., & Stern, E. (2014). Health care provider perspectives on pregnancy and parenting in HIV positive individuals in South Africa. *BMC Health Services Research, 14*, 384.

Morrell, R. (Ed.). (2001). *Changing Men in Southern Africa.* Pietermaritzburg: University of KwaZulu-Natal and Zed Press.

Moustakas, C. (1994). *Phenomenological Research Methods.* London or Thousand Oaks, CA: Sage.

Moynihan, C. (1998). Theories in health care and research: Theories of masculinity. *BMJ, 317*, 1072–1075.

Msemburi, W., Pillay-van Wyk, V., Dorrington, R., Neethling, I., Nannan, N., Groenewald, P., et al. (2016). *Second National Burden of Disease Study for South Africa: Cause-of-Death Profile for South Africa, 1997–2012.* Cape Town: South African Medical Research Council.

Mullick, S., Teffo-Menziwa, M., Williams, E., & Jina, R. (2010). Women and sexual violence. In F. Padarath (Ed.), *South African Health Review 2010.* Durban: Health Systems Trust.

Murray, C., & Lopez, A. (Eds.). (1996). *The Global Burden of Disease: A Comprehensive Assessment of Mortality and Disability from Diseases, Injuries, and Risk Factors in 1990 and Projected to 2020.* Cambridge: Harvard University Press.

Murshid, N., Akincigil, A., & Zippay, A. (2016). Microfinance participation and domestic violence in Bangladesh: Results from a nationally representative survey. *Journal of Interpersonal Violence, 31*(9), 1579–1596.

Myers, B., Jones, H., Doherty, I., Kline, T., Key, M., Johnson, K., et al. (2015). Correlates of lifetime trauma exposure among pregnant women from Cape Town, South Africa. *International Journal of Mental Health and Addiction, 13*(3), 307–321.

Nachega, J., Uthman, O., Anderson, J., Peltzer, K., Wampold, S., Cotton, M., et al. (2012). Adherence to antiretroviral therapy during and after pregnancy in low-income, middle-income, and high-income countries: A systematic review and meta analysis. *AIDS, 26*(16), 2039–2052.

Nagel, T. (1979). *Mortal Questions.* Cambridge: Cambridge University Press.

Narasimhan, M., Orza, L., Welbourn, A., Bewley, S., Crone, T., & Vazquez, M. (2016). Sexual and reproductive health and human rights of women living with HIV: A global community survey. *Bulletin of the World Health Organization, 94*(4), 243–249.

Nass, S., Levit, L., & Gostin, L. (Eds.). (2009). *Beyond the HIPAA Privacy Rule: Enhancing Privacy, Improving Health Through Research*. Washington, DC: National Academies Press, Institute of Medicine Committee on Health Research and the Privacy of Health Information.

Nattrass, N. (2004). *The Moral Economy of AIDS in South Africa*. Cambridge: Cambridge University Press.

Negin, J., & Cumming, R. (2010). HIV infection in older adults in sub-Saharan Africa: Extrapolating prevalence from existing data. *Bulletin of the World Health Organization, 88*, 847–853.

Neuman, L. (2007). *Social Research Methods: Qualitative and Quantitative Approaches* (5th ed.). Boston, MA: Allyn and Bacon.

Nussbaum, M. (1988a). Nature, function and capability: Aristotle on political distribution. *Oxford Studies in Ancient Philosophy, 1*(1), S145–S184.

Nussbaum, M. (1988b). Non-relative virtues: An Aristotelian approach. *Midwest Studies in Philosophy, 13*, 32–53.

Nussbaum, M. (1992). Human functioning and social justice: In defense of Aristotelian essentialism. *Political Theory, 20*, 202–246.

Nussbaum, M. (2000). *Women and Human Development: The Capabilities Approach*. Cambridge: Cambridge University Press.

Nussbaum, M. (2002). Capabilities and social justice. *International Studies Review, 4*(2), 123–135.

Nussbaum, M. (2003). Capabilities as fundamental entitlements: Sen and social justice. *Feminist Economics, 9*(2–3), 33–59.

Nussbaum, M. (2007). Human rights and human capabilities: Twentieth century reflections. *Harvard Human Rights Journal, 20*, 21–24.

Nussbaum, M. (2008). Foreword: Constitutions and capabilities: Perception against Lofty Formalism, The Supreme Court 2006 Term. *Harvard Law Review, 121*(4), 1–79.

Nussbaum, M. (2011). *Creating Capabilities*. Cambridge: Harvard University Press.

Nussbaum, M. (2006). Women's bodies: Violence, security, capabilities. *Journal of Human Development, 6*(2), 167–183. Published online 17 August.

Olsen, W., Holborn, M., & Haralambos, U. (Eds.). (2004). Triangulation in social research: Qualitative and quantitative methods can really be mixed. In *Developments in Sociology*. Harlow: Causeway Press.

Orton, L., Pennington, A., Nayak, S., Sowden, A., White, M., & Whitehead, M. (2016). Group-based microfinance for collective empowerment: A systematic review of health impacts. *Bulletin of the World Health Organization, 94*(9), 694–704A.

Orza, L., Bewley, S., Logie, C. H., Crone, E. T., Moroz, S., Strachan, S., et al. (2015). How does living with HIV impact on women's mental health? Voices from a global survey. *Journal of the International AIDS Society, 18*(Suppl. 5), 20289.

Osmani, S., & Sen, A. (2003). The hidden penalties of gender inequality: Fetal origins of ill-health. *Economics and Human Biology, 1*, 105–121.

Östlin, P., Sen, G., & George, A. (2001). Gender, health and equity—The intersections. In T. Evans, M. Whitehead, F. Diderichsen, A. Bhuiya, & M. Wirth (Eds.), *Challenging Inequities to Health: From Ethics to Action*. Oxford: Oxford University Press.

Otieno, P., Kohler, P., Bosire, R., Brown, E., Macharia, S., & John-Stewart, G. (2010). Determinants of failure to access care in mothers referred to HIV treatment programs in Nairobi, Kenya. *AIDS Care, 22*(6), 729–736.

Ottersen, O., Dasgupta, J., Blouin, C., Buss, P., Chongsuvivatwong, V., Frenk, J., et al. (2014). The political origins of health inequity: Prospects for change. *Lancet, 383*(9917), 630–667.

Otwombe, K., Petzold, M., Modisenyane, T., Martinson, N., & Chirwa, T. (2014). Factors associated with mortality in HIV-infected people in rural and urban South Africa. *Global Health Action, 7*, 25488.

Ouzgane, L., & Morrell, R. (Eds.). (2005). *African Masculinities: Men in Africa from the Late Nineteenth Century to the Present*. New York: Palgrave.

Padian, N., McCoy, S., Balkus, J., & Wasserheit, J. (2010). Weighing the gold in the gold standard: Challenges in HIV prevention research. *AIDS, 24*, 621–635.

Parker, R. (2003). Building the foundations for the response for HIV/AIDS in Brazil: The development of HIV/AIDS policy, 1992–1996. *Divulgaçao em Saúde para Debate, 27*, 143–183.

Parkhurst, J. (2014). Structural approaches for prevention of sexually transmitted HIV in general populations: Definitions and an operational approach. *Journal of the International AIDS Society, 17*(1), 19052.

Pattinson, R. (2007). Maternal health. In *South African Health Review 2006* (pp. 89–99). Durban: Health Systems Trust.

Peltzer, K., Friend-du Preez, N., Ramlagan, S., & Anderson, J. (2010). Antiretroviral treatment adherence among HIV patients in KwaZulu-Natal, South Africa. *BMC Public Health, 10*, 111. https://doi.org/10.1186/1471-2458-10-111

Petchesky, R. (2003). *Global Prescriptions: Gendering Health and Human Rights*. New York: Zed Books.

Peter, F. (2000). *Health Equity and Social Justice*. Cambridge: Harvard Center for Population and Development Studies.

Peter, F. (2004). Health equity and social justice. In S. Anand, F. Peter, & A. Sen (Eds.), *Public Health, Ethics, and Equity* (pp. 93–106). Oxford: Oxford University Press.

Peter, F., & Evans, T. (2001). Ethical dimensions of health equity. In T. Evans, M. Whitehead, F. Diderichsen, A. Bhuiya, & M. Wirth (Eds.), *Challenging Inequities to Health: From Ethics to Action* (pp. 25–33). Oxford: Oxford University Press.

Pettifor, A., MacPhail, C., Anderson, A., & Maman, S. (2012). "If I buy the Kellogg's then he should [buy] the milk": Young women's perspectives on relationship dynamics, gender power and HIV risk in Johannesburg, South Africa. *Culture, Health & Sexuality, 14*(5), 477–490.

Pilane, P. (2016). Sugar daddies: Shame the blessers, not the blessed. [online]. *Mail & Guardian* (South Africa). Retrieved May 5, 2017, from http://mg.co.za/article/2016-05-19-shame-the-blessers-not-the-blessed

Piot, P. (2006). AIDS: From crisis to sustained response. *Lancet, 368*, 526–530.

Pogge, T. (2004). Relational conceptions of justice: Responsibilities for health outcomes. In S. Anand, F. Peter, & A. Sen (Eds.), *Public Health, Ethics, and Equity* (pp. 135–161). Oxford: Oxford University Press.

Popay, J., & Graves, K. (2000). 'Narrative' in research on gender inequalities in health. In E. Annandale & K. Hunt (Eds.), *Gender Inequalities in Health* (pp. 64–89). Philadelphia: Open University Press.

Power, S. (2003). The AIDS Rebel. [online]. *The New Yorker*. Retrieved February 2, 2017, from http://www.newyorker.com/magazine/2003/05/19/the-aids-rebel

Preston-Whyte, E. (2003). Contexts of vulnerability: Sex, secrecy and HIV/AIDS. *African Journal of AIDS Research, 2*(2), 89–94.

Probst, C., Parry, C., & Rehm, J. (2016). Socioeconomic differences in HIV/AIDS mortality in South Africa. *Tropical Medicine and International Health, 21*(7), 846–855.

Pronyk, P., Hargreaves, J., Kim, J., Morison, L., Phetla, G., Watts, C., et al. (2006). Effect of a structural intervention for the prevention of intimate partner violence and HIV in rural South Africa: A cluster randomised trial. *Lancet, 368*, 1973–1983.

Pronyk, P., Kim, J., Abramsky, T., Phetla, G., Hargreaves, J., Morison, L., et al. (2008). A combined microfinance and training intervention can reduce HIV risk behavior in young female participants. *AIDS, 22*, 1659–1665.

Pronyk, P., Kim, J., Hargreaves, J., Makhubele, M., Morison, L., Watts, C., et al. (2005). Microfinance and HIV prevention—Emerging lessons from rural South Africa. *Small Enterprise Development, 16*(3), 26–38.

Psaros, C., Remmert, J., Bangsberg, D., Safren, S., & Smit, J. (2015). Adherence to HIV care after pregnancy among women in sub-Saharan Africa: Falling off the cliff of the treatment cascade. *Current HIV/AIDS Reports, 12*(1), 1–5.

Punpanich, W., Ungchusak, K., & Detels, R. (2004). Thailand's response to the HIV epidemic: Yesterday, today, and tomorrow. *AIDS Education and Prevention, 16*(Suppl. 3A), 119–136.

Quillen, C. (2001). Feminist theory, justice and the lure of the human. *Signs, 27*(1), 87–122.

Quinn, T., & Overbaugh, J. (2005). HIV/AIDS in women: An expanding epidemic. *Science, 308*(5728), 1582–1583.

Rabe, M. (2003). Revisiting 'insiders' and 'outsiders' as social researchers. *African Sociological Review, 7*(2), 149–161.

Ramjee, G., & Daniels, B. (2013). Women and HIV in sub-Saharan Africa. *AIDS Research and Therapy, 10*(1), 30.

Ramjee, G., Kamali, A., & McCormack, S. (2010). The last decade of microbicide clinical trials in Africa: From hypothesis to facts. *AIDS, 24*(Suppl. 4), S40–S49.

Ramjee, G., Kapiga, S., Weiss, S., Peterson, L., Leburg, C., Kelly, C., et al. (2008). The value of site preparedness studies for future implementation of phase 2/IIb/III HIV prevention trials: Experience from the HPTN 055 study. *Journal of the Acquired Immune Deficiency Syndromes, 47*(1), 93–100.

Ramkissoon, A., Coutsoudis, A., Coovadia, H., Mthembu, P., Hlazo, J., & Smit, J. (2006). Options for HIV positive women. In *South African Health Review 2006* (pp. 315–332). Durban: Health Systems Trust.

Rand, M., & Saltzman, L. (2003). The nature and extent of recurring intimate partner violence against women in the United States. *Journal of Comparative Family Studies, 34*, 137–149.

Rawizza, H., Chan, C., Chaplin, B., Ahmed, I., Meloni, S., Oyebode, T., et al. (2015). Loss to follow-up within the prevention of mother-to-child transmission care cascade in a large ART program in Nigeria. *Current HIV Research, 13*(3), 201–209.

Rawls, J. (1971). *A Theory of Justice*. Cambridge, MA: Harvard University Press.

Rawls, J. (1993). *Political Liberalism*. New York: Columbia University Press.

Rhodes, T., Singer, M., Bourgois, P., Friedman, S., & Strathdee, S. (2005). The social structural production of HIV risk among drug users. *Social Science & Medicine, 61*(5), 1026–1044.

Richter, L., Komarek, A., Desmond, C., Celentano, D., Morin, S., Sweat, M., et al. (2014). Reported physical and sexual abuse in childhood and adult HIV risk behaviour in three African countries: Findings from Project Accept (HPTN-043). *AIDS and Behavior, 18*(2), 381–389.

Richter, M. (2013). *Characteristics, sexual behaviour and access to health care services for sex workers in South Africa and Kenya*. Doctoral thesis, Ghent University.

Ritchie, J., & Lewis, J. (Eds.). (2012). *Qualitative Research Practice: A Guide for Social Science Students and Researchers* (2nd ed.). Thousand Oaks: Sage.

Robeyns, I. (2003). Capability ethics. In H. LaFollette & I. Persson (Eds.), *The Blackwell Guide to Ethical Theory* (2nd ed.). New York: Blackwell.

Robson, C. (1993). *Real World Research: A Resource for Social Scientists and Practitioner-Researchers*. Oxford: Blackwell.

Rochat, T., Bland, R., Tomlinson, M., & Stein, A. (2011). The prevalence and clinical presentation of antenatal depression in rural South Africa. *Journal of Affective Disorders, 135*, 362–373.

Ronsmans, C., & Graham, W. (2006). Maternal mortality: Who, when, where, and why. *Lancet, 368*, 1189–2000.

Rosenberg, T. (2001). Drug companies are vincible. The AIDS crisis is solvable. *The New York Times Magazine*.

Ruger, J. (2004a). Health and social justice. *Lancet, 364*, 1075–1080.

Ruger, J. (2004b). Ethics of the social determinants of health. *Lancet, 364*, 1092–1097.

Ruger, J. (2006). Ethics and governance of global health inequalities. *Journal of Epidemiological and Community Health, 60*, 998–1003.

Ruger, J. (2010). *Health and Social Justice*. Oxford: Oxford University Press.

Russell, B. (2004). *History of Western Philosophy*. New York: Simon & Schuster.

Saracci, R. (1997). The World Health Organisation needs to reconsider its definition of health. *BMJ, 314*(7091), 1409–1410.

Scanlon, M. L., MacNaughton, G., & Sprague, C. (2017). Neglected disease, neglected right: Children living with HIV and their right to science. *Health & Human Rights Journal, 19*(2), 169–181.

Schneider, H., Barron, P., & Fonn, S. (2006). The promise and practice of transformation in South Africa's Health System. In S. Buhlungu, J. Daniel, R. Southall, & J. Lutchman (Eds.), *State of the Nation: South Africa 2007* (pp. 289–341). Cape Town: HSRC.

Selikow, T., Ahmed, N., Flisher, A., Mathews, C., & Mukoma, W. (2009). I am not "Umqwayito:" A qualitative study of peer pressure and sexual risk behaviour among young adolescents in Cape Town, South Africa. *Scandinavian Journal of Public Health, 37*, 107–112.

Selikow, T., Zulu, B., & Cedras, E. (2002). The Ingagara, the Regte and the Cherry: HIV/AIDS and youth culture in contemporary urban townships. *Agenda, 53*, 22–32.

Sen, A. (1985). *Commodities and Capabilities*. Amsterdam: North Holland.

Sen, A. (1990). More than 100 million women are missing. *New York Review of Books, 37*(20), 20 December 1990 [online]. Retrieved January 11, 2018, from http://ucatlas.ucsc.edu/gender/sen100m.html

Sen, A. (1992). *Inequality Re-Examined*. Cambridge: Harvard University Press.

Sen, A. (1999). *Development as Freedom*. New York: Random House.

Sen, A. (2001). Health equity, perspectives, measurability and criteria. In T. Evans, M. Whitehead, F. Diderichsen, A. Bhuiya, & M. Wirth (Eds.), *Challenging Inequities to Health: From Ethics to Action* (pp. 69–75). Oxford: Oxford University Press.

Sen, A. (2002). Why health equity? *Health Economics, 11*, 659–666.

Sen, A. (2004a). Why health equity? In S. Anand, F. Peter, & A. Sen (Eds.), *Public Health, Ethics, and Equity* (pp. 21–34). Oxford: Oxford University Press.

Sen, A. (2004b). Health achievement and equity: External and internal perspectives. In S. Anand, F. Peter, & A. Sen (Eds.), *Public Health, Ethics, and Equity* (pp. 263–268). Oxford: Oxford University Press.

Sen, A. (2005). Human rights and capabilities. *Journal of Human Development, 6*(2), 151–166.

Sen, A. (2009). *The Idea of Justice*. Cambridge: Harvard University Press.

Sen, G., Östlin, P., & George, A. (2007). Unequal, unfair, ineffective and inefficient gender inequity in health: Why it exists and how we can change it. In *Report of the Women and Gender Equity Knowledge Network of the Commission on Social Determinants of Health, Final Report to the Commission on Social Determinants of Health*. Geneva: WHO.

Sewell, W. (1992). A theory of structure: Duality, agency and transformation. *The American Journal of Sociology, 98*(1), 1–29.

Sexual Violence Research Initiative. (2015). *Guidelines for the Prevention and Management of Vicarious Trauma Among Researchers of Sexual and Intimate Partner v Violence*. Pretoria: Sexual Violence Research Initiative.

Shai, N., & Sikweyiya, Y. (2015). Programmes for change: Addressing sexual and intimate partner violence in South Africa. *South Africa Crime Quarterly, 51*, 31–41.

Shamu, S., Abrahams, N., Temmerman, M., Musekiwa, A., & Zarowsky, C. (2011). A systematic review of African studies on intimate partner violence against pregnant women: Prevalence and risk factors. *PLoS ONE, 6*(3), e17591.

Shilts, R. (1988). *And the Band Played On*. New York: St. Martin's Press.

Shisana, O., Rehle, T., Simbayi, L., Parker, W., Zuma, K., Bhana, A., et al. (2005). *South African National HIV Prevalence, Incidence and Communication Survey*. Cape Town: HSRC Press.

Shisana, O., Rehle, T., Simbayi, L., Zuma, K., Jooste, S., Pillay-van Wyk, V., et al. (2009). *South African National HIV Prevalence, Incidence and Communication Survey, 2008. A Turning Tide Among Teenagers?* Cape Town: HSRC Press.

Shisana, O., Rehle, T., Simbayi, L., Zuma, K., Jooste, S., Zungu, N., et al. (2014). *South African National HIV Prevalence, Incidence and Behaviour Survey, 2012*. Cape Town: HSRC Press.

Silverman, J. (2010). Key to prevent HIV in women: Reduce gender-based violence. *Lancet, 376*(9734), 6–7.

Skevington, S., Sovetkina, E., & Gillison, F. (2013). A systematic review to quantitatively evaluate 'Stepping Stones': A participatory community-based HIV/AIDS prevention intervention. *AIDS and Behavior, 17*(3), 1025–1039.

Small Enterprise Foundation. (2016). About Small Enterprise Foundation. [online]. Retrieved January 2, 2017, from http://www.sef.co.za/about-sef

Smith, A. (2010). *The Theory of Moral Sentiments*. London: Penguin.

Smith, K., Bambra, C., & Hill, S. (Eds.). (2015). *Health Inequalities: Critical Perspectives*. Oxford: Oxford University Press.

Solar, O., & Irwin, A. (2007). *A Conceptual Framework for Action on the Social Determinants of Health*. Discussion paper for the Commission on Social Determinants of Health (April). Geneva: WHO.

Soman, K. (1997). Picture of Women's Health: Three stories. *Economic and Political Weekly, 32*(8), 396–398.

South Africa Every Death Counts Writing Group. (2008a). Every death counts: Use of mortality audit data for decision making to save the lives of mothers, babies, and children in South Africa. *Lancet, 371*, 1294–1304.

South Africa Every Death Counts Writing Group. (2008b). *Every Death Counts: Saving the Lives of Mothers, Babies, and Children in South Africa*. Cape Town: National Department of Health, Medical Research Council, University of Pretoria, Save the Children and UNICEF.

South African National AIDS Council (SANAC). (2014). *Progress Report on the National Strategic Plan for HIV, TB and STIs 2012–2016*. Pretoria: South African National AIDS Council.

South African National AIDS Council (SANAC). (2016). *Enhanced Progress Report, National Strategic Plan for HIV, TB and STIs 2012–2016*. Pretoria: SANAC.

SANAC Women's Sector. (2015). Make a plan to stop GBV. [online]. Retrieved February 24, 2017, from http://sanacws.org.za/make-a-plan-to-stop-gbv/

Sprague, C. (2009). *Cui Bono: A Capabilities Approach to Understanding HIV 1192 Prevention and Treatment for Pregnant Women and Children in South Africa.* 1193 Doctoral thesis, University of the Witwatersrand.

Sprague, C., & Brown, S. (2016). Introduction: Local and global HIV aging demographics and research. In R. DeMarco & M. Brennan-Ing (Eds.), *HIV and Aging* (pp. 1–10). Basel: S. Karger.

Sprague, C., Chersich, M., & Black, V. (2011). Health systems weaknesses constrain access to PMTCT and maternal HIV services in South Africa: A qualitative enquiry. *AIDS Research and Therapy, 8*, 10.

Sprague, C., Hatcher, A., Woollett, N., & Black, V. (2015). How nurses in Johannesburg address intimate partner violence in female patients: Understanding IPV responses in low and middle-income country health systems. *Journal of Interpersonal Violence, 32*(11), 1591–1619, Epub ahead of print.

Sprague, C., Hatcher, A., Woollett, N., Sommers, T., & Black, V. (2016). They can't report abuse; they can't move out. They are at the mercy of these men: Exploring connections between intimate partner violence, gender and HIV in South African clinical settings. *Culture, Health & Sexuality, 18*(5), 567–581. Epub, 2016.

Sprague, C., Hatcher, A., Woollett, N., Sommers, T., & Black, V. (2016a). "They can't report abuse; they can't move out. They are at the mercy of these men." Exploring connections between intimate partner violence, gender and HIV in South African clinical settings. *Culture, Health & Sexuality, 27*, 1–15, Epub 2015.

Sprague, C., Radhakrishnan, B., Brown, S., Sommers, T. E., & Pantalone, D. (2017a). Southern women at risk: Narratives of familial and social HIV risk in justice-involved US women in Alabama. *Violence & Victims, 32*(4), 728–753, Epub 2016.

Sprague, C., Scanlon, M., & Pantalone, D. W. (2017b). Qualitative methods to advance research on health inequities among previously incarcerated women living with HIV in Alabama. *Health Education & Behavior, 44*(5), 716–727.

Sprague, C., Scanlon, M., Radhakrishnan, B., & Pantalone, D. W. (2017c). The HIV prison paradox: Agency and HIV positive women's experiences in jail and prison in Alabama. *Qualitative Health Research, 27*(10), 1427–1444, Epub 2016.

Sprague, C., & Simon, S. (2014). Understanding HIV care delays in the US South and the role of the social-level in HIV care engagement/retention: A qualitative study. *International Journal for Equity in Health, 13*(28), 1–14.

Sprague, C., Woollett, N., Parpart, J., Hatcher, A., Sommers, T., Brown, S., et al. (2016b). When nurses are also patients: Intimate partner violence and the health system as an enabler of women's health and institutional agency in Johannesburg. *Global Public Health, 11*(1–2), 169–183, Epub 2015.

Sprague, C., & Woolman, S. (2006). Moral luck: Exploiting South Africa's policy environment for an effective national antiretroviral treatment programme. *South African Journal on Human Rights, 22*(3), 337–379.

Starfield, B. (2006). State of the art in research on equity in health. *Journal of Health Politics, Policy and Law, 31*(1), 11–32.

Statistics South Africa (Stats SA). (2015). *Mid-Year Population Estimates 2015, Statistical Release P0302*. Pretoria: South Africa.

Stats SA. (2016a). *Mid-Year Population Estimates 2016, Statistical Release P0302*. Pretoria: Statistics South Africa.

Stats SA. (2016b). *Labour-Force Survey, Quarter 2*. Pretoria: Statistics South Africa.

Stats SA. (2016c). *Community Survey 2016*. Pretoria: Statistics South Africa.

Staton-Tindall, M. (n.d.). *Female Offender Drug Use and Related Issues*. [online]. Retrieved January 22, 2017, from http://www.nij.gov/topics/drugs/markets/adam/documents/staton-paper.pdf

Steinberg, J. (2008). *Three-Letter Plague. A Young Man's Journey Through a Great Epidemic*. Johannesburg: Jonathan Ball.

Stern, D. (2013). Intersubjectivity. In E. Person, A. Cooper, & G. Gabbard (Eds.), *The American Psychiatric Publishing Text—Book of Psychoanalysis* (pp. 77–92). Arlington, TX: American Psychiatric Publishing.

Stern, E., Buikema, R., & Cooper, D. (2016). South African women's agency in relation to hegemonic masculinity in the context of intimate partner violence. *Global Public Health, 11*(1–2), 135–152.

Stern, E., & Cooper, D. (2014). Experiences and conceptualizations of sexual debut from the narratives of South African men and women in the context of HIV/AIDS. *African Journal of AIDS Research, 13*(2), 121–131.

Stop Stockouts Project. (2016). *2015 Stock Outs National Survey, 3rd Annual Report—South Africa*. Johannesburg: Medecins Sans Frontieres, Southern African HIV Clinicians Society, Section 27, Rudasa, Treatment Action Campaign, Rural Health Advocacy Project.

Stuart, E., & Woodroffe, J. (2016). Leaving no-one behind: Can the sustainable development goals succeed where the millennium development goals lacked? *Gender and Development, 24*(1), 69–81.

Tazreiter, C., Weber, L., Pickering, S., Segrave, M., & McKernan, H. (2016). *Fluid Security in the Asia Pacific: Transnational Lives, Human Rights and State Control*. London: Palgrave Macmillan.

Technau, K., Kalk, E., Coovadia, A., Black, V., Pickerill, S., Mellins, C., et al. (2014). Timing of maternal HIV testing and uptake of prevention of mother-to-child transmission interventions among women and their infected infants in Johannesburg, South Africa. *Journal of Acquired Immune Deficiency Syndromes, 65*(5), e170–e178.

Teixeira, P. (2003). Universal access to AIDS medicines: The Brazilian experience. *Divulgaçao em Saúde para Debate, 27*, 184–191.

The Guardian. (2006, May 8). Jacob Zuma cleared of rape. Retrieved July 1, 2017, from https://www.theguardian.com/world/2006/may/08/aids.southafrica

Tinker, A. (2000). Women's health: The unfinished agenda. *International Journal of Gynecology and Obstetrics, 70*, 149–158.

Titmuss, R. (1974). *Social Policy*. London: Allen and Unwin.

Treves-Kagan, S., Steward, W., Ntswane, L., Haller, R., Gilvydis, J. M., Gulati, H., et al. (2016). Why increasing availability of ART is not enough: A rapid, community-based study on how HIV-related stigma impacts engagement to care in rural South Africa. *BMC Public Health, 16*, 87.

Tuhiwai Smith, L. (1999). *Decolonizing Methodologies*. New York: Zed Books.

UNAIDS. (1998). *Mother to Child Transmission of HIV: UNAIDS Technical Update*. Geneva: UNAIDS.

UNAIDS. (2004). *Greater Involvement of People Living with HIV and AIDS Policy Brief.* [online]. New York: UNAIDS. Retrieved February 2, 2016, from http://data.unaids.org/pub/BriefingNote/2007/jc1299_policy_brief_gipa.pdf

UNAIDS. (2005). *Epidemiological Fact Sheets on HIV/AIDS and Sexually Transmitted Infections, 2005 Update (South Africa)*. Geneva: UNAIDS.

UNAIDS. (2013). *HIV and Aging: Special Supplement to the UNAIDS Report on the Global AIDS Epidemic 2013*. Geneva: UNAIDS.

UNAIDS. (2014a). *90-90-90: An Ambitious Treatment Target to Help End the AIDS Epidemic*. Geneva: UNAIDS.

UNAIDS. (2014b). *The Gap Report*. Geneva: UNAIDS.

UNAIDS. (2016a). *UNAIDS 2016 Estimates*. [online]. Geneva: UNAIDS. Retrieved February 8, 2017, from http://www.unaids.org/en/resources/documents/2016/HIV_estimates_with_uncertainty_bounds_1990-2015

UNAIDS. (2016b). *UNAIDS 2016 Guidance: HIV Prevention Among Adolescent Girls and Young Women. Putting HIV Prevention Among Adolescent Girls and Young Women on the Fast-Track and Engaging Men and Boys*. [online]. Geneva: UNAIDS. Retrieved February 8, 2017, from http://www.unaids.org/sites/default/files/media_asset/UNAIDS_HIV_prevention_among_adolescent_girls_and_young_women.pdf

UNAIDS. (2016c). *Global AIDS Update 2016*. Geneva: UNAIDS.

UNAIDS/WHO. (2008). *Sub-Saharan Africa AIDS Epidemic Update Regional Summary*. Geneva: UNAIDS/WHO.

UNDP. (2011). "Basic capabilities". From UNDP website [no longer accessible]. Retrieved February 2, 2017, from http://hdr.undp.org/en/humandev

UNICEF. (2007). *State of the World's Children*. New York: UNICEF.

UNICEF South Africa/Department of Social Development. (2012). *The South African Child Support Grant Impact Assessment: Evidence from a Survey of Children, Adolescents, and Their Households*. Pretoria: UNICEF South Africa.

UN Office of the Special Adviser on Gender Issues and the Advancement of Women. (2001). Important concepts underlying gender mainstreaming: Concepts and definitions. Retrieved June 16, 2017, from http://www.un.org/womenwatch/osagi/conceptsandefinitions.htm

UN Statistical Division/UN Population Division. (n.d.-a). *South Africa, Life Expectancy at Birth (Female), 1960–2014*. [online]. New York: United Nations. Retrieved January 15, 2018, from http://data.worldbank.org/indicator/SP.DYN.LE00.FE.IN?locations=ZA

UN Statistical Division/UN Population Division. (n.d.-b). *World Life Expectancy at Birth, 1960–2014*. [online]. New York: United Nations. Retrieved January 15, 2018, from http://data.worldbank.org/indicator/SP.DYN.LE00.IN

Uthman, O., Magidson, J., Safren, S., & Nachega, J. (2014). Depression and adherence to antiretroviral therapy in low-, middle- and high-income countries: A systematic review and meta-analysis. *Current HIV/AIDS Reports, 11*(3), 291–307.

van der Linde, I. (2013). *HIV/AIDS in South Africa: At Last the Glass is Half Full*. [online]. Pretoria: HSRC. Retrieved January 15, 2018, from http://www.hsrc.ac.za/en/media-briefs/hiv-aids-stis-and-tb/plenary-session-3-20-june-2013-hiv-aids-in-south-africa-at-last-the-glass-is-half-full

Vaughan, B. (2001). Handle with care: On the use of structuration theory within criminology. *British Journal of Criminology, 41*(1), 185–200.

Vearey, J. (2010). *The persistent urban challenges of migration and informal settlements in the context of HIV*. Doctoral thesis, University of the Witwatersrand, Johannesburg, South Africa.

Velkoff, V., & Kowal, P. (2007). *Population Aging in Sub-Saharan Africa: Demographic Dimensions 2006*. Washington, DC: US Census Bureau.

Venkatapuram, S. (2011). *Health Justice*. Cambridge: Polity Press.

Villegas, L., McKay, K., Dennis, C., & Ross, L. (2011). Postpartum depression among rural women from developed and developing countries: A systematic review. *Journal of Rural Health, 27*(3), 278–288.

Walensky, R., Paltiel, A., & Losina, E. (2006). The survival benefits of AIDS treatment in the United States. *Journal of Infectious Diseases, 194*(1), 11–19.

Wang, B., Losina, E., Stark, R., Munro, A., Walensky, R. P., Wilke, M., et al. (2011). Loss to follow-up in a community clinic in South Africa—Roles of gender, pregnancy and CD4 count. *South African Medical Journal, 101*(4), 253–257.

Wang, C., & Geale, S. (2015). The power of story: Narrative inquiry as a methodology in nursing research. *International Journal of Nursing Sciences, 2*, 195–198.

Wasserheit, J. (1992). Epidemiologic synergy: Interrelationships between human immunodeficiency virus infection and other sexually transmitted diseases. *Sexually Transmitted Diseases, 9*, 61–77.

Welbourn, A., & Bollinger, A. (2015). The original Stepping Stones—What is it? The Stepping Stones Feedback Project. [online]. Retrieved February 16, 2017, from http://www.steppingstonesfeedback.org/index.php/About/What_is_it/gb

Wettstein, C., Mugglin, C., Egger, M., Blaser, N., Vizcaya, L. S., Estill, J., et al. (2012). Missed opportunities to prevent mother-to-child-transmission: Systematic review and meta-analysis. *AIDS, 26*(18), 2361–2373.

Whitehead, M. (1990). *The Concepts and Principles of Equity in Health*. Copenhagen: WHO Regional Office for Europe.

Whitehead, M. (1992). The concepts and principles of equity in health. *International Journal of Health Services, 22*(3), 429–435.

Whyte, D. (1994). *The Heart Aroused*. New York: Doubleday.

Wikler, D. (2004). Personal and social responsibility for health. In S. Anand, F. Peter, & A. Sen (Eds.), *Public Health, Ethics, and Equity* (pp. 109–134). Oxford: Oxford University Press.

Williams, A. (1998). If we are going to get a fair innings, someone will need to keep the score. In M. L. Barer, T. E. Getzen, & G. L. Stoddart (Eds.), *Health, Health Care and Economics* (pp. 319–330). New York: Wiley.

Wilkinson, R., & Marmot, M. (Eds.). (2003). *Social Determinants of Health: The Solid Facts*. Copenhagen: WHO Regional Office for Europe.

Woldesenbet, S., Jackson, D., Lombard, C., Dinh, T. H., Puren, A., Sherman, G., et al. (2015). Missed opportunities along the prevention of mother-to-child transmission services cascade in South Africa: Uptake, determinants, and attributable risk (the SAPMTCTE). *PLoS ONE, 10*(7), e0132425.

Wolffers, I. (2000). Biomedical and development paradigms in AIDS prevention. *Bulletin of the World Health Organization, 78*(2), 267–273.

Wood, K., Maforah, F., & Jewkes, R. (1998). 'He forced me to love him': Putting violence on the adolescent sexual health agenda. *Social Science & Medicine, 47*, 233–242.

Woolman, S. (2008). *Constitutional Law of South Africa* (2nd ed.). Cape Town: Juta Press.

Woolman, S., & Sprague, C. (2015). Nowhere to run, nowhere to hide: The absence of public policy as to how health care professionals should address intimate partner violence constitutes a breach of the rights to health and bodily integrity under the South African Constitution. *Cardozo Journal of Law & Gender, 22*(1), 29–74.

Woolman, S., Sprague, C., & Black, V. (2009). Why state policies that undermine HIV lay counsellors constitute retrogressive measures that violate the right of access to health care for pregnant women and infants. *South African Journal on Human Rights, 24*, 102–123.

World Health Organisation [WHO]. (1946). *Preamble to the Constitution of the World Health Organization*. [online]. Geneva: WHO. Retrieved June 2, 2017, from http://www.who.int/suggestions/faq/en/print.html

WHO. (1988). WHO: From Small Beginnings, Interview with Dr Szeming Sze. *World Health Forum, 9*, 29–34. Retrieved October 19, 2017, from http://apps.who.int/iris/bitstream/10665/46414/1/WHF_1988_9_1_p29-34.pdf

WHO. (2002). *The World Health Report, 2002: Reducing Risks, Promoting Healthy Life*. Geneva: WHO.

WHO. (2006a). *Sexual and Reproductive Health for Women Living with HIV/AIDS: Guidelines on Care, Treatment and Support for Women Living with HIV/AIDS and Their Children in Resource-Constrained Settings*. Geneva: WHO.

WHO. (2006b). *Defining Sexual Health: Report of a Technical Consultation on Sexual Health*. Geneva: WHO.

WHO. (2010). *A Conceptual Framework for Action on the Social Determinants of Health. Discussion Paper 2: Debates, Policy and Practice*. Geneva: WHO. Retrieved June 10, 2017, from http://www.who.int/sdhconference/resources/ConceptualframeworkforactiononSDH_eng.pdf

WHO. (2013a). *Responding to Intimate Partner Violence and Sexual Violence Against Women, WHO Clinical and Policy Guidelines*. Geneva: WHO.

WHO. (2013b). *Global and Regional Estimates of Violence Against Women: Prevalence and Health Effects of Intimate Partner Violence and Non-Partner Sexual Violence*. Geneva: WHO.

WHO. (2013c). *16 Ideas for Addressing Violence Against Women in the Context of the HIV Epidemic a Programming Tool*. Geneva: WHO.

WHO (2014a). Women's health. Fact sheet number 334 (September). Retrieved May 30, 2017, from http://www.who.int/mediacentre/factsheets/fs334/en/

WHO. (2014b). *World Health Statistics, 2014*. Geneva: WHO.

WHO. (2014c). *Civil Registration: Why Counting Births and Deaths Is Important. Fact Sheet No. 324*. Geneva: WHO.

WHO. (2014d). *MDG 5: Improve Maternal Health*. [online]. Geneva: WHO. Retrieved November 6, 2014, from http://www.who.int/topics/millennium_development_goals/maternal_health/en/

WHO. (2014e). *Risk Factors*. [online]. Geneva: WHO. Retrieved November 6, 2014, from http://www.who.int/topics/risk_factors/en/

WHO. (2015). *Global Health Observatory Data*. [online]. Geneva: WHO. Retrieved January 14, 2017, from http://www.who.int/gho/database/en/

WHO. (2016a). *World Health Statistics 2016: Monitoring Health for the SDGs*. Geneva: WHO.

WHO. (2016b). Violence against women, intimate partner and sexual violence against women fact sheet, updated November 2016. [online]. Geneva: WHO. Retrieved January 22, 2017, from http://www.who.int/mediacentre/factsheets/fs239/en/

WHO. (2016c). *Consolidated Guidelines on the Use of Antiretroviral Drugs for Treating and Preventing HIV Infection: Recommendations for a Public Health Approach—Second Edition*. Geneva: WHO.

WHO. (2016d). *About the Global Burden of Disease (GBD) Project*. [online]. Geneva: WHO. Retrieved October 28, 2016, from http://www.who.int/healthinfo/global_burden_disease/about/en/

WHO. (2017). *The Ecological Framework*. [online]. Geneva: WHO. Retrieved June 15, 2017, from http://www.who.int/violenceprevention/approach/ecology/en/

WHO. (n.d.). Maternal and perinatal health. Retrieved June 30, 2017, from http://www.who.int/maternal_child_adolescent/topics/maternal/maternal_perinatal/en/

WHO Quality of Life (WHOQOL). (2012). *WHOQOL BREF Instrument*. Geneva: WHO.

WHO Regional Office for Europe. (2013). *Health 2020: The European Policy for Health and Well-Being*. Copenhagen: WHO.

Wouters, E., Heunis, C., Michielsen, J., Van Loon, F., & Meulemans, H. (2011). The long road to universal antiretroviral treatment coverage in South Africa. *Future Virology, 6*(7), 801–812.

Yang, L. H., Kleinman, A., Link, B. G., Phelan, J. C., Lee, S., & Good, B. (2007). Culture and stigma: Adding moral experience to stigma theory. *Social Science & Medicine, 64*(7), 1524–1535.

Index[1]

[1] Note: Page numbers followed by 'n' refer to notes.

C. Sprague, *Gender and HIV in South Africa*, Global Research in Gender, Sexuality and Health, https://doi.org/10.1057/978-1-137-55997-5

CPSIA information can be obtained
at www.ICGtesting.com
Printed in the USA
BVHW040218210219
540813BV00003B/12/P

9 781137 559968